THE NINE BOOKS

OF

THE DANISH HISTORY

OF

SAXO GRAMMATICUS

IN

ONE VOLUME

Translated by Oliver Elton

With Some Considerations
on Saxo's Sources,
Historical Methods
and Folk-Lore

By Frederick York Powell

Oliver Elton's Translation of the Nine Books of The Danish
History of Saxo Grammaticus was published in two volumes
by the Norroena Society in 1905, and is now in the public
domain. It is available in various digital formats from a
number of sources on the internet. The contents of this book
are of great interest to Heathens. Our goal was to make
Saxo's writings available in print at an affordable price. We've
included Frederick Powell's introductory materials and all of
the illustrations from the original 1905 edition of the book.
The appendixes and index of the 1905 edition have been
excluded.

Any profits made from this book, will go directly to our fund to
build a Hof and Hall in the Heartland of the United States.

Published by Jotun's Bane Kindred
Temple of Our Heathen Gods
P.O. Box 618
Liberty, MO 64069
http://heathengods.com

mark@heathengods.com

TABLE OF CONTENTS

INTRODUCTION TO SAXO GRAMMATICUS
By Frederick York Powell

THE DANISH HISTORY OF SAXO GRAMMATICUS
Translated by Oliver Elton

Saxo Grammaticus

INTRODUCTION TO SAXO GRAMMATICUS

SAXO'S POSITION

Saxo Grammaticus, or "The Lettered", one of the notable historians of the Middle Ages, may fairly be called not only the earliest chronicler of Denmark, but her earliest writer. In the latter half of the twelfth century, when Iceland was in the flush of literary production, Denmark lingered behind. No literature in her vernacular, save a few Runic inscriptions, has survived. Monkish annals, devotional works, and lives were written in Latin; but the chronicle of Roskild, the necrology of Lund, the register of gifts to the cloister of Sora, are not literature. Neither are the half-mythological genealogies of kings; and besides, the mass of these, though doubtless based on older verses that are lost, are not proved to be, as they stand, prior to Saxo. One man only, Saxo's elder contemporary, Sueno Aggonis, or Sweyn (Svend) Aageson, who wrote about 1185, shares or anticipates the credit of attempting a connected record. His brief draft of annals is written in rough mediocre Latin. It names but a few of the kings recorded by Saxo, and tells little that Saxo does not. Yet there is a certain link between the two writers. Sweyn speaks of Saxo with respect; he not obscurely leaves him the task of filling up his omissions. Both writers, servants of the brilliant Bishop Absalon, and probably set by him upon their task, proceed, like Geoffrey of Monmouth, by gathering and editing mythical matter. This they more or less embroider, and arrive in due course insensibly at actual history. Both, again, thread their stories upon a genealogy of kings in part legendary. Both write at the spur of patriotism, both to let Denmark linger in the race for light and learning, and desirous to save her glories, as other nations have saved theirs, by a record. But while Sweyn only made a skeleton chronicle, Saxo leaves a memorial in which historian and philologist find their account. His seven later books are the chief Danish authority for the times which they relate; his first nine, here translated, are a treasure of myth and folk-lore. Of the songs and stories which Denmark possessed from the common Scandinavian stock, often her only native record is in Saxo's Latin. Thus, as a chronicler both of truth and fiction, he had in his own land no predecessor, nor had he any literary tradition behind him. Single-handed, therefore, he may be said to have lifted the dead-weight against him, and given Denmark a writer. The nature of his work will be discussed presently.

LIFE OF SAXO

Of Saxo little is known but what he himself indicates, though much doubtful supposition has gathered round his name.

That he was born a Dane his whole language implies; it is full of a glow of aggressive patriotism. He also often praises the Zealanders at the expense of other Danes, and Zealand as the centre of Denmark; but that is the whole contemporary evidence for the statement that he was a Zealander. This statement is freely taken for granted three centuries afterwards by Urne in the first edition of the book (1514), but is not traced further back than an epitomator, who wrote more than 200 years after Saxo's death. Saxo tells us that his father and grandfather fought for Waldemar the First of Denmark, who reigned from 1157 to 1182. Of these men we know nothing further, unless the Saxo whom he names as one of Waldemar's admirals be his grandfather, in which case his family was one of some distinction and his father and grandfather probably "King's men". But Saxo was a very common name, and we shall see the licence of hypothesis to which this fact has given rise. The notice, however, helps us approximately towards Saxo's birth-year. His grandfather, if he fought for Waldemar, who began to reign in 1157, can hardly have been born before 1100, nor can Saxo himself have been born before 1145 or 1150. But he was undoubtedly born before 1158, since he speaks of the death of Bishop Asker, which took place in that year, as occurring "in our time". His life therefore covers and overlaps the last half of the twelfth century.

His calling and station in life are debated. Except by the anonymous Zealand chronicler, who calls him Saxo "the Long", thus giving us the one personal detail we have, he has been universally known as Saxo "Grammaticus" ever since the epitomator of 1431 headed his compilation with the words, "A certain notable man of letters ("grammaticus"), a Zealander by birth, named Saxo, wrote," etc. It is almost certain that this general term, given only to men of signal gifts and learning, became thus for the first time, and for good, attached to Saxo's name. Such a title, in the Middle Ages, usually implied that its owner was a churchman, and Saxo's whole tone is devout, though not conspicuously professional.

But a number of Saxos present themselves in the same surroundings with whom he has been from time to time identified. All he tells us himself is, that Absalon, Archbishop of Lund from 1179 to 1201, pressed him, who was "the least of his companions, since all the rest refused the task", to write the history of Denmark, so that it might record its glories like other nations. Absalon was previously, and also after his promotion,

Bishop of Roskild, and this is the first circumstance giving colour to the theory—which lacks real evidence—that Saxo the historian was the same as a certain Saxo, Provost of the Chapter of Roskild, whose death is chronicled in a contemporary hand without any mark of distinction. It is unlikely that so eminent a man would be thus barely named; and the appended eulogy and verses identifying the Provost and the historian are of later date. Moreover, the Provost Saxo went on a mission to Paris in 1165, and was thus much too old for the theory. Nevertheless, the good Bishop of Roskild, Lave Urne, took this identity for granted in the first edition, and fostered the assumption. Saxo was a cleric; and could such a man be of less than canonical rank? He was (it was assumed) a Zealander; he was known to be a friend of Absalon, Bishop of Roskild. What more natural than that he should have been the Provost Saxo? Accordingly this latter worthy had an inscription in gold letters, written by Lave Urne himself, affixed to the wall opposite his tomb.

Even less evidence exists for identifying our Saxo with the scribe of that name—a comparative menial—who is named in the will of Bishop Absalon; and hardly more warranted is the theory that he was a member, perhaps a subdeacon, of the monastery of St. Laurence, whose secular canons formed part of the Chapter of Lund. It is true that Sweyn Aageson, Saxo's senior by about twenty years, speaks (writing about 1185) of Saxo as his "contubernalis". Sweyn Aageson is known to have had strong family connections with the monastery of St. Laurence; but there is only a tolerably strong probability that he, and therefore that Saxo, was actually a member of it. ("Contubernalis" may only imply comradeship in military service.) Equally doubtful is the consequence that since Saxo calls himself "one of the least" of Absalon's "followers" ("comitum"), he was probably, if not the inferior officer, who is called an "acolitus", at most a sub-deacon, who also did the work of a superior "acolitus". This is too poor a place for the chief writer of Denmark, high in Absalon's favor, nor is there any direct testimony that Saxo held it.

His education is unknown, but must have been careful. Of his training and culture we only know what his book betrays. Possibly, like other learned Danes, then and afterwards, he acquired his training and knowledge at some foreign University. Perhaps, like his contemporary Anders Suneson, he went to Paris; but we cannot tell. It is not even certain that he had a degree; for there is really little to identify him with the "M(agister) Saxo" who witnessed the deed of Absalon founding the monastery at Sora.

3

SAXO'S DANISH HISTORY

How he was induced to write his book has been mentioned. The expressions of modesty Saxo uses, saying that he was "the least" of Absalon's "followers", and that "all the rest refused the task", are not to be taken to the letter. A man of his parts would hardly be either the least in rank, or the last to be solicited. The words, however, enable us to guess an upward limit for the date of the inception of the work. Absalon became Archbishop in 1179, and the language of the Preface (written, as we shall see, last) implies that he was already Archbishop when he suggested the History to Saxo. But about 1185 we find Sweyn Aageson complimenting Saxo, and saying that Saxo "had `determined' to set forth all the deeds" of Sweyn Estridson, in his eleventh book, "at greater length in a more elegant style". The exact bearing of this notice on the date of Saxo's History is doubtful. It certainly need not imply that Saxo had already written ten books, or indeed that he had written any, of his History. All we call say is, that by 1185 a portion of the history was planned. The order in which its several parts were composed, and the date of its completion, are not certainly known, as Absalon died in 1201. But the work was not then finished; for, at the end of Bk. XI, one Birger, who died in 1202, is mentioned as still alive.

We have, however, a yet later notice. In the Preface, which, as its whole language implies, was written last, Saxo speaks of Waldemar II having "encompassed (`complexus') the ebbing and flowing waves of Elbe." This language, though a little vague, can hardly refer to anything but an expedition of Waldemar to Bremen in 1208. The whole History was in that case probably finished by about 1208. As to the order in which its parts were composed, it is likely that Absalon's original instruction was to write a history of Absalon's own doings. The fourteenth and succeeding books deal with these at disproportionate length, and Absalon, at the expense even of Waldemar, is the protagonist. Now Saxo states in his Preface that he "has taken care to follow the statements ("asserta") of Absalon, and with obedient mind and pen to include both his own doings and other men's doings of which he learnt."

The latter books are, therefore, to a great extent, Absalon's personally communicated memoirs. But we have seen that Absalon died in 1201, and that Bk. xi, at any rate, was not written after 1202. It almost certainly follows that the latter books were written in Absalon's life; but the Preface, written after them, refers to events in 1208. Therefore, unless we suppose that the issue was for some reason delayed, or that Saxo spent seven years in polishing—which is not impossible—there is some reason to surmise that he began with that portion of his work which was nearest to his own time, and added the previous (especially the first nine, or mythical) books, as a completion, and possibly as an afterthought. But this is a point which there is no real means of settling. We do not know how late the Preface was written, except that it must have been some time between 1208 and 1223, when Anders Suneson ceased to be Archbishop; nor do we know when Saxo died.

LITERARY HISTORY OF SAXO'S WORK

Nothing is stranger than that a work of such force and genius, unique in Danish letters, should have been forgotten for three hundred years, and have survived only in an epitome and in exceedingly few manuscripts. The history of the book is worth recording. Doubtless its very merits, its "marvellous vocabulary, thickly-studded maxims, and excellent variety of images," which Erasmus admired long afterwards, sealed it to the vulgar. A man needed some Latin to appreciate it, and Erasmus' natural wonder "how a Dane at that day could have such a force of eloquence" is a measure of the rarity both of the gift and of a public that could appraise it. The epitome (made about 1430) shows that Saxo was felt to be difficult, its author saying: "Since Saxo's work is in many places diffuse, and many things are said more for ornament than for historical truth, and moreover his style is too obscure on account of the number of terms ("plurima vocabula") and sundry poems, which are unfamiliar to modern times, this opuscle puts in clear words the more notable of the deeds there related, with the addition of some that happened after Saxo's death." A Low-German version of this epitome, which appeared in 1485, had a considerable vogue, and the two together "helped to drive the history out of our libraries, and explains why the annalists and geographers of the Middle Ages so seldom quoted it." This neglect appears to have been greatest of all in Denmark, and to have lasted until the appearance of the "First Edition" in 1511.

The first impulse towards this work by which Saxo was saved, is found in a letter from the Bishop of Roskild, Lave Urne, dated May 1512, to Christian Pederson, Canon of Lund, whom he compliments as a lover of letters, antiquary, and patriot, and urges to edit and publish "tam divinum latinae eruditionis culmen et splendorem Saxonem nostrum". Nearly two years afterwards Christian Pederson sent Lave Urne a copy of the first edition, now all printed, with an account of its history. "I do not think that any mortal was more inclined and ready for" the task. "When living at Paris, and paying heed to good literature, I twice sent a messenger at my own charges to buy a faithful copy at any cost, and bring it back to me. Effecting nothing thus, I went back to my country for this purpose; I visited and turned over all the libraries, but still could not pull out a Saxo, even covered with beetles, bookworms, mould, and dust. So stubbornly had all the owners locked it away." A worthy prior, in compassion offered to get a copy and transcribe it with his own hand, but Christian, in respect for the prior's rank, absurdly declined. At last Birger, the Archbishop of Lund, by some strategy, got a copy, which King Christian the Second allowed to be taken to Paris on condition of its being wrought at "by an instructed and skilled graver (printer)." Such a person was found in Jodocus Badius Ascenshls, who adds a third letter written by himself to Bishop Urne, vindicating his application to Saxo of the title Grammaticus, which he well defines as "one who knows how to speak or write with diligence, acuteness, or knowledge." The beautiful book he produced was worthy of the zeal, and unsparing, unweariable pains, which had been spent on it by the band of enthusiasts, and it was truly a little triumph of humanism. Further editions were reprinted during the sixteenth century at Basic and at Frankfort-on-Main, but they did not improve in any way upon the first; and the next epoch in the study of Saxo was made by the edition and notes of Stephanus Johansen Stephanius, published at Copenhagen in the middle of the seventeenth century (1644). Stephanius, the first commentator on Saxo, still remains the best upon his language. Immense knowledge of Latin, both good and bad (especially of the authors Saxo imitated), infinite and prolix industry, a sharp eye for the text, and continence in emendation, are not his only virtues. His very bulkiness and leisureliness are charming; he writes like a man who had eternity to write in, and who knew enough to fill it, and who expected readers of an equal leisure. He also prints some valuable notes signed with the famous name of Bishop Bryniolf of Skalholt, a man of force and talent, and others by Casper Barth, "corculum Musarum", as Stephanius calls him, whose textual and other comments are sometimes of use, and who worked with a MS. of Saxo. The edition of Klotz, 1771, based on that of Stephanius, I have but seen; however, the first standard commentary is that begun by P. E. Muller, Bishop of Zealand, and finished after his death by Johan Velschow, Professor of History at Copenhagen, where the first part of the work, containing text and notes, was published in 1839; the second, with prolegomena and fuller notes, appearing in 1858. The standard edition, containing bibliography, critical apparatus based on all the editions and MS. fragments, text, and index, is the admirable one of that indefatigable veteran, Alfred Holder, Strasburg, 1886.

Hitherto the translations of Saxo have been into Danish. The first that survives, by Anders Soffrinson Vedel, dates from 1575, some sixty years after the first edition. In such passages as I have examined it is vigorous, but very free, and more like a paraphrase than a translation, Saxo's verses being put into loose prose. Yet it has had a long life, having been modified by Vedel's grandson, John Laverentzen, in 1715, and reissued in 1851. The present version has been much helped by the translation of Seier Schousbolle, published at Copenhagen in 1752. It is true that the verses, often the hardest part, are put into periphrastic verse (by Laurentius Thura, c. 1721), and Schousbolle often does not face a difficulty; but he gives the sense of Saxo simply and concisely. The lusty paraphrase by the enthusiastic Nik. Fred. Sev. Grundtvig, of which there have been several editions, has also been of occasional use. No other translations, save of a scrap here and there into German, seem to be extant.

MANUSCRIPT FRAGMENTS

It will be understood, from what has been said, that no complete MS. of Saxo's History is known. The epitomator in the fourteenth century, and Krantz in the seventeenth, had MSS. before them; and there was that one which Christian Pedersen found and made the basis of the first edition, but which has disappeared. Barth had two manuscripts, which are said to have been burnt in 1636. Another, possessed by a Swedish parish priest, Aschaneus, in 1630, which Stephenhis unluckily did not know of, disappeared in the Royal Archives of Stockholm after his death. These are practically the only MSS. of which we have sure information, excepting the four fragments that are now preserved. Of these by far the most interesting is the "Angers Fragment."

This was first noticed in 1863, in the Angers Library, where it was found degraded into the binding of a number of devotional works and a treatise on metric, dated 1459, and once the property of a priest at Alencon. In 1877 M. Gaston Paris called the attention of the learned to it, and the result was that the Danish Government received it next year in exchange for a valuable French manuscript which was in the Royal Library at Copenhagen. This little national treasure, the only piece of contemporary writing of the History, has been carefully photographed and edited by that enthusiastic and urbane scholar, Christian Bruun. In the opinion both of Dr. Vigfusson and M. Paris, the writing dates from about 1200; and this date, though difficult to determine, owing to the paucity of Danish MSS. of the 12th and early lath centuries, is confirmed by the character of the contents. For there is little doubt that the Fragment shows us Saxo in the labour of composition. The MSS. looks as if expressly written for interlineation. Besides a marginal gloss by a later, fourteenth century hand, there are two distinct sets of variants, in different writings, interlined and running over into the margin. These variants are much more numerous in the prose than in the verse. The first set are in the same hand as the text, the second in another hand: but both of them have the character, not of variants from some other MSS., but of alternative expressions put down tentatively. If either hand is Saxo's it is probably the second. He may conceivably have dictated both at different times to different scribes. No other man would tinker the style in this fashion. A complete translation of all these changes has been deemed unnecessary in these volumes; there is a full collation in Holder's "Apparatus Criticus". The verdict of the Angers-Fragment, which, for the very reason mentioned, must not be taken as the final form of the text, nor therefore, despite its antiquity, as conclusive against the First Edition where the two differ, is to confirm, so far as it goes, the editing of Ascensius and Pederson. There are no vital differences, and the care of the first editors, as well as the authority of their source, is thus far amply vindicated.

A sufficient account of the other fragments will be found in Holder's list. In 1855 M. Kall-Rasmussen found in the private archives at Kronborg a scrap of fourteenth century MS., containing a short passage from Bk. vii. Five years later G. F. Lassen found, at Copenhagen, a fragment of Bk. vi believed to be written in North Zealand, and in the opinion of Bruun belonging to the same codex as Kall-Rasmussen's fragment. Of another longish piece, found in Copenhagen at the end of the seventeenth century by Johannes Laverentzen, and belonging to a codex burnt in the fire of 1728, a copy still extant in the Copenhagen Museum, was made by Otto Sperling. For fragments, either extant or alluded to, of the later books, the student should consult the carefully collated text of Holder. The whole MS. material, therefore, covers but a little of Saxo's work, which was practically saved for Europe by the perseverance and fervour for culture of a single man, Bishop Urne.

SAXO AS A WRITER

Saxo's countrymen have praised without stint his remarkable style, for he has a style. It is often very bad; but he writes, he is not in vain called Grammaticus, the man of letters. His style is not merely remarkable considering its author's difficulties; it is capable at need of pungency and of high expressiveness. His Latin is not that of the Golden Age, but neither is it the common Latin of the Middle Ages. There are traces of his having read Virgil and Cicero. But two writers in particular left their mark on him. The first and most influential is Valerius Maximus, the mannered author of the "Memorabilia", who lived in the first half of the first century, and was much relished in the Middle Ages. From him Saxo borrowed a multitude of phrases, sometimes apt but often crabbed and deformed, as well as an exemplary and homiletic turn of narrative. Other idioms, and perhaps the practice of interspersing verses amid prose (though this also was a twelfth century Icelandic practice), Saxo found in a fifth-century writer, Martianus Capella, the pedantic author of the "De Nuptiis Philologiae et Mercurii" Such models may have saved him from a base mediaeval vocabulary; but they were not worthy of him, and they must answer for some of his falsities of style. These are apparent. His accumulation of empty and motley phrase, like a garish bunch of coloured bladders; his joy in platitude and pomposity, his proneness to say a little thing in great words, are only too easy to translate. We shall be well content if our version also gives some inkling of his qualities; not only of what Erasmus called his "wonderful vocabulary, his many pithy sayings, and the excellent variety of his images"; but also of his feeling for grouping, his barbaric sense of colour, and his stateliness. For he moves with resource and strength both in prose and verse, and is often only hindered by his own wealth. With no kind of critical tradition to chasten him, his force is often misguided and his work shapeless; but he stumbles into many splendours.

FOLK LORE INDEX

The mass of archaic incidents, beliefs, and practices recorded by the 12th-century writer seemed to need some other classification than a bare alphabetic index. The present plan, a subject-index practically, has been adopted with a view to the needs of the anthropologist and folk-lorist. Its details have been largely determined by the bulk and character of the entries themselves. No attempt has been made to supply full parallels from any save the more striking and obvious old Scandinavian sources, the end being to classify material rather than to point out its significance of geographic distribution. With regard to the first three heads, the reader who wishes to see how Saxo compares with the Old Northern poems may be referred to the Grimm Centenary papers, Oxford, 1886, and the Corpus Poeticurn Boreale, Oxford, 1883.

POLITICAL INSTITUTIONS

King—As portrayed by Saxo, the ideal king should be (as in "Beowulf's Lay") generous, brave and just. He should be a man of accomplishments, of unblemished body, presumably of royal kin (peasant-birth is considered a bar to the kingship), usually a son or a nephew, or brother of his foregoer (though no strict rule of succession seems to appear in Saxo), and duly chosen and acknowledged at the proper place of election. In Denmark this was at a stone circle, and the stability of these stones was taken as an omen for the king's reign.

There are exceptional instances noted, as the serf-king Eormenric (cf. Guthred-Canute of Northumberland), whose noble birth washed out this blot of his captivity, and there is a curious tradition of a conqueror setting his hound as king over a conquered province in mockery.

The king was of age at twelve. A king of seven years of age has twelve Regents chosen in the Moot, in one case by lot, to bring him up and rule for him till his majority. Regents are all appointed in Denmark, in one case for lack of royal blood, one to Scania, one to Zealand, one to Funen, two to Jutland. Underkings and Earls are appointed by kings, and though the Earl's office is distinctly official, succession is sometimes given to the sons of faithful fathers. The absence of a settled succession law leads (as in Muslim States) to rebellions and plots.

Kings sometimes abdicated, giving up the crown perforce to a rival, or in high age to a kinsman. In heathen times, kings, as Thiodwulf tells us in the case of Domwald and Yngwere, were sometimes sacrificed for better seasons (African fashion), and Wicar of Norway perishes, like Iphigeneia, to procure fair winds. Kings having to lead in war, and sometimes being willing to fight wagers of battle, are short-lived as a rule, and assassination is a continual peril, whether by fire at a time of feast, of which there are numerous examples, besides the classic one on which Biarea-mal is founded and the not less famous one of Hamlet's vengeance, or whether by steel, as with Hiartuar, or by trick, as in Wicar's case above cited. The reward for slaying a king is in one case 120 gold lbs.; 19 "talents" of gold from each ringleader, 1 oz. of gold from each commoner, in the story of Godfred, known as Ref's gild, "i.e., Fox tax". In the case of a great king, Frode, his death is concealed for three years to avoid disturbance within and danger from without. Captive kings were not as a rule well treated. A Slavonic king, Daxo, offers Ragnar's son Whitesark his daughter and half his realm, or death, and the captive strangely desires death by fire. A captive king is exposed, chained to wild beasts, thrown into a serpent-pit, wherein Ragnar is given the fate of the elder Gunnar in the Eddic Lays, Atlakvida. The king is treated with great respect by his people, he is finely clad, and his commands are carried out, however abhorrent or absurd, as long as they do not upset customary or statute law. The king has slaves in his household, men and women, besides his guard of housecarles and his bearsark champions. A king's daughter has thirty slaves with her, and the footmaiden existed exactly as in the stories of the Wicked Waiting Maid. He is not to be awakened in his slumbers (cf. St. Olaf's Life, where the naming of King Magnus is the result of adherence to this etiquette). A champion weds the king's leman.

His thanes are created by the delivery of a sword, which the king bolds by the blade and the thane takes by the hilt. (English earls were created by the girding with a sword. "Taking treasure, and weapons and horses, and feasting in a hall with the king" is synonymous with thane-hood or gesith-ship in "Beowulf's Lay"). A king's thanes must avenge him if he falls, and owe him allegiance. (This was paid in the old English monarchies by kneeling and laying the head down at the lord's knee.)

The trick by which the Mock-king, or King of the Beggars (parallel to our Boy-bishop, and perhaps to that enigmatic churls' King of the "O. E. Chronicle", s.a. 1017, Eadwiceorla-kyning) gets allegiance paid to him, and so secures himself in his attack on the real king, is cleverly devised. The king, besides being a counsel giver himself, and speaking the law, has "counsellors", old and wise men, "sapientes" (like the O. E. Thyle). The aged warrior counsellor, as Starcad here and Master Hildebrand in the "Nibelungenlied", is one type of these persons, another is the false counsellor, as Woden in guise of Bruni, another the braggart, as Hunferth in "Beowulf's Lay". At "moots" where laws are made, kings and regents chosen, cases judged, resolutions taken of national importance, there are discussions, as in that armed most the host.

The king has, beside his estates up and down the country, sometimes (like Hrothgar with his palace Heorot in "Beowulf's Lay") a great fort and treasure house, as Eormenric, whose palace may well have really existed. There is often a primitive and negroid character about dwellings of formidable personages, heads placed on stakes adorn their exterior, or shields are ranged round the walls.

The provinces are ruled by removable earls appointed by the king, often his own kinsmen, sometimes the heads of old ruling families. The "hundreds" make up the province or subkingdom. They may be granted to king's thanes, who became "hundred-elders". Twelve hundreds are in one case bestowed upon a man.

The "yeoman's" estate is not only honourable but useful, as Starcad generously and truly acknowledges. Agriculture should be fostered and protected by the king, even at the cost of his life.

But gentle birth and birth royal place certain families above the common body of freemen (landed or not); and for a commoner to pretend to a king's daughter is an act of presumption, and generally rigorously resented.

The "smith" was the object of a curious prejudice, probably akin to that expressed in St. Patrick's "Lorica", and derived from the smith's having inherited the functions of the savage weapon-maker with his poisons and charms. The curious attempt to distinguish smiths into good and useful swordsmiths and base and bad goldsmiths seems a merely modern explanation: Weland could both forge swords and make ornaments of metal. Starcad's loathing for a smith recalls the mockery with which the Homeric gods treat Hephaistos.

Slavery—As noble birth is manifest by fine eyes and personal beauty, courage and endurance, and delicate behaviour, so the slave nature is manifested by cowardice, treachery, unbridled lust, bad manners, falsehood, and low physical traits. Slaves had, of course, no right either of honour, or life, or limb. Captive ladies are sent to a brothel; captive kings cruelly put to death. Born slaves were naturally still less considered, they were flogged; it was disgraceful to kill them with honourable steel; to accept a slight service from a slave-woman was beneath old Starcad's dignity. A man who loved another man's slave-woman, and did base service to her master to obtain her as his consort, was looked down on. Slaves frequently ran away to escape punishment for carelessness, or fault, or to gain liberty.

CUSTOMARY LAW

The evidence of Saxo to archaic law and customary institutions is pretty much (as we should expect) that to be drawn from the Icelandic Sagas, and even from the later Icelandic rimur and Scandinavian kaempe-viser. But it helps to complete the picture of the older stage of North Teutonic Law, which we are able to piece together out of our various sources, English, Icelandic, and Scandinavian. In the twilight of Yore every glowworm is a helper to the searcher.
There are a few MAXIMS of various times, but all seemingly drawn from custom cited or implied by Saxo as authoritative:—

"It is disgraceful to be ruled by a woman."—The great men of Teutonic nations held to this maxim. There is no Boudicea or Maidhbh in our own annals till after the accession of the Tudors, when Great Eliza rivals her elder kins-women's glories. Though Tacitus expressly notices one tribe or confederacy, the Sitones, within the compass of his Germania, ruled by a woman, as an exceptional case, it was contrary to the feeling of mediaeval Christendom for a woman to be emperor; it was not till late in the Middle Ages that Spain saw a queen regnant, and France has never yet allowed such rule. It was not till long after Saxo that the great queen of the North, Margaret, wielded a wider sway than that rejected by Gustavus' wayward daughter.

"The suitor ought to urge his own suit."—This, an axiom of the most archaic law, gets evaded bit by bit till the professional advocate takes the place of the plaintiff. "Njal's Saga", in its legal scenes, shows the transition period, when, as at Rome, a great and skilled chief was sought by his client as the supporter of his cause at the Moot. In England, the idea of representation at law is, as is well known, late and largely derived from canon law practice.

"To exact the blood-fine was as honourable as to take vengeance."— This maxim, begotten by Interest upon Legality, established itself both in Scandinavia and Arabia. It marks the first stage in a progress which, if carried out wholly, substitutes law for feud. In the society of the heathen Danes the maxim was a novelty; even in Christian Denmark men sometimes preferred blood to fees.

MARRIAGE.—There are many reminiscences of "archaic marriage customs in Saxo." The capture marriage has left traces in the guarded king's daughters, the challenging of kings to fight or hand over their daughters, in the promises to give a daughter or sister as a reward to a hero who shall accomplish some feat. The existence of polygamy is attested, and it went on till the days of Charles the Great and Harold Fairhair in singular instances, in the case of great kings, and finally disappeared before the strict ecclesiastic regulations.

But there are evidences also of later customs, such as "marriage by purchase", already looked on as archaic in Saxo's day; and the free women in Denmark had clearly long had a veto or refusal of a husband for some time back, and sometimes even free choice. "Go-betweens" negotiate marriages.

Betrothal was of course the usage. For the groom to defile an espoused woman is a foul reproach. Gifts made to father-in-law after bridal by bridegroom seem to denote the old bride-price. Taking the bride home in her car was an important ceremony, and a bride is taken to her future husband's by her father. The wedding-feast, as in France in Rabelais' time, was a noisy and drunken and tumultuous rejoicing, when bone-throwing was in favor, with other rough sports and jokes. The three days after the bridal and their observance in "sword-bed" are noticed below.

A commoner or one of slave-blood could not pretend to wed a high-born lady. A woman would sometimes require some proof of power or courage at her suitor's hands; thus Gywritha, like the famous lady who weds Harold Fairhair, required her husband Siwar to be over-king of the whole land. But in most instances the father or brother betrothed the girl, and she consented to their choice. Unwelcome suitors perish.

The prohibited degrees were, of course, different from those established by the mediaeval church, and brother weds brother's widow in good archaic fashion. Foster-sister and foster-brother may marry, as Saxo notices carefully. The Wolsung incest is not noticed by Saxo. He only knew, apparently, the North-German form of the Niflung story. But the reproachfulness of incest is apparent.

Birth and beauty were looked for in a bride by Saxo's heroes, and chastity was required. The modesty of maidens in old days is eulogised by Saxo, and the penalty for its infraction was severe: sale abroad into slavery to grind the quern in the mud of the yard. One of the tests of virtue is noticed, "lac in ubere".

That favourite "motif", the "Patient Grizzle", occurs, rather, however, in the Border ballad than the Petrarcan form.

"Good wives" die with their husbands as they have vowed, or of grief for their loss, and are wholly devoted to their interests. Among "bad wives" are those that wed their husband's slayer, run away from their husbands, plot against their husbands' lives. The penalty for adultery is death to both, at husband's option—disfigurement by cutting off the nose of the guilty woman, an archaic practice widely spread. In one case the adulterous lady is left the choice of her own death. Married women's Homeric duties are shown.

There is a curious story, which may rest upon fact, and not be merely typical, where a mother who had suffered wrong forced her daughter to suffer the same wrong.

Captive women are reduced to degrading slavery as "harlots" in one case, according to the eleventh century English practice of Gytha.

THE FAMILY AND BLOOD REVENGE.—This duty, one of the strongest links of the family in archaic Teutonic society, has left deep traces in Saxo.

To slay those most close in blood, even by accident, is to incur the guilt of parricide, or kin-killing, a bootless crime, which can only be purged by religious ceremonies; and which involves exile, lest the gods' wrath fall on the land, and brings the curse of childlessness on the offender until he is forgiven.

BOOTLESS CRIMES.—As among the ancient Teutons, botes and were-gilds satisfy the injured who seek redress at law rather than by the steel. But there are certain bootless crimes, or rather sins, that imply "sacratio", devotion to the gods, for the clearing of the community. Such are treason, which is punishable by hanging; by drowning in sea.

Rebellion is still more harshly treated by death and forfeiture; the rebels' heels are bored and thonged under the sinew, as Hector's feet were, and they are then fastened by the thongs to wild bulls, hunted by hounds, till they are dashed to pieces (for which there are classic parallels), or their feet are fastened with thongs to horses driven apart, so that they are torn asunder.

For "parricide", i.e., killing within near degrees, the criminal is hung up, apparently by the heels, with a live wolf (he having acted as a wolf which will slay its fellows). Cunning avoidance of the guilt by trick is shown.

For "arson" the appropriate punishment is the fire.

For "incestuous adultery" of stepson with his stepmother, hanging is awarded to the man. In the same case Swanwhite, the woman, is punished, by treading to death with horses. A woman accomplice in adultery is treated to what Homer calls a "stone coat." Incestuous adultery is a foul slur.

For "witchcraft", the horror of heathens, hanging was the penalty.

"Private revenge" sometimes deliberately inflicts a cruel death for atrocious wrong or insult, as when a king, enraged at the slaying of his son and seduction of his daughter, has the offender hanged, an instance famous in Nathan's story, so that Hagbard's hanging and hempen necklace were proverbial.

For the slayer by a cruel death of their captive father, Ragnar's sons act the blood-eagle on Ella, and salt his flesh. There is an undoubted instance of this act of vengeance (the symbolic meaning of which is not clear as yet) in the "Orkney Saga".

But the story of Daxo and of Ref's gild show that for such wrongs were-gilds were sometimes exacted, and that they were considered highly honourable to the exactor.

Among OFFENCES NOT BOOTLESS, and left to individual pursuit, are:—

"Highway robbery".—There are several stories of a type such as that of Ingemund and Ioknl (see "Landnamaboc") told by Saxo of highwaymen;

and an incident of the kind that occurs in the Theseus story (the Bent-tree, which sprung back and slew the wretch bound to it) is given. The romantic trick of the mechanic bed, by which a steel-shod beam is let fall on the sleeping traveller, also occurs. Slain highwaymen are gibbeted as in Christian days.

"Assassination", as distinct from manslaughter in vengeance for a wrong, is not very common. A hidden mail-coat foils a treacherous javelin-cast (cf. the Story of Olaf the Stout and the Blind King, Hrorec); murderers lurk spear-armed at the threshold, sides, as in the Icelandic Sagas; a queen hides a spear-head in her gown, and murders her husband (cf. Olaf Tryggvason's Life). Godfred was murdered by his servant (and Ynglingatal).

"Burglary".—The crafty discovery of the robber of the treasury by Hadding is a variant of the world-old Rhampsinitos tale, but less elaborate, possibly abridged and cut down by Saxo, and reduced to a mere moral example in favour of the goldenness of silence and the danger of letting the tongue feed the gallows.

Among other disgraceful acts, that make the offender infamous, but do not necessarily involve public action:—

"Manslaughter in Breach of Hospitality".—Probably any gross breach of hospitality was disreputable and highly abhorred, but "guest-slaughter" is especially mentioned. The ethical question as to whether a man should slay his guest or forego his just vengeance was often a "probleme du jour" in the archaic times to which these traditions witness. Ingeld prefers his vengeance, but Thuriswend, in the Lay cited by Paul the Deacon, chooses to protect his guest. Heremod slew his messmates in his wrath, and went forth alone into exile. ("Beowulf's Lay".)

"Suicide".—This was more honourable than what Earl Siward of Northumberland called a "cow-death." Hadding resolves to commit suicide at his friend's death. Wermund resolves to commit suicide if his son be slain (in hopelessness of being able to avenge him, cf. "Njal's Saga", where the hero, a Christian, prefers to perish in his burning house than live dishonoured, "for I am an old man and little fitted to avenge my sons, but I will not live in shame"). Persons commit suicide by slaying each other in time of famine; while in England (so Baeda tells) they "decliffed" themselves in companies, and, as in the comic little Icelandic tale Gautrec's birth, a Tarpeian death is noted as the customary method of relieving folks from the hateful starvation death. It is probable that the violent death relieved the ghost or the survivors of some inconveniences which a "straw death" would have brought about.

"Procedure by Wager of Battle".—This archaic process pervades Saxo's whole narrative. It is the main incident of many of the sagas from which he drew. It is one of the chief characteristics of early Teutonic custom-law, and along with "Cormac's Saga", "Landnamaboc", and the Walter Saga, our author has furnished us with most of the information we have upon its principles and practice.

Steps in the process are the Challenge, the Acceptance and Settlement of Conditions, the Engagement, the Treatment of the vanquished, the Reward of the conqueror, and there are rules touching each of these, enough almost to furnish a kind of "Galway code".

A challenge could not, either to war or wager of battle, be refused with honor, though a superior was not bound to fight an inferior in rank. An ally might accept for his principal, or a father for a son, but it was not honourable for a man unless helpless to send a champion instead of himself.

Men were bound to fight one to one, and one man might decline to fight two at once. Great champions sometimes fought against odds.

The challenged man chose the place of battle, and possibly fixed the time. This was usually an island in the river.

The regular weapons were swords and shields for men of gentle blood. They fought by alternate separate strokes; the senior had the first blow. The fight must go on face to face without change of place; for the ground was marked out for the combatants, as in our prize ring, though one can hardly help fancying that the fighting ground so carefully described in "Cormac's Saga", ch. 10, may have been Saxo's authority. The combatants change places accidentally in the struggle in one story.

The combat might last, like Cuchullin's with Ferdia, several days; a nine days' fight occurs; but usually a few blows settled the matter. Endurance was important, and we are told of a hero keeping himself in constant training by walking in a mail coat.

The conqueror ought not to slay his man if he were a stripling, or maimed, and had better take his were-gild for his life, the holmslausn or ransom of "Cormac's Saga" (three marks in Iceland); but this was a mere concession to natural pity, and he might without loss of honor finish his man, and cut off his head, though it was proper, if the slain adversary has been a man of honor, to bury him afterward.

The stakes are sometimes a kingdom or a kingdom's tribute, often a lady, or the combatants fought for "love" or the point of honor. Giants and noted champions challenge kings for their daughters (as in the fictitious parts of the Icelandic family sagas) in true archaic fashion, and in true archaic fashion the prince rescues the lady from a disgusting and evil fate by his prowess.

The champion's fee or reward when he was fighting for his principal and came off successful was heavy—many lands and sixty slaves. Bracelets are given him; a wound is compensated for at ten gold pieces; a fee for killing a king is 120 of the same.

Of the incidents of the combat, beside fair sleight of fence, there is the continual occurrence of the sword-blunting spell, often cast by the eye of the sinister champion, and foiled by the good hero, sometimes by covering his blade with thin skin, sometimes by changing the blade, sometimes by using a mace or club.

The strength of this tradition sufficiently explains the necessity of the great oath against magic taken by both parties in a wager of battle in Christian England.

The chief combats mentioned by Saxo are:—

Sciold v. Attila.
Sciold v. Scate, for the hand of Alfhild.
Gram v. Swarin and eight more, for the crown of the Swedes.
Hadding v. Toste, by challenge.
Frode v. Hunding, on challenge.
Frode v. Hacon, on challenge.
Helge v. Hunding, by challenge at Stad.
Agnar v. Bearce, by challenge.
Wizard v. Danish champions, for truage of the Slavs.
Wizard v. Ubbe, for truage of the Slavs.
Coll v. Horwendill, on challenge.
Athisl v. Frowine, meeting in battle.
Athisl v. Ket and Wig, on challenge.
Uffe v. Prince of Saxony and Champion, by challenge.
Frode v. Froger, on challenge.
Eric v. Grep's brethren, on challenge, twelve a side.
Eric v. Alrec, by challenge.
Hedin v. Hogni, the mythic everlasting battle.
Arngrim v. Scalc, by challenge.
Arngrim v. Egtheow, for truage of Permland.

Arrow-Odd and Hialmar v. twelve sons of Arngrim Samsey fight.
Ane Bow-swayer v. Beorn, by challenge.
Starkad v. Wisin, by challenge.
Starkad v. Tanlie, by challenge.
Starkad v. Wasce—Wilzce, by challenge.
Starkad v. Hame, by challenge.
Starkad v. Angantheow and eight of his brethren, on challenge.
Halfdan v. Hardbone and six champions, on challenge.
Halfdan v. Egtheow, by challenge.
Halfdan v. Grim, on challenge.
Halfdan v. Ebbe, on challenge, by moonlight.
Halfdan v. Twelve champions, on challenge.
Halfdan v. Hildeger, on challenge.
Ole v. Skate and Hiale, on challenge.
Homod and Thole v. Beorn and Thore, by challenge.
Ref. v. Gaut, on challenge.
Ragnar and three sons v. Starcad of Sweden and seven sons, on
challenge.

CIVIL PROCEDURE.—"Oaths" are an important art of early procedure,
and noticed by Saxo; one calling the gods to witness and therefor, it is
understood, to avenge perjury if he spake not truth.

"Testification", or calling witnesses to prove the steps of a legal action,
was known, "Glum's Saga" and "Landnamaboc", and when a manslayer
proceeded (in order to clear himself of murder) to announce the
manslaughter as his act, he brings the dead man's head as his proof,
exactly as the hero in the folk-tales brings the dragon's head or tongue
as his voucher.

A "will" is spoken of. This seems to be the solemn declaration of a
childless man to his kinsfolk, recommending some person as his
successor. Nothing more was possible before written wills were
introduced by the Christian clergy after the Roman fashion.

STATUTE LAWS

"Lawgivers".—The realm of Custom had already long been curtailed by
the conquests of Law when Saxo wrote, and some epochs of the
invasion were well remembered, such as Canute's laws. But the
beginnings were dim, and there were simply traditions of good and bad
lawyers of the past; such were "Sciold" first of all the arch-king, "Frode"
the model lawgiver, "Helge" the tyrant, "Ragnar" the shrewd conqueror.

"Sciold", the patriarch, is made by tradition to fulfil, by abolishing evil customs and making good laws, the ideal of the Saxon and Frankish Coronation oath formula (which may well go back with its two first clauses to heathen days). His fame is as widely spread. However, the only law Saxo gives to him has a story to it that he does not plainly tell. Sciold had a freedman who repaid his master's manumission of him by the ingratitude of attempting his life. Sciold thereupon decrees the unlawfulness of manumissions, or (as Saxo puts it), revoked all manumissions, thus ordaining perpetual slavery on all that were or might become slaves. The heathen lack of pity noticed in Alfred's preface to "Gregory's Handbook" is illustrated here by contrast with the philosophic humanity of the Civil Law, and the sympathy of the mediaeval Church.

But FRODE (known also to the compiler of "Beowulf's Lay", 2025) had, in the Dane's eyes, almost eclipsed Sciold as conqueror and lawgiver. His name Frode almost looks as if his epithet Sapiens had become his popular appellation, and it befits him well. Of him were told many stories, and notably the one related of our Edwin by Bede (and as it has been told by many men of many rulers since Bede wrote, and before). Frode was able to hang up an arm-ring of gold in three parts of his kingdom that no thief for many years dared touch. How this incident (according to our version preserved by Saxo), brought the just king to his end is an archaic and interesting story. Was this ring the Brosinga men?

Saxo has even recorded the Laws of Frode in four separate bits, which we give as A, B, C, D.

A. is mainly a civil and military code of archaic kind:

(a) The division of spoil shall be—gold to captains, silver to privates, arms to champions, ships to be shared by all. Cf. Jomswickinga S. on the division of spoil by the law of the pirate community of Jom.

(b) No house stuff to be locked; if a man used a lock he must pay a gold mark.

(c) He who spares a thief must bear his punishment.

(d) The coward in battle is to forfeit all rights (cf. "Beowulf", 2885).

(e) Women to have free choice (or, at least, veto) in taking husbands.

20

(f) A free woman that weds a slave loses rank and freedom (cf. Roman Law).

(g) A man must marry a girl he has seduced.

(h) An adulterer to be mutilated at pleasure of injured husband.

(i) Where Dane robbed Dane, the thief to pay double and peace-breach.

(k) Receivers of stolen goods suffer forfeiture and flogging at most.

(l) Deserter bearing shield against his countrymen to lose life and property.

(m) Contempt of fyrd-summons or call to military service involves outlawry and exile.

(n) Bravery in battle to bring about increase in rank (cf. the old English "Ranks of Men").

(o) No suit to lie on promise and pledge; fine of a gold lb. for asking pledge.
(p) Wager of battle is to be the universal mode of proof.

(q) If an alien kill a Dane two aliens must suffer. (This is practically the same principle as appears in the half weregild of the Welsh in West Saxon Law.)

B. An illustration of the more capricious of the old enactments and the jealousy of antique kings.

(a) Loss of gifts sent to the king involves the official responsible; he shall be hanged. (This is introduced as illustration of the cleverness of Eric and the folly of Coll.)

C. Saxo associates another set of enactments with the completion of a successful campaign of conquest over the Ruthenians, and shows Frode chiefly as a wise and civilising statesman, making conquest mean progress.

(a) Every free householder that fell in war was to be set in his barrow with horse and arms (cf. "Vatzdaela Saga", ch. 2).

The body-snatcher was to be punished by death and the lack of sepulture.

Earl or king to be burned in his own ship.

Ten sailors may be burnt on one ship.

(b) Ruthenians to have the same law of war as Danes.

(c) Ruthenians must adopt Danish sale-marriage. (This involves the abolition of the Baltic custom of capture-marriage. That capture-marriage was a bar to social progress appears in the legislation of Richard II, directed against the custom as carried out on the borders of the Palatine county of Chester, while cases such as the famous one of Rob Roy's sons speak to its late continuance in Scotland. In Ireland it survived in a stray instance or two into this century, and songs like "William Riley" attest the sympathy of the peasant with the eloping couple.)

(d) A veteran, one of the Doughty, must be such a man as will attack one foe, will stand two, face three without withdrawing more than a little, and be content to retire only before four. (One of the traditional folk-sayings respecting the picked men, the Doughty or Old Guard, as distinguished from the Youth or Young Guard, the new-comers in the king's Company of House-carles. In Harald Hardrede's Life the Norwegians dread those English house-carles, "each of whom is a match for four," who formed the famous guard that won Stamford Bridge and fell about their lord, a sadly shrunken band, at Senlake.)

(f) The house-carles to have winter-pay. The house-carle three pieces of silver, a hired soldier two pieces, a soldier who had finished his service one piece.

(The treatment of the house-carles gave Harald Harefoot a reputation long remembered for generosity, and several old Northern kings have won their nicknames by their good or ill feeding and rewarding their comitatus.)

D. Again a civil code, dealing chiefly with the rights of travellers.

(a) Seafarers may use what gear they find (the "remis" of the text may include boat or tackle).

(b) No house is to be locked, nor coffer, but all thefts to be compensated threefold. (This, like A, b, which it resembles, seems a popular tradition intended to show the absolute security of Frode's reign of seven or three hundred years. It is probably a gloss wrongly repeated.)

(c) A traveller may claim a single supper; if he take more he is a thief (the mark of a prae-tabernal era when hospitality was waxing cold through misuse).

(d) Thief and accomplices are to be punished alike, being hung up by a line through the sinews and a wolf fastened beside. (This, which contradicts A, i, k, and allots to theft the punishment proper for parricide, seems a mere distorted tradition.)

But beside just Frode, tradition spoke of the unjust Kinge HELGE, whose laws represent ill-judged harshness. They were made for conquered races, (a) the Saxons and (b) the Swedes.

(a) Noble and freedmen to have the same were-gild (the lower, of course, the intent being to degrade all the conquered to one level, and to allow only the lowest were-gild of a freedman, fifty pieces, probably, in the tradition).

(b) No remedy for wrong done to a Swede by a Dane to be legally recoverable. (This is the traditional interpretation of the conqueror's haughty dealing; we may compare it with the Middle-English legends of the pride of the Dane towards the conquered English. The Tradition sums up the position in such concrete forms as this Law of Helge's.)

Two statutes of RAGNAR are mentioned:—

(a) That any householder should give up to his service in war the worst of his children, or the laziest of his slaves (a curious tradition, and used by Saxo as an opportunity for patriotic exaltation).

(b) That all suits shall be absolutely referred to the judgment of twelve chosen elders (Lodbroc here appearing in the strange character of originator of trial by jury).

"Tributes".—Akin to laws are the tributes decreed and imposed by kings and conquerors of old. Tribute infers subjection in archaic law. The poll-tax in the fourteenth century in England was unpopular, because of its seeming to degrade Englishmen to the level of Frenchmen, who paid tribute like vanquished men to their absolute lord, as well as for other reasons connected with the collection of the tax.

The old fur tax (mentioned in "Egil's Saga") is here ascribed to FRODE, who makes the Finns pay him, every three years, a car full or sledge full of skins for every ten heads; and extorts one skin per head from the Perms. It is Frode, too (though Saxo has carved a number of Frodes out of one or two kings of gigantic personality), that made the Saxons pay a poll-tax, a piece of money per head, using, like William the Conqueror, his extraordinary revenue to reward his soldiers, whom he first regaled with double pay. But on the conquered folks rebelling, he marked their reduction by a tax of a piece of money on every limb a cubit long, a "limb-geld" still more hateful than the "neb-geld."

HOTHERUS (Hodr) had set a tribute on the Kurlanders and Swedes, and HROLF laid a tribute on the conquered Swedes.

GODEFRIDUS-GOTRIC is credited with a third Saxon tribute, a heriot of 100 snow-white horses payable to each Danish king at his succession, and by each Saxon chief on his accession: a statement that, recalling sacred snow-white horses kept in North Germany of yore makes one wish for fuller information. But Godefridus also exacted from the Swedes the "Ref-gild", or Fox-money; for the slaying of his henchman Ref, twelve pieces of gold from each man of rank, one from every commoner. And his Friesland tribute is stranger still, nor is it easy to understand from Saxo's account. There was a long hall built, 240 feet, and divided up into twelve "chases" of 20 feet each (probably square). There was a shield set up at one end, and the taxpayers hurled their money at it; if struck so as to sound, it was good; if not, it was forfeit, but not reckoned in the receipt. This (a popular version, it may be, of some early system of treasury test) was abolished, so the story goes, by Charles the Great.

RAGNAR'S exaction from Daxo, his son's slayer, was a yearly tribute brought by himself and twelve of his elders barefoot, resembling in part such submissions as occur in the Angevin family history, the case of the Calais burgesses, and of such criminals as the Corporation of Oxford, whose penance was only finally renounced by the local patriots in our own day.

24

WAR

"Weapons".—The sword is the weapon par excellence in Saxo's narrative, and he names several by name, famous old blades like our royal Curtana, which some believed was once Tristrem's, and that sword of Carlus, whose fortunes are recorded in Irish annals. Such are "Snyrtir", Bearce's sword; "Hothing", Agnar's blade; "Lauf", or "Leaf", Bearce's sword; "Screp", Wermund's sword, long buried and much rust-eaten, but sharp and trusty, and known by its whistle; Miming's sword ("Mistletoe"), which slew Balder. Wainhead's curved blade seems to be a halbert; "Lyusing" and "Hwiting", Ragnald of Norway's swords; "Logthe", the sword of Ole Siward's son.

The "war-club" occurs pretty frequently. But it is usually introduced as a special weapon of a special hero, who fashions a gold-headed club to slay one that steel cannot touch, or who tears up a tree, like the Spanish knight in the ballad, or who uses a club to counteract spells that blunt steel. The bat-shapen archaic rudder of a ship is used as a club in the story of the Sons of Arngrim.

The "spear" plays no particular part in Saxo: even Woden's spear Gungne is not prominent.

"Bows and arrows" are not often spoken of, but archer heroes, such as Toki, Ane Bow-swayer, and Orwar-Odd, are known. Slings and stones are used.

The shield, of all defensive armour, is far the most prominent. They were often painted with devices, such as Hamlet's shield, Hildiger's Swedish shield. Dr. Vigfusson has shown the importance of these painted shields in the poetic history of the Scandinavians.

A red shield is a signal of peace. Shields are set round ramparts on land as round ships at sea.

"Mail-coats" are worn. Frode has one charmed against steel. Hother has another; a mail-coat of proof is mentioned and their iron meshes are spoken of.

"Helmets" are used, but not so carefully described as in "Beowulf's Lay"; crested helmets and a gilded helmet occur in Bearca-mal and in another poem.

"Banners" serve as rallying points in the battle and on the march. The

Huns' banners are spoken of in the classic passage for the description of a huge host invading a country. Bearcamal talks of golden banners.

"Horns" (1) were blown up at the beginning of the engagement and for signalling. The gathering of the host was made by delivery of a wooden arrow painted to look like iron.

"Tactics".—The hand-to-hand fight of the wager of battle with sword and shield, and the fighting in ranks and the wedge-column at close quarters, show that the close infantry combat was the main event of the battle. The preliminary hurling of stones, and shooting of arrows, and slinging of pebbles, were harassing and annoying, but seldom sufficiently important to affect the result of the main engagement.

Men ride to battle, but fight on foot; occasionally an aged king is car-borne to the fray, and once the car, whether by Saxo's adorning hand, or by tradition, is scythe-armed.

The gathered host is numbered, once, where, as with Xerxes, counting was too difficult, by making each man as he passed put a pebble in a pile (which piles survive to mark the huge size of Frode's army). This is, of course, a folktale, explaining the pebble-hills and illustrating the belief in Frode's power; but armies were mustered by such expedients of old. Burton tells of an African army each man of whom presented an egg, as a token of his presence and a means of taking the number of the host.

We hear of men marching in light order without even scabbards, and getting over the ice in socks.

The war equipment and habits of the Irish, light armoured, clipped at back of head, hurling the javelin backwards in their feigned flight; of the Slavs, small blue targets and long swords; of the Finns, with their darts and skees, are given.

Watches are kept, and it is noted that "uht", the early watch after midnight, is the worst to be attacked in (the duke's two-o'clock-in-the-morning courage being needed, and the darkness and cold helping the enemy).

Spies were, of course, slain if discovered. But we have instances of kings and heroes getting into foeman's camps in disguise (cf. stories of Alfred and Anlaf).

The order of battle of Bravalla fight is given, and the ideal array of a host. To Woden is ascribed the device of the boar's head, hamalt fylking (the swine-head array of Manu's Indian kings), the terrible column with wedge head which could cleave the stoutest line.

The host of Ring has men from Wener, Wermland, Gotaelf, Thotn, Wick, Thelemark, Throndham, Sogn, Firths, Fialer, Iceland; Sweden, Gislamark, Sigtun, Upsala, Pannonia.

The host of Harold had men from Iceland, the Danish provinces, Frisia, Lifland; Slavs, and men from Jom, Aland, and Sleswick.

The battle of Bravalla is said to have been won by the Gotland archers and the men of Throndham, and the Dales. The death of Harald by treachery completed the defeat, which began when Ubbe fell (after he had broken the enemy's van) riddled with arrows.

The defeated, unless they could fly, got little quarter. One-fifth only of the population of a province are said to have survived an invasion. After sea-battles (always necessarily more deadly) the corpses choke the harbours. Seventy sea-kings are swept away in one sea-fight. Heads seem to have been taken in some cases, but not as a regular Teutonic usage, and the practice, from its being attributed to ghosts and aliens, must have already been considered savage by Saxo, and probably by his informants and authorities.

Prisoners were slaves; they might be killed, put to cruel death, outraged, used as slaves, but the feeling in favour of mercy was growing, and the cruelty of Eormenric, who used tortures to his prisoners, of Rothe, who stripped his captives, and of Fro, who sent captive ladies to a brothel in insult, is regarded with dislike.

Wounds were looked on as honourable, but they must be in front or honourably got. A man who was shot through the buttocks, or wounded in the back, was laughed at and disgraced. We hear of a mother helping her wounded son out of battle.

That much of human interest centered round war is evident by the mass of tradition that surrounds the subject in Saxo, both in its public and private aspects. Quaint is the analysis of the four kinds of warriors: (a) The Veterans, or Doughty, who kill foes and spare flyers; (b) the Young men who kill foes and flyers too; (c) the well-to-do, landed, and propertied men of the main levy, who neither fight for fear nor fly for shame; (d) the worthless, last to fight and first to fly; and curious are the remarks about married and unmarried troops, a matter which Chaka pondered over in later days. Homeric speeches precede the fight.

27

"Stratagems of War" greatly interested Saxo (probably because Valerius Maximus, one of his most esteemed models, was much occupied with such matters), so that he diligently records the military traditions of the notably skillful expedients of famous commanders of old.

There is the device for taking a town by means of the "pretended death" of the besieging general, a device ascribed to Hastings and many more commanders (see Steenstrup Normannerne); the plan of "firing" a besieged town by fire-bearing birds, ascribed here to Fridlev, in the case of Dublin to Hadding against Duna (where it was foiled by all tame birds being chased out of the place).

There is the "Birnam Wood" stratagem, by which men advanced behind a screen of boughs, which is even used for the concealment of ships, and the curious legend (occurring in Irish tradition also, and recalling Capt. B. Hall's "quaker gun" story) by which a commander bluffs off his enemy by binding his dead to stakes in rows, as if they were living men.

Less easy to understand are the "brazen horses" or "machines" driven into the close lines of the enemy to crush and open them, an invention of Gewar. The use of hooked weapons to pull down the foes' shields and helmets was also taught to Hother by Gewar.

The use of black tents to conceal encampment; the defence of a pass by hurling rocks from the heights; the bridge of boats across the Elbe; and the employment of spies, and the bold venture, ascribed in our chronicles to Alfred and Anlaf, of visiting in disguise the enemy's camp, is here attributed to Frode, who even assumed women's clothes for the purpose.

Frode is throughout the typical general, as he is the typical statesman and law-giver of archaic Denmark.

There are certain heathen usages connected with war, as the hurling of a javelin or shooting of an arrow over the enemy's ranks as a "sacratio" to Woden of the foe at the beginning of a battle. This is recorded in the older vernacular authorities also, in exact accordance with the Homeric usage, "Odyssey" xxiv, 516-595.

The dedication of part of the spoils to the god who gave good omens for the war is told of the heathen Baltic peoples; but though, as Sidonius records, it had once prevailed among the Saxons, and, as other witnesses add, among the Scandinavian people, the tradition is not clearly preserved by Saxo.

"Sea and Sea Warfare."—As might be expected, there is much mention of Wicking adventure and of maritime warfare in Saxo.

Saxo tells of Asmund's huge ship (Gnod), built high that he might shoot down on the enemy's craft; he speaks of a ship (such as Godwin gave as a gift to the king his master), and the monk of St. Bertin and the court-poets have lovingly described a ship with gold-broidered sails, gilt masts, and red-dyed rigging. One of his ships has, like the ships in the Chansons de Geste, a carbuncle for a lantern at the masthead. Hedin signals to Frode by a shield at the masthead. A red shield was a peace signal, as noted above. The practice of "strand-hewing", a great feature in Wicking-life (which, so far as the victualling of raw meat by the fishing fleets, and its use raw, as Mr. P. H. Emerson informs me, still survives), is spoken of. There was great fear of monsters attacking them, a fear probably justified by such occasional attacks of angry whales as Melville (founding his narrative on repeated facts) has immortalised. The whales, like Moby Dick, were uncanny, and inspired by troll-women or witches (cf. "Frithiof Saga" and the older "Lay of Atle and Rimegerd"). The clever sailing of Hadding, by which he eludes pursuit, is tantalising, for one gathers that, Saxo knows the details that he for some reason omits. Big fleets of 150 and a monster armada of 3,000 vessels are recorded.

The ships were moved by oars and sails; they had rudders, no doubt such as the Gokstad ship, for the hero Arrow-Odd used a rudder as a weapon.

"Champions".—Professed fighting men were often kept by kings and earls about their court as useful in feud and fray. Harald Fairhair's champions are admirably described in the contemporary Raven Song by Hornclofe—

> "Wolf-coats they call them that in battle
> Bellow into bloody shields.
> They wear wolves' hides when they come into the fight,
> And clash their weapons together."

and Saxo's sources adhere closely to this pattern.

These "bear-sarks", or wolf-coats of Harald give rise to an O. N. term, "bear-sarks' way", to describe the frenzy of fight and fury which such champions indulged in, barking and howling, and biting their shield-rims (like the ferocious "rook" in the narwhale ivory chessmen in the British Museum) till a kind of state was produced akin to that of the Malay when he has worked himself up to "run-a-muck." There seems to have

29

been in the 10th century a number of such fellows about unemployed, who became nuisances to their neighbours by reason of their bullying and highhandedness. Stories are told in the Icelandic sagas of the way such persons were entrapped and put to death by the chiefs they served when they became too troublesome. A favourite (and fictitious) episode in an "edited" Icelandic saga is for the hero to rescue a lady promised to such a champion (who has bullied her father into consent) by slaying the ruffian. It is the same "motif" as Guy of Warwick and the Saracen lady, and one of the regular Giant and Knight stories.

Beside men-warriors there were "women-warriors" in the North, as Saxo explains. He describes shield-maidens, as Alfhild, Sela, Rusila (the Ingean Ruadh, or Red Maid of the Irish Annals, as Steenstrup so ingeniously conjectures); and the three she-captains, Wigbiorg, who fell on the field, Hetha, who was made queen of Zealand, and Wisna, whose hand Starcad cut off, all three fighting manfully at Bravalla fight.

SOCIAL LIFE AND MANNERS

"Feasts".—The hall-dinner was an important feature in the old Teutonic court-life. Many a fine scene in a saga takes place in the hall while the king and his men are sitting over their ale. The hall decked with hangings, with its fires, lights, plate and provisions, appears in Saxo just as in the Eddic Lays, especially Rigsmal, and the Lives of the Norwegian Kings and Orkney Earls.

The order of seats is a great point of archaic manners. Behaviour at table was a matter of careful observance. The service, especially that of the cup-bearer, was minutely regulated by etiquette. An honoured guest was welcomed by the host rising to receive him and giving him a seat near himself, but less distinguished visitors were often victims to the rough horseplay of the baser sort, and of the wanton young gentleman at court. The food was simple, boiled beef and pork, and mutton without sauce, ale served in horns from the butt. Roast meat, game, sauces, mead, and flagons set on the table, are looked on by Starcad as foreign luxuries, and Germany was credited with luxurious cookery.

"Mimes and jugglers", who went through the country or were attached to the lord's court to amuse the company, were a despised race because of their ribaldry, obscenity, cowardice, and unabashed self-debasement; and their newfangled dances and piping were loathsome to the old court-poets, who accepted the harp alone as an instrument of music.

The story that once a king went to war with his jugglers and they ran away, would represent the point of view of the old house-carle, who was neglected, though "a first-class fighting man", for these debauched foreign buffoons.

SUPERNATURAL BEINGS

GODS AND GODDESSES.—The gods spring, according to Saxo's belief, from a race of sorcerers, some of whom rose to pre-eminence and expelled and crushed the rest, ending the "wizard-age", as the wizards had ended the monster or "giant-age". That they were identic with the classic gods he is inclined to believe, but his difficulty is that in the week-days we have Jove : Thor; Mercury : Woden; whereas it is perfectly well known that Mercury is Jove's son, and also that Woden is the father of Thor—a comic "embarras". That the persians the heathens worshipped as gods existed, and that they were men and women false and powerful, Saxo plainly believes. He has not Snorre's appreciation of the humorous side of the mythology. He is ironic and scornful, but without the kindly, naive fun of the Icelander.
The most active god, the Dane's chief god (as Frey is the Swede's god, and patriarch), is "Woden". He appears in heroic life as patron of great heroes and kings. Cf. "Hyndla-Lay", where it is said of Woden:—

"Let us pray the Father of Hosts to be gracious to us!
He granteth and giveth gold to his servants,
He gave Heremod a helm and mail-coat,
And Sigmund a sword to take.
He giveth victory to his sons, to his followers wealth,
Ready speech to his children and wisdom to men.
Fair wind to captains, and song to poets;
He giveth luck in love to many a hero."

He appears under various disguises and names, but usually as a one-eyed old man, cowled and hooded; sometimes with another, bald and ragged, as before the battle Hadding won; once as "Hroptr", a huge man skilled in leechcraft, to Ragnar's son Sigfrid.

Often he is a helper in battle or doomer of feymen. As "Lysir", a rover of the sea, he helps Hadding. As veteran slinger and archer he helps his favourite Hadding; as charioteer, "Brune", he drives Harald to his death in battle. He teaches Hadding how to array his troops. As "Yggr" the prophet he advises the hero and the gods. As "Wecha" (Waer) the leech he woos Wrinda. He invented the wedge array. He can grant charmed lives to his favourites against steel. He prophesies their victories and death. He snatches up one of his disciples, sets him on his magic horse that rides over seas in the air, as in Skida-runa the god takes the beggar over the North Sea. His image (like that of Frey in the Swedish story of Ogmund dytt and Gunnar helming, "Flatey book", i, 335) could speak by magic power.

Of his life and career Saxo gives several episodes.

Woden himself dwelt at Upsala and Byzantium (Asgard); and the northern kings sent him a golden image ring-bedecked, which he made to speak oracles. His wife Frigga stole the bracelets and played him false with a servant, who advised her to destroy and rob the image. When Woden was away (hiding the disgrace brought on him by Frigga his wife), an imposter, Mid Odin, possibly Loke in disguise, usurped his place at Upsala, instituted special drink-offerings, fled to Finland on Woden's return, and was slain by the Fins and laid in barrow. But the barrow smote all that approached it with death, till the body was unearthed, beheaded, and impaled, a well-known process for stopping the haunting of an obnoxious or dangerous ghost.

Woden had a son Balder, rival of Hother for the love of Nanna, daughter of King Gewar. Woden and Thor his son fought for him against Hother, but in vain, for Hother won the laity and put Balder to shameful flight; however, Balder, half-frenzied by his dreams of Nanna, in turn drove him into exile (winning the lady); finally Hother, befriended hy luck and the Wood Maidens, to whom he owed his early successes and his magic coat, belt, and girdle (there is obvious confusion here in the text), at last met Balder and stabbed him in the side. Of this wound Balder died in three days, as was foretold by the awful dream in which Proserpina (Hela) appeared to him. Balder's grand burial, his barrow, and the magic flood which burst from it when one Harald tried to break into it, and terrified the robbers, are described.

The death of Balder led Woden to seek revenge. Hrossthiof the wizard, whom he consulted, told him he must beget a son by "Wrinda" (Rinda, daughter of the King of the Ruthenians), who should avenge his half-brother.

Woden's wooing is the best part of this story, half spoilt, however, by euhemeristic tone and lack of epic dignity. He woos as a victorious warrior, and receives a cuff; as a generous goldsmith, and gets a buffet; as a handsome soldier, earning a heavy knock-down blow; but in the garb of a women as Wecha (Wakr), skilled in leechcraft, he won his way by trickery; and ("Wale") "Bous" was born, who, after some years, slew Hother in battle, and died himself of his wounds. Bous' barrow in

Bohusland, Balder's haven, Balder's well, are named as local attestations of the legend, which is in a late form, as it seems.

The story of Woden's being banished for misbehaviour, and especially for sorcery and for having worn woman's attire to trick Wrinda, his replacement by "Wuldor" ("Oller"), a high priest who assumed Woden's name and flourished for ten years, but was ultimately expelled by the returning Woden, and killed by the Danes in Sweden, is in the same style. But Wuldor's bone vessel is an old bit of genuine tradition mangled. It would cross the sea as well as a ship could, by virtue of certain spells marked on it.

Of "Frey", who appears as "satrapa" of the gods at Upsala, and as the originator of human sacrifice, and as appeased by black victims, at a sacrifice called Froblod (Freys-blot) instituted by Hadding, who began it as an atonement for having slain a sea-monster, a deed for which he had incurred a curse. The priapic and generative influences of Frey are only indicated by a curious tradition mentioned. It almost looks as if there had once been such an institution at Upsala as adorned the Phoenician temples, under Frey's patronage and for a symbolic means of worship.

"Thunder", or "Thor", is Woden's son, strongest of gods or men, patron of Starcad, whom he turned, by pulling off four arms, from a monster to a man.

He fights by Woden's side and Balder's against Hother, by whose magic wand his club (hammer) was lopped off part of its shaft, a wholly different and, a much later version than the one Snorre gives in the prose Edda. Saxo knows of Thor's journey to the haunt of giant Garfred (Geirrod) and his three daughters, and of the hurling of the iron "bloom", and of the crushing of the giantesses, though he does not seem to have known of the river-feats of either the ladies or Thor, if we may judge (never a safe thing wholly) by his silence.

Whether "Tew" is meant by the Mars of the Song of the Voice is not evident. Saxo may only be imitating the repeated catch-word "war" of the original.

"Loke" appears as Utgard-Loke, Loke of the skirts of the World, as it were; is treated as a venomous giant bound in agony under a serpent-haunted cavern (no mention is made of "Sigyn" or her pious ministry).

"Hela" seems to be meant by Saxo's Proserpina.

"Nanna" is the daughter of Gewar, and Balder sees her bathing and falls in love with her, as madly as Frey with Gertha in Skirnismal.

"Freya", the mistress of Od, the patroness of Othere the homely, the sister of Frey-Frode, and daughter of Niord-Fridlaf, appears as Gunwara Eric's love and Syritha Ottar's love and the hair-clogged maiden, as Dr. Rydberg has shown.

The gods can disguise their form, change their shape, are often met in a mist, which shrouds them save from the right person; they appear and disappear at will. For the rest they have the mental and physical characteristics of the kings and queens they protect or persecute so capriciously. They can be seen by making a magic sign and looking through a witch's arm held akimbo. They are no good comates for men or women, and to meddle with a goddess or nymph or giantess was to ensure evil or death for a man. The god's loves were apparently not always so fatal, though there seems to be some tradition to that effect. Most of the god-sprung heroes are motherless or unborn (i.e., born like Macduff by the Caesarean operation)—Sigfred, in the Eddic Lays for instance.

Besides the gods, possibly older than they are, and presumably mightier, are the "Fates" (Norns), three Ladies who are met with together, who fulfil the parts of the gift-fairies of our Sleeping Beauty tales, and bestow endowments on the new-born child, as in the beautiful "Helge Lay", a point of the story which survives in Ogier of the Chansons de Geste, wherein Eadgar (Otkerus or Otgerus) gets what belonged to Holger (Holge), the Helga of "Beowulf's Lay". The caprices of the Fates, where one corrects or spoils the others' endowments, are seen in Saxo, when beauty, bounty, and meanness are given together. They sometimes meet heroes, as they met Helgi in the Eddic Lay (Helgi and Sigrun Lay), and help or begift them; they prepare the magic broth for Balder, are charmed with Hother's lute-playing, and bestow on him a belt of victory and a girdle of splendour, and prophesy things to come.

The verse in Biarca-mal, where "Pluto weaves the dooms of the mighty and fills Phlegethon with noble shapes," recalls Darrada-liod, and points to Woden as death-doomer of the warrior.

"Giants".—These are stupid, mischievous, evil and cunning in Saxo's eyes. Oldest of beings, with chaotic force and exuberance, monstrous in extravagant vitality.

The giant nature of the older troll-kind is abhorrent to man and woman. But a giantess is enamoured of a youth she had fostered, and giants

34

carry off king's daughters, and a three-bodied giant captures young children.

Giants live in caves by the sea, where they keep their treasure. One giant, Unfoot (Ofoti), is a shepherd, like Polyphemus, and has a famous dog which passed into the charge of Biorn, and won a battle; a giantess is keeping goats in the wilds. A giant's fury is so great that it takes twelve champions to control him, when the rage is on him. The troll (like our Puss-in-Boots Ogre) can take any shape.

Monstrous apparitions are mentioned, a giant hand (like that in one story of Finn) searching for its prey among the inmates of a booth in the wilds. But this Grendel-like arm is torn off by a giantess, Hardgrip, daughter of Wainhead and niece possibly of Hafle.

The voice heard at night prophesying is that of some god or monster, possibly Woden himself.

"Dwarves".—These Saxo calls Satyrs, and but rarely mentions. The dwarf Miming, who lives in the desert, has a precious sword of sharpness (Mistletoe?) that could even pierce skin-hard Balder, and a ring (Draupnir) that multiplied itself for its possessor. He is trapped by the hero and robbed of his treasures.

FUNERAL RITES AND MAN'S FUTURE STATE

"Barrow-burials".—The obsequies of great men (such as the classic funeral of "Beowulf's Lay", 3138-80) are much noticed by Saxo, and we might expect that he knew such a poem (one similar to Ynglingatal, but not it) which, like the Books of the Kings of Israel and Judah, recorded the deaths and burials, as well as the pedigrees and deeds, of the Danish kings.

The various stages of the "obsequy by fire" are noted; the byre sometimes formed out of a ship; the "sati"; the devoted bower-maidens choosing to die with their mistress, the dead man's beloved (cf. The Eddic funerals of Balder, Sigfred, and Brunhild, in the Long "Brunhild's Lay", Tregrof Gudrumar and the lost poem of Balder's death paraphrased in the prose Edda); the last message given to the corpse on the pyre (Woden's last words to Balder are famous); the riding round the pyre; the eulogium; the piling of the barrow, which sometimes took whole days, as the size of many existing grass mounds assure us; the funeral feast, where an immense vat of ale or mead is drunk in honor of the dead; the epitaph, like an ogham, set up on a stone over the barrow.

The inclusion of a live man with the dead in a barrow, with the live or fresh-slain beasts (horse and bound) of the dead man, seems to point to a time or district when burning was not used. Apparently, at one time, judging from Frode's law, only chiefs and warriors were burnt.

Not to bury was, as in Hellas, an insult to the dead, reserved for the bodies of hated foes. Conquerors sometimes show their magnanimity (like Harald Godwineson) by offering to bury their dead foes.

The buried "barrow-ghost" was formidable; he could rise and slay and eat, vampire-like, as in the tale of Asmund and Aswit. He must in such case be mastered and prevented doing further harm by decapitation and thigh-forking, or by staking and burning. So criminals' bodies were often burnt to stop possible haunting.

Witches and wizards could raise corpses by spells to make them prophesy. The dead also appeared in visions, usually foretelling death to the person they visited.

OTHER WORLDS.—The "Land of Undeath" is spoken of as a place reached by an exiled hero in his wanderings. We know it from Eric the traveller's S., Helge Thoreson's S., Herrand and Bose S., Herwon S., Thorstan Baearmagn S., and other Icelandic sources. But the voyage to the Other Worlds are some of the most remarkable of the narratives Saxo has preserved for us.

"Hadding's Voyage Underground".—(a) A woman bearing in her lap angelica fresh and green, though it was deep winter, appears to the hero at supper, raising her head beside the brazier. Hadding wishes to know where such plants grow.

(b) She takes him with her, under cover of her mantle, underground.

(c) They pierce a mist, get on a road worn by long use, pass nobly-clad men, and reach the sunny fields that bear the angelica:—

> "Through griesly shadowes by a beaten path,
> Into a garden goodly garnished."
> —F.Q. ii. 7, 51.

(d) Next they cross, by a bridge, the "River of Blades", and see "two armies fighting", ghosts of slain soldiers.

(e) Last they came to a high wall, which surrounds the land of Life, for a cock the woman brought with her, whose neck she wrung and tossed over this wall, came to life and crowed merrily.

Here the story breaks off. It is unfinished, we are only told that Hadfling got back. Why he was taken to this under-world? Who took him? What followed therefrom? Saxo does not tell. It is left to us to make out.

That it is an archaic story of the kind in the Thomas of Ercildoune and so many more fairy-tales, e.g., Kate Crack-a-Nuts, is certain. The "River of Blades" and "The Fighting Warriors" are known from the Eddic Poems. The angelica is like the green birk of that superb fragment, the ballad of the Wife of Usher's Well—a little more frankly heathen, of course—

"It fell about the Martinmas, when nights are long and mirk,
The carline wife's three sons cam hame, and their hats were
o' the birk.
It neither grew in syke nor dyke, nor yet in ony sheugh,
But at the gates o' Paradise that birk grew fair eneuch."

The mantel is that of Woden when he bears the hero over seas; the cock is a bird of sorcery the world over; the black fowl is the proper gift to the Underground powers—a heriot really, for did not the Culture god steal all the useful beasts out of the underground world for men's use?

Dr. Rydberg has shown that the "Seven Sleepers" story is an old Northern myth, alluded to here in its early pre-Christian form, and that with this is mixed other incidents from voyages of Swipdag, the Teutonic Odusseus.

"Thorkill's Second Voyage to Outgarth-Loke to get Knowledge".—(a) Guthrum is troubled as to the immortality and fate of the soul, and the reward of piety after death. To spite Thorkill, his enviers advised the king to send him to consult Outgarth-Loke. He required of the king that his enemies should be sent with him.

(b) In one well-stored and hide-defended ship they set out, reached a sunless, starless land, without fuel; ate raw food and suffered. At last, after many days, a fire was seen ashore. Thorkill, setting a jewel at the mast-head to be able to regain his vessel easily, rows ashore to get fire.

(c) In a filthy, snake-paved, stinking cavern he sees two horny-nebbed giants, (2) making a fire. One of the giants offers to direct him to Loke if he will say three true things in three phrases, and this done, tells him to row four days and then he would reach a Dark and Grassless Land. For three more true sayings he obtains fire, and gets back to his vessel.

(d) With good wind they make Grassless Land, go ashore, find a huge, rocky cavern, strike a flint to kindle a fire at the entrance as a safeguard against demons, and a torch to light them as they explored the cavern.

(e) First appears iron seats set amid crawling snakes.

(f) Next is sluggish water flowing over sand.

(g) Last a steep, sloping cavern is reached, in a chamber of which lay Outgarth-Loke chained, huge and foul.

(h) Thorkill plucks a hair of his beard "as big as a cornel-wood spear." The stench that arose was fearful; the demens and snakes fell upon the invaders at once; only Thorkill and five of the crew, who had sheltered themselves with hides against the virulent poison the demons and snakes cast, which would take a head off at the neck if it fell upon it, got back to their ship.

(i) By vow to the "God that made the world", and offerings, a good voyage was made back, and Germany reached, where Thorkill became a Christian. Only two of his men survived the effects of the poison and stench, and he himself was scarred and spoilt in the face.

(k) When he reached the king, Guthrum would not listen to his tale, because it was prophesied to him that he would die suddenly if he heard it; nay, he even sent men to smite him as he lay in bed, but, by the device of laying a log in his place, he escaped, and going to the king as he sat at meat, reproached him for his treachery.

(l) Guthrum bade him tell his story, but died of horror at hearing his god Loke foully spoken of, while the stench of the hair that Thorkill produced, as Othere did his horn for a voucher of his speech, slew many bystanders.

This is the regular myth of Loke, punished by the gods, lying bound with his own soils' entrails on three sharp stones and a sword-blade, (this latter an addition, when the myth was made stones were the only blades), with snakes' venom dripping on to him, so that when it falls on him he shakes with pain and makes earthquakes—a Titan myth in answer to the question, "Why does the earth quake?" The vitriolic power of the poison is excellently expressed in the story. The plucking

of the hair as a token is like the plucking of a horn off the giant or devil
that occurs in some folk-tale.

MAGIC AND FOLK-SCIENCE

There is a belief in magic throughout Saxo's work, showing how fresh
heathendom still was in men's minds and memories. His explanations,
when he euhemerizes, are those of his day.

By means of spells all kinds of wonders could be effected, and the
powers of nature forced to work for the magician or his favourite.

"Skin-changing" (so common in "Landnamaboc") was as well known as
in the classic world of Lucian and Apuleius; and, where Frode perishes
of the attacks of a witch metamorphosed into a walrus.

"Mist" is induced by spells to cover and hide persons, as in Homer, and
"glamour" is produced by spells to dazzle foemen's sight. To cast
glamour and put confusion into a besieged place a witch is employed by
the beleaguerer, just as William the Conqueror used the witch in the
Fens against Hereward's fortalice. A soothsayer warns Charles the
Great of the coming of a Danish fleet to the Seine's mouth.

"Rain and bad weather" may be brought on, as in a battle against the
enemy, but in this, as in other instances, the spell may be counteracted.

"Panic Terror" may be induced by the spell worked with a dead horse's
head set up on a pole facing the antagonist, but the spell may be met
and combatted by silence and a counter-curse.

"Magic help" may be got by calling on the friendly magician's name. The
magician has also the power of summoning to him anyone, however
unwilling, to appear.

Of spells and magic power to blunt steel there are several instances;
they may be counteracted (as in the Icelandic Sagas) by using the hilt,
or a club, or covering the blade with fine skin. In another case the
champion can only be overcome by one that will take up some of the
dust from under his feet. This is effected by the combatants shifting their
ground and exchanging places. In another case the foeman can only be
slain by gold, whereupon the hero has a gold-headed mace made and
batters the life out of him therewith. The brothers of Swanhild cannot be
cut by steel, for their mail was charmed by the witch Gudrun, but
Woden taught Eormenric, the Gothic king, how to overcome them with

stones (which apparently cannot, as archaic weapons, be charmed against at all, resisting magic like wood and water and fire). Jordanis tells the true history of Ermanaric, that great Gothic emperor whose rule from the Dnieper to the Baltic and Rhine and Danube, and long reign of prosperity, were broken by the coming of the Huns. With him vanished the first great Teutonic empire.

Magic was powerful enough even to raise the dead, as was practised by the Perms, who thus renewed their forces after a battle. In the Everlasting battle the combatants were by some strange trick of fate obliged to fulfil a perennial weird (like the unhappy Vanderdecken). Spells to wake the dead were written on wood and put under the corpses' tongue. Spells (written on bark) induce frenzy.

"Charms" would secure a man against claw or tooth.

"Love philtres" (as in the long "Lay of Gudrun) appear as everywhere in savage and archaic society.

"Food", porridge mixed with the slaver of tortured snakes, gives magic strength or endues the eater with eloquence and knowledge of beast and bird speech (as Finn's broiled fish and Sigfred's broiled dragon-heart do).

"Poison" like these hell-broths are part of the Witch or Obi stock-in-trade, and Frode uses powdered gold as an antidote.

"Omens" are observed; tripping as one lands is lucky (as with our William the Norman). Portents, such as a sudden reddening of the sea where the hero is drowned, are noticed and interpreted.

"Dreams" (cf. Eddic Lays of Attila, and the Border ballads) are prophetic (as nine-tenths of Europeans firmly believe still); thus the visionary flame-spouting dragon is interpreted exactly as Hogne's and Attila's dreams. The dreams of the three first bridals nights (which were kept hallowed by a curious superstition, either because the dreams would then bold good, or as is more likely, for fear of some Asmodeus) were fateful. Animals and birds in dreams are read as persons, as nowadays.

A "curse" is powerful unless it can be turned back, when it will harm its utterer, for harm someone it must. The "curse" of a dying man on his slayer, and its lack of effect, is noted.

Sometimes "magic messengers" are sent, like the swans that bore a token and uttered warning songs to the hero.

40

"Witches and wizards" (as belonging to the older layer of archaic beliefs) are hateful to the gods, and Woden casts them out as accursed, though he himself was the mightiest of wizards. Heathen Teutonic life was a long terror by reason of witchcraft, as is the heathen African life to-day, continual precautions being needful to escape the magic of enemies. The Icelandic Sagas, such as Gretter's, are full of magic and witchcraft. It is by witchcraft that Gretter is first lamed and finally slain; one can see that Glam's curse, the Beowulf motif, was not really in the original Gretter story.

"Folk-medicine" is really a branch of magic in old days, even to such pioneers of science as Paracelsus.

Saxo's traditions note drinking of a lion's blood that eats men as a means of gaining might and strength; the drinking of bear's blood is also declared to give great bodily power.

The tests for "madness" are of a primitive character, such as those applied to Odusseus, who, however, was not able, like Hamlet, to evade them.

The test for death is the red-hot iron or hot brand (used by the Abyssinians of to-day, as it was supposed in the thirteenth century to have been used by Grimhild. "And now Grimhild goes and takes a great brand, where the house had burnt, and goes to Gernot her brother, and thrusts the burning brand in his mouth, and will know whether he is dead or living. But Gernot was clearly dead. And now she goes to Gislher and thrusts the firebrand in his mouth. He was not dead before, but Gislher died of that. Now King Thidrec of Bern saw what Grimhild is doing, and speaks to King Attila. `See how that devil Grimhild, thy wife, is killing her brothers, the good warriors, and how many men have lost their lives for her sake, and how many good men she has destroyed, Huns and Amalungs and Niflungs; and in the same way would she bring thee and me to hell, if she could do it?' Then spake King Attila, `Surely she is a devil, and slay thou her, and that were a good work if thou had done it seven nights ago! Then many a gallant fellow were whole that is now dead.' Now King Thidrec springs at Grimhild and swings up his sword Eckisax, and hews her asunder at the middle").

It was believed (as in Polynesia, where "Captain Cook's path" was shown in the grass) that the heat of the hero's body might blast the grass; so Starcad's entrails withered the grass.

It was believed that a severed head might bite the ground in rage, and there were certainly plenty of opportunities for observation of such cases.

It was believed that a "dumb man" might be so wrought on by passion that he would speak, and wholly acquire speech-power.

Little is told of "surgery", but in one case of intestines protruding owing to wounds, withies were employed to bind round the trunk and keep the bowels from risk till the patient could be taken to a house and his wounds examined and dressed. It was considered heroic to pay little heed to wounds that were not dangerous, but just to leave them to nature.

Personal "cleanliness" was not higher than among savages now. A lover is loused by his lady after the mediaeval fashion.

CHRISTIANITY—In the first nine books of Saxo, which are devoted to heathendom, there is not much save the author's own Christian point of view that smacks of the New Faith. The apostleships of Ansgarius in Denmark, the conversion of King Eric, the Christianity of several later Danish Kings, one of whom was (like Olaf Tryggwason) baptised in Britain are also noticed.

Of "Christian legends" and beliefs, besides the euhemerist theory, widely held, of the heathen gods there are few hints, save the idea that Christ was born in the reign of Frode, Frode having been somehow synchronised with Augustus, in whose reign also there was a world-peace.

Of course the christening of Scandinavia is history, and the mythic books are little concerned with it. The episode in Adam of Bremen, where the king offers the people, if they want a new god, to deify Eric, one of their hero-kings, is eminently characteristic and true.

FOLK-TALES

There might be a classification of Saxo's stories akin to that of the Irish poets, Battles, Sieges, Voyages, Rapes, Cattle Forays, etc.; and quite apart from the historic element, however faint and legendary, there are a set of stories ascribed by him, or rather his authorities, to definite persons, which had, even in his day, probably long been the property of Tis, their original owners not being known owing to lapse of time and the wear of memory, and the natural and accidental catastrophies that impair the human record. Such are the "Dragon-Slayer" stories. In one

42

type of these the hero (Frithlaf) is cast on a desolate island, and warned by a dream to attack and slay a dragon guarding treasure. He wakes, sees the dragon arise out of the waves, apparently, to come ashore and go back to the cavern or mound wherein the treasure lay. His scales are too hard to pierce; he is terribly strong, lashing trees down with his tail, and wearing a deep path through the wood and over the stones with his huge and perpetual bulk; but the hero, covered with hide-wrapped shield against the poison, gets down into the hollow path, and pierces the monster from below, afterward rifling its underground store and carrying off its treasure.

Again the story is repeated; the hero (Frode Haddingsson) is warned by a countryman of the island-dragon and its hoard, is told to cover his shield and body with bulls' hides against the poison, and smite the monster's belly. The dragon goes to drink, and, as it is coming back, it is attacked, slain, and its treasure lifted precisely as before. The analogies with the Beowulf and Sigfred stories are evident; but no great poet has arisen to weave the dragon-slaying intimately into the lives of Frode and Frithlaf as they have been woven into the tragedy of Sigfred the wooer of Brunhild and, if Dr. Vigffisson be right the conqueror of Varus, or into the story of Beowulf, whose real engagements were with sea-monsters, not fiery dragons.

Another type is that of the "Loathly Worm". A king out hunting (Herod or Herraud, King of Sweden), for some unexplained reason brings home two small snakes as presents for his daughter. They wax wonderfully, have to be fed a whole ox a day, and proceed to poison and waste the countryside. The wretched king is forced to offer his daughter (Thora) to anyone who will slay them. The hero (Ragnar) devises a dress of a peculiar kind (by help of his nurse, apparently), in this case, woolly mantle and hairy breeches all frozen and ice-covered to resist the venom, then strapping his spear to his hand, he encounters them boldly alone. The courtiers hide "like frightened little girls", and the king betakes him to a "narrow shelter", an euphemism evidently of Saxo's, for the scene is comic. The king comes forth when the hero is victorious, and laughing at his hairy legs, nick-names him Shaggy-breech, and bids him to the feast. Ragnar fetches up his comrades, and apparently seeks out the frightened courtiers (no doubt with appropriate quip, omitted by Saxo, who hurries on), feasts, marries the king's daughter, and begets on her two fine sons.

Of somewhat similar type is the proud "Maiden guarded" by Beasts. Here the scene is laid in Gaulardale in Norway. The lady is Ladgerda, the hero Ragnar. Enamoured of the maiden by seeing her prowess in war, he accepts no rebuffs, but leaving his followers, enters the house,

43

slays the guardian Bear and Dog, thrusting one through with a spear and throttling the other with his hand. The lady is won and wed, and two daughters and a son (Frithlaf) duly begotten. The story of Alf and Alfhild combines several types. There are the tame snakes, the baffled suitors' heads staked to terrify other suitors, and the hero using red-hot iron and spear to slay the two reptiles.

The "Proud Lady", (cf. Kudrun and the Niebelungen, and Are's story of the queen that burnt her suitors) appears in Hermintrude, Queen of Scotland, who battles and slays her lovers, but is out-witted by the hero (Hamlet), and, abating her arrogance, agrees to wed him. This seems an obvious accretion in the original Hamlet story, and probably owing not to Saxo, but to his authority.

The "Beggar that stole the Lady" (told of Snio Siwaldson and the daughter of the King of the Goths), with its brisk dialogue, must have been one of the most artful of the folk-tales worked on by Saxo or his informants; but it is only half told, unfortunately.

The "Crafty Soaker" is another excellent comic folk-tale. A terrible famine made the king (Snio) forbid brewing to save the barley for bread, and abolished all needless toping. The Soaker baffled the king by sipping, never taking a full draught. Rebuked, he declared that he never drank, but only sucked a drop. This was forbidden him for the future, so he sopped his bread in ale, and in that inconvenient manner continued to get drunk, excusing himself with the plea that though it was forbidden to drink or sip beer, it was not forbidden to eat it. When this was in turn prohibited, the Soaker gave up any pretence, and brewed and drank unabashed, telling the angry king that he was celebrating his approaching funeral with due respect, which excuse led to the repeal of the obnoxious decree. A good Rabelaisian tale, that must not have been wide-spread among the Danish topers, whose powers both Saxo and Shakespeare have celebrated, from actual experience no doubt.

The "Magician's tricks to elude pursuit", so common an incident in our fairy tales, e.g., Michael Scot's flight, is ascribed here to the wonder-working and uncanny Finns, who, when pursued, cast behind them successively three pebbles, which become to their enemies' eyes mountains, then snow, which appeared like a roaring torrent. But they could not cast the glamour on Arngrim a third time, and were forced to submit. The glamour here and in the case of the breaking of Balder's barrow is akin to that which the Druid puts on the sons of Uisnach.

The tale of the king who shuts up his daughter in an "earth-house" or underground chamber with treasures (weapons and gold and silver), in fear of invasion, looks like a bit of folk-tale, such as the "Hind in the Wood", but it may have a traditional base of some kind here.

A folk-tale, very imperfectly narrated, is the "Clever King's Daughter", who evidently in the original story had to choose her suitor by his feet (as the giantess in the prose Edda chooses her husband), and was able to do so by the device she had practised of sewing up her ring in his leg sometime before, so that when she touched the flesh she could feel the hardness of the ring beneath the scar.

Bits of folk-tales are the "Device for escaping threatened death by putting a log in one's bed" (as in our Jack the Giant-Killer). The device, as old as David's wife, of dressing up a dummy (here a basket with a dog inside, covered outside with clothes), while the hero escapes, is told of Eormenric, the mighty Gothic King of Kings, who, like Walter of Aquitaine, Theodoric of Varona, Ecgherht, and Arminius, was an exile in his youth. This traditional escape of the two lads from the Scyths should be compared with the true story in Paul the Deacon of his little ancestor's captivity and bold and successful stroke for freedom.

"Disguise" plays a great part in the folk-tales used by Saxo. Woden disguises himself in a cowl on his earthly travels, and heroes do the same; a king disguises himself as a slave at his rival's court, to try and find occasion of slaying him; a hero wraps himself up in skins, like Alleleirah.

"Escaped recognition" is accordingly a feature in many of these simple but artistic plots. A son is not known by his mother in the story of Hrolf.

Other "Devices" are exemplified, such as the "booby-trap" loaded with a millstone, which slays a hateful and despised tyrant, imposed by a foreign conqueror; evasion by secret passages, and concealment in underground vaults or earth-houses. The feigning of madness to escape death occurs, as well as in the better-known Hamlet story. These stratagems are universal in folk-history.

To Eric, the clever and quick of speech, is ascribed an excellent sailor's smuggling trick to hide slaughtered cattle, by sinking them till the search is over.

The "Hero's Mighty Childhood" (like David's) of course occurs when he binds a bear with his girdle. Sciold is full grown at fifteen, and Hadding is full grown in extreme youth. The hero in his boyhood slays a full-grown man and champion. The cinder-biting, lazy stage of a mighty youth is exemplified.

The "fierce eyes" of the hero or heroine, which can daunt an assassin as could the piercing glance of Marius, are the "falcon eyes" of the Eddic Lays.

The shining, effulgent, "illuminating hair" of the hero, which gives light in the darkness, is noticed here, as it obtains in Cuaran's thirteenth century English legend.

The wide-spread tale of the "City founded on a site marked out by a hide cut into finest thongs", occurs, told of Hella and Iwarus exactly as our Kentishmen told it of Hengist, and as it is also told of Dido.

The incidents of the "hero sleeping by a rill", of the guarded king's daughter, with her thirty attendants, the king's son keeping sheep, are part of the regular stock incidents in European folk-tales. So are the Nausicaa incident of the "king's daughter going a washing", the hero disguising himself as a woman and winding wool (like a second Heracles).

There are a certain number of stories, which only occur in Saxo and in our other Northern sources with attributions, though they are of course legendary; such are:

The "Everlasting Battle" between Hedhin and Hogne, a legend connected with the great Brisinga-men story, and paralleled by the Cordelia-tale among the Britons.

The story of the "Children preserved" is not very clearly told, and Saxo seems to have euhemerized. It is evidently of the same type as the Lionel-Lancelot story in the Arthurian cycle. Two children, ordered to be killed, are saved by the slaying of other children in their place; and afterwards by their being kept and named as dogs; they come to their own and avenge their wrongs.

The "Journey to Hell" story is told of Eric, who goes to a far land to fetch a princess back, and is successful. It is apparently an adventure of Swipdag, if everyone had their rights. It is also told of Thorkill, whose adventures are rather of the "True Thomas" type.

The "Test of Endurance" by sitting between fires, and the relief of the tortured and patient hero by a kindly trick, is a variant of the famous Eddic Lays concerning Agnar.

The "Robbers of the Island", evidently comes from an Icelandic source

46

(cf. The historic "Holmveria Saga" and Icelandic folk-tales of later date), the incident of the hero slaying his slave, that the body might be mistaken for his, is archaic in tone; the powerful horse recalls Grani, Bayard, and even Sleipner; the dog which had once belonged to Unfoot (Ofote), the giant shepherd (cf. its analogues in old Welsh tales), is not quite assimilated or properly used in this story. It seems (as Dr. Rydberg suspects) a mythical story coloured by the Icelandic relater with memory full of the robber-hands of his own land.

The stratagem of "Starcad", who tried even in death to slay his slayer, seems an integral part of the Starcad story; as much as the doom of three crimes which are to be the price for the threefold life that a triple man or giant should enjoy. The noose story in Starcad (cf. that told of Bicce in the Eormenric story), is also integral.

SAXO'S MYTHOLOGY

No one has commented upon Saxo's mythology with such brilliancy, such minute consideration, and such success as the Swedish scholar, Victor Rydberg. More than occasionally he is over-ingenious and over-anxious to reduce chaos to order; sometimes he almost loses his faithful reader in the maze he treads so easily and confidently, and sometimes he stumbles badly. But he has placed the whole subject on a fresh footing, and much that is to follow will be drawn from his "Teutonic Mythology" (cited here from the English version by Rasmus B. Anderson, London, 1889, as "T.M.").

Let us take first some of the incontestable results of his investigations that affect Saxo.

SCIOLD is the father of Gram in Saxo, and the son of Sceaf in other older authorities. Dr. Rydberg (97-101) forms the following equations for the Sciolding patriarchs:—

a. Scef—Heimdal—Rig.
b. Sciold—Borgar—Jarl.
c. Gram—Halfdan—Koming.

Chief among the mythic tales that concern Saxo are the various portions of the Swipdag-Myth, which Dr. Rydberg has been able to complete with much success. They may be resumed briefly as follows:—

Swipdag, helped by the incantations of his dead mother, whom he had raised from the dead to teach him spells of protection, sets forth on his quests. He is the Odusseus of the Teutonic mythology. He desires to avenge his father on Halfdan that slew him. To this end he must have a weapon of might against Halfdan's club. The Moon-god tells him of the blade Thiasse has forged. It has been stolen by Mimer, who has gone out into the cold wilderness on the rim of the world. Swipdag achieves the sword, and defeats and slays Halfdan. He now buys a wife, Menglad, of her kinsmen the gods by the gift of the sword, which thus passes into Frey's hands.

How he established a claim upon Frey, and who Menglad was, is explained in Saxo's story of Eric, where the characters may be identified thus:—

    Swipdag—Eric
    Freya—Gunwara
    Frey—Frode III
    Niord—Fridlaf
    Wuldor—Roller
    Thor—Brac
    Giants—The Greps
    Giants—Coller.

Frey and Freya had been carried off by the giants, and Swipdag and his faithful friend resolve to get them back for the Anses, who bewail their absence. They journey to Monster-land, win back the lady, who ultimately is to become the hero's wife, and return her to her kindred; but her brother can only be rescued by his father Niord. It is by wit rather than by force that Swipdag is successful here.

The third journey of Swipdag is undertaken on Frey's behalf; he goes under the name of Scirner to woo giant Gymer's daughter Gerth for his brother-in-law, buying her with the sword that he himself had paid to Frey as his sister's bride-price. So the sword gets back to the giants again.

Swipdag's dead foe Halfdan left two young "avengers", Hadding and Guthorm, whom he seeks to slay. But Thor-Brache gives them in charge of two giant brothers. Wainhead took care of Hadding, Hafle of Guthorm. Swipdag made peace with Guthorm, in a way not fully explained to us, but Hadding took up the blood-feud as soon as he was old enough.

Hadding was befriended by a woman, who took him to the Underworld —the story is only half told in Saxo, unluckily—and by Woden, who took him over-sea wrapt in his mantle as they rode Sleipner over the waves; but here again Saxo either had not the whole story before him, or he wished to abridge it for some reason or prejudice, and the only result of this astonishing pilgrimage is that Woden gives the young hero some useful counsels. He falls into captivity, entrapped by Loke (for what reason again we are left to guess), and is exposed to wild beasts, but he slays the wolf that attacks him, and eating its heart as Woden had bidden him, he gains wisdom and foresight.

Prepared by these adventures, he gets Guthorm to join him (how or why the peace between him and Swipdag was broken, we know not), and they attack their father's slayer, but are defeated, though Woden sunk Asmund Swipdag's son's ship, Grio, at Hlessey, and Wainhead and Hardgrip his daughter fought for Hadding.

Hadding wanders off to the East with his foster-sister and mistress and Hardgrip, who is slain protecting him against an angry ghost raised from the Underworld by her spells. However, helped by Heimdal and Woden (who at this time was an exile), Hadding's ultimate success is assured.

When Woden came back to power, Swipdag, whose violence and pride grew horribly upon him, was exiled, possibly by some device of his foes, and took upon him, whether by will or doom, a sea-monster's shape. His faithful wife follows him over land and sea, but is not able to save him. He is met by Hadding and, after a fierce fight, slain. Swipdag's wife cursed the conqueror, and he was obliged to institute an annual sacrifice to Frey (her brother) at Upsale, who annuls the curse. Loke, in seal's guise, tried to steal the necklace of Freya at the Reef of Treasures, where Swipdag was slain, but Haimdal, also in sealskin, fought him, and recovered it for the gods.

Other myths having reference to the goddesses appear in Saxo. There is the story of "Heimdall and Sol", which Dr. Rydberg has recognised in the tale of Alf and Alfhild. The same tale of how the god won the sun for his wife appears in the mediaeval German King Ruther (in which title Dr. Ryuberg sees Hrutr, a name of the ram-headed god).

The story of "Othar" (Od) and "Syritha" (Sigrid) is obviously that of Freya and her lover. She has been stolen by the giants, owing to the wiles of her waiting-maid, Loke's helper, the evil witch Angrbode. Od seeks her, finds her, slays the evil giant who keeps her in the cave; but she is still bewitched, her hair knotted into a hard, horny mass, her eyes void of brightness. Unable to gain recognition he lets her go, and she is made by a giantess to herd her flocks. Again found by Od, and again refusing to recognise him, she is let go again. But this time she flies to

49

the world of men, and takes service with Od's mother and father. Here, after a trial of her love, she and Od are reconciled. Sywald (Sigwald), her father, weds Od's sister.

The tale of the vengeance of Balder is more clearly given by the Dane, and with a comic force that recalls the Aristophanic fun of Loka-senna. It appears that the story had a sequel which only Saxo gives. Woden had the giantess Angrbode, who stole Freya, punished. Frey, whose mother-in-law she was, took up her quarrel, and accusing Woden of sorcery and dressing up like a woman to betray Wrind, got him banished. While in exile Wuldor takes Woden's place and name, and Woden lives on earth, part of the time at least, with Scathe Thiasse's daughter, who had parted from Niord.

The giants now resolved to attack Ansegard; and Woden, under the name of Yggr, warned the gods, who recall him after ten years' exile.

But for Saxo this part of the story of the wars of the gods would be very fragmentary.

The "Hildiger story", where a father slays his son unwittingly, and then falls at his brother's hand, a tale combining the Rustam and the Balin-Balan types, is one of the Hilding tragedies, and curiously preserved in the late "Saga of Asmund the Champions' bane". It is an antithesis, as Dr. Rydberg remarks, to the Hildebrand and Hadubrand story, where father and son must fight and are reconciled.

The "story of Orwandel" (the analogue of Orion the Hunter) must be gathered chiefly from the prose Edda. He was a huntsman, big enough and brave enough to cope with giants. He was the friend of Thor, the husband of Groa, the father of Swipdag, the enemy of giant Coller and the monster Sela. The story of his birth, and of his being blinded, are lost apparently in the Teutonic stories, unless we may suppose that the bleeding of Robin Hood till he could not see by the traitorous prioress is the last remains of the story of the great archer's death.

Great part of the troubles which befell the gods arose from the antagonism of the sons of Iwalde and the brethren Sindre and Brokk (Cinder and Brank), rival artist families; and it was owing to the retirement of their artist foster-parents that Frey and Freya were left among the giants. The Hniflung hoard is also supposed to have consisted of the treasures of one band of primaeval artists, the Iwaldings.

Whether we have here the phenomenon of mythological doublets belonging to different tribes, or whether we have already among these early names that descent of story which has led to an adventure of Moses being attributed to Garibaldi, given to Theodoric the king the adventures of Theodoric the god, taken Arthur to Rome, and Charles the Great to Constantinople, it is hard to say.

The skeleton-key of identification, used even as ably as Dr. Rydberg uses it, will not pick every mythologic lock, though it undoubtedly has opened many hitherto closed. The truth is that man is a finite animal; that he has a limited number of types of legend; that these legends, as long as they live and exist, are excessively prehensile; that, like the opossum, they can swing from tree to tree without falling; as one tree dies out of memory they pass on to another. When they are scared away by what is called exact intelligence from the tall forest of great personalities, they contrive to live humbly clinging to such bare plain stocks and poles (Tis and Jack and Cinderella) as enable them to find a precarious perch.

To drop similitudes, we must be prepared, in unravelling our tangled mythology, to go through several processes. We must, of course, note the parallelisms and get back to the earliest attribution-names we can find. But all system is of late creation, it does not begin till a certain political stage, a stage where the myths of coalescing clans come into contact, and an official settlement is attempted by some school of poets or priests. Moreover, systematization is never so complete that it effaces all the earlier state of things. Behind the official systems of Homer and Hesiod lies the actual chaos of local faiths preserved for us by Pausanias and other mythographers. The common factors in the various local faiths are much the majority among the factors they each possess; and many of these common factors are exceedingly primitive, and resolve themselves into answers to the questions that children still ask, still receiving no answer but myth—that is, poetic and subjective hypothesis, containing as much truth as they can receive or their inventors can grasp.

Who were our forbears? How did day and night, sun and moon, earth and water, and fire come? How did the animals come? Why has the bear no tail? Why are fishes dumb, the swallow cleft-tail? How did evil come? Why did men begin to quarrel? How did death arise? What will the end be? Why do dead persons come back? What do the dead do? What is the earth shaped like? Who invented tools and weapons, and musical instruments, and how? When did kings and chiefs first come?

From accepted answers to such questions most of the huge mass of mythology arises. Man makes his gods in his own image, and the doctrines of omen, coincidence, and correspondence helped by incessant and imperfect observation and logic, bring about a system of religious observance, of magic and ritual, and all the masses of folly and cruelty, hope and faith, and even charity, that group about their inventions, and seem to be the necessary steps in the onward path of progressive races.

When to these we add the true and exaggerated memories of actual heroes, the material before the student is pretty completely comprised. Though he must be prepared to meet the difficulties caused in the contact of races, of civilisations, by the conversion of persons holding one set of mythical ideas to belief in another set of different, more attractive, and often more advanced stage.

The task of arriving at the scientific, speculative ethic, and the actual practice of our remote ancestry (for to that end is the student of mythology and folk-lore aiming) is not therefore easy. Nor is the record perfect, though it is not so poor in most cases as was once believed. The Brothers Grimm, patriarchs alike as mythologists and folk-lorists, the Castor and Pollox of our studies, have proved this as regards the Teutonic nations, just as they showed us, by many a striking example, that in great part folk-lore was the mythology of to-day, and mythology the folk-lore of yesterday.

In many cases we are helped by quite modern material to make out some puzzle that an old tale presents, and there is little doubt but that the present activity in the field of folklore will not only result in fresh matter but in fresh methods freshly applied.

The Scandinavian material, at all events, is particularly rich: there is the extensive Icelandic written literature touching the ninth and tenth and eleventh centuries; the noble, if fragmentary remains of Old Northern poetry of the Wickingtide; and lastly, the mass of tradition which, surviving in oral form, and changing in colour from generation to generation, was first recorded in part in the seventeenth, and again in part, in the present century; and all these yield a plentiful field for research. But their evidence gains immensely by the existence of Saxo's nine books of traditional and mythic lore, collected and written down in an age when much that was antique and heathen was passing away forever. The gratitude due to the Welshman of the twelfth century, whose garnered hoard has enriched so many poets and romances from his day to now, is no less due to the twelfth-century Dane, whose faithful and eloquent enthusiasm has swept much dust from antique time, and saved us such a story as Shakespeare has not disdained to consecrate to highest use. Not only Celtic and Teutonic lore are the

52

richer for these two men, but the whole Western world of thought and speech. In the history of modern literature, it is but right that by the side of Geoffrey an honourable place should be maintained for Saxo, and

"awake remembrance of these mighty dead."

ENDNOTES:

(1) A horn and a tusk of great size are described as things of price, and great uroch's horns are mentioned in Thorkill's Second Journey. Horns were used for feast as well as fray.

(2) Such bird-beaked, bird-legged figures occur on the Cross at Papil, Burra Island, Shetland. Cf. Abbey Morne Cross, and an Onchan Cross, Isle of Man.

A Pleader at the Thing

THE DANISH HISTORY OF SAXO GRAMMATICUS

PREFACE

Forasmuch as all other nations are wont to vaunt the glory of their achievements, and reap joy from the remembrance of their forefathers: Absalon, Chief Pontiff of the Danes, whose zeal ever burned high for the glorification of our land, and who would not suffer it to be defrauded of like renown and record, cast upon me, the least of his followers—since all the rest refused the task—the work of compiling into a chronicle the history of Denmark, and by the authority of his constant admonition spurred my weak faculty to enter on a labour too heavy for its strength. For who could write a record of the deeds of Denmark? It had but lately been admitted to the common faith: it still languished as strange to Latin as to religion. But now that the holy ritual brought also the command of the Latin tongue, men were as slothful now as they were unskilled before, and their sluggishness proved as faultful as that former neediness. Thus it came about that my lowliness, though perceiving itself too feeble for the aforesaid burden, yet chose rather to strain beyond its strength than to resist his bidding; fearing that while our neighbours rejoiced and transmitted records of their deeds, the repute of our own people might appear not to possess any written chronicle, but rather to be sunk in oblivion and antiquity. Thus I, forced to put my shoulder, which was unused to the task, to a burden unfamiliar to all authors of preceding time, and dreading to slight his command, have obeyed more boldly than effectually, borrowing from the greatness of my admonisher that good heart which the weakness of my own wit denied me.

And since, ere my enterprise reached its goal, his death outran it; I entreat thee chiefly, Andrew, who wast chosen by a most wholesome and accordant vote to be successor in the same office and to headship of spiritual things, to direct and inspire my theme; that I may baulk by the defence of so great an advocate that spiteful detraction which ever reviles what is most conspicuous. For thy breast, very fruitful in knowledge, and covered with great store of worshipful doctrines, is to be deemed a kind of shrine of heavenly treasures. Thou who hast searched through Gaul and Italy and Britain also in order to gather knowledge of letters and amass them abundantly, didst after thy long wandering obtain a most illustrious post in a foreign school, and proved such a pillar thereof, that thou seemedst to confer more grace on thy degree than it did on thee. Then being made, on account of the height of thy honours and the desert of thy virtues, Secretary to the King, thou didst adorn that employment, in itself bounded and insignificant, with such works of wisdom as to leave it a piece of promotion for men of greatest rank to covet afterwards, when thou wert transferred to that office which now thou holdest. Wherefore Skaane has been found to leap for joy that she has borrowed a Pontiff from her neighbours rather than chosen one from her own people; inasmuch as she both elected nobly and deserved joy of her election. Being a shining light, therefore, in lineage, in letters, and in parts, and guiding the people with the most fruitful labours of thy teaching, thou hast won the deepest love of thy flock, and by thy boldness in thy famous administration hast conducted the service thou hast undertaken unto the summit of renown. And lest thou shouldst seem to acquire ownership on the strength of prescription, thou hast, by a pious and bountiful will, made over a very rich inheritance to Holy Church; choosing rather honourably to reject riches (which are covered with the rust of cares) than to be shackled with the greed of them and with their burden. Likewise thou hast set about an amazing work upon the reverend tenets of the faith; and in thy zeal to set the service of public religion before thy private concerns, hast, by the lesson of thy wholesome admonitions, driven those men who refused payment of the dues belonging to religion to do to holy things the homage that they ought; and by thy pious gift of treasure hast atoned for the ancient neglect of sacred buildings. Further, those who pursued a wanton life, and yielded to the stress of incontinence above measure, thou hast redeemed from nerveless sloth to a more upright state of mind, partly by continuing instant in wholesome reproof, and partly by the noble example of simple living; leaving it in doubt whether thou hast edified them more by word or deed. Thus thou, by mere counsels of wisdom, hast achieved what it was not granted to any of thy forerunners to obtain.

And I would not have it forgotten that the more ancient of the Danes, when any notable deeds of mettle had been done, were filled with emulation of glory, and imitated the Roman style; not only by relating in a choice kind of composition, which might be called a poetical work, the roll of their lordly deeds; but also by having graven upon rocks and cliffs, in the characters of their own language, the works of their forefathers, which were commonly known in poems in the mother tongue. In the footsteps of these poems, being as it were classic books of antiquity, I have trod; and keeping true step with them as I translated, in the endeavour to preserve their drift, I have taken care to render verses by verses; so that the chronicle of what I shall have to write, being founded upon these, may thus be known, not for a modern fabrication, but for the utterance of antiquity; since this present work promises not a trumpery dazzle of language, but faithful information concerning times past.

Moreover, how many histories must we suppose that men of such genius would have written, could they have had skill in Latin and so slaked their thirst for writing! Men who though they lacked acquaintance with, the speech of Rome, were yet seized with such a passion for bequeathing some record of their history, that they encompassed huge boulders instead of scrolls, borrowing rocks for the usage of books.

Nor may the pains of the men of Thule be blotted in oblivion; for though they lack all that can foster luxury (so naturally barren is the soil), yet they make up for their neediness by their wit, by keeping continually every observance of soberness, and devoting every instant of their lives to perfecting our knowledge of the deeds of foreigners. Indeed, they account it a delight to learn and to consign to remembrance the history of all nations, deeming it as great a glory to set forth the excellences of others as to display their own. Their stores, which are stocked with attestations of historical events, I have examined somewhat closely, and have woven together no small portion of the present work by following their narrative, not despising the judgment of men whom I know to be so well versed in the knowledge of antiquity. And I have taken equal care to follow the statements of Absalon, and with obedient mind and pen to include both his own doings and other men's doings of which he learnt; treasuring the witness of his August narrative as though it were some teaching from the skies.

Wherefore, Waldemar, (1) healthful Prince and Father of us all, shining light of thy land, whose lineage, most glorious from times of old, I am to relate, I beseech thee let thy grace attend the faltering course of this work; for I am fettered under the weight of my purpose, and dread that I may rather expose my unskillfulness and the feebleness of my parts, than portray thy descent as I duly should. For, not to speak of thy rich inheritance from thy fathers, thou hast nobly increased thy realm by conquering thy neighbours, and in the toil of spreading thy sovereignty hast encompassed the ebbing and flowing waves of Elbe, thus adding to thy crowded roll of honours no mean portion of fame. And after outstripping the renown and repute of thy forerunners by the greatness of thy deeds, thou didst not forbear to make armed, assault even upon part of the Roman empire. And though thou art deemed to be well endowed with courage and generosity, thou hast left it in doubt whether thou dost more terrify to thy foes in warfare or melt thy people by thy mildness. Also thy most illustrious grandsire, who was sanctioned with the honours of public worship, and earned the glory of immortality by an unmerited death, now dazzles by the refulgence of his holiness those whom living he annexed in his conquests. And from his most holy wounds more virtue than blood hath flowed.

Moreover I, bound by an old and inherited duty of obedience, have set my heart on fighting for thee, if it be only with all the forces of my mind; my father and grandfather being known to have served thy illustrious sire in camp with loyal endurance of the toils of war. Relying therefore on thy guidance and regard, I have resolved to begin with the position and configuration of our own country; for I shall relate all things as they come more vividly, if the course of this history first traverse the places to which the events belong, and take their situation as the starting-point for its narrative.

The extremes, then, of this country are partly bounded by a frontier of another land, and partly enclosed by the waters of the adjacent sea. The interior is washed and encompassed by the ocean; and this, through the circuitous winds of the interstices, now straitens into the narrows of a firth, now advances into ampler bays, forming a number of islands. Hence Denmark is cut in pieces by the intervening waves of ocean, and has but few portions of firm and continuous territory; these being divided by the mass of waters that break them up, in ways varying with the different angle of the bend of the sea. Of all these, Jutland, being the largest and first settled, holds the chief place in the Danish kingdom. It both lies fore-most and stretches furthest, reaching to the frontiers of Teutonland, from contact with which it is severed by the bed of the river Eyder. Northwards it swells somewhat in breadth, and runs out to the shore of the Noric Channel (Skagerrak). In this part is to be found the fjord called Liim, which is so full of fish that it seems to yield the natives as much food as the whole soil.

Close by this fjord also lies Lesser (North) Friesland, which curves in from the promontory of Jutland in a cove of sinking plains and shelving lap, and by the favour of the flooding ocean yields immense crops of grain. But whether this violent inundation bring the inhabitants more profit or peril, remains a vexed question. For when the (dykes of the) estuaries, whereby the waves of the sea are commonly checked among that people, are broken through by the greatness of the storm, such a mass of waters is wont to overrun the fields that it sometimes overwhelms not only the tilled lands, but people and their dwellings likewise.

Eastwards, after Jutland, comes the Isle of Funen, cut off from the mainland by a very narrow sound of sea. This faces Jutland on the west, and on the east Zealand, which is famed for its remarkable richness in the necessaries of life. This latter island, being by far the most delightful of all the provinces of our country, is held to occupy the heart of Denmark, being divided by equal distances from the extreme frontier; on its eastern side the sea breaks through and cuts off the western side of Skaane; and this sea commonly yields each year an abundant haul to the nets of the fishers. Indeed, the whole sound is apt to be so thronged with fish that any craft which strikes on them is with difficulty got off by hard rowing, and the prize is captured no longer by tackle, but by simple use of the hands.

Moreover, Halland and Bleking, shooting forth from the mass of the Skaane like two branches from a parent trunk, are linked to Gothland and to Norway, though with wide deviations of course, and with various gaps consisting of fjords. Now in Bleking is to be seen a rock which travellers can visit, dotted with letters in a strange character. For there stretches from the southern sea into the desert of Vaarnsland a road of rock, contained between two lines a little way apart and very prolonged, between which is visible in the midst a level space, graven all over with characters made to be read. And though this lies so unevenly as sometimes to break through the tops of the hills, sometimes to pass along the valley bottoms, yet it can be discerned to preserve continuous traces of the characters. Now Waldemar, well-starred son of holy Canute, marvelled at these, and desired to know their purport, and sent men to go along the rock and gather with close search the series of the characters that were to be seen there; they were then to denote them with certain marks, using letters of similar shape. These men could not gather any sort of interpretation of them, because owing to the hollow space of the graving being partly smeared up with mud and partly worn by the feet of travellers in the trampling of the road, the long line that had been drawn became blurred. Hence it is plain that crevices, even in the solid rock, if long drenched with wet, become choked either by the solid washings of dirt or the moistening drip of showers.

But since this country, by its closeness of language as much as of position, includes Sweden and Norway, I will record their divisions and their climates also as I have those of Denmark. These territories, lying under the northern pole, and facing Bootes and the Great Bear, reach with their utmost outlying parts the latitude of the freezing zone; and beyond these the extraordinary sharpness of the cold suffers not human habitation. Of these two, Norway has been allotted by the choice of nature a forbidding rocky site. Craggy and barren, it is beset all around by cliffs, and the huge desolate boulders give it the aspect of a rugged and a gloomy land; in its furthest part the day-star is not hidden even by night; so that the sun, scorning the vicissitudes of day and night, ministers in unbroken presence an equal share of his radiance to either season.

On the west of Norway comes the island called Iceland, with the mighty ocean washing round it: a land very squalid to dwell in, but noteworthy for marvels, both strange occurrences and objects that pass belief. A spring is there which, by the malignant reek of its water, destroys the original nature of anything whatsoever. Indeed, all that is sprinkled with the breath of its vapour is changed into the hardness of stone. It remains a doubt whether it be more marvellous or more perilous, that soft and flowing water should be invested with such a stiffness, as by a sudden change to transmute into the nature of stone whatsoever is put to it and drenched with its reeking fume, nought but the shape surviving. Here also are said to be other springs, which now are fed with floods of rising water, and, overflowing in full channels, cast a mass of spray upwards; and now again their bubbling flags, and they can scarce be seen below at the bottom, and are swallowed into deep hiding far under ground. Hence, when they are gushing over, they bespatter everything about them with the white spume, but when they are spent the sharpest eye cannot discern them. In this island there is likewise a mountain, whose floods of incessant fire make it look like a glowing rock, and which, by belching out flames, keeps its crest in an everlasting blaze. This thing awakens our wonder as much as those aforesaid; namely, when a land lying close to the extreme of cold can have such abundance of matter to keep up the heat, as to furnish eternal fires with unseen fuel, and supply an endless provocative to feed the burning. To this isle also, at fixed and appointed seasons, there drifts a boundless mass of ice, and when it approaches and begins to dash upon the rugged reefs, then, just as if the cliffs rang reply, there is heard from the deep a roar of voices and a changing din of extraordinary clamour. Whence it is supposed that spirits, doomed to torture for the iniquity of their guilty life, do here pay, by that bitter cold, the penalty of their sins. And so any portion of this mass that is cut off when the aforesaid ice breaks away from the land, soon slips its bonds and bars, though it be made fast with ever so great joins and knots. The mind stands dazed in wonder, that a thing which is covered with bolts past picking, and shut in by manifold and intricate barriers, should so depart after that mass whereof it was a portion, as by its enforced and inevitable flight to baffle the wariest watching. There also, set among the ridges and crags of the mountains, is another kind of ice which is known periodically to change and in a way reverse its position, the upper parts sinking to the bottom, and the lower again returning to the top. For proof of this story it is told that certain men, while they chanced to be running over the level of ice, rolled into the abyss before them, and into the depths of the yawning crevasses, and were a little later picked up dead without the smallest chink of ice above them. Hence it is common for many to imagine that the urn of the sling of ice first swallows them, and then a little after turns upside down and restores them. Here also, is reported to bubble up the water of a pestilent flood, which if a man taste, he falls struck as though by poison. Also there are other springs, whose gushing waters are said to resemble the quality of the bowl of Ceres. There are also fires, which, though they cannot consume linen, yet devour so fluent a thing as water. Also there is a rock, which flies over mountain-steeps, not from any outward impulse, but of its innate and proper motion.

And now to unfold somewhat more thoroughly our delineation of Norway. It should be known that on the east it is conterminous with Sweden and Gothland, and is bounded on both sides by the waters of the neighbouring ocean. Also on the north it faces a region whose position and name are unknown, and which lacks all civilisation, but teems with peoples of monstrous strangeness; and a vast interspace of flowing sea severs it from the portion of Norway opposite. This sea is found hazardous for navigation, and suffers few that venture thereon to return in peace.

Moreover, the upper bend of the ocean, which cuts through Denmark and flows past it, washes the southern side of Gothland with a gulf of some width; while its lower channel, passing the northern sides of Gothland and Norway, turns eastwards, widening much in breadth, and is bounded by a curve of firm land. This limit of the sea the elders of our race called Grandvik. Thus between Grandvik and the Southern Sea there lies a short span of mainland, facing the seas that wash on either shore; and but that nature had set this as a boundary where the billows almost meet, the tides of the two seas would have flowed into one, and cut off Sweden and Norway into an island. The regions on the east of these lands are inhabited by the Skric-Finns. This people is used to an extraordinary kind of carriage, and in its passion for the chase strives to climb untrodden mountains, and attains the coveted ground at the cost of a slippery circuit. For no crag juts out so high, but they can reach its crest by fetching a cunning compass. For when they first leave the deep valleys, they glide twisting and circling among the bases of the rocks, thus making the route very roundabout by dint of continually swerving aside, until, passing along the winding curves of the tracks, they conquer the appointed summit. This same people is wont to use the skins of certain beasts for merchandise with its neighbours.

Now Sweden faces Denmark and Norway on the west, but on the south and on much of its eastern side it is skirted by the ocean. Past this eastward is to be found a vast accumulation of motley barbarism.

That the country of Denmark was once cultivated and worked by giants, is attested by the enormous stones attached to the barrows and caves of the ancients. Should any man question that this is accomplished by superhuman force, let him look up at the tops of certain mountains and say, if he knows how, what man hath carried such immense boulders up to their crests. For anyone considering this marvel will mark that it is inconceivable how a mass, hardly at all or but with difficulty movable upon a level, could have been raised to so mighty a peak of so lofty a mountain by mere human effort, or by the ordinary exertion of human strength. But as to whether, after the Deluge went forth, there existed giants who could do such deeds, or men endowed beyond others with bodily force, there is scant tradition to tell us.

But, as our countrymen aver, those who even to-day are said to dwell in that rugged and inaccessible desert aforesaid, are, by the mutable nature of their bodies, vouchsafed the power of being now near, now far, and of appearing and vanishing in turn. The approach to this desert is beset with perils of a fearful kind, and has seldom granted to those who attempted it an unscathed return. Now I will let my pen pass to my theme.

ENDNOTES:

(1) Waldemar the Second (1203-42); Saxo does not reach his history.

BOOK ONE

Now Dan and Angul, with whom the stock of the Danes begins, were begotten of Humble, their father, and were the governors and not only the founders of our race. (Yet Dudo, the historian of Normandy, considers that the Danes are sprung and named from the Danai.) And these two men, though by the wish and favour of their country they gained the lordship of the realm, and, owing to the wondrous deserts of their bravery, got the supreme power by the consenting voice of their countrymen, yet lived without the name of king: the usage whereof was not then commonly resorted to by any authority among our people.

Of these two, Angul, the fountain, so runs the tradition, of the beginnings of the Anglian race, caused his name to be applied to the district which he ruled. This was an easy kind of memorial wherewith to immortalise his fame: for his successors a little later, when they gained possession of Britain, changed the original name of the island for a fresh title, that of their own land. This action was much thought of by the ancients: witness Bede, no mean figure among the writers of the Church, who was a native of England, and made it his care to embody the doings of his country in the most hallowed treasury of his pages;

deeming it equally a religious duty to glorify in writing the deeds of his land, and to chronicle the history of the Church.

From Dan, however, so saith antiquity; the pedigrees of our kings have flowed in glorious series, like channels from some parent spring. Grytha, a matron most highly revered among the Teutons, bore him two sons, HUMBLE and LOTHER.

The ancients, when they were to choose a king, were wont to stand on stones planted in the ground, and to proclaim their votes, in order to foreshadow from the steadfastness of the stones that the deed would be lasting. By this ceremony Humble was elected king at his father's death, thus winning a novel favour from his country; but by the malice of ensuing fate he fell from a king into a common man. For he was taken by Lother in war, and bought his life by yielding up his crown; such, in truth, were the only terms of escape offered him in his defeat. Forced, therefore, by the injustice of a brother to lay down his sovereignty, he furnished the lesson to mankind, that there is less safety, though more pomp, in the palace than in the cottage. Also, he bore his wrong so meekly that he seemed to rejoice at his loss of title as though it were a blessing; and I think he had a shrewd sense of the quality of a king's estate. But Lother played the king as insupportably as he had played the soldier, inaugurating his reign straightway with arrogance and crime; for he counted it uprightness to strip all the most eminent of life or goods, and to clear his country of its loyal citizens, thinking all his equals in birth his rivals for the crown. He was soon chastised for his wickedness; for he met his end in an insurrection of his country; which had once bestowed on him his kingdom, and now bereft him of his life.

SKIOLD, his son, inherited his natural bent, but not his behaviour; avoiding his inborn perversity by great discretion in his tender years, and thus escaping all traces of his father's taint. So he appropriated what was alike the more excellent and the earlier share of the family character; for he wisely departed from his father's sins, and became a happy counterpart of his grandsire's virtues. This man was famous in his youth among the huntsmen of his father for his conquest of a monstrous beast: a marvellous incident, which augured his future prowess. For he chanced to obtain leave from his guardians, who were rearing him very carefully, to go and see the hunting. A bear of extraordinary size met him; he had no spear, but with the girdle that he commonly wore he contrived to bind it, and gave it to his escort to kill. More than this, many champions of tried prowess were at the same time of his life vanquished by him singly; of these Attal and Skat were renowned and famous. While but fifteen years of age he was of unusual bodily size and displayed mortal strength in its perfection, and so mighty were the proofs of his powers that the rest of the kings of the Danes were called after him by a common title, the SKIOLDUNG'S. Those who were wont to live an abandoned and flaccid life, and to sap their self-control by wantonness, this man vigilantly spurred to the practice of virtue in an active career. Thus the ripeness of Skiold's spirit outstripped the fulness of his strength, and he fought battles at which one of his tender years could scarce look on. And as he thus waxed in years and valour he beheld the perfect beauty of Alfhild, daughter of the King of the Saxons, sued for her hand, and, for her sake, in the sight of the armies of the Teutons and the Danes, challenged and fought with Skat, governor of Allemannia, and a suitor for the same maiden; whom he slew, afterwards crushing the whole nation of the Allemannians, and forcing them to pay tribute, they being subjugated by the death of their captain. Skiold was eminent for patriotism as well as arms. For he annulled unrighteous laws, and most heedfully executed whatsoever made for the amendment of his country's condition. Further, he regained by his virtue the realm that his father's wickedness had lost. He was the first to proclaim the law abolishing manumissions. A slave, to whom he had chanced to grant his freedom, had attempted his life by stealthy treachery, and he exacted a bitter penalty; as though it were just that the guilt of one freedman should be visited upon all. He paid off all men's debts from his own treasury, and contended, so to say, with all other monarchs in courage, bounty, and generous dealing. The sick he used to foster, and charitably gave medicines to those sore stricken; bearing witness that he had taken on him the care of his country and not of himself. He used to enrich his nobles not only with home taxes, but also with plunder taken in war; being wont to aver that the prize-money should flow to the soldiers, and the glory to the general.

Thus delivered of his bitterest rival in wooing, he took as the prize of combat the maiden, for the love of whom he had fought, and wedded her in marriage. Soon after, he had by her a son, GRAM, whose wondrous parts savoured so strongly of his father's virtues that he was deemed to tread in their very footsteps. The days of Gram's youth were enriched with surpassing gifts of mind and body, and he raised them to the crest of renown. Posterity did such homage to his greatness that in the most ancient poems of the Danes royal dignity is implied in his very name. He practiced with the most zealous training whatsoever serves to sharpen and strengthen the bodily powers. Taught by the fencers, he trained himself by sedulous practice to parrying and dealing blows. He took to wife the daughter of his upbringer, Roar, she being his foster-sister and of his own years, in order the better to show his gratefulness for his nursing. A little while after he gave her in marriage to a certain Bess, since he had ofttimes used his strenuous service. In this partner of his warlike deeds he put his trust; and he has left it a question whether he has won more renown by Bess's valour or his own.

Gram, chancing to hear that Groa, daughter of Sigtryg, King of the Swedes, was plighted to a certain giant, and holding accursed an union so unworthy of the blood royal, entered on a Swedish war; being destined to emulate the prowess of Hercules in resisting the attempts of monsters. He went into Gothland, and, in order to frighten people out of his path, strode on clad in goats' skins, swathed in the motley hides of beasts, and grasping in his right hand a dreadful weapon, thus feigning the attire of a giant; when he met Groa herself riding with a very small escort of women on foot, and making her way, as it chanced, to the forest-pools to bathe, she thought it was her betrothed who had hastened to meet her, and was scared with feminine alarm at so strange a garb: so, flinging up the reins, and shaking terribly all over, she began in the song of her country, thus:

"I see that a giant, hated of the king, has come, and darkens the highways with his stride. Or my eyes play me false; for it has oft befallen bold warriors to skulk behind the skin of a beast."

Then began Bess: "Maiden, seated on the shoulders of the steed, tell me, pouring forth in thy turn words of answer, what is thy name, and of what line art thou born?"

Groa replied: "Groa is my name; my sire is a king, glorious in blood, gleaming in armour. Disclose to us, thou also, who thou art, or whence sprung!"

To whom Bess: "I am Bess, brave in battle, ruthless to foes, a terror to nations, and oft drenching my right hand in the blood of foes."

Then said Groa: "Who, prithee, commands your lines? Under what captain raise ye the war-standards? What prince controls the battle? Under whose guidance is the war made ready?"

Bess in answer: "Gram, the blest in battle, rules the array: force nor fear can swerve him; flaming pyre and cruel sword and ocean billow have never made him afraid. Led by him, maiden, we raise the golden standards of war."

Groa once more: "Turn your feet and go back hence, lest Sigtryg vanquish you all with his own array, and fasten you to a cruel stake, your throats haltered with the cord, and doom your carcases to the stiff noose, and, glaring evilly, thrust out your corpses to the hungry raven."

Bess again: "Gram, ere he shall shut his own eyes in death, shall first make him a ghost, and, smiting him on the crest, shall send him to Tartarus. We fear no camp of the Swedes. Why threaten us with ghastly dooms, maiden?"

Groa answered him: "Behold, I will ride thence to see again the roof of my father which I know, that I may not rashly set eyes on the array of my brother who is coming. And I pray that your death-doom may tarry for you who abide."
Bess replied: "Daughter, to thy father go back with good cheer; nor imprecate swift death upon us, nor let choler shake thy bosom. For often has a woman, harsh at first and hard to a wooer, yielded the second time."

Whereupon Gram could brook no longer to be silent, and pitching his tones gruffly, so as to mimic a gruesome and superhuman voice, accosted the maiden thus:

"Let not the maiden fear the brother of the fleet giant, nor turn pale because I am nigh her. For I am sent by Grip, and never seek the couch and embrace of damsels save when their wish matches mine."

Groa answered: "Who so mad as to wish to be the leman of giants? Or what woman could love the bed that genders monsters? Who could be the wife of demons, and know the seed whose fruit is monstrous? Or who would fain share her couch with a barbarous giant? Who caresses thorns with her fingers? Who would mingle honest kisses with mire? Who would unite shaggy limbs to smooth ones which correspond not? Full ease of love cannot be taken when nature cries out against it: nor doth the love customary in the use of women sort with monsters."

Gram rejoined: "Oft with conquering hand I have tamed the necks of mighty kings, defeating with stronger arm their insolent pride. Thence take red-glowing gold, that the troth may be made firm by the gift, and that the faith to be brought to our wedlock may stand fast."

Thus speaking, he cast off his disguises, and revealed his natural comeliness; and by a single sight of him he filled the damsel with well-nigh as much joy as he had struck her with fear before at his counterfeit. She was even incited to his embraces by the splendour of his beauty; nor did he fail to offer her the gifts of love.

Having won Groa, Bess proceeded and learnt that the road was beset by two robbers. These he slew simply by charging them as they rushed covetously forth to despoil him. This done, loth to seem to have done any service to the soil of an enemy, he put timbers under the carcases of the slain, fastened them thereto, and stretched them so as to counterfeit an upright standing position; so that in their death they might menace in seeming those whom their life had harmed in truth; and that, terrible even after their decease, they might block the road in effigy as much as they had once in deed. Whence it appears that in slaying the robbers he took thought for himself and not for Sweden: for he betokened by so singular an act how great a hatred of Sweden filled him. Having heard from the diviners that Sigtryg could only be conquered by gold, he straightway fixed a knob of gold to a wooden mace, equipped himself therewith in the war wherein he attacked the king, and obtained his desire. This exploit was besung by Bess in a most zealous strain of eulogy:

"Gram, the fierce wielder of the prosperous mace, knowing not the steel, rained blows on the outstretched sword, and with a stock beat off the lances of the mighty.

"Following the decrees and will of the gods, he brought low the glory of the powerless Swedes, doing their king to death and crushing him with the stiff gold.

"For he pondered on the arts of war: he wielded in his clasp the ruddy-flashing wood, and victoriously with noble stroke made their fallen captain writhe.

"Shrewdly he conquered with the hardness of gold him whom fate forbade should be slain by steel; unsworded, waging war with the worthier metal.

"This treasure, for which its deviser claims glory and the height of honour, shall abide yet more illustrious hereafter, known far and wide in ampler fame."

Having now slain Sigtryg, the King of Sweden, Gram desired to confirm his possession of the empire which he had won in war; and therefore, suspecting Swarin the governor of Gothland of aspiring to the crown, he challenged him to combat, and slew him. This man's brethren, of whom he had seven lawfully born, and nine the sons of a concubine, sought to avenge their brother's death, but Gram, in an unequal contest, cut them off.

Gram, for his marvellous prowess, was granted a share in the sovereignty by his father, who was now in extreme age, and thought it better and likewise more convenient to give his own blood a portion of the supremacy of the realm, than now in the setting of his life to administer it without a partner. Therefore Ring, a nobly-born Zealander, stirred the greater part of the Danes with desire for insurrection; fancying that one of these men was unripe for his rank, and that the other had run the course of his powers, alleging the weakness in years of both, and declaring that the wandering wit of an old man made the one, and that of a boy the other, unfit for royal power. But they fought and crushed him, making him an example to all men, that no season of life is to be deemed incompatible with valour.

Many other deeds also King Gram did. He declared war against Sumble, King of the Finns; but when he set eyes upon the King's daughter, Signe, he laid down his arms, the foeman turned into the suitor, and, promising to put away his own wife, he plighted troth with her. But, while much busied with a war against Norway, which he had taken up against King Swipdag for debauching his sister and his daughter, he heard from a messenger that Signe had, by Sumble's treachery, been promised in marriage to Henry, King of Saxony. Then, inclining to love the maiden more than his soldiers, he left his army, privily made his way to Finland, and came in upon the wedding, which was already begun. Putting on a garb of the utmost meanness, he lay down at the table in a seat of no honour. When asked what he brought, he professed skill in leechcraft. At last, when all were drenched in drunkenness, he gazed at the maiden, and amid the revels of the riotous banquet, cursing deep the fickleness of women, and vaunting loud his own deeds of valour, he poured out the greatness of his wrath in a song like this:

"Singly against eight at once I drove the darts of death, and smote nine with a back-swung sword, when I slew Swarin, who wrongfully assumed his honours and tried to win fame unmerited; wherefore I have oft dyed in foreign blood my blade red with death and reeking with slaughter, and have never blenched at the clash of dagger or the sheen of helmet. Now Signe, the daughter of Sumble, vilely spurns me, and endures vows not mine, cursing her ancient troth; and, conceiving an ill-ordered love, commits a notable act of female lightness; for she entangles, lures, and bestains princes, rebuffing beyond all others the lordly of birth; yet remaining firm to none, but ever wavering, and bringing to birth impulses doubtful and divided."

And as he spoke he leapt up from where he lay, and there he cut Henry down while at the sacred board and the embraces of his friends, carried off his bride from amongst the bridesmaids, felled most of the guests, and bore her off with him in his ship. Thus the bridal was turned into a funeral; and the Finns might learn the lesson, that hands should not be laid upon the loves of other men.

After this SWIPDAG, King of Norway, destroyed Gram, who was attempting to avenge the outrage on his sister and the attempt on his daughter's chastity. This battle was notable for the presence of the Saxon forces, who were incited to help Swipdag, not so much by love of him, as by desire to avenge Henry.

GUTHORM and HADDING, the son of Gram (Groa being the mother of the first and Signe of the second), were sent over to Sweden in a ship by their foster-father, Brage (Swipdag being now master of Denmark), and put in charge of the giants Wagnhofde and Hafle, for guard as well as rearing.

As I shall have briefly to relate doings of these folk, and would fain not seem to fabricate what conflicts with common belief or outsteps the faithful truth, it is worth the knowing that there were in old times three kinds of magicians who by diverse sleights practiced extraordinary marvels. The first of these were men of monstrous stock, termed by antiquity giants; these by their exceeding great bodily stature surpassed the size natural to mankind. Those who came after these were the first who gained skill in divination from entrails, and attained the Pythonic art. These surpassed the former in briskness of mental parts as much as they fell behind them in bodily condition. Constant wars for the supremacy were waged between these and the giants; till at last the sorcerers prevailed, subdued the tribe of giants by arms, and acquired not merely the privilege of ruling, but also the repute of being divine. Both of these kinds had extreme skill in deluding the eyesight, knowing how to obscure their own faces and those of others with divers semblances, and to darken the true aspects of things with beguiling shapes. But the third kind of men, springing from the natural union of the first two, did not answer to the nature of their parents either in bodily size or in practice of magic arts; yet these gained credit for divinity with minds that were befooled by their jugglings.

Nor must we marvel if, tempted by the prodigious miracles of these folk, the barbaric world fell to worshipping a false religion, when others like unto these, who were mere mortals, but were reverenced with divine honours, beguiled even the shrewdness of the Latins. I have touched on these things lest, when I relate of sleights and marvels, I be checked by the disbelief of the reader. Now I will leave these matters and return to my theme.

Swipdag, now that he had slain Gram, was enriched with the realms of Denmark and Sweden; and because of the frequent importunities of his wife he brought back from banishment her brother Guthorm, upon his promising tribute, and made him ruler of the Danes. But Hadding preferred to avenge his father rather than take a boon from his foe.

This man's nature so waxed and throve that in the early season of his youth he was granted the prime of manhood. Leaving the pursuit of pleasure, he was constantly zealous in warlike exercises; remembering that he was the son of a fighting father, and was bound to spend his whole span of life in approved deeds of warfare. Hardgrep, daughter of Wagnhofde, tried to enfeeble his firm spirit with her lures of love, contending and constantly averring that he ought to offer the first dues of the marriage bed in wedlock with her, who had proffered to his childhood most zealous and careful fostering, and had furnished him with his first rattle.

Nor was she content with admonishing in plain words, but began a strain of song as follows:

"Why doth thy life thus waste and wander? Why dost thou pass thy years unwed, following arms, thirsting for throats? Nor does my beauty draw thy vows. Carried away by excess of frenzy, thou art little prone to love. Steeped in blood and slaughter, thou judgest wars better than the bed, nor refreshest thy soul with incitements. Thy fierceness finds no leisure; dalliance is far from thee, and savagery fostered. Nor is thy hand free from blasphemy while thou loathest the rites of love. Let this hateful strictness pass away, let that loving warmth approach, and plight the troth of love to me, who gave thee the first breasts of milk in childhood, and helped thee, playing a mother's part, duteous to thy needs."

When he answered that the size of her body was unwieldy for the embraces of a mortal, since doubtless her nature was framed in conformity to her giant stock, she said:

"Be not moved by my unwonted look of size. For my substance is sometimes thinner, sometimes ampler; now meagre, now abundant; and I alter and change at my pleasure the condition of my body, which is at one time shrivelled up and at another time expanded: now my tallness rises to the heavens, and now I settle down into a human being, under a more bounded shape."

As he still faltered, and was slow to believe her words, she added the following song:

"Youth, fear not the converse of my bed. I change my bodily outline in

70

twofold wise, and am wont to enjoin a double law upon my sinews. For I conform to shapes of different figure in turn, and am altered at my own sweet will: now my neck is star-high, and soars nigh to the lofty Thunderer; then it falls and declines to human strength, and plants again on earth that head which was near the firmament. Thus I lightly shift my body into diverse phases, and am beheld in varying wise; for changefully now cramped stiffness draws in my limbs, now the virtue of my tall body unfolds them, and suffers them to touch the cloud-tops. Now I am short and straitened, now stretch out with loosened knee; and I have mutably changed myself like wax into strange aspects. He who knows of Proteus should not marvel at me. My shape never stays the same, and my aspect is twofold: at one time it contrasts its outstretched limbs, at another shoots them out when closed; now disentangling the members and now rolling them back into a coil. I dart out my ingathered limbs, and presently, while they are strained, I wrinkle them up, dividing my countenance between shapes twain, and adopting two forms; with the greater of these I daunt the fierce, while with the shorter I seek the embraces of men."

By thus averring she obtained the embraces of Hadding; and her love for the youth burned so high that when she found him desirous of revisiting his own land, she did not hesitate to follow him in man's attire, and counted it as joy to share his hardships and perils. While upon the journey she had undertaken, she chanced to enter in his company, in order to pass the night, a dwelling, the funeral of whose dead master was being conducted with melancholy rites. Here, desiring to pry into the purposes of heaven by the help of a magical espial, she graved on wood some very dreadful spells, and caused Hadding to put them under the dead man's tongue; thus forcing him to utter, with the voice so given, a strain terrible to hear:

"Perish accursed he who hath dragged me back from those below, let him be punished for calling a spirit out of bale!

"Whoso hath called me, who am lifeless and dead, back from the abode below, and hath brought me again into upper air, let him pay full penalty with his own death in the dreary shades beneath livid Styx. Behold, counter to my will and purpose, I must declare some bitter tidings. For as ye go away from this house ye will come to the narrow path of a grove, and will be a prey to demons all about. Then she who hath brought our death back from out of void, and has given us a sight of this light once more, by her prayers wondrously drawing forth the ghost and casting it into the bonds of the body, shall bitterly bewail her rash enterprise.

"Perish accursed he who hath dragged me back from those below, let him be punished for calling a spirit out of bale!

"For when the black pestilence of the blast that engenders monsters has crushed out the inmost entrails with stern effort, and when their hand has swept away the living with cruel nail, tearing off limbs and rending ravished bodies; then Hadding, thy life shall survive, nor shall the nether realms bear off thy ghost, nor thy spirit pass heavily to the waters of Styx; but the woman who hath made the wretched ghost come back hither, crushed by her own guilt, shall appease our dust; she shall be dust herself.

"Perish accursed he who hath dragged me back from those below, let him be punished for calling a spirit out of bale!"

So, while they were passing the night in the forest foretold them, in a shelter framed of twigs, a hand of extraordinary size was seen to wander over the inside of the dwelling. Terrified at this portent, Hadding entreated the aid of his nurse. Then Hardgrep, expanding her limbs and swelling to a mighty bigness, gripped the hand fast and held it to her foster-child to hew off. What flowed from the noisesome wounds he dealt was not so much blood as corrupt matter. But she paid the penalty of this act, presently being torn in pieces by her kindred of the same stock; nor did her constitution or her bodily size help her against feeling the attacks of her foes' claws.

Hadding, thus bereft of his foster-mother, chanced to be made an ally in a solemn covenant to a rover, Lysir, by a certain man of great age that had lost an eye, who took pity on his loneliness. Now the ancients, when about to make a league, were wont to besprinkle their footsteps with blood of one another, so to ratify their pledge of friendship by reciprocal barter of blood. Lysir and Hadding, being bound thus in the strictest league, declared war against Loker, the tyrant of the Kurlanders. They were defeated; and the old man aforementioned took Hadding, as he fled on horseback, to his own house, and there refreshed him with a certain pleasant draught, telling him that he would find himself quite brisk and sound in body. This prophetic advice he confirmed by a song as follows:

"As thou farest hence, a foe, thinking thee a deserter, will assail thee, that he may keep thee bound and cast thee to be devoured by the mangling jaws of beasts. But fill thou the ears of the warders with divers tales, and when they have done the feast and deep sleep holds them, snap off the fetters upon thee and the loathly chains. Turn thy feet thence, and when a little space has fled, with all thy might rise up

72

against a swift lion who is wont to toss the carcases of the prisoners, and strive with thy stout arms against his savage shoulders, and with naked sword search his heart-strings. Straightway put thy throat to him and drink the steaming blood, and devour with ravenous jaws the banquet of his body. Then renewed strength will come to thy limbs, then shall undreamed-of might enter thy sinews, and an accumulation of stout force shall bespread and nerve thy frame through-out. I myself will pave the path to thy prayers, and will subdue the henchmen in sleep, and keep them snoring throughout the lingering night."

And as he spoke, he took back the young man on his horse, and set him where he had found him. Hadding cowered trembling under his mantle; but so extreme was his wonder at the event, that with keen vision he peered through its holes. And he saw that before the steps of the horse lay the sea; but was told not to steal a glimpse of the forbidden thing, and therefore turned aside his amazed eyes from the dread spectacle of the roads that he journeyed. Then he was taken by Loker, and found by very sure experience that every point of the prophecy was fulfilled upon him. So he assailed Handwan, king of the Hellespont, who was entrenched behind an impregnable defence of wall in his city Duna, and withstood him not in the field, but with battlements. Its summit defying all approach by a besieger, he ordered that the divers kinds of birds who were wont to nest in that spot should be caught by skilled fowlers, and he caused wicks which had been set on fire to be fastened beneath their wings. The birds sought the shelter of their own nests, and filled the city with a blaze; all the townsmen flocked to quench it, and left the gates defenceless. He attacked and captured Handwan, but suffered him to redeem his life with gold for ransom. Thus, when he might have cut off his foe, he preferred to grant him the breath of life; so far did his mercy qualify his rage.

After this he prevailed over a great force of men of the East, and came back to Sweden. Swipdag met him with a great fleet off Gottland; but Hadding attacked and destroyed him. And thus he advanced to a lofty pitch of renown, not only by the fruits of foreign spoil, but by the trophies of his vengeance for his brother and his father. And he exchanged exile for royalty, for he became king of his own land as soon as he regained it.

At this time there was one Odin, who was credited over all Europe with the honour, which was false, of godhead, but used more continually to sojourn at Upsala; and in this spot, either from the sloth of the inhabitants or from its own pleasantness, he vouchsafed to dwell with somewhat especial constancy. The kings of the North, desiring more zealously to worship his deity, embounded his likeness in a golden image; and this statue, which betokened their homage, they transmitted with much show of worship to Byzantium, fettering even the effigied arms with a serried mass of bracelets. Odin was overjoyed at such notoriety, and greeted warmly the devotion of the senders. But his queen Frigga, desiring to go forth more beautified, called smiths, and had the gold stripped from the statue. Odin hanged them, and mounted the statue upon a pedestal, which by the marvellous skill of his art he made to speak when a mortal touched it. But still Frigga preferred the splendour of her own apparel to the divine honours of her husband, and submitted herself to the embraces of one of her servants; and it was by this man's device she broke down the image, and turned to the service of her private wantonness that gold which had been devoted to public idolatry. Little thought she of practicing unchastity, that she might the easier satisfy her greed, this woman so unworthy to be the consort of a god; but what should I here add, save that such a godhead was worthy of such a wife? So great was the error that of old befooled the minds of men. Thus Odin, wounded by the double trespass of his wife, resented the outrage to his image as keenly as that to his bed; and, ruffled by these two stinging dishonours, took to an exile overflowing with noble shame, imagining so to wipe off the slur of his ignominy.

When he had retired, one Mit-othin, who was famous for his juggling tricks, was likewise quickened, as though by inspiration from on high, to seize the opportunity of feigning to be a god; and, wrapping the minds of the barbarians in fresh darkness, he led them by the renown of his jugglings to pay holy observance to his name. He said that the wrath of the gods could never be appeased nor the outrage to their deity expiated by mixed and indiscriminate sacrifices, and therefore forbade that prayers for this end should be put up without distinction, appointing to each of those above his especial drink-offering. But when Odin was returning, he cast away all help of jugglings, went to Finland to hide himself, and was there attacked and slain by the inhabitants. Even in his death his abominations were made manifest, for those who came nigh his barrow were cut off by a kind of sudden death; and after his end, he spread such pestilence that he seemed almost to leave a filthier record in his death than in his life: it was as though he would extort from the guilty a punishment for his slaughter. The inhabitants, being in this trouble, took the body out of the mound, beheaded it, and impaled it through the breast with a sharp stake; and herein that people found relief.

The death of Odin's wife revived the ancient splendour of his name, and seemed to wipe out the disgrace upon his deity; so, returning from exile, he forced all those, who had used his absence to assume the honours of divine rank, to resign them as usurped; and the gangs of sorcerers that had arisen he scattered like a darkness before the advancing glory of his godhead. And he forced them by his power not only to lay down their divinity, but further to quit the country, deeming that they, who tried to foist themselves so iniquitously into the skies, ought to be outcasts from the earth.

Meanwhile Asmund, the son of Swipdag, fought with Hadding to avenge his father. And when he heard that Henry his son, his love for whom he set even before his own life, had fallen fighting valiantly, his soul longed for death, and loathed the light of day, and made a song in a strain like this:

"What brave hath dared put on my armour? The sheen of the helmet serves not him who tottereth, nor doth the breastplate fitly shelter him that is sore spent. Our son is slain, let us riot in battle; my eager love for him driveth me to my death, that I may not be left outliving my dear child. In each hand I am fain to grasp the sword; now without shield let us ply our warfare bare-breasted, with flashing blades. Let the rumour of our rage beacon forth: boldly let us grind to powder the column of the foe; nor let the battle be long and chafe us; nor let our onset be shattered in rout and be still."

When he had said this, he gripped his hilt with both hands, and, fearless of peril, swung his shield upon his back and slew many. Hadding therefore called on the powers with which he was allied to protect him, and on a sudden Wagnhofde rode up to fight on his side. And when Asmund saw his crooked sword, he cried out, and broke into the following strain:

"Why fightest thou with curved sword? The short sword shall prove thy doom, the javelin shall be flung and bring forth death. Thou shouldst conquer thy foe by thy hand, but thou trustest that he can be rent by spells; thou trustest more in words than rigour, and puttest thy strength in thy great resource. Why dost thus beat me back with thy shield, threatening with thy bold lance, when thou art so covered with wretched crimes and spotted all over? Thus hath the brand of shame bestained thee, rotting in sin, lubber-lipped."

While he thus clamoured, Hadding, flinging his spear by the thong, pierced him through. But Asmund lacked not comfort even for his death; for while his life flickered in the socket he wounded the foot of his slayer, and by this short instant of revenge he memorized his fall, punishing the other with an incurable limp. Thus crippling of a limb befell one of them and loss of life the other. Asmund's body was buried in solemn state at Upsala and attended with royal obsequies. His wife

Gunnhild, loth to outlive him, cut off her own life with the sword, choosing rather to follow her lord in death than to forsake him by living. Her friends, in consigning her body to burial, laid her with her husband's dust, thinking her worthy to share the mound of the man, her love for whom she had set above life. So there lies Gunnhild, clasping her lord somewhat more beautifully in the tomb than she had ever done in the bed.

After this Hadding, now triumphant, wasted Sweden. But Asmund's son, named Uffe, shrinking from a conflict, transported his army into Denmark, thinking it better to assail the house of his enemy than to guard his own, and deeming it a timely method of repelling his wrongs to retaliate upon his foe what he was suffering at his hands. Thus the Danes had to return and defend their own, preferring the safety of their land to lordship of a foreign realm; and Uffe went back to his own country, now rid of an enemy's arms.

Hadding, on returning from the Swedish war, perceived that his treasury, wherein he was wont to store the wealth he had gotten by the spoils of war, had been forced and robbed, and straightway hanged its keeper Glumer, proclaiming by a crafty device, that, if any of the culprits brought about the recovery of the stolen goods, he should have the same post of honour as Glumer had filled. Upon this promise, one of the guilty men became more zealous to reap the bounty than to hide his crime, and had the money brought back to the king. His confederates fancied he had been received into the king's closest friendship, and believed that the honours paid him were as real as they were lavish; and therefore they also, hoping to be as well rewarded, brought back their moneys and avowed their guilt. Their confession was received at first with promotion and favours, and soon visited with punishment, thus bequeathing a signal lesson against being too confiding. I should judge that men, whose foolish blabbing brought them to destruction, when wholesome silence could have ensured their safety, well deserved to atone upon the gallows for their breach of reticence.

After this Hadding passed the whole winter season in the utmost preparation for the renewal of the war. When the frosts had been melted by the springtime sun, he went back to Sweden and there spent five years in warfare. By dint of this prolonged expedition, his soldiers, having consumed all their provision, were reduced almost to the extremity of emaciation, and began to assuage their hunger with mushrooms from the wood. At last, under stress of extreme necessity, they devoured their horses, and finally satisfied themselves with the carcases of dogs. Worse still, they did not scruple to feed upon human limbs. So, when the Danes were brought unto the most desperate

76

straits, there sounded in the camp, in the first sleep of the night, and no man uttering it, the following song:

"With foul augury have ye left the abode of your country, thinking to harry these fields in War. What idle notion mocks your minds? What blind self-confidence has seized your senses, that ye think this soil can thus be won. The might of Sweden cannot yield or quail before the War of the stranger; but the whole of your column shall melt away when it begins to assault our people in War. For when flight has broken up the furious onset, and the straggling part of the fighters wavers, then to those who prevail in the War is given free scope to slay those who turn their backs, and they have earned power to smite the harder when fate drives the renewer of the war headlong. Nor let him whom cowardice deters aim the spears."

This prophecy was accomplished on the morrow's dawn by a great slaughter of the Danes. On the next night the warriors of Sweden heard an utterance like this, none knowing who spake it:

"Why doth Uffe thus defy me with grievous rebellion? He shall pay the utmost penalty. For he shall be buried and transpierced under showers of lances, and shall fall lifeless in atonement for his insolent attempt. Nor shall the guilt of his wanton rancour be unpunished; and, as I forebode, as soon as he joins battle and fights, the points shall fasten in his limbs and strike his body everywhere, and his raw gaping wounds no bandage shall bind up; nor shall any remedy heal over thy wide gashes."

On that same night the armies fought; when two hairless old men, of appearance fouler than human, and displaying their horrid baldness in the twinkling starlight, divided their monstrous efforts with opposing ardour, one of them being zealous on the Danish side, and the other as fervent for the Swedes. Hadding was conquered and fled to Helsingland, where, while washing in the cold sea-water his body which was scorched with heat, he attacked and cut down with many blows a beast of unknown kind, and having killed it had it carried into camp. As he was exulting in this deed a woman met him and addressed him in these words:

"Whether thou tread the fields afoot, or spread canvas overseas, thou shalt suffer the hate of the gods, and through all the world shalt behold the elements oppose thy purposes. Afield thou shalt fall, on sea thou shalt be tossed, an eternal tempest shall attend the steps of thy wandering, nor shall frost-bind ever quit thy sails; nor shall thy roof-tree roof thee, but if thou seekest it, it shall fall smitten by the hurricane; thy herd shall perish of bitter chill. All things shall be tainted, and shall lament that thy lot is there. Thou shalt be shunned like a pestilent tetter, nor shall any plague be fouler than thou. Such chastisement doth the power of heaven mete out to thee, for truly thy sacrilegious hands have slain one of the dweller's above, disguised in a shape that was not his: thus here art thou, the slayer of a benignant god! But when the sea receives thee, the wrath of the prison of Eolus shall be loosed upon thy head. The West and the furious North, the South wind shall beat thee down, shall league and send forth their blasts in rivalry; until with better prayers thou hast melted the sternness of heaven, and hast lifted with appeasement the punishment thou hast earned."

So, when Hadding went back, he suffered all things after this one fashion, and his coming brought disquiet upon all peaceful places. For when he was at sea a mighty storm arose and destroyed his fleet in a great tempest: and when, a shipwrecked man, he sought entertainment, he found a sudden downfall of that house. Nor was there any cure for his trouble, ere he atoned by sacrifice for his crime, and was able to return into favour with heaven. For, in order to appease the deities, he sacrificed dusky victims to the god Frey. This manner of propitiation by sacrifice he repeated as an annual feast, and left posterity to follow. This rite the Swedes call Froblod (the sacrifice or feast of Frey).

Hadding chanced to hear that a certain giant had taken in troth Ragnhild, daughter of Hakon, King of the Nitherians; and, loathing so ignominious a state of affairs, and utterly abominating the destined union, he forestalled the marriage by noble daring. For he went to Norway and overcame by arms him that was so foul, a lover for a princess. For he thought so much more of valour than of ease, that, though he was free to enjoy all the pleasures of a king, he accounted it sweeter than any delight to repel the wrongs done, not only to himself, but to others. The maiden, not knowing him, ministered with healing tendance to the man that had done her kindness and was bruised with many wounds. And in order that lapse of time might not make her forget him, she shut up a ring in his wound, and thus left a mark on his leg. Afterwards her father granted her freedom to choose her own husband; so when the young men were assembled at banquet, she went along them and felt their bodies carefully, searching for the tokens she had stored up long ago. All the rest she rejected, but Hadding she discovered by the sign of the secret ring; then she embraced him, and gave herself to be the wife of him who had not suffered a giant to win her in marriage.

While Hadding was sojourning with her a marvellous portent befell him. While he was at supper, a woman bearing hemlocks was seen to raise her head beside the brazier, and, stretching out the lap of her robe, seemed to ask, "in what part of the world such fresh herbs had grown in winter?" The king desired to know; and, wrapping him in her mantle, she drew him with her underground, and vanished. I take it that the nether gods purposed that he should pay a visit in the flesh to the regions whither he must go when he died. So they first pierced through a certain dark misty cloud, and then advancing along a path that was worn away with long thoroughfaring, they beheld certain men wearing rich robes, and nobles clad in purple; these passed, they at last approached sunny regions which produced the herbs the woman had brought away. Going further, they came on a swift and tumbling river of leaden waters, whirling down on its rapid current divers sorts of missiles, and likewise made passable by a bridge. When they had crossed this, they beheld two armies encountering one another with might and main. And when Hadding inquired of the woman about their estate: "These," she said, "are they who, having been slain by the sword, declare the manner of their death by a continual rehearsal, and enact the deeds of their past life in a living spectacle." Then a wall hard to approach and to climb blocked their further advance. The woman tried to leap it, but in vain, being unable to do so even with her slender wrinkled body; then she wrung off the head of a cock which she chanced to be taking down with her, and flung it beyond the barrier of the walls; and forthwith the bird came to life again, and testified by a loud crow to recovery of its breathing. Then Hadding turned back and began to make homewards with his wife; some rovers bore down on him, but by swift sailing he baffled their snares; for though it was almost the same wind that helped both, they were behind him as he clove the billows, and, as they had only just as much sail, could not overtake him.

Meantime Uffe, who had a marvellously fair daughter, decreed that the man who slew Hadding should have her. This sorely tempted one Thuning, who got together a band of men of Perm (Byarmenses), being fain so to win the desired advancement. Hadding was going to fall upon him, but while he was passing Norway in his fleet he saw upon the beach an old man signing to him, with many wavings of his mantle, to put into shore. His companions opposed it, and declared that it would be a ruinous diversion from their journey; but he took the man on board, and was instructed by him how to order his army. For this man, in arranging the system of the columns, used to take special care that the front row consisted of two, the second of four, while the third increased and was made up to eight, and likewise each row was double that in front of it. Also the old man bade the wings of the slingers go back to the extremity of the line, and put with them the ranks of the archers. So when the squadrons were arranged in the wedge, he stood himself behind the warriors, and from the wallet which was slung round his neck drew an arbalist. This seemed small at first, but soon projected with more prolonged tip, and accommodated ten arrows to its string at once, which were shot all at once at the enemy in a brisk volley, and inflicted as many wounds. Then the men of Perm, quitting arms for cunning, by their spells loosed the sky in clouds of rain, and melted the joyous visage of the air in dismal drenching showers. But the old man, on the other hand, drove back with a cloud the heavy mass of storm which had arisen, and checked the dripping rain by this barrier of mist. Thus Hadding prevailed. But the old man, when he parted from him, foretold that the death whereby he would perish would be inflicted, not by the might of an enemy, but by his own hand. Also he forbade him to prefer obscure wars to such as were glorious, and border wars to those remote.

Hadding, after leaving him, was bidden by Uffe to Upsala on pretence of a interview; but lost all his escort by treachery, and made his escape sheltered by the night. For when the Danes sought to leave the house into which they had been gathered on pretext of a banquet, they found one awaiting them, who mowed off the head of each of them with his sword as it was thrust out of the door. For this wrongful act Hadding retaliated and slew Uffe; but put away his hatred and consigned his body to a sepulchre of notable handiwork, thus avowing the greatness of his foe by his pains to beautify his tomb, and decking in death with costly distinctions the man whom he used to pursue in his life with hot enmity. Then, to win the hearts of the people he had subdued, he appointed Hunding, the brother of Uffe, over the realm, that the sovereignty might seem to be maintained in the house of Asmund, and not to have passed into the hand of a stranger.

Thus his enemy was now removed, and he passed several years without any stirring events and in utter disuse of arms; but at last he pleaded the long while he had been tilling the earth, and the immoderate time he had forborne from exploits on the seas; and seeming to think war a merrier thing than peace, he began to upbraid himself with slothfulness in a strain like this:

"Why loiter I thus in darksome hiding, in the folds of rugged hills, nor follow seafaring as of old? The continual howling of the band of wolves, and the plaintive cry of harmful beasts that rises to heaven, and the fierce impatient lions, all rob my eyes of sleep. Dreary are the ridges and the desolation to hearts that trusted to do wilder work. The stark rocks and the rugged lie of the ground bar the way to spirits who are wont to love the sea. It were better service to sound the firths with the oars, to revel in plundered wares, to pursue the gold of others for my coffer, to gloat over sea-gotten gains, than to dwell in rough lands and winding woodlands and barren glades."

Then his wife, loving a life in the country, and weary of the marin harmony of the sea-birds, declared how great joy she found in frequenting the woodlands, in the following strain:

"The shrill bird vexes me as I tarry by the shore, and with its chattering rouses me when I cannot sleep. Wherefore the noisy sweep of its boisterous rush takes gentle rest from my sleeping eye, nor doth the loud-chattering sea-mew suffer me to rest in the night, forcing its wearisome tale into my dainty ears; nor when I would lie down doth it suffer me to be refreshed, clamouring with doleful modulation of its ill-boding voice. Safer and sweeter do I deem the enjoyment of the woods. How are the fruits of rest plucked less by day or night than by tarrying tossed on the shifting sea?"

At this time one Toste emerged, from the obscure spot of Jutland where he was born, into bloody notoriety. For by all manner of wanton attacks upon the common people he spread wide the fame of his cruelty, and gained so universal a repute for rancour, that he was branded with the name of the Wicked. Nor did he even refrain from wrongdoing to foreigners, but, after foully harrying his own land, went on to assault Saxony. The Saxon general Syfrid, when his men were hard put to it in the battle, entreated peace. Toste declared that he should have what he asked, but only if he would promise to become his ally in a war against Hadding. Syfrid demurred, dreading to fulfill the condition, but by sharp menaces Toste induced him to promise what he asked. For threats can sometimes gain a request which soft-dealing cannot compass. Hadding was conquered by this man in an affair by land; but in the midst of his flight he came on his enemy's fleet, and made it unseaworthy by boring the sides; then he got a skiff and steered it out to sea. Toste thought he was slain, but though he sought long among the indiscriminate heaps of dead, could not find him, and came back to his fleet; when he saw from afar off a light boat tossing on the ocean billows. Putting out some vessels, he resolved to give it chase, but was brought back by peril of shipwreck, and only just reached the shore. Then he quickly took some sound craft, and accomplished the journey which he had before begun. Hadding, seeing he was caught, proceeded to ask his companion whether he was a skilled and practised swimmer; and when the other said he was not, Hadding despairing of flight, deliberately turned the vessel over and held on inside to its hollow, thus making his pursuers think him dead. Then he attacked Toste, who, careless and unaware, was greedily watching over the remnants of his spoil; cut down his army, forced him to quit his plunder, and avenged his own rout by that of Toste.

But Toste lacked not heart to avenge himself. For, not having store enough in his own land to recruit his forces—so heavy was the blow he had received—he went to Britain, calling himself an ambassador. Upon his outward voyage, for sheer wantonness, he got his crew together to play dice, and when a wrangle arose from the throwing of the cubes, he taught them to wind it up with a fatal affray. And so, by means of this peaceful sport, he spread the spirit of strife through the whole ship, and the jest gave place to quarrelling, which engendered bloody combat. Also, fain to get some gain out of the misfortunes of others, he seized the moneys of the slain, and attached to him a certain rover then famous, named Koll; and a little after returned in his company to his own land, where he was challenged and slain by Hadding, who preferred to hazard his own fortune rather than that of his soldiers. For generals of antique valour were loth to accomplish by general massacre what could be decided by the lot of a few.

After these deeds the figure of Hadding's dead wife appeared before him in his sleep, and sang thus:

"A monster is born to thee that shall tame the rage of wild beasts, and crush with fierce mouth the fleet wolves."

Then she added a little: "Take thou heed; from thee hath issued a bird of harm, in choler a wild screech-owl, in tongue a tuneful swan."

On the morrow the king, when he had shaken off slumber, told the vision to a man skilled in interpretations, who explained the wolf to denote a son that would be truculent and the word swan as signifying a daughter; and foretold that the son would be deadly to enemies and the daughter treacherous to her father. The result answered to the prophecy. Hadding's daughter, Ulfhild, who was wife to a certain private person called Guthorm, was moved either by anger at her match, or with aspirations to glory, and throwing aside all heed of daughterly love, tempted her husband to slay her father; declaring that she preferred the name of queen to that of princess. I have resolved to set forth the manner of her exhortation almost in the words in which she uttered it; they were nearly these:

"Miserable am I, whose nobleness is shadowed by an unequal yoke! Hapless am I, to whose pedigree is bound the lowliness of a peasant! Luckless issue of a king, to whom a common man is equal by law of marriage! Pitiable daughter of a prince, whose comeliness her spiritless father hath made over to base and contemptible embraces! Unhappy child of thy mother, with thy happiness marred by consorting with this bed! thy purity is handled by the impurity of a peasant, thy nobility is bowed down by ignoble commonness, thy high birth is impaired by the estate of thy husband! But thou, if any pith be in thee, if valour reign in thy soul at all, if thou deem thyself fit husband for a king's daughter, wrest the sceptre from her father, retrieve thy lineage by thy valour, balance with courage thy lack of ancestry, requite by bravery thy detriment of blood. Power won by daring is more prosperous than that won by inheritance. Boldness climbs to the top better than inheritance, and worth wins power better than birth. Moreover, it is no shame to overthrow old age, which of its own weight sinks and totters to its fall. It shall be enough for my father to have borne the sceptre for so long; let the dotard's power fall to thee; if it elude thee, it will pass to another. Whatsoever rests on old age is near its fall. Think that his reign has been long enough, and be it thine, though late in the day, to be first. Further, I would rather have my husband than my father king—would rather be ranked a king's wife than daughter. It is better to embrace a monarch in one's home, than to give him homage from afar; it is nobler to be a king's bride than his courtier. Thou, too, must surely prefer thyself to thy wife's father for bearing the sceptre; for nature has made each one nearest to himself. If there be a will for the deed, a way will open; there is nothing but yields to the wit of man. The feast must be kept, the banquet decked, the preparations looked to, and my father bidden. The path to treachery shall be smoothed by a pretence of friendship, for nothing cloaks a snare better than the name of kindred. Also his soddenness shall open a short way to his slaughter; for when the king shall be intent upon the dressing of his hair, and his hand is upon his beard and his mind upon stories; when he has parted his knotted locks, either with hairpin or disentangling comb, then let him feel the touch of the steel in his flesh. Busy men commonly devise little precaution. Let thy hand draw near to punish all his sins. It is a righteous deed to put forth thy hand to avenge the wretched!"

Thus Ulfhild importuned, and her husband was overcome by her promptings, and promised his help to the treachery. But meantime Hadding was warned in a dream to beware of his son-in-law's guile. He went to the feast, which his daughter had made ready for him with a show of love, and posted an armed guard hard by to use against the treachery when need was. As he ate, the henchman who was employed to do the deed of guile silently awaited a fitting moment for his crime, his dagger hid under his robe. The king, remarking him, blew on the trumpet a signal to the soldiers who were stationed near; they straightway brought aid, and he made the guile recoil on its deviser.

Meanwhile Hunding, King of the Swedes, heard false tidings that Hadding was dead, and resolved to greet them with obsequies. So he gathered his nobles together, and filled a jar of extraordinary size with ale, and had this set in the midst of the feasters for their delight, and, to omit no mark of solemnity, himself assumed a servant's part, not hesitating to play the cupbearer. And while he was passing through the palace in fulfilment of his office, he stumbled and fell into the jar, and, being choked by the liquor, gave up the ghost; thus atoning either to Orcus, whom he was appeasing by a baseless performance of the rites, or to Hadding, about whose death he had spoken falsely. Hadding, when he heard this, wished to pay like thanks to his worshipper, and, not enduring to survive his death, hanged himself in sight of the whole people.

BOOK TWO

HADDING was succeeded by FRODE, his son, whose fortunes were many and changeful. When he had passed the years of a stripling, he displayed the fulness of a warrior's prowess; and being loth that this should be spoilt by slothfulness, he sequestered his mind from delights and perseveringly constrained it to arms. Warfare having drained his father's treasury, he lacked a stock of pay to maintain his troops, and cast about diligently for the supplies that he required; and while thus employed, a man of the country met him and roused his hopes by the following strain:

"Not far off is an island rising in delicate slopes, hiding treasure in its hills and ware of its rich booty. Here a noble pile is kept by the occupant of the mount, who is a snake wreathed in coils, doubled in many a fold, and with tail drawn out in winding whorls, shaking his manifold spirals and shedding venom. If thou wouldst conquer him, thou must use thy shield and stretch thereon bulls' hides, and cover thy body with the skins of kine, nor let thy limbs lie bare to the sharp poison; his slaver burns up what it bespatters. Though the three-forked tongue flicker and leap out of the gaping mouth, and with awful yawn menace ghastly wounds remember to keep the dauntless temper of thy mind; nor let the point of the jagged tooth trouble thee, nor the starkness of the beast, nor the venom spat from the swift throat. Though the force of his scales spurn thy spears, yet know there is a place under his lowest belly whither thou mayst plunge the blade; aim at this with thy sword, and thou shalt probe the snake to his centre. Thence go fearless up to the hill, drive the mattock, dig and ransack the holes; soon fill thy pouch with treasure, and bring back to the shore thy craft laden."

Frode believed, and crossed alone to the island, loth to attack the beast with any stronger escort than that wherewith it was the custom for champions to attack. When it had drunk water and was repairing to its cave, its rough and sharp hide spurned the blow of Frode's steel. Also the darts that he flung against it rebounded idly, foiling the effort of the thrower. But when the hard back yielded not a whit, he noted the belly heedfully, and its softness gave entrance to the steel. The beast tried to retaliate by biting, but only struck the sharp point of its mouth upon the shield. Then it shot out its flickering tongue again and again, and gasped away life and venom together.

The money which the King found made him rich; and with this supply he approached in his fleet the region of the Kurlanders, whose king Dorn, dreading a perilous war, is said to have made a speech of the following kind to his soldiers:

"Nobles! Our enemy is a foreigner, begirt with the arms and the wealth of almost all the West; let us, by endeavouring to defer the battle for our profit, make him a prey to famine, which is all inward malady; and he will find it very hard to conquer a peril among his own people. It is easy to oppose the starving. Hunger will be a better weapon against our foe than arms; famine will be the sharpest lance we shall hurl at him. For lack of food nourishes the pestilence that eats away men's strength, and lack of victual undermines store of weapons. Let this whirl the spears while we sit still; let this take up the prerogative and the duty of fighting. Unimperilled, we shall be able to imperil others; we can drain their blood and lose no drop of ours. One may defeat an enemy by inaction. Who would not rather fight safely than at a loss? Who would strive to suffer chastisement when he may contend unhurt? Our success in arms will be more prosperous if hunger joins battle first. Let hunger captain us, and so let us take the first chance of conflict. Let it decide the day in our stead, and let our camp remain free from the stir of war; if hunger retreat beaten, we must break off idleness. He who is fresh easily overpowers him who is shaken with languor. The hand that is flaccid and withered will come fainter to the battle. He whom any hardship has first wearied, will bring slacker hands to the steel. When he that is wasted with sickness engages with the sturdy, the victory hastens. Thus, undamaged ourselves, we shall be able to deal damage to others."

Having said this, he wasted all the places which he saw would be hard to protect, distrusting his power to guard them, and he so far forestalled the ruthlessness of the foe in ravaging his own land, that he left nothing untouched which could be seized by those who came after. Then he shut up the greater part of his forces in a town of undoubted strength, and suffered the enemy to blockade him. Frode, distrusting his power of attacking this town, commanded several trenches of unwonted depth to

85

be made within the camp, and the earth to be secretly carried out in baskets and cast quietly into the river bordering the walls. Then he had a mass of turf put over the trenches to hide the trap: wishing to cut off the unwary enemy by tumbling them down headlong, and thinking that they would be overwhelmed unawares by the slip of the subsiding earth. Then he feigned a panic, and proceeded to forsake the camp for a short while. The townsmen fell upon it, missed their footing everywhere, rolled forward into the pits, and were massacred by him under a shower of spears.

Thence he travelled and fell in with Trannon, the monarch of the Ruthenians. Desiring to spy out the strength of his navy, he made a number of pegs out of sticks, and loaded a skiff with them; and in this he approached the enemy's fleet by night, and bored the hulls of the vessels with an auger. And to save them from a sudden influx of the waves, he plugged up the open holes with the pegs he had before provided, and by these pieces of wood he made good the damage done by the auger. But when he thought there were enough holes to drown the fleet, he took out the plugs, thus giving instant access to the waters, and then made haste to surround the enemy's fleet with his own. The Ruthenians were beset with a double peril, and wavered whether they should first withstand waves or weapons. Fighting to save their ships from the foe, they were shipwrecked. Within, the peril was more terrible than without: within, they fell back before the waves, while drawing the sword on those without. For the unhappy men were assaulted by two dangers at once; it was doubtful whether the swiftest way of safety was to swim or to battle to the end; and the fray was broken off at its hottest by a fresh cause of doom. Two forms of death advanced in a single onset; two paths of destruction offered united peril: it was hard to say whether the sword or the sea hurt them more. While one man was beating off the swords, the waters stole up silently and took him. Contrariwise, another was struggling with the waves, when the steel came up and encompassed him. The flowing waters were befouled with the gory spray. Thus the Ruthenians were conquered, and Frode made his way back home.

Finding that some envoys, whom he had sent into Russia to levy tribute, had been horribly murdered through the treachery of the inhabitants, Frode was stung by the double wrong and besieged closely their town Rotel. Loth that the intervening river should delay his capture of the town, he divided the entire mass of the waters by making new and different streams, thus changing what had been a channel of unknown depth into passable fords; not ceasing till the speed of the eddy, slackened by the division of its outlet, rolled its waves onward in fainter current, and winding along its slender reaches, slowly thinned and dwindled into a shallow. Thus he prevailed over the river; and the town, which lacked natural defences, he overthrew, his soldiers breaking in without resistance. This done, he took his army to the city of Paltisca. Thinking no force could overcome it, he exchanged war for guile. He went into a dark and unknown hiding-place, only a very few being in the secret, and ordered a report of his death to be spread abroad, so as to inspire the enemy with less fear; his obsequies being also held, and a barrow raised, to give the tale credit. Even the soldiers bewailed his supposed death with a mourning which was in the secret of the trick. This rumour led Vespasins, the king of the city, to show so faint and feeble a defence, as though the victory was already his, that the enemy got a chance of breaking in, and slew him as he sported at his ease.

Frode, when he had taken this town, aspired to the Empire of the East, and attacked the city of Handwan. This king, warned by Hadding's having once fired his town, accordingly cleared the tame birds out of all his houses, to save himself from the peril of like punishment. But Frode was not at a loss for new trickery. He exchanged garments with a serving-maid, and feigned himself to be a maiden skilled in fighting; and having thus laid aside the garb of man and imitated that of woman, he went to the town, calling himself a deserter. Here he reconnoitred everything narrowly, and on the next day sent out an attendant with orders that the army should be up at the walls, promising that he would see to it that the gates were opened. Thus the sentries were eluded and the city despoiled while it was buried in sleep; so that it paid for its heedlessness with destruction, and was more pitiable for its own sloth than by reason of the valour of the foe. For in warfare nought is found to be more ruinous than that a man, made foolhardy by ease, should neglect and slacken his affairs and doze in arrogant self-confidence.

Handwan, seeing that the fortunes of his country were lost and overthrown, put all his royal wealth on shipboard and drowned it in the sea, so as to enrich the waves rather than his enemy. Yet it had been better to forestall the goodwill of his adversaries with gifts of money than to begrudge the profit of it to the service of mankind. After this, when Frode sent ambassadors to ask for the hand of his daughter, he answered, that he must take heed not to be spoiled by his thriving fortunes, or to turn his triumph into haughtiness; but let him rather bethink him to spare the conquered, and in this their abject estate to respect their former bright condition; let him learn to honour their past fortune in their present pitiable lot. Therefore, said Handwan, he must mind that he did not rob of his empire the man with whom he sought alliance, nor bespatter her with the filth of ignobleness whom he desired to honour with marriage: else he would tarnish the honour of the union with covetousness. The courtliness of this saying not only won him his conqueror for son-in-law, but saved the freedom of his realm.

Meantime Thorhild, wife of Hunding, King of the Swedes, possessed with a boundless hatred for her stepsons Ragnar and Thorwald, and fain to entangle them in divers perils, at last made them the king's shepherds. But Swanhwid, daughter of Hadding, wished to arrest by woman's wit the ruin of natures so noble; and taking her sisters to serve as retinue, journeyed to Sweden. Seeing the said youths beset with sundry prodigies while busy watching at night over their flocks, she forbade her sisters, who desired to dismount, in a poem of the following strain:

"Monsters I behold taking swift leaps and flinging themselves over the night places. The demon is at war, and the unholy throng, devoted to the mischievous fray, battles in the mid-thoroughfare. Prodigies of aspect grim to behold pass by, and suffer no mortal to enter this country. The ranks galloping in headlong career through the void bid us stay our advance in this spot; they warn us to turn our rein and hold off from the accursed fields, they forbid us to approach the country beyond. A scowling horde of ghosts draws near, and scurries furiously through the wind, bellowing drearily to the stars. Fauns join Satyrs, and the throng of Pans mingles with the Spectres and battles with fierce visage. The Swart ones meet the Woodland Spirits, and the pestilent phantoms strive to share the path with the Witches. Furies poise themselves on the leap, and on them huddle the Phantoms, whom Foreboder (Fantua) joined to the Flatnoses (Satyrs), jostles. The path that the footfarer must tread brims with horror. It were safer to burden the back of the tall horse."

Thereon Ragnar declared that he was a slave of the king, and gave as reason of his departure so far from home that, when he had been banished to the country on his shepherd's business, he had lost the flock of which he had charge, and despairing to recover it, had chosen rather to forbear from returning than to incur punishment. Also, loth to say nothing about the estate of his brother, he further spoke the following poem:

"Think us men, not monsters; we are slaves who drove our lingering flocks for pasture through the country. But while we took our pastime in gentle sports, our flock chanced to stray and went into far-off fields. And when our hope of finding them, our long quest failed, trouble came upon the mind of the wretched culprits. And when sure tracks of our kine were nowhere to be seen, dismal panic filled our guilty hearts. That is why, dreading the penal stripe of the rod, we thought it doleful to return to our own roof. We supposed it safer to hold aloof from the familiar hearth than to bear the hand of punishment. Thus we are fain to put off the punishment; we loathe going back and our wish is to lie hid here and escape our master's eye. This will aid us to elude the avenger of his neglected flock; and this is the one way of escape that remains safe for us."

Then Swanhwid gazed intently, and surveying his features, which were very comely, admired them ardently, and said:

"The radiant flashing of thine eyes is eloquent that thou art of kingly and not of servile stock. Beauty announces blood, and loveliness of soul glitters in the flash of the eyes. A keen glance betokens lordly birth, and it is plain that he whom fairness, that sure sign of nobleness, commends, is of no mean station. The outward alertness of thine eyes signifies a spirit of radiance within. Face vouches for race; and the lustre of forefathers is beheld in the brightness of the countenance. For an aspect so benign and noble could never have issued from base parentage. The grace of thy blood makes thy brow mantle with a kindred grace, and the estate of thy birth is reflected in the mirror of thy countenance. It is no obscure craftsman, therefore, that has finished the portrait of so choice a chasing. Now therefore turn aside with all speed, seek constantly to depart out of the road, shun encounters with monsters, lest ye yield your most gracious bodies to be the prey and pasture of the vilest hordes."

But Ragnar was seized with great shame for his unsightly attire, which he thought was the only possible device to disguise his birth. So he rejoined, "That slaves were not always found to lack manhood; that a strong hand was often hidden under squalid raiment, and sometimes a stout arm was muffled trader a dusky cloak; thus the fault of nature was retrieved by valour, and deficiency in race requited by nobleness of spirit. He therefore feared the might of no supernatural prowess, save of the god Thor only, to the greatness of whose force nothing human or divine could fitly be compared. The hearts of men ought not to be terrified at phantoms, which were only awful from their ghastly foulness, and whose semblances, marked by counterfeit ghostliness, were wont for a moment to borrow materiality from the fluent air. Swanhwid therefore erred in trying, womanlike, to sap the firm strength of men, and to melt in unmanly panic that might which knew not defeat."

Swanhwid marvelled at the young man's steadfastness, and cast off the cloud of mist which overshadowed her, dispelling the darkness which shrouded her face, till it was clear and cloudless. Then, promising that she would give him a sword fitted for diver's kinds of battle, she revealed the marvellous maiden beauty of her lustrous limbs. Thus was the youth kindled, and she plighted her troth with him, and proffering the sword, she thus began:

"King, in this sword, which shall expose the monsters to thy blows, take the first gift of thy betrothed. Show thyself duly deserving hereof; let hand rival sword, and aspire to add lustre to its weapon. Let the might of steel strengthen the defenceless point of thy wit, and let spirit know how to work with hand. Let the bearer match the burden: and that thy deed may sort with thy blade, let equal weight in each be thine. What avails the javelin when the breast is weak and faint, and the quivering hands have dropped the lance? Let steel join soul, and be both the body's armour! Let the right hand be linked with its hilt in alliance. These fight famous battles, because they always keep more force when together; but less when parted. Therefore if it be joy to thee to win fame by the palm of war, pursue with daring whatsoever is hard pressed by thy hand."

After thus discoursing long in harmoniously-adjusted strains, she sent away her retinue, and passed all the night in combat against the foulest throngs of monsters; and at return of daybreak she perceived fallen all over the fields diverse shapes of phantoms, and figures extraordinary to look on; and among them was seen the semblance of Thorhild herself covered with wounds. All these she piled in a heap and burnt, kindling a huge pyre, lest the foul stench of the filthy carcases might spread in pestilent vapour and hurt those who came nigh with its taint of corruption. This done, she won the throne of Sweden for Ragnar, and Ragnar for her husband. And though he deemed it uncomely to inaugurate his first campaign with a wedding, yet, moved by gratitude for the preservation of his safety, he kept his promise.

Meantime one Ubbe, who had long since wedded Ulfhild the sister of Frode, trusting in the high birth of his wife, seized the kingdom of Denmark, which he was managing carelessly as deputy. Frode was thus forced to quit the wars of the East and fought a great battle in Sweden with his sister Swanhwid, in which he was beaten. So he got on board a skiff, and sailed stealthily in a circuit, seeking some way of boring through the enemy's fleet. When surprised by his sister and asked why he was rowing silently and following divers meandering courses, he cut short her inquiry by a similar question; for Swanhwid had also, at the same time of the night, taken to sailing about alone, and was stealthily searching out all the ways of approach and retreat through devious and dangerous windings. So she reminded her brother of the freedom he had given her long since, and went on to ask him that he should allow her full enjoyment of the husband she had taken; since, before he started on the Russian war, he had given her the boon of marrying as she would; and that he should hold valid after the event what he had himself allowed to happen. These reasonable entreaties touched Frode, and he made a peace with Ragnar, and forgave, at his sister's request, the wrongdoing which Ragnar, seemed to have begun because of her wantonness. They presented him with a force equal to that which they had caused him to lose: a handsome gift in which he rejoiced as compensation for so ugly a reverse.

Ragnar, entering Denmark, captured Ubbe, had him brought before him, and pardoned him, preferring to visit his ill deserts with grace rather than chastisement; because the man seemed to have aimed at the crown rather at his wife's instance than of his own ambition, and to have been the imitator and not the cause of the wrong. But he took Ulfhild away from him and forced her to wed his friend Scot, the same man that founded the Scottish name; esteeming change of wedlock a punishment for her. As she went away he even escorted her in the royal chariot, requiting evil with good; for he regarded the kinship of his sister rather than her disposition, and took more thought for his own good name than of her iniquity. But the fair deeds of her brother did not make her obstinate and wonted hatred slacken a whit; she wore the spirit of her new husband with her design of slaying Frode and mastering the sovereignty of the Danes. For whatsoever design the mind has resolutely conceived, it is slow to quit; nor is a sin that is long schemed swept away by the stream of years. For the temper of later life follows the mind of childhood; nor do the traces easily fade of vices which have been stamped upon the character in the impressible age. Finding the ears of her husband deaf, she diverted her treachery from her brother against her lord, hiring bravoes to cut his throat while he slept. Scot was told about this by a waiting-woman, and retired to bed in his cuirass on the night on which he had heard the deed of murder was to be wrought upon him. Ulfhild asked him why he had exchanged his wonted ways to wear the garb of steel; he rejoined that such was just then his fancy. The agents of the treachery, when they imagined him in a deep sleep, burst in; but he slipped from his bed and cut them down. The result was, that he prevented Ulfhild from weaving plots against her brother, and also left a warning to others to beware of treachery from their wives.

Meantime the design occurred to Frode of a campaign against Friesland; he was desirous to dazzle the eyes of the West with the glory he had won in conquering the East. He put out to ocean, and his first contest was with Witthe, a rover of the Frisians; and in this battle he bade his crews patiently bear the first brunt of the enemy's charge by merely opposing their shields, ordering that they should not use their missiles before they perceived that the shower of the enemy's spears was utterly silent. This the Frisians hurled as vehemently as the Danes received it impassively; for Witthe supposed that the long-suffering of Frode was due to a wish for peace. High rose the blast of the trumpet, and loud whizzed the javelins everywhere, till at last the heedless Frisians had not a single lance remaining, and they were conquered, overwhelmed by the missiles of the Danes. They fled hugging the shore, and were cut to pieces amid the circuitous windings of the canals. Then Frode explored the Rhine in his fleet, and laid hands on the farthest parts of Germany. Then he went back to the ocean, and attacked the Frisian fleet, which had struck on shoals; and thus he crowned shipwreck with slaughter. Nor was he content with the destruction of so great an army of his foes, but assailed Britain, defeated its king, and attacked Melbrik, the Governor of the Scottish district. Just as he was preparing to fight him, he heard from a scout that the King of the Britons was at hand, and could not look to his front and his rear both at once. So he assembled the soldiers, and ordered that they should abandon their chariots, fling away all their goods, and scatter everywhere over the fields the gold which they had about them; for he declared that their one chance was to squander their treasure; and that, now they were hemmed in, their only remaining help was to tempt the enemy from combat to covetousness. They ought cheerfully to spend on so extreme a need the spoil they had gotten among foreigners; for the enemy would drop it as eagerly, when it was once gathered, as they would snatch it when they first found it; for it would be to them more burden than profit.

Then Thorkill, who was a more notable miser and a better orator than them all, dishelming and leaning on his shield, said:

"O King! Most of us who rate high what we have bought with our life-blood find thy bidding hard. We take it ill that we should fling away what we have won with utmost hazard; and men are loth to forsake what they have purchased at peril of their lives. For it is utter madness to spurn away like women what our manly hearts and hands have earned, and enrich the enemy beyond their hopes. What is more odious than to anticipate the fortune of war by despising the booty which is ours, and, in terror of an evil that may never come, to quit a good which is present and assured? Shall we scatter our gold upon the earth, ere we have set eyes upon the Scots? Those who faint at the thought of warring when they are out for war, what manner of men are they to be thought in the battle? Shall we be a derision to our foes, we who were their terror? Shall we take scorn instead of glory? The Briton will marvel that he was conquered by men whom he sees fear is enough to conquer. We struck them before with panic; shall we be panic-stricken by them? We scorned them when before us; shall we dread them when they are not here? When will our bravery win the treasure which our cowardice rejects? Shall we shirk the fight, in scorn of the money which we fought to win, and enrich those whom we should rightly have impoverished? What deed more despicable can we do than to squander gold on those whom we should smite with steel? Panic must never rob us of the spoils of valour; and only war must make us quit what in warfare we have won. Let us sell our plunder at the price at which we bought it; let the purchase-money be weighed out in steel. It is better to die a noble death, than to molder away too much in love with the light life. In a fleeting instant of time life forsakes us, but shame pursues us past the grave. Further, if we cast away this gold, the greater the enemy thinks our fear, the hotter will be his chase. Besides, whichever the issue of the day, the gold is not hateful to us. Conquerors, we shall triumph in the treasure which now we bear; conquered, we shall leave it to pay our burying."

So spoke the old man; but the soldiers regarded the advice of their king rather than of their comrade, and thought more of the former than of the latter counsel. So each of them eagerly drew his wealth, whatever he had, from his pouch; they unloaded their ponies of the various goods they were carrying; and having thus cleared their money-bags, girded on their arms more deftly. They went on, and the Britons came up, but broke away after the plunder which lay spread out before them. Their king, when he beheld them too greedily busied with scrambling for the treasure, bade them "take heed not to weary with a load of riches those hands which were meant for battle, since they ought to know that a victory must be culled ere it is counted. Therefore let them scorn the gold and give chase to the possessors of the gold; let them admire the lustre, not of lucre, but of conquest; remembering, that a trophy gave more reward than gain. Courage was worth more than dross, if they measured aright the quality of both; for the one furnished outward adorning, but the other enhanced both outward and inward grace. Therefore they must keep their eyes far from the sight of money, and their soul from covetousness, and devote it to the pursuits of war. Further, they should know that the plunder had been abandoned by the enemy of set purpose, and that the gold had been scattered rather to betray them than to profit them. Moreover, the honest lustre of the silver was only a bait on the barb of secret guile. It was not thought to be that they, who had first forced the Britons to fly, would lightly fly themselves. Besides, nothing was more shameful than riches which betrayed into captivity the plunderer whom they were supposed to enrich. For the Danes thought that the men to whom they pretended to have offered riches ought to be punished with sword and slaughter. Let them therefore feel that they were only giving the enemy a weapon if they seized what he had scattered. For if they were caught by the look of the treasure that had been exposed, they must lose, not only that, but any of their own money that might remain. What could it profit them to gather what they must straightway disgorge? But if they refuse to abase themselves before money, they would doubtless abase the foe. Thus it was better for them to stand erect in valour than be grovelling in greed; with their souls not sinking into covetousness, but up and doing for renown. In the battle they would have to use not gold but swords."

As the king ended, a British knight, shewing them all his lapful of gold, said:

"O King! From thy speech can be gathered two feelings; and one of them witnesses to thy cowardice and the other to thy ill will: inasmuch as thou forbiddest us the use of the wealth because of the enemy, and also thinkest it better that we should serve thee needy than rich. What is more odious than such a wish? What more senseless than such a counsel? We recognise these as the treasures of our own homes, and having done so, shall we falter to pick them up? We were on our way to regain them by fighting, we were zealous to win them back by our blood: shall we shun them when they are restored unasked? Shall we hesitate to claim our own? Which is the greater coward, he who squanders his winnings, or he who is fearful to pick up what is squandered? Look how chance has restored what compulsion took! These are, not spoils from the enemy, but from ourselves; the Dane took gold from Britain, he brought none. Beaten and loth we lost it; it comes back for nothing, and shall we run away from it? Such a gift of fortune it were a shame to take in an unworthy spirit. For what were madder than to spurn wealth that is set openly before us, and to desire it when it is shut up and kept from us? Shall we squeamishly yield what is set under our eyes, and clutch at it when it vanishes? Shall we seek distant and foreign treasure, refraining from what is made public property? If we disown what is ours, when shall we despoil the goods of others? No anger of heaven can I experience which can force me to unload of its lawful burden the lap which is filled with my father's and my grandsire's gold. I know the wantonness of the Danes: never would they have left jars full of wine had not fear forced them to flee. They would rather have sacrificed their life than their liquor. This passion we share with them, and herein we are like them. Grant that their flight is feigned; yet they will light upon the Scots ere they can come back. This gold shall never rust in the country, to be trodden underfoot of swine or brutes: it will better serve the use of men. Besides, if we plunder the spoil of the army that prevailed over us, we transfer the luck of the conqueror to ourselves. For what surer omen of triumph could be got, than to bear off the booty before the battle, and to capture ere the fray the camp which the enemy have forsaken? Better conquer by fear than by steel."

The knight had scarce ended, when behold; the hands of all were loosed upon the booty and everywhere plucked up the shining treasure. There you might have marvelled at their disposition of filthy greed, and watched a portentous spectacle of avarice. You could have seen gold and grass clutched up together; the birth of domestic discord; fellow-countrymen in deadly combat, heedless of the foe; neglect of the bonds of comradeship and of reverence for ties; greed the object of all minds, and friendship of none.

Meantime Frode traversed in a great march the forest which separates Scotland and Britain, and bade his soldiers arm. When the Scots beheld his line, and saw that they had only a supply of light javelins, while the Danes were furnished with a more excellent style of armour, they forestalled the battle by flight. Frode pursued them but a little way, fearing a sally of the British, and on returning met Scot, the husband of Ulfhild, with a great army; he had been brought from the utmost ends of Scotland by the desire of aiding the Danes. Scot entreated him to abandon the pursuit of the Scottish and turn back into Britain. So he eagerly regained the plunder which he had cunningly sacrificed; and got back his wealth with the greater ease, that he had so tranquilly let it go. Then did the British repent of their burden and pay for their covetousness with their blood. They were sorry to have clutched at greed with insatiate arms, and ashamed to have hearkened to their own avarice rather than to the counsel of their king.

Then Frode attacked London, the most populous city of Britain; but the strength of its walls gave him no chance of capturing it. Therefore he reigned to be dead, and his guile strengthened him. For Daleman, the governor of London, on hearing the false news of his death, accepted the surrender of the Danes, offered them a native general, and suffered them to enter the town, that they might choose him out of a great throng. They feigned to be making a careful choice, but beset Daleman in a night surprise and slew him.

When he had done these things, and gone back to his own land, one Skat entertained him at a banquet, desirous to mingle his toilsome warfare with joyous licence. Frode was lying in his house, in royal fashion, upon cushions of cloth of gold, and a certain Hunding challenged him to fight. Then, though he had bent his mind to the joys of wassail, he had more delight in the prospect of a fray than in the presence of a feast, and wound up the supper with a duel and the duel with a triumph. In the combat he received a dangerous wound; but a taunt of Hakon the champion again roused him, and, slaying his challenger, he took vengeance for the disturbance of his rest. Two of his chamber-servants were openly convicted of treachery, and he had them tied to vast stones and drowned in the sea; thus chastising the weighty guilt of their souls by fastening boulders to their bodies. Some relate that Ulfhild gave him a coat which no steel could pierce, so that when he wore it no missile's point could hurt him. Nor must I omit how Frode was wont to sprinkle his food with brayed and pounded atoms of gold, as a resource against the usual snares of poisoners. While he was attacking Ragnar, the King of Sweden, who had been falsely accused of treachery, he perished, not by the spears, but stifled in the weight of his arms and by the heat of his own body.

Frode left three sons, Halfdan, Ro, and Skat, who were equal in valour, and were seized with an equal desire for the throne. All thought of sway, none was constrained by brotherly regard: for love of others forsaketh him who is eaten up with love of self, nor can any man take thought at once for his own advancement and for his friendship with others. Halfdan, the eldest son, disgraced his birth with the sin of slaying his brethren, winning his kingdom by the murder of his kin; and, to complete his display of cruelty, arrested their adherents, first confining them in bonds, and presently hanging them. The most notable thing in the fortunes of Halfdan was this, that though he devoted every instant of his life to the practice of cruel deeds, yet he died of old age, and not by the steel.

Halfdan's sons were Ro and Helge. Ro is said to have been the founder of Roskild, which was later increased in population and enhanced in power by Sweyn, who was famous for the surname Forkbeard. Ro was short and spare, while Helge was rather tall of stature. Dividing the realm with his brother, Helge was allotted the domain of the sea; and attacking Skalk, the King of Sklavia, with his naval force, he slew him. Having reduced Sklavia into a province, he scoured the various arms of the sea in a wandering voyage. Savage of temper as Helge was, his cruelty was not greater than his lust. For he was so immoderately prone to love, that it was doubtful whether the heat of his tyranny or of his concupiscence was the greater. In Thorey he ravished the maiden Thora, who bore a daughter, to whom she afterwards gave the name of Urse. Then he conquered in battle, before the town of Stad, the son of Syrik, King of Saxony, Hunding, whom he challenged, attacked, and slew in duel. For this he was called Hunding's-Bane, and by that name gained glory of his victory. He took Jutland out of the power of the Saxons, and entrusted its management to his generals, Heske, Eyr, and Ler. In Saxony he enacted that the slaughter of a freedman and of a noble should be visited with the same punishment; as though he wished it to be clearly known that all the households of the Teutons were held in equal slavery, and that the freedom of all was tainted and savoured equally of dishonour.

Then Helge went freebooting to Thorey. But Thora had not ceased to bewail her lost virginity, and planned a shameful device in abominable vengeance for her rape. For she deliberately sent down to the beach her daughter, who was of marriageable age, and prompted her father to deflower her. And though she yielded her body to the treacherous lures of delight, yet she must not be thought to have abjured her integrity of soul, inasmuch as her fault had a ready excuse by virtue of her ignorance. Insensate mother, who allowed the forfeiture of her child's chastity in order to avenge her own; caring nought for the purity of her own blood, so she might stain with incest the man who had cost her her own maidenhood at first! Infamous-hearted woman, who, to punish her defiler, measured out as it were a second defilement to herself, whereas she clearly by the selfsame act rather swelled than lessened the transgression! Surely, by the very act wherewith she thought to reach her revenge, she accumulated guilt; she added a sin in trying to remove a crime: she played the stepdame to her own offspring, not sparing her daughter abomination in order to atone for her own disgrace. Doubtless her soul was brimming over with shamelessness, since she swerved so far from shamefastness, as without a blush to seek solace for her wrong in her daughter's infamy. A great crime, with but one atonement; namely, that the guilt of this intercourse was wiped away by a fortunate progeny, its fruits being as delightful as its repute was evil.

ROLF, the son of Urse, retrieved the shame of his birth by signal deeds of valour; and their exceeding lustre is honoured with bright laudation by the memory of all succeeding time. For lamentation sometimes ends in laughter, and foul beginnings pass to fair issues. So that the father's fault, though criminal, was fortunate, being afterwards atoned for by a son of such marvellous splendour.

Meantime Ragnar died in Sweden; and Swanhwid his wife passed away soon after of a malady which she had taken from her sorrow, following in death the husband from whom she had not endured severance in life. For it often happens that some people desire to follow out of life those whom they loved exceedingly when alive. Their son Hothbrodd succeeded them. Fain to extend his empire, he warred upon the East, and after a huge massacre of many peoples begat two sons, Athisl and Hother, and appointed as their tutor a certain Gewar, who was bound to him by great services. Not content with conquering the East, he assailed Denmark, challenged its king, Ro, in three battles, and slew him. Helge, when he heard this, shut up his son Rolf in Leire, wishing, however he might have managed his own fortunes, to see to the safety of his heir. When Hothbrodd sent in governors, wanting to free his country from alien rule, he posted his people about the city and prevailed and slew them. Also he annihilated Hothbrodd himself and all his forces in a naval battle; so avenging fully the wrongs of his country as well as of his brother. Hence he who had before won a nickname for slaying Hunding, now bore a surname for the slaughter of Hothbrodd. Besides, as if the Swedes had not been enough stricken in the battles, he punished them by stipulating for most humiliating terms; providing by law that no wrong done to any of them should receive amends according to the form of legal covenants. After these deeds, ashamed of his former infamy, he hated his country and his home, went back to the East, and there died. Some think that he was affected by the disgrace which was cast in his teeth, and did himself to death by falling upon his drawn sword.

He was succeeded by his son Rolf, who was comely with every gift of mind and body, and graced his mighty stature with as high a courage. In his time Sweden was subject to the sway of the Danes; wherefore Athisl, the son of Hothbrodd, in pursuit of a crafty design to set his country free, contrived to marry Rolf's mother, Urse, thinking that his kinship by marriage would plead for him, and enable him to prompt his stepson more effectually to relax the tribute; and fortune prospered his wishes. But Athisl had from his boyhood been imbued with a hatred of liberality, and was so grasping of money, that he accounted it a disgrace to be called openhanded. Urse, seeing him so steeped in filthy covetousness, desired to be rid of him; but, thinking that she must act by cunning, veiled the shape of her guile with a marvellous skill. Feigning to be unmotherly, she spurred on her husband to grasp his freedom, and urged and tempted him to insurrection; causing her son to be summoned to Sweden with a promise of vast gifts. For she thought that she would best gain her desire if, as soon as her son had got his stepfather's gold, she could snatch up the royal treasures and flee, robbing her husband of bed and money to boot. For she fancied that the best way to chastise his covetousness would be to steal away his wealth. This deep guilefulness was hard to detect, from such recesses of cunning did it spring; because she dissembled her longing for a change of wedlock under a show of aspiration for freedom. Blind-witted husband, fancying the mother kindled against the life of the son, never seeing that it was rather his own ruin being compassed! Doltish lord, blind to the obstinate scheming of his wife, who, out of pretended hatred of her son, devised opportunity for change of wedlock! Though the heart of woman should never be trusted, he believed in a woman all the more insensately, because he supposed her faithful to himself and treacherous to her son.

Accordingly, Rolf, tempted by the greatness of the gifts, chanced to enter the house of Athisl. He was not recognised by his mother owing to his long absence and the cessation of their common life; so in jest he first asked for some victual to appease his hunger. She advised him to ask the king for a luncheon. Then he thrust out a torn piece of his coat, and begged of her the service of sewing it up. Finding his mother's ears shut to him, he observed, "That it was hard to discover a friendship that was firm and true, when a mother refused her son a meal, and a sister refused a brother the help of her needle." Thus he punished his mother's error, and made her blush deep for her refusal of kindness. Athisl, when he saw him reclining close to his mother at the banquet, taunted them both with wantonness, declaring that it was an impure intercourse of brother and sister. Rolf repelled the charge against his honour by an appeal to the closest of natural bonds, and answered, that it was honourable for a son to embrace a beloved mother. Also, when the feasters asked him what kind of courage he set above all others, he named Endurance. When they also asked Athisl, what was the virtue which above all he desired most devotedly, he declared, Generosity. Proofs were therefore demanded of bravery on the one hand and munificence on the other, and Rolf was asked to give an evidence of courage first. He was placed to the fire, and defending with his target the side that was most hotly assailed, had only the firmness of his endurance to fortify the other, which had no defence. How dexterous, to borrow from his shield protection to assuage the heat, and to guard his body, which was exposed to the flames, with that which sometime sheltered it amid the hurtling spears! But the glow was hotter than the fire of spears; as though it could not storm the side that was entrenched by the shield, yet it assaulted the flank that lacked its protection. But a waiting-maid who happened to be standing near the hearth, saw that he was being roasted by the unbearable heat upon his ribs; so taking the stopper out of a cask, she spilt the liquid and quenched the flame, and by the timely kindness of the shower checked in its career the torturing blaze. Rolf was lauded for supreme endurance, and then came the request for Athisl's gifts. And they say that he showered treasures on his stepson, and at last, in order to crown the gift, bestowed on him an enormously heavy necklace.

Now Urse, who had watched her chance for the deed of guile, on the third day of the banquet, without her husband ever dreaming of such a thing, put all the king's wealth into carriages, and going out stealthily, stole away from her own dwelling and fled in the glimmering twilight, departing with her son. Thrilled with fear of her husband's pursuit, and utterly despairing of escape beyond, she begged and bade her companions to cast away the money, declaring that they must lose either life or riches; the short and only path to safety lay in flinging away the treasure, nor could any aid to escape be found save in the loss of their possessions. Therefore, said she, they must follow the example of the manner in which Frode was said to have saved himself among the Britons. She added, that it was not paying a great price to lay down the Swedes' own goods for them to regain; if only they could themselves gain a start in flight, by the very device which would check the others in their pursuit, and if they seemed not so much to abandon their own possessions as to restore those of other men. Not a moment was lost; in order to make the flight swifter, they did the bidding of the queen. The gold is cleared from their purses; the riches are left for the enemy to seize. Some declare that Urse kept back the money, and strewed the tracks of her flight with copper that was gilt over. For it was thought credible that a woman who could scheme such great deeds could also have painted with lying lustre the metal that was meant to be lost, mimicking riches of true worth with the sheen of spurious gold. So Athisl, when he saw the necklace that he had given to Rolf left among the other golden ornaments, gazed fixedly upon the dearest treasure of his avarice, and, in order to pick up the plunder, glued his knees to the earth and deigned to stoop his royalty unto greed. Rolf, seeing him lie abjectly on his face in order to gather up the money, smiled at the sight of a man prostrated by his own gifts, just as if he were seeking covetously to regain what he had craftily yielded up. The Swedes were content with their booty, and Rolf quickly retired to his ships, and managed to escape by rowing violently.

Now they relate that Rolf used with ready generosity to grant at the first entreaty whatsoever he was begged to bestow, and never put off the request till the second time of asking. For he preferred to forestall repeated supplication by speedy liberality, rather than mar his kindness by delay. This habit brought him a great concourse of champions; valour having commonly either rewards for its food or glory for its spur.

At this time, a certain Agnar, son of Ingild, being about to wed Rute, the sister of Rolf, celebrated his bridal with a great banquet. The champions were rioting at this banquet with every sort of wantonness, and flinging from all over the room knobbed bones at a certain Hjalte; but it chanced that his messmate, named Bjarke, received a violent blow on the head through the ill aim of the thrower; at whom, stung both by the pain and the jeering, he sent the bone back, so that he twisted the front of his head to the back, and wrung the back of it to where the front had been; punishing the wryness of the man's temper by turning his face sidelong. This deed moderated their wanton and injurious jests, and drove the champions to quit the place. The bridegroom, nettled at this affront to the banquet, resolved to fight Bjarke, in order to seek vengeance by means of a duel for the interruption of their mirth. At the outset of the duel there was a long dispute, which of them ought to have the chance of striking first. For of old, in the ordering of combats, men did not try to exchange their blows thick and fast; but there was a pause, and at the same time a definite succession in striking: the contest being carried on with few strokes, but those terrible, so that honour was paid more to the mightiness than to the number of the blows. Agnar, being of higher rank, was put first; and the blow which he dealt is said to have been so furious, that he cut through the front of the helmet, wounded the skin on the scalp, and had to let go his sword, which became locked in the vizor-holes. Then Bjarke, who was to deal the return-stroke, leaned his foot against a stock, in order to give the freer poise to his steel, and passed his fine-edged blade through the midst of Agnar's body. Some declare that Agnar, in supreme suppression of his pain, gave up the ghost with his lips relaxed into a smile. The champions passionately sought to avenge him, but were visited by Bjarke with like destruction; for he used a sword of wonderful sharpness and unusual length which he called Lovi. While he was triumphing in these deeds of prowess, a beast of the forest furnished him fresh laurels. For he met a huge bear in a thicket, and slew it with a javelin; and then bade his companion Hjalte put his lips to the beast and drink the blood that came out, that he might be the stronger afterwards. For it was believed that a draught of this sort caused an increase of bodily strength. By these valorous achievements he became intimate with the most illustrious nobles, and even, became a favourite of the king; took to wife his sister Rute, and had the bride of the conquered as the prize of the conquest. When Rolf was harried by Athisl he avenged himself on him in battle and overthrew Athisl in war. Then Rolf gave his sister Skulde in marriage to a youth of keen wit, called Hiartuar, and made him governor of Sweden, ordaining a yearly tax; wishing to soften the loss of freedom to him by the favour of an alliance with himself.

Here let me put into my work a thing that it is mirthful to record. A youth named Wigg, scanning with attentive eye the bodily size of Rolf, and smitten with great wonder thereat, proceeded to inquire in jest who was that "Krage" whom Nature in her beauty had endowed with such towering stature? Meaning humorously to banter his uncommon tallness. For "Krage" in the Danish tongue means a tree-trunk, whose branches are pollarded, and whose summit is climbed in such wise that the foot uses the lopped timbers as supports, as if leaning on a ladder, and, gradually advancing to the higher parts, finds the shortest way to the top. Rolf accepted this random word as though it were a name of honour for him, and rewarded the wit of the saying with a heavy bracelet. Then Wigg, thrusting out his right arm decked with the bracelet, put his left behind his back in affected shame, and walked with a ludicrous gait, declaring that he, whose lot had so long been poverty-stricken, was glad of a scanty gift. When he was asked why he was behaving so, he said that the arm which lacked ornament and had no splendour to boast of was mantling with the modest blush of poverty to behold the other. The ingenuity of this saying won him a present to match the first. For Rolf made him bring out to view, like the other, the hand which he was hiding. Nor was Wigg heedless to repay the kindness; for he promised, uttering a strict vow, that, if it befell Rolf to perish by the sword, he would himself take vengeance on his slayers. Nor should it be omitted that in old time nobles who were entering. The court used to devote to their rulers the first-fruits of their service by vowing some mighty exploit; thus bravely inaugurating their first campaign.

Meantime, Skulde was stung with humiliation at the payment of the tribute, and bent her mind to devise deeds of horror. Taunting her husband with his ignominious estate, she urged and egged him to break off his servitude, induced him to weave plots against Rolf, and filled his mind with the most abominable plans of disloyalty, declaring that everyone owed more to their freedom than to kinship. Accordingly, she ordered huge piles of arms to be muffled up under divers coverings, to be carried by Hiartuar into Denmark, as if they were tribute: these would furnish a store wherewith to slay the king by night. So the vessels were loaded with the mass of pretended tribute, and they proceeded to Leire, a town which Rolf had built and adorned with the richest treasure of his realm, and which, being a royal foundation and a royal seat, surpassed in importance all the cities of the neighbouring districts. The king welcomed the coming of Hiartuar with a splendid banquet, and drank very deep, while his guests, contrary to their custom, shunned immoderate tippling. So, while all the others were sleeping soundly, the Swedes, who had been kept from their ordinary rest by their eagerness on their guilty purpose, began furtively to slip down from their sleeping-rooms. Straightway uncovering the hidden heap of weapons, each girded on his arms silently and then went to the palace. Bursting into its recesses, they drew their swords upon the sleeping figures. Many awoke; but, invaded as much by the sudden and dreadful carnage as by the drowsiness of sleep, they faltered in their resistance; for the night misled them and made it doubtful whether those they met were friends or foes. Hjalte, who was foremost in tried bravery among the nobles of the king, chanced to have gone out in the dead of that same night into the country and given himself to the embraces of a harlot. But when his torpid hearing caught from afar the rising din of battle, preferring valour to wantonness, he chose rather to seek the deadly perils of the War-god than to yield to the soft allurements of Love. What a love for his king, must we suppose, burned in this warrior! For he might have excused his absence by feigning not to have known; but he thought it better to expose his life to manifest danger than save it for pleasure. As he went away, his mistress asked him how aged a man she ought to marry if she were to lose him? Then Hjalte bade her come closer, as though he would speak to her more privately; and, resenting that she needed a successor to his love, he cut off her nose and made her unsightly, punishing the utterance of that wanton question with a shameful wound, and thinking that the lecherousness of her soul ought to be cooled by outrage to her face. When he had done this, he said he left her choice free in the matter she had asked about. Then he went quickly back to the town and plunged into the densest of the fray, mowing down the opposing ranks as he gave blow for blow. Passing the sleeping-room of Bjarke, who was still slumbering, he bade him wake up, addressing him as follows:

"Let him awake speedily, whoso showeth himself by service or avoweth himself in mere loyalty, a friend of the king! Let the princes shake off slumber, let shameless lethargy begone; let their spirits awake and warm to the work; each man's own right hand shall either give him to glory, or steep him in sluggard shame; and this night shall be either end or vengeance of our woes.

"I do not now bid ye learn the sports of maidens, nor stroke soft cheeks, nor give sweet kisses to the bride and press the slender breasts, nor desire the flowing wine and chafe the soft thigh and cast eyes upon snowy arms. I call you out to the sterner fray of War. We need the battle, and not light love; nerveless languor has no business here: our need calls for battles. Whoso cherishes friendship for the king, let him take up arms. Prowess in war is the readiest appraiser of men's spirits. Therefore let warriors have no fearfulness and the brave no fickleness: let pleasure quit their soul and yield place to arms. Glory is now appointed for wages; each can be the arbiter of his own renown, and shine by his own right hand. Let nought here be tricked out with wantonness: let all be full of sternness, and learn how to rid them of this calamity. He who covets the honours or prizes of glory must not be faint with craven fear, but go forth to meet the brave, nor whiten at the cold steel."

At this utterance, Bjarke, awakened, roused up his chamber-page Skalk speedily, and addressed him as follows:

"Up, lad, and fan the fire with constant blowing; sweep the hearth clear of wood, and scatter the fine ashes. Strike out sparks from the fire, rouse the fallen embers, draw out the smothered blaze. Force the slackening hearth to yield light by kindling the coals to a red glow with a burning log. It will do me good to stretch out my fingers when the fire is

103

brought nigh. Surely he that takes heed for his friend should have warm hands, and utterly drive away the blue and hurtful chill."

Hjalte said again: "Sweet is it to repay the gifts received from our lord, to grip the swords, and devote the steel to glory. Behold, each man's courage tells him loyally to follow a king of such deserts, and to guard our captain with fitting earnestness. Let the Teuton swords, the helmets, the shining armlets, the mail-coats that reach the heel, which Rolf of old bestowed upon his men, let these sharpen our mindful hearts to the fray. The time requires, and it is just, that in time of war we should earn whatsoever we have gotten in the deep idleness of peace, that we should not think more of joyous courses than of sorrowful fortunes, or always prefer prosperity to hardship. Being noble, let us with even soul accept either lot, nor let fortune sway our behaviour, for it beseems us to receive equably difficult and delightsome days; let us pass the years of sorrow with the same countenance wherewith we took the years of joy. Let us do with brave hearts all the things that in our cups we boasted with sodden lips; let us keep the vows which we swore by highest Jove and the mighty gods. My master is the greatest of the Danes: let each man, as he is valorous, stand by him; far, far hence be all cowards! We need a brave and steadfast man, not one that turns his back on a dangerous pass, or dreads the grim preparations for battle. Often a general's greatest valour depends on his soldiery, for the chief enters the fray all the more at ease that a better array of nobles throngs him round. Let the thane catch up his arms with fighting fingers, setting his right hand on the hilt and holding fast the shield: let him charge upon the foes, nor pale at any strokes. Let none offer himself to be smitten by the enemy behind, let none receive the swords in his back: let the battling breast ever front the blow. `Eagles fight brow foremost', and with swift gaping beaks speed onward in the front: be ye like that bird in mien, shrinking from no stroke, but with body facing the foe.

"See how the enemy, furious and confident overduly, his limbs defended by the steel, and his face with a gilded helmet, charges the thick of the battle-wedges, as though sure of victory, fearless of rout and invincible by any endeavour. Ah, misery! Swedish assurance spurns the Danes. Behold, the Goths with savage eyes and grim aspect advance with crested helms and clanging spears: wreaking heavy slaughter in our blood, they wield their swords and their battle-axes hone-sharpened.

"Why name thee, Hiartuar, whom Skulde hath filled with guilty purpose, and hath suffered thus to harden in sin? Why sing of thee, villain, who hast caused our peril, betrayer of a noble king? Furious lust of sway hath driven thee to attempt an abomination, and, stung with frenzy, to screen thyself behind thy wife's everlasting guilt. What error hath made thee to hurt the Danes and thy lord, and hurled thee into such foul crime as this? Whence entered thy heart the treason framed with such careful guile?

"Why do I linger? Now we have swallowed our last morsel. Our king perishes, and utter doom overtakes our hapless city. Our last dawn has risen, unless perchance there be one here so soft that he fears to offer himself to the blows, or so unwarlike that he dares not avenge his lord, and disowns all honours worthy of his valour.

"Thou, Ruta, rise and put forth thy snow-white head, come forth from thy hiding into the battle. The carnage that is being done without calls thee. By now the council-chamber is shaken with warfare, and the gates creak with the dreadful fray. Steel rends the mail-coats, the woven mesh is torn apart, and the midriff gives under the rain of spears. By now the huge axes have hacked small the shield of the king; by now the long swords clash, and the battle-axe clatters its blows upon the shoulders of men, and cleaves their breasts. Why are your hearts afraid? Why is your sword faint and blunted? The gate is cleared of our people, and is filled with the press of the strangers."

And when Hjalte had wrought very great carnage and stained the battle with blood, he stumbled for the third time on Bjarke's berth, and thinking he desired to keep quiet because he was afraid, made trial of him with such taunts at his cowardice as these:

"Bjarke, why art thou absent? Doth deep sleep hold thee? I prithee, what makes thee tarry? Come out, or the fire will overcome thee. Ho! Choose the better way, charge with me! Bears may be kept off with fire; let us spread fire in the recesses, and let the blaze attack the door-posts first. Let the firebrand fall upon the bedchamber, let the falling roof offer fuel for the flames and serve to feed the fire. It is right to scatter conflagration on the doomed gates. But let us who honour our king with better loyalty form the firm battle-wedges, and, having measured the phalanx in safe rows, go forth in the way the king taught us: our king, who laid low Rorik, the son of Bok the covetous, and wrapped the coward in death. He was rich in wealth, but in enjoyment poor, stronger in gain than bravery; and thinking gold better than warfare, he set lucre above all things, and ingloriously accumulated piles of treasure, scorning the service of noble friends. And when he was attacked by the navy of Rolf, he bade his servants take the gold from the chests and spread it out in front of the city gates, making ready bribes rather than battle, because he knew not the soldier, and thought that the foe should be attempted with gifts and not with arms: as though he could fight with wealth alone, and prolong the war by using, not men, but wares! So he undid the heavy coffers and the rich chests; he brought forth the polished bracelets and the heavy caskets; they only fed his destruction. Rich in treasure, poor in warriors, he left his foes to take away the prizes which he forebore to give to the friends of his own land. He who once shrank to give little rings of his own will, now unwillingly squandered his masses of wealth, rifling his hoarded heap. But our king in his wisdom spurned him and the gifts he proffered, and took from him life and goods at once; nor was his foe profited by the useless wealth which he had greedily heaped up through long years. But Rolf the righteous assailed him, slew him, and captured his vast wealth, and shared among worthy friends what the hand of avarice had piled up in all those years; and, bursting into the camp which was wealthy but not brave, gave his friends a lordly booty without bloodshed. Nothing was so fair to him that he would not lavish it, or so dear that he would not give it to his friends, for he used treasure like ashes, and measured his years by glory and not by gain. Whence it is plain that the king who hath died nobly lived also most nobly, that the hour of his doom is beautiful, and that he graced the years of his life with manliness. For while he lived his glowing valour prevailed over all things, and he was allotted might worthy of his lofty stature. He was as swift to war as a torrent tearing down to sea, and as speedy to begin battle as a stag is to fly with cleft foot upon his fleet way.

"See now, among the pools dripping with human blood, the teeth struck out of the slain are carried on by the full torrent of gore, and are polished on the rough sands. Dashed on the slime they glitter, and the torrent of blood bears along splintered bones and flows above lopped limbs. The blood of the Danes is wet, and the gory flow stagnates far around, and the stream pressed out of the steaming veins rolls back the scattered bodies. Tirelessly against the Danes advances Hiartuar, lover of battle, and challenges the fighters with outstretched spear. Yet here, amid the dangers and dooms of war, I see Frode's grandson smiling joyously, who once sowed the fields of Fyriswald with gold. Let us also be exalted with an honourable show of joy, following in death the doom of our noble father. Be we therefore cheery in voice and bold in daring; for it is right to spurn all fear with words of courage, and to meet our death in deeds of glory. Let fear quit heart and face; in both let us avow our dauntless endeavours, that no sign anywhere may show us to betray faltering fear. Let our drawn sword measure the weight of our service. Fame follows us in death, and glory shall outlive our crumbling ashes! And that which perfect valour hath achieved during its span shall not fade for ever and ever. What want we with closed floors? Why doth the locked bolt close the folding-gates? For it is now the third cry, Bjarke, that calls thee, and bids thee come forth from the barred room."

Bjarke rejoined: "Warlike Hjalte, why dost thou call me so loud? I am the son-in-law of Rolf. He who boasts loud and with big words challenges other men to battle, is bound to be venturous and act up to his words, that his deed may avouch his vaunt. But stay till I am armed and have girded on the dread attire of war.

"And now I tie my sword to my side, now first I get my body guarded with mail-coat and headpiece, the helm keeping my brows and the stout iron shrouding my breast. None shrinks more than I from being burnt a prisoner inside, and made a pyre together with my own house: though an island brought me forth, and though the land of my birth be bounded, I shall hold it a debt to repay to the king the twelve kindreds which he added to my honours. Hearken, warriors! Let none robe in mail his body that shall perish; let him last of all draw tight the woven steel; let the shields go behind the back; let us fight with bared breasts, and load all your arms with gold. Let your right hands receive the bracelets, that they may swing their blows the more heavily and plant the grievous wound. Let none fall back! Let each zealously strive to meet the swords of the enemy and the threatening spears, that we may avenge our beloved master. Happy beyond all things is he who can mete out revenge for such a crime, and with righteous steel punish the guilt of treacheries.

"Lo, methinks I surely pierced a wild stag with the Teutonic sword which is called Snyrtir: from which I won the name of Warrior, when I felled Agnar, son of Ingild, and brought the trophy home. He shattered and broke with the bite the sword Hoding which smote upon my head, and would have dealt worse wounds if the edge of his blade had held out better. In return I clove asunder his left arm and part of his left side and his right foot, and the piercing steel ran down his limbs and smote deep into his ribs. By Hercules! No man ever seemed to me stronger than he. For he sank down half-conscious, and, leaning on his elbow, welcomed death with a smile, and spurned destruction with a laugh, and passed rejoicing in the world of Elysium. Mighty was the man's courage, which knew how with one laugh to cover his death-hour, and with a joyous face to suppress utter anguish of mind and body!

"Now also with the same blade I searched the heart of one sprung from an illustrious line, and plunged the steel deep in his breast. He was a king's son, of illustrious ancestry, of a noble nature, and shone with the brightness of youth. The mailed metal could not avail him, nor his sword, nor the smooth target-boss; so keen was the force of my steel, it knew not how to be stayed by obstacles.

"Where, then, are the captains of the Goths, and the soldiery of

Hiartuar? Let them come, and pay for their might with their life-blood. Who can cast, who whirl the lance, save scions of kings? War springs from the nobly born: famous pedigrees are the makers of war. For the perilous deeds which chiefs attempt are not to be done by the ventures of common men. Renowned nobles are passing away. Lo! Greatest Rolf, thy great ones have fallen, thy holy line is vanishing. No dim and lowly race, no low-born dead, no base souls are Pluto's prey, but he weaves the dooms of the mighty, and fills Phlegethon with noble shapes.

"I do not remember any combat wherein swords were crossed in turn and blow dealt out for blow more speedily. I take three for each I give; thus do the Goths requite the wounds I deal them, and thus doth the stronger hand of the enemy avenge with heaped interest the punishment that they receive. Yet singly in battle I have given over the bodies of so many men to the pyre of destruction, that a mound like a hill could grow up and be raised out of their lopped limbs, and the piles of carcases would look like a burial-barrow. And now what doeth he, who but now bade me come forth, vaunting himself with mighty praise, and chafing others with his arrogant words, and scattering harsh taunts, as though in his one body he enclosed twelve lives?"

Hjalte answered: "Though I have but scant help, I am not far off. Even here, where I stand, there is need of aid, and nowhere is a force or a chosen band of warriors ready for battle wanted more. Already the hard edges and the spear-points have cleft my shield in splinters, and the ravening steel has rent and devoured its portions bit by bit in the battle. The first of these things testifies to and avows itself. Seeing is better than telling, eyesight faithfuller than hearing. For of the broken shield only the fastenings remain, and the boss, pierced and broken in its circle, is all left me. And now, Bjarke, thou art strong, though thou hast come forth more tardily than was right, and thou retrievest by bravery the loss caused by thy loitering."

But Bjarke said: "Art thou not yet weary of girding at me and goading me with taunts? Many things often cause delay. The reason why I tarried was the sword in my path, which the Swedish foe whirled against my breast with mighty effort. Nor did the guider of the hilt drive home the sword with little might; for though the body was armed he smote it as far as one may when it is bare or defenceless; he pierced the armour of hard steel like yielding waters; nor could the rough, heavy breastplate give me any help.

"But where now is he that is commonly called Odin, the mighty in battle, content ever with a single eye? If thou see him anywhere, Rute, tell me."

Rute replied: "Bring thine eye closer and look under my arm akimbo: thou must first hallow thine eyes with the victorious sign, if thou wilt safely know the War-god face to face."

Then said Bjarke: "If I may look on the awful husband of Frigg, howsoever he be covered with his white shield, and guide his tall steed, he shall in no wise go safe out of Leire; it is lawful to lay low in war the war-waging god. Let a noble death come to those that fall before the eyes of their king. While life lasts, let us strive for the power to die honourably and to reap a noble end by our deeds. I will die overpowered near the head of my slain captain, and at his feet thou also shalt slip on thy face in death, so that whoso scans the piled corpses may see in what wise we rate the gold our lord gave us. We shall be the prey of ravens and a morsel for hungry eagles, and the ravening bird shall feast on the banquet of our body. Thus should fall princes dauntless in war, clasping their famous king in a common death."

I have composed this particular series of harangues in metrical shape, because the gist of the same thoughts is found arranged in a short form in a certain ancient Danish song, which is repeated by heart by many conversant with antiquity.

Now, it came to pass that the Goths gained the victory and all the array of Rolf fell, no man save Wigg remaining out of all those warriors. For the soldiers of the king paid this homage to his noble virtues in that battle, that his slaying inspired in all the longing to meet their end, and union with him in death was accounted sweeter than life.

HIARTUAR rejoiced, and had the tables spread for feasting, bidding the banquet come after the battle, and fain to honour his triumph with a carouse. And when he was well filled therewith, he said that it was matter of great marvel to him, that out of all the army of Rolf no man had been found to take thought for his life by flight or fraud. Hence, he said, it had been manifest with what zealous loyalty they had kept their love for their king, because they had not endured to survive him. He also blamed his ill fortune, because it had not suffered the homage of a single one of them to be left for himself: protesting that he would very willingly accept the service of such men. Then Wigg came forth, and Hiartuar, as though he were congratulating him on the gift, asked him if he were willing to fight for him. Wigg assenting, he drew and proferred him a sword. But Wigg refused the point, and asked for the hilt, saying first that this had been Rolf's custom when he handed forth a sword to his soldiers. For in old time those who were about to put themselves in dependence on the king used to promise fealty by touching the hilt of the sword. And in this wise Wigg clasped the hilt, and then drove the point through Hiartuar; thus gaining the vengeance which he had promised Rolf to accomplish for him. When he had done this, and the soldiers of Hiartuar rushed at him, he exposed his body to them eagerly and exultantly, shouting that he felt more joy in the slaughter of the tyrant than bitterness at his own. Thus the feast was turned into a funeral, and the wailing of burial followed the joy of victory. Glorious, ever memorable hero, who valiantly kept his vow, and voluntarily courted death, staining with blood by his service the tables of the despot! For the lively valour of his spirit feared not the hands of the slaughterers, when he had once beheld the place where Rolf had been wont to live bespattered with the blood of his slayer. Thus the royalty of Hiartuar was won and ended on the same day. For whatsoever is gotten with guile melts away in like fashion as it is sought, and no fruits are long-lasting that have been won by treachery and crime. Hence it came to pass that the Swedes, who had a little before been the possessors of Denmark, came to lose even their own liberty. For they were straightway cut off by the Zealanders, and paid righteous atonement to the injured shades of Rolf. In this way does stern fortune commonly avenge the works of craft and cunning.

BOOK THREE

After Hiartuar, HOTHER, whom I mentioned above, the brother of Athisl, and also the fosterling of King Gewar, became sovereign of both realms. It will be easier to relate his times if I begin with the beginning of his life. For if the earlier years of his career are not doomed to silence, the latter ones can be more fully and fairly narrated.

When Helgi had slain Hodbrodd, his son Hother passed the length of his boyhood under the tutelage of King Gewar. While a stripling, he excelled in strength of body all his foster-brethren and compeers. Moreover, he was gifted with many accomplishments of mind. He was very skilled in swimming and archery, and also with the gloves; and further was as nimble as such a youth could be, his training being equal to his strength. Though his years were unripe, his richly-dowered spirit surpassed them. None was more skilful on lyre or harp; and he was cunning on the timbrel, on the lute, and in every modulation of string instruments. With his changing measures he could sway the feelings of men to what passions he would; he knew how to fill human hearts with joy or sadness, with pity or with hatred, and used to enwrap the soul with the delight or terror of the ear. All these accomplishments of the youth pleased Nanna, the daughter of Gewar, mightily, and she began to seek his embraces. For the valour of a youth will often kindle a maid, and the courage of those whose looks are not so winning is often acceptable. For love hath many avenues; the path of pleasure is opened to some by grace, to others by bravery of soul, and to some by skill in accomplishments. Courtesy brings to some stores of Love, while most are commended by brightness of beauty. Nor do the brave inflict a shallower wound on maidens than the comely.

Now it befell that Balder the son of Odin was troubled at the sight of Nanna bathing, and was seized with boundless love. He was kindled by her fair and lustrous body, and his heart was set on fire by her manifest beauty; for nothing exciteth passion like comeliness. Therefore he resolved to slay with the sword Hother, who, he feared, was likeliest to baulk his wishes; so that his love, which brooked no postponement, might not be delayed in the enjoyment of its desire by any obstacle.

About this time Hother chanced, while hunting, to be led astray by a mist, and he came on a certain lodge in which were wood-maidens; and when they greeted him by his own name, he asked who they were. They declared that it was their guidance and government that mainly determined the fortunes of war. For they often invisibly took part in battles, and by their secret assistance won for their friends the coveted victories. They averted, indeed, that they could win triumphs and inflict defeats as they would; and further told him how Balder had seen his foster-sister Nanna while she bathed, and been kindled with passion for her; but counselled Hother not to attack him in war, worthy as he was of his deadliest hate, for they declared that Balder was a demigod, sprung secretly from celestial seed. When Hother had heard this, the place melted away and left him shelterless, and he found himself standing in the open and out in the midst of the fields, without a vestige of shade. Most of all he marvelled at the swift flight of the maidens, the shifting of the place, and the delusive semblance of the building. For he knew not that all that had passed around him had been a mere mockery and an unreal trick of the arts of magic.

Returning thence, he related to Gewar the mystification that had followed on his straying, and straightway asked him for his daughter. Gewar answered that he would most gladly favour him, but that he feared if he rejected Balder he would incur his wrath; for Balder, he said, had proffered him a like request. For he said that the sacred strength of Balder's body was proof even against steel; adding, however, that he knew of a sword which could deal him his death, which was fastened up in the closest bonds; this was in the keeping of Miming, the Satyr of the woods, who also had a bracelet of a secret and marvellous virtue, that used to increase the wealth of the owner. Moreover, the way to these regions was impassable and filled with obstacles, and therefore hard for mortal men to travel. For the greater part of the road was perpetually beset with extraordinary cold. So he advised him to harness a car with reindeer, by means of whose great speed he could cross the hard-frozen ridges. And when he had got to the place, he should set up his tent away from the sun in such wise that it should catch the shadow of the cave where Miming was wont to be; while he should not in return cast a shade upon Miming, so that no unaccustomed darkness might be thrown and prevent the Satyr from going out. Thus both the bracelet and the sword would be ready to his hand, one being attended by fortune in wealth and the other by fortune in war, and each of them thus bringing a great prize to the owner. Thus much said Gewar; and Hother was not slow to carry out his instructions. Planting his tent in the manner aforesaid, he passed the nights in anxieties and the days in hunting. But through either season he remained very wakeful and sleepless, allotting the divisions of night and day so as to devote the one to reflection on events, and to spend the other in providing food for his body. Once as he watched all night, his spirit was drooping and dazed with anxiety, when the Satyr cast a shadow on his tent. Aiming a spear at him, he brought him down with the blow, stopped him, and bound him, while he could not make his escape. Then in the most dreadful words he threatened him with the worst, and demanded the sword and bracelets. The Satyr was not slow to tender him the ransom of his life for which he was asked. So surely do all prize life beyond wealth; for nothing is ever cherished more among mortals than the breath of their own life. Hother, exulting in the treasure he had gained, went home enriched with trophies which, though few, were noble.

When Gelder, the King of Saxony, heard that Hother had gained these things, he kept constantly urging his soldiers to go and carry off such glorious booty; and the warriors speedily equipped a fleet in obedience to their king. Gewar, being very learned in divining and an expert in the knowledge of omens, foresaw this; and summoning Hother, told him, when Gelder should join battle with him, to receive his spears with patience, and not let his own fly until he saw the enemy's missiles exhausted; and further, to bring up the curved scythes wherewith the vessels could be rent and the helmets and shields plucked from the soldiers. Hother followed his advice and found its result fortunate. For he bade his men, when Gelder began to charge, to stand their ground and defend their bodies with their shields, affirming that the victory in that battle must be won by patience. But the enemy nowhere kept back their missiles, spending them all in their extreme eagerness to fight; and the more patiently they found Hother bear himself in his reception of their spears and lances, the more furiously they began to hurl them. Some of these stuck in the shields and some in the ships, and few were the wounds they inflicted; many of them were seen to be shaken off idly and to do no hurt. For the soldiers of Hother performed the bidding of their king, and kept off the attack of the spears by a penthouse of interlocked shields; while not a few of the spears smote lightly on the bosses and fell into the waves. When Gelder was emptied of all his store, and saw the enemy picking it up, and swiftly hurling it back at him, he covered the summit of the mast with a crimson shield, as a signal of peace, and surrendered to save his life. Hother received him with the friendliest face and the kindliest words, and conquered him as much by his gentleness as he had by his skill.

At this time Helgi, King of Halogaland, was sending frequent embassies to press his suit for Thora, daughter of Kuse, sovereign of the Finns and Perms. Thus is weakness ever known by its wanting help from others. For while all other young men of that time used to sue in marriage with their own lips, this man was afflicted with so faulty an utterance that he was ashamed to be heard not only by strangers, but by those of his own house. So much doth calamity shun all witnesses; for natural defects are the more vexing the more manifest they are. Kuse despised his embassy, answering that that man did not deserve a wife who trusted too little to his own manhood, and borrowed by entreaty the aid of others in order to gain his suit. When Helgi heard this, he besought Hother, whom he knew to be an accomplished pleader, to favour his desires, promising that he would promptly perform whatsoever he should command him. The earnest entreaties of the youth prevailed on Hother, and he went to Norway with an armed fleet, intending to achieve by arms the end which he could not by words. And when he had pleaded for Helgi with the most dulcet eloquence, Kuse rejoined that his daughter's wish must be consulted, in order that no paternal strictness might forestall anything against her will. He called her in and asked her whether she felt a liking for her wooer; and when she assented he promised Helgi her hand. In this way Hother, by the sweet sounds of his fluent and well-turned oratory, opened the ears of Kuse, which were before deaf to the suit he urged.

While this was passing in Halogaland, Balder entered the country of Gewar armed, in order to sue for Nanna. Gewar bade him learn Nanna's own mind; so he approached the maiden with the most choice and cajoling words; and when he could win no hearing for his prayers, he persisted in asking the reason of his refusal. She replied, that a god could not wed with a mortal, because the vast difference of their natures prevented any bond of intercourse. Also the gods sometimes used to break their pledges; and the bond contracted between unequals was apt to snap suddenly. There was no firm tie between those of differing estate; for beside the great, the fortunes of the lowly were always dimmed. Also lack and plenty dwelt in diverse tents, nor was there any fast bond of intercourse between gorgeous wealth and obscure poverty. In fine, the things of earth would not mate with those of heaven, being sundered by a great original gulf through a difference in nature; inasmuch as mortal man was infinitely far from the glory of the divine majesty. With this shuffling answer she eluded the suit of Balder, and shrewdly wove excuses to refuse his hand.

When Hother heard this from Gewar, he complained long to Helgi of Balder's insolence. Both were in doubt as to what should be done, and beat their brains over divers plans; for converse with a friend in the day of trouble, though it removeth not the peril, yet maketh the heart less sick. Amid all the desires of their souls the passion of valour prevailed, and a naval battle was fought with Balder. One would have thought it a contest of men against gods, for Odin and Thor and the holy array of the gods fought for Balder. There one could have beheld a war in which divine and human might were mingled. But Hother was clad in his steel-defying tunic, and charged the closest bands of the gods, assailing them as vehemently as a son of earth could assail the powers above. However, Thor was swinging his club with marvellous might, and shattered all interposing shields, calling as loudly on his foes to attack him as upon his friends to back him up. No kind of armour withstood his onset, no man could receive his stroke and live. Whatsoever his blow fended off it crushed; neither shield nor helm endured the weight of its dint; no greatness of body or of strength could serve. Thus the victory would have passed to the gods, but that Hother, though his line had already fallen back, darted up, hewed off the club at the haft, and made it useless. And the gods, when they had lost this weapon, fled incontinently. But that antiquity vouches for it, it were quite against common belief to think that men prevailed against gods. (We call them gods in a supposititious rather than in a real sense; for to such we give the title of deity by the custom of nations, not because of their nature.)

As for Balder, he took to flight and was saved. The conquerors either hacked his ships with their swords or sunk them in the sea; not content to have defeated gods, they pursued the wrecks of the fleet with such rage, as if they would destroy them to satiate their deadly passion for war. Thus doth prosperity commonly whet the edge of licence. The haven, recalling by its name Balder's flight, bears witness to the war. Gelder, the King of Saxony, who met his end in the same war, was set by Hother upon the corpses of his oarsmen, and then laid on a pyre built of vessels, and magnificently honoured in his funeral by Hother, who not only put his ashes in a noble barrow, treating them as the remains of a king, but also graced them with most reverent obsequies. Then, to prevent any more troublesome business delaying his hopes of marriage, he went back to Gewar and enjoyed the coveted embraces of Nanna. Next, having treated Helgi and Thora very generously, he brought his new queen back to Sweden, being as much honoured by all for his victory as Balder was laughed at for his flight.

At this time the nobles of the Swedes repaired to Demnark to pay their tribute; but Hother, who had been honoured as a king by his countrymen for the splendid deeds of his father, experienced what a lying pander Fortune is. For he was conquered in the field by Balder, whom a little before he had crushed, and was forced to flee to Gewar, thus losing while a king that victory which he had won as a common man. The conquering Balder, in order to slake his soldiers, who were parched with thirst, with the blessing of a timely draught, pierced the earth deep and disclosed a fresh spring. The thirsty ranks made with gaping lips for the water that gushed forth everywhere. The traces of these springs, eternised by the name, are thought not quite to have dried up yet, though they have ceased to well so freely as of old. Balder was continually harassed by night phantoms feigning the likeness of Nanna, and fell into such ill health that he could not so much as walk, and began the habit of going his journeys in a two horse car or a four-wheeled carriage. So great was the love that had steeped his heart and now had brought him down almost to the extremity of decline. For he thought that his victory had brought him nothing if Nanna was not his prize. Also Frey, the regent of the gods, took his abode not far from Upsala, where he exchanged for a ghastly and infamous sin-offering the old custom of prayer by sacrifice, which had been used by so many ages and generations. For he paid to the gods abominable offerings, by beginning to slaughter human victims.

Meantime Hother (1) learned that Denmark lacked leaders, and that Hiartuar had swiftly expiated the death of Rolf; and he used to say that chance had thrown into his hands that to which he could scarce have aspired. For first, Rolf, whom he ought to have killed, since he remembered that Rolf's father had slain his own, had been punished by the help of another; and also, by the unexpected bounty of events, a chance had been opened to him of winning Denmark. In truth, if the pedigree of his forefathers were rightly traced, that realm was his by ancestral right! Thereupon he took possession, with a very great fleet, of Isefjord, a haven of Zealand, so as to make use of his impending fortune. There the people of the Danes met him and appointed him king; and a little after, on hearing of the death of his brother Athisl, whom he had bidden rule the Swedes, he joined the Swedish empire to that of Denmark. But Athisl was cut off by an ignominious death. For whilst, in great jubilation of spirit, he was honouring the funeral rites of Rolf with a feast, he drank too greedily, and paid for his filthy intemperance by his sudden end. And so, while he was celebrating the death of another with immoderate joviality, he forced on his own apace.

While Hother was in Sweden, Balder also came to Zealand with a fleet; and since he was thought to be rich in arms and of singular majesty, the Danes accorded him with the readiest of voices whatever he asked concerning the supreme power. With such wavering judgment was the opinion of our forefathers divided. Hother returned from Sweden and attacked him. They both coveted sway, and the keenest contest for the sovereignty began between them; but it was cut short by the flight of Hother. He retired to Jutland, and caused to be named after him the village in which he was wont to stay. Here he passed the winter season, and then went back to Sweden alone and unattended. There he summoned the grandees, and told them that he was weary of the light of life because of the misfortunes wherewith Balder had twice victoriously stricken him. Then he took farewell of all, and went by a circuitous path to a place that was hard of access, traversing forests uncivilised. For it oft happens that those upon whom has come some inconsolable trouble of spirit seek, as though it were a medicine to drive away their sadness, far and sequestered retreats, and cannot bear the greatness of their grief amid the fellowship of men; so dear, for the most part, is solitude to sickness. For filthiness and grime are chiefly pleasing to those who have been stricken with ailments of the soul. Now he had been wont to give out from the top of a hill decrees to the people when they came to consult him; and hence when they came they upbraided the sloth of the king for hiding himself, and his absence was railed at by all with the bitterest complaints.

But Hother, when he had wandered through remotest byways and crossed an uninhabited forest, chanced to come upon a cave where dwelt some maidens whom he knew not; but they proved to be the same who had once given him the invulnerable coat. Asked by them wherefore he had come thither, he related the disastrous issue of the war. So he began to bewail the ill luck of his failures and his dismal misfortunes, condemning their breach of faith, and lamenting that it had not turned out for him as they had promised him. But the maidens said that though he had seldom come off victorious, he had nevertheless inflicted as much defeat on the enemy as they on him, and had dealt as much carnage as he had shared in. Moreover, the favour of victory would be speedily his, if he could first lay hands upon a food of extraordinary delightsomeness which had been devised to increase the strength of Balder. For nothing would be difficult if he could only get hold of the dainty which was meant to enhance the rigour of his foe.

Hard as it sounded for earthborn endeavours to make armed assault upon the gods, the words of the maidens inspired Hother's mind with instant confidence to fight with Balder. Also some of his own people said that he could not safely contend with those above; but all regard for their majesty was expelled by the boundless fire of his spirit. For in brave souls vehemence is not always sapped by reason, nor doth counsel defeat rashness. Or perchance it was that Hother remembered how the might of the lordliest oft proveth unstable, and how a little clod can batter down great chariots.

On the other side, Balder mustered the Danes to arms and met Hother in the field. Both sides made a great slaughter; the carnage of the opposing parties was nearly equal, and night stayed the battle. About the third watch, Hother, unknown to any man, went out to spy upon the enemy, anxiety about the impending peril having banished sleep. This strong excitement favours not bodily rest, and inward disquiet suffers not outward repose. So, when he came to the camp of the enemy he heard that three maidens had gone out carrying the secret feast of Balder. He ran after them (for their footsteps in the dew betrayed their flight), and at last entered their accustomed dwelling. When they asked him who he was, he answered, a lutanist, nor did the trial belie his profession. For when the lyre was offered him, he tuned its strings, ordered and governed the chords with his quill, and with ready modulation poured forth a melody pleasant to the ear. Now they had three snakes, of whose venom they were wont to mix a strengthening compound for the food of Balder, and even now a flood of slaver was dripping on the food from the open mouths of the serpents. And some of the maidens would, for kindness sake, have given Hother a share of the dish, had not eldest of the three forbidden them, declaring that Balder would be cheated if they increased the bodily powers of his enemy. He had said, not that he was Hother, but that he was one of his company. Now the same nymphs, in their gracious kindliness, bestowed on him a belt of perfect sheen and a girdle which assured victory.

Retracing the path by which he had come, he went back on the same road, and meeting Balder plunged his sword into his side, and laid him low half dead. When the news was told to the soldiers, a cheery shout of triumph rose from all the camp of Hother, while the Danes held a public mourning for the fate of Balder. He, feeling no doubt of his impending death, and stung by the anguish of his wound, renewed the battle on the morrow; and, when it raged hotly, bade that he should be borne on a litter into the fray, that he might not seem to die ignobly within his tent. On the night following, Proserpine was seen to stand by him in a vision, and to promise that on the morrow he should have her

117

embrace. The boding of the dream was not idle; for when three days had passed, Balder perished from the excessive torture of his wound; and his body given a royal funeral, the army causing it to be buried in a barrow which they had made.

Certain men of our day, Chief among whom was Harald, (2) since the story of the ancient burial-place still survived, made a raid on it by night in the hope of finding money, but abandoned their attempt in sudden panic. For the hill split, and from its crest a sudden and mighty torrent of loud-roaring waters seemed to burst; so that its flying mass, shooting furiously down, poured over the fields below, and enveloped whatsoever it struck upon, and at its onset the delvers were dislodged, flung down their mattocks, and fled divers ways; thinking that if they strove any longer to carry through their enterprise they would be caught in the eddies of the water that was rushing down. Thus the guardian gods of that spot smote fear suddenly into the minds of the youths, taking them away from covetousness, and turning them to see to their safety; teaching them to neglect their greedy purpose and be careful of their lives. Now it is certain that this apparent flood was not real but phantasmal; not born in the bowels of the earth (since Nature suffereth not liquid springs to gush forth in a dry place), but produced by some magic agency. All men afterwards, to whom the story of that breaking in had come down, left this hill undisturbed. Wherefore it has never been made sure whether it really contains any wealth; for the dread of peril has daunted anyone since Harald from probing its dark foundations.

But Odin, though he was accounted the chief of the gods, began to inquire of the prophets and diviners concerning the way to accomplish vengeance for his son, as well as all others whom he had beard were skilled in the most recondite arts of soothsaying. For godhead that is incomplete is oft in want of the help of man. Rostioph (Hrossthiof), the Finn, foretold to him that another son must be born to him by Rinda (Wrinda), daughter of the King of the Ruthenians; this son was destined to exact punishment for the slaying of his brother. For the gods had appointed to the brother that was yet to be born the task of avenging his kinsman. Odin, when he heard this, muffled his face with a cap, that his garb might not betray him, and entered the service of the said king as a soldier; and being made by him captain of the soldiers, and given an army, won a splendid victory over the enemy. And for his stout achievement in this battle the king admitted him into the chief place in his friendship, distinguishing him as generously with gifts as with honours. A very little while afterwards Odin routed the enemy single-handed, and returned, at once the messenger and the doer of the deed. All marvelled that the strength of one man could deal such slaughter upon a countless host. Trusting in these services, he privily let the king into the secret of his love, and was refreshed by his most gracious favour; but when he sought a kiss from the maiden, he received a cuff. But he was not driven from his purpose either by anger at the slight or by the odiousness of the insult.

Next year, loth to quit ignobly the quest he had taken up so eagerly, he put on the dress of a foreigner and went back to dwell with the king. It was hard for those who met him to recognise him; for his assumed filth obliterated his true features, and new grime hid his ancient aspect. He said that his name was Roster (Hrosstheow), and that he was skilled in smithcraft. And his handiwork did honour to his professions: for he portrayed in bronze many and many a shape most beautifully, so that he received a great mass of gold from the king, and was ordered to hammer out the ornaments of the matrons. So, after having wrought many adornments for women's wearing, he at last offered to the maiden a bracelet which he had polished more laboriously than the rest and several rings which were adorned with equal care. But no services could assuage the wrath of Rinda; when he was fain to kiss her she cuffed him; for gifts offered by one we hate are unacceptable, while those tendered by a friend are far more grateful: so much doth the value of the offering oft turn on the offerer. For this stubborn-hearted maiden never doubted that the crafty old man was feigning generosity in order to seize an opening to work his lust. His temper, moreover, was keen and indomitable; for she knew that his homage covered guile, and that under the devotion of his gifts there lay a desire for crime. Her father fell to upbraiding her heavily for refusing the match; but she loathed to wed an old man, and the plea of her tender years lent her some support in her scorning of his hand; for she said that a young girl ought not to marry prematurely.

But Odin, who had found that nothing served the wishes of lovers more than tough persistency, though he was stung with the shame of his double rebuff, nevertheless, effacing the form he had worn before, went to the king for the third time, professing the completest skill in soldiership. He was led to take this pains not only by pleasure but by the wish to wipe out his disgrace. For of old those who were skilled in magic gained this power of instantly changing their aspect and exhibiting the most different shapes. Indeed, they were clever at imitating any age, not only in its natural bodily appearance, but also in its stature; and so the old man, in order to exhibit his calling agreeably, used to ride proudly up and down among the briskest of them. But not even such a tribute could move the rigour of the maiden; for it is hard for the mind to come back to a genuine liking for one against whom it has once borne heavy dislike. When he tried to kiss her at his departure, she repulsed him so that he tottered and smote his chin upon the ground. Straightway he touched her with a piece of bark whereon spells were written, and made her like unto one in frenzy: which was a gentle revenge to take for all the insults he had received.

But still he did not falter in the fulfilment of his purpose; for trust in his divine majesty buoyed him up with confidence; so, assuming the garb of a maiden, this indefatigable journeyer repaired for the fourth time to the king, and, on being received by him, showed himself assiduous and even forward. Most people believed him to be a woman, as he was dressed almost in female attire. Also he declared that his name was Wecha, and his calling that of a physician: and this assertion he confirmed by the readiest services. At last he was taken into the household of the queen, and played the part of a waiting-woman to the princess, and even used to wash the soil off her feet at eventide; and as he was applying the water he was suffered to touch her calves and the upper part of the thighs. But fortune goes with mutable steps, and thus chance put into his hand what his address had never won. For it happened that the girl fell sick, and looked around for a cure; and she summoned to protect her health those very hands which aforetime she had rejected, and appealed for preservation to him whom she had ever held in loathing. He examined narrowly all the symptoms of the trouble, and declared that, in order to check the disease as soon as possible, it was needful to use a certain drugged draught; but that it was so bitterly compounded, that the girl could never endure so violent a cure unless she submitted to be bound; since the stuff of the malady must be ejected from the very innermost tissues. When her father heard this he did not hesitate to bind his daughter; and laying her on the bed, he bade her endure patiently all the applications of the doctor. For the king was tricked by the sight of the female dress, which the old man was using to disguise his persistent guile; and thus the seeming remedy became an opportunity of outrage. For the physician seized the chance of love, and, abandoning his business of healing, sped to the work, not of expelling the fever, but of working his lust; making use of the sickness of the princess, whom in sound health he had found adverse to him. It will not be wearisome if I subjoin another version of this affair. For there are certain who say that the king, when he saw the physician groaning with love, but despite all his expense of mind and body accomplishing nothing, did not wish to rob of his due reward one who had so well earned it, and allowed him to lie privily with his daughter. So doth the wickedness of the father sometimes assail the child, when vehement passion perverts natural mildness. But his fault was soon followed by a remorse that was full of shame, when his daughter bore a child.

But the gods, whose chief seat was then at Byzantium, (Asgard), seeing that Odin had tarnished the fair name of godhead by divers injuries to its majesty, thought that he ought to be removed from their society. And they had him not only ousted from the headship, but outlawed and stripped of all worship and honour at home; thinking it better that the power of their infamous president should be overthrown than that public religion should be profaned; and fearing that they might themselves be involved in the sin of another, and though guiltless be punished for the crime of the guilty. For they saw that, now the derision of their great god was brought to light, those whom they had lured to proffer them divine honours were exchanging obeisance for scorn and worship for shame; that holy rites were being accounted sacrilege, and fixed and regular ceremonies deemed so much childish raving. Fear was in their souls, death before their eyes, and one would have supposed that the fault of one was visited upon the heads of all. So, not wishing Odin to drive public religion into exile, they exiled him and put one Oller (Wulder?) in his place, to bear the symbols not only Of royalty but also of godhead, as though it had been as easy a task to create a god as a king. And though they had appointed him priest for form's sake, they endowed him actually with full distinction, that he might be seen to be the lawful heir to the dignity, and no mere deputy doing another's work. Also, to omit no circumstance of greatness, they further gave his the name of Odin, trying by the prestige of that title to be rid of the obloquy of innovation. For nearly ten years Oller held the presidency of the divine senate; but at last the gods pitied the horrible exile of Odin, and thought that he had now been punished heavily enough; so he exchanged his foul and unsightly estate for his ancient splendour; for the lapse of time had now wiped out the brand of his earlier disgrace. Yet some were to be found who judged that he was not worthy to approach and resume his rank, because by his stage-tricks and his assumption of a woman's work he had brought the foulest scandal on the name of the gods. Some declare that he bought back the fortune of his lost divinity with money; flattering some of the gods and mollifying some with bribes; and that at the cost of a vast sum he contrived to get back to the distinction which he had long quitted. If you ask how much he paid for them, inquire of those who have found out what is the price of a godhead. I own that to me it is but little worth.

Thus Oller was driven out from Byzantium by Odin and retired into Sweden. Here, while he was trying, as if in a new world, to repair the records of his glory, the Danes slew him. The story goes that he was such a cunning wizard that he used a certain bone, which he had marked with awful spells, wherewith to cross the seas, instead of a vessel; and that by this bone he passed over the waters that barred his way as quickly as by rowing.

But Odin, now that he had regained the emblems of godhead, shone over all parts of the world with such a lustre of renown that all nations welcomed him as though he were light restored to the universe; nor was any spot to be found on the earth which did not hornage to his might. Then finding that Boe, his son by Rhlda, was enamoured of the hardships of war, he called him, and bade him bear in mind the slaying of his brother: saying that it would be better for him to take vengeande on the murderers of Balder than to overcome them in battle; for warfare was most fitting and wholesome when a holy occasion for waging it was furnished by a righteous opening for vengeande.

News came meantime that Gewar had been slain by the guile of his own satrap (jarl), Gunne. Hother determined to visit his murder with the strongest and sharpest revenge. So he surprised Gunne, cast him on a blazing pyre, and burnt him; for Gunne had himself treacherously waylaid Gewar, and burnt him alive in the night. This was his offering of vengeance to the shade of his foster-father; and then he made his sons, Herlek and Gerit, rulers of Norway.

Then he summoned the elders to assembly, and told them that he would perish in the war wherein he was bound to meet Boe, and said that he knew this by no doubtful guesswork, but by sure prophecies of seers. So he besought them to make his son RORIK king, so that the judgment of wicked men should not transfer the royalty to strange and unknown houses; averring that he would reap more joy from the succession of his son than bitterness from his own impending death. This request was speedily granted. Then he met Boe in battle and was killed; but small joy the victory gave Boe. Indeed, he left the battle so sore stricken that he was lifted on his shield and carried home by his foot-soldiers supporting him in turn, to perish next day of the pain of his wounds. The Ruthenian army gave his body a gorgeous funeral and buried it in a splendid howe, which it piled in his name, to save the record of so mighty a warrior from slipping out of the recollection of after ages.

So the Kurlanders and the Swedes, as though the death of Hother set them free from the burden of their subjection, resolved to attack Denmark, to which they were accustomed to do homage with a yearly tax. By this the Slavs also were emboldened to revolt, and a number of others were turned from subjects into foes. Rorik, in order to check this wrongdoing, summoned his country to arms, recounted the deeds of his forefathers, and urged them in a passionate harangue unto valorous deeds. But the barbarians, loth to engage without a general, and seeing that they needed a head, appointed a king over them; and, displaying all the rest of their military force, hid two companies of armed men in a dark spot. But Rorik saw the trap; and perceiving that his fleet was wedged in a certain narrow creek among the shoal water, took it out from the sands where it was lying, and brought it forth to sea; lest it should strike on the oozy swamps, and be attacked by the foe on different sides. Also, he resolved that his men should go into hiding during the day, where they could stay and suddenly fall on the invaders of his ships. He said that perchance the guile might in the end recoil on the heads of its devisors. And in fact the barbarians who had been appointed to the ambuscade knew nothing of the wariness of the Danes, and sallying against them rashly, were all destroyed. The remaining force of the Slavs, knowing nothing of the slaughter of their friends, hung in doubt wondering over the reason of Rorik's tarrying. And after waiting long for him as the months wearily rolled by, and finding delay every day more burdensome, they at last thought they should attack him with their fleet.

Now among them there was a man of remarkable stature, a wizard by calling. He, when he beheld the squadrons of the Danes, said: "Suffer a private combat to forestall a public slaughter, so that the danger of many may be bought off at the cost of a few. And if any of you shall take heart to fight it out with me, I will not flinch from these terms of conflict. But first of all I demand that you accept the terms I prescribe, the form whereof I have devised as follows: If I conquer, let freedom be granted us from taxes; if I am conquered, let the tribute be paid you as of old: For to-day I will either free my country from the yoke of slavery by my victory or bind her under it by my defeat. Accept me as the surety and the pledge for either issue." One of the Danes, whose spirit was stouter than his strength, heard this, and proceeded to ask Rorik, what would be the reward for the man who met the challenger in combat? Rorik chanced to have six bracelets, which were so intertwined that they could not be parted from one another, the chain of knots being inextricaly laced; and he promised them as a reward for the man who would venture on the combat. But the youth, who doubted his fortune, said: "Rorik, if I prove successful, let thy generosity award the prize of the conqueror, do thou decide and allot the palm; but if my enterprise go little to my liking, what prize canst thou owe to the beaten, who will be wrapped either in cruel death or in bitter shame? These things commonly go with feebleness, these are the wages of the defeated, for whom naught remains but utter infamy. What guerdon must be paid, what thanks offered, to him who lacks the prize of courage? Who has ever garlanded with ivy the weakling in War, or decked him with a conqueror's wage? Valour wins the prize, not sloth, and failure lacks renown. For one is followed by triumph and honour, the other by an unsightly life or by a stagnant end. I, who know not which way the issue of this duel inclines, dare not boldly anticipate that as a reward, of which I know not whether it be rightly mine. For one whose victory is doubtful may not seize the assured reward of the victor. I forbear, while I am not sure of the day, to claim firmly the title to the wreath. I refuse the gain, which may be the wages of my death as much as of my life. It is folly to lay hands on the fruit before it is ripe, and to be fain to pluck that which one is not yet sure is one's title. This hand shall win me the prize, or death." Having thus spoken, he smote the barbarian with his sword; but his fortune was tardier than his spirit; for the other smote him back, and he fell dead under the force of the first blow. Thus he was a sorry sight unto the Danes, but the Slavs granted their triumphant comrade a great procession, and received him with splendid dances. On the morrow the same man, whether he was elated with the good fortune of his late victory, or was fired with the wish to win another, came close to the enemy, and set to girding at them in the words of his former challenge. For, supposing that he had laid low the bravest of the Danes, he did not think that any of them would have any heart left to fight further with him upon his challenge. Also, trusting that, now one champion had fallen, he had shattered the strength of the whole army, he thought that naught would be hard to achieve upon which his later endeavours were bent. For nothing pampers arrogance more than success, or prompts to pride more surely than prosperity.

So Rorik was vexed that the general courage should be sapped by the impudence of one man; and that the Danes, with their roll of victories, should be met presumptuously by those whom they had beaten of old; nay, should be ignominiously spurned; further, that in all that host not one man should be found so quick of spirit or so vigorous of arm, that he longed to sacrifice his life for his country. It was the high-hearted Ubbe who first wiped off this infamous reproach upon the hesitating Danes. For he was of great bodily strength and powerful in incantations. He also purposely asked the prize of the combat, and the king promised him the bracelets. Then said he: "How can I trust the promise when thou keepest the pledge in thine own hands, and dost not deposit the gift in the charge of another? Let there be some one to whom thou canst entrust the pledge, that thou mayst not be able to take thy promise back. For the courage of the champion is kindled by the irrevocable certainty of the prize." Of course it was plain that he had said this in jest; sheer courage had armed him to repel the insult to his country. But Rorik thought he was tempted by avarice, and was loth to seem as if, contrary to royal fashion, he meant to take back the gift or revoke his promise; so, being stationed on his vessel, he resolved to shake off the bracelets, and with a mighty swing send them to the asker. But his attempt was baulked by the width of the gap between them; for the bracelets fell short of the intended spot, the impulse being too faint and slack, and were reft away by the waters. For this nickname of Slyngebond, (swing-bracelet) clung to Rorik. But this event testified much to the valour of Ubbe. For the loss of his drowned prize never turned his mind from his bold venture; he would not seem to let his courage be tempted by the wages of covetousness. So he eagerly went to fight, showing that he was a seeker of honour and not the slave of lucre, and that he set bravery before lust of pelf; and intent to prove that his confidence was based not on hire, but on his own great soul. Not a moment is lost; a ring is made; the course is thronged with soldiers; the champions engage; a din arises; the crowd of onlookers shouts in discord, each backing his own. And so the valour of the champions blazes to white-heat; falling dead under the wounds dealt by one another, they end together the combat and their lives. I think that it was a provision of fortune that neither of them should reap joy and honour by the other's death. This event won back to Rorik the hearts of the insurgents and regained him the tribute.

At this time Horwendil and Feng, whose father Gerwendil had been governor of the Jutes, were appointed in his place by Rorik to defend Jutland. But Horwendil held the monarchy for three years, and then, to will the height of glory, devoted himself to roving. Then Koller, King of Norway, in rivalry of his great deeds and renown, deemed it would be a handsome deed if by his greater strength in arms he could bedim the far-famed glory of the rover; and cruising about the sea, he watched for Horwendil's fleet and came up with it. There was an island lying in the middle of the sea, which each of the rovers, bringing his ships up on either side, was holding. The captains were tempted by the pleasant look of the beach, and the comeliness of the shores led them to look through the interior of the springtide woods, to go through the glades, and roam over the sequestered forests. It was here that the advance of Koller and Horwendil brought them face to face without any witness. Then Horwendil endeavoured to address the king first, asking him in what way it was his pleasure to fight, and declaring that one best which needed the courage of as few as possible. For, said he, the duel was the surest of all modes of combat for winning the meed of bravery, because it relied only upon native courage, and excluded all help from the hand of another. Koller marvelled at so brave a judgment in a youth, and said: "Since thou hast granted me the choice of battle, I think it is best to employ that kind which needs only the endeavours of two, and is free from all the tumult. Certainly it is more venturesome, and allows of a speedier award of the victory. This thought we share, in this opinion we agree of our own accord. But since the issue remains doubtful, we must pay some regard to gentle dealing, and must not give way so far to our inclinations as to leave the last offices undone. Hatred is in our hearts; yet let piety be there also, which in its due time may take the place of rigour. For the rights of nature reconcile us, though we are parted by differences of purpose; they link us together, howsoever rancour estrange our spirit. Let us, therefore, have this pious stipulation, that the conqueror shall give funeral rites to the conquered. For all allow that these are the last duties of human kind, from which no righteous man shrinks. Let each army lay aside its sternness and perform this function in harmony. Let jealousy depart at death, let the feud be buried in the tomb. Let us not show such an example of cruelty as to persecute one another's dust, though hatred has come between us in our lives. It will be a boast for the victor if he has borne his beaten foe in a lordly funeral. For the man who pays the rightful dues over his dead enemy wins the goodwill of the survivor; and whoso devotes gentle dealing to him who is no more, conquers the living by his kindness. Also there is another disaster, not less lamentable, which sometimes befalls the living—the loss of some part of their body; and I think that succor is due to this just as much as to the worst hap that may befall. For often those who fight keep their lives safe, but suffer maiming; and this lot is commonly thought more dismal than any death; for death cuts off memory of all things, while the living cannot forget the devastation of his own body. Therefore this mischief also must be helped somehow; so let it be agreed, that the injury of either of us by the other shall be made good with ten talents (marks) of gold. For if it be righteous to have compassion on the calamities of another, how much more is it to pity one's own? No man but obeys nature's prompting; and he who slights it is a self-murderer."

After mutually pledging their faiths to these terms, they began the battle. Nor was their strangeness his meeting one another, nor the sweetness of that spring-green spot, so heeded as to prevent them from the fray. Horwendil, in his too great ardour, became keener to attack his enemy than to defend his own body; and, heedless of his shield, had grasped his sword with both hands; and his boldness did not fail. For by his rain of blows he destroyed Koller's shield and deprived him of it, and at last hewed off his foot and drove him lifeless to the ground. Then, not to fail of his compact, he buried him royally, gave him a howe of lordly make and pompous obsequies. Then he pursued and slew Koller's sister Sela, who was a skilled warrior and experienced in roving.

He had now passed three years in valiant deeds of war; and, in order to win higher rank in Rorik's favour, he assigned to him the best trophies and the pick of the plunder. His friendship with Rorik enabled him to woo and will in marriage his daughter Gerutha, who bore him a son Amleth.

Such great good fortune stung Feng with jealousy, so that he resolved treacherously to waylay his brother, thus showing that goodness is not safe even from those of a man's own house. And behold, when a chance came to murder him, his bloody hand sated the deadly passion of his soul. Then he took the wife of the brother he had butchered, capping unnatural murder with incest. For whoso yields to one iniquity, speedily falls an easier victim to the next, the first being an incentive to the second. Also, the man veiled the monstrosity of his deed with such hardihood of cunning, that he made up a mock pretence of goodwill to excuse his crime, and glossed over fratricide with a show of righteousness. Gerutha, said he, though so gentle that she would do no man the slightest hurt, had been visited with her husband's extremest hate; and it was all to save her that he had slain his brother; for he thought it shameful that a lady so meek and unrancorous should suffer the heavy disdain of her husband. Nor did his smooth words fail in their intent; for at courts, where fools are sometimes favoured and backbiters preferred, a lie lacks not credit. Nor did Feng keep from shameful embraces the hands that had slain a brother; pursuing with equal guilt both of his wicked and impious deeds.

Amleth beheld all this, but feared lest too shrewd a behaviour might make his uncle suspect him. So he chose to feign dulness, and pretend an utter lack of wits. This cunning course not only concealed his intelligence but ensured his safety. Every day he remained in his mother's house utterly listless and unclean, flinging himself on the ground and bespattering his person with foul and filthy dirt. His discoloured face and visage smutched with slime denoted foolish and grotesque madness. All he said was of a piece with these follies; all he did savoured of utter lethargy. In a word, you would not have thought him a man at all, but some absurd abortion due to a mad fit of destiny. He used at times to sit over the fire, and, raking up the embers with his hands, to fashion wooden crooks, and harden them in the fire, shaping at their lips certain barbs, to make them hold more tightly to their fastenings. When asked what he was about, he said that he was preparing sharp javelins to avenge his father. This answer was not a little scoffed at, all men deriding his idle and ridiculous pursuit; but the thing helped his purpose afterwards. Now it was his craft in this matter that first awakened in the deeper observers a suspicion of his cunning. For his skill in a trifling art betokened the hidden talent of the craftsman; nor could they believe the spirit dull where the hand had acquired so cunning a workmanship. Lastly, he always watched with the most punctual care over his pile of stakes that he had pointed in the fire. Some people, therefore, declared that his mind was quick enough, and fancied that he only played the simpleton in order to hide his understanding, and veiled some deep purpose under a cunning feint. His wiliness (said these) would be most readily detected, if a fair woman were put in his way in some secluded place, who should provoke his mind to the temptations of love; all men's natural temper being too blindly amorous to be artfully dissembled, and this passion being also too impetuous to be checked by cunning. Therefore, if his lethargy were feigned, he would seize the opportunity, and yield straightway to violent delights. So men were commissioned to draw the young man in his rides into a remote part of the forest, and there assail him with a temptation of this nature. Among these chanced to be a foster-brother of Amleth, who had not ceased to have regard to their common nurture; and who esteemed his present orders less than the memory of their past fellowship. He attended Amleth among his appointed train, being anxious not to entrap, but to warn him; and was persuaded that he would suffer the worst if he showed the slightest glimpse of sound reason, and above all if he did the act of love openly. This was also plain enough to Amleth himself. For when he was bidden mount his horse, he deliberately set himself in such a fashion that he turned his back to the neck and faced about, fronting the tail; which he proceeded to encompass with the reins, just as if on that side he would check the horse in its furious pace. By this cunning thought he eluded the trick, and overcame the treachery of his uncle. The reinless steed galloping on, with rider directing its tail, was ludicrous enough to behold.

Amleth went on, and a wolf crossed his path amid the thicket. When his companions told him that a young colt had met him, he retorted, that in Feng's stud there were too few of that kind fighting. This was a gentle but witty fashion of invoking a curse upon his uncle's riches. When they averred that he had given a cunning answer, he answered that he had spoken deliberately; for he was loth, to be thought prone to lying about any matter, and wished to be held a stranger to falsehood; and accordingly he mingled craft and candour in such wise that, though his words did lack truth, yet there was nothing to betoken the truth and betray how far his keenness went.

Again, as he passed along the beach, his companions found the rudder of a ship, which had been wrecked, and said they had discovered a huge knife. "This," said he, "was the right thing to carve such a huge ham;" by which he really meant the sea, to whose infinitude, he thought, this enormous rudder matched. Also, as they passed the sandhills, and bade him look at the meal, meaning the sand, he replied that it had been ground small by the hoary tempests of the ocean. His companions praising his answer, he said that he had spoken it wittingly. Then they purposely left him, that he might pluck up more courage to practise wantonness. The woman whom his uncle had dispatched met him in a dark spot, as though she had crossed him by chance; and he took her and would have ravished her, had not his foster-brother, by a secret device, given him an inkling of the trap. For this man, while pondering the fittest way to play privily the prompter's part, and forestall the young man's hazardous lewdness, found a straw on the ground and fastened it underneath the tail of a gadfly that was flying past; which he then drove towards the particular quarter where he knew Amleth to be: an act which served the unwary prince exceedingly well. The token was interpreted as shrewdly as it had been sent. For Amleth saw the gadfly, espied with curiosity the straw which it wore embedded in its tail, and perceived that it was a secret warning to beware of treachery. Alarmed, scenting a trap, and fain to possess his desire in greater safety, he caught up the woman in his arms and dragged her off to a distant and impenetrable fen. Moreover, when they had lain together, he conjured her earnestly to disclose the matter to none, and the promise of silence was accorded as heartily as it was asked. For both of them had been under the same fostering in their childhood; and this early rearing in common had brought Amleth and the girl into great intimacy.

So, when he had returned home, they all jeeringly asked him whether he had given way to love, and he avowed that he had ravished the maid. When he was next asked where he did it, and what had been his pillow, he said that he had rested upon the hoof of a beast of burden, upon a cockscomb, and also upon a ceiling. For, when he was starting into temptation, he had gathered fragments of all these things, in order to avoid lying. And though his jest did not take aught of the truth out of the story, the answer was greeted with shouts of merriment from the bystanders. The maiden, too, when questioned on the matter, declared that he had done no such thing; and her denial was the more readily credited when it was found that the escort had not witnessed the deed. Then he who had marked the gadfly in order to give a hint, wishing to show Amleth that to his trick he owed his salvation, observed that latterly he had been singly devoted to Amleth. The young man's reply was apt. Not to seem forgetful of his informant's service, he said that he had seen a certain thing bearing a straw flit by suddenly, wearing a stalk of chaff fixed in its hinder parts. The cleverness of this speech, which made the rest split with laughter, rejoiced the heart of Amleth's friend.

Thus all were worsted, and none could open the secret lock of the young man's wisdom. But a friend of Feng, gifted more with assurance than judgment, declared that the unfathomable cunning of such a mind could not be detected by any vulgar plot, for the man's obstinacy was so great that it ought not to be assailed with any mild measures; there were many sides to his wiliness, and it ought not to be entrapped by any one method. Accordingly, said he, his own profounder acuteness had hit on a more delicate way, which was well fitted to be put in practice, and would effectually discover what they desired to know. Feng was purposely to absent himself, pretending affairs of great import. Amleth should be closeted alone with his mother in her chamber; but a man should first be commissioned to place himself in a concealed part of the room and listen heedfully to what they talked about. For if the son had any wits at all he would not hesitate to speak out in the hearing of his mother, or fear to trust himself to the fidelity of her who bore him. The speaker, loth to seem readier to devise than to carry out the plot, zealously proffered himself as the agent of the eavesdropping. Feng rejoiced at the scheme, and departed on pretence of a long journey. Now he who had given this counsel repaired privily to the room where Amleth was shut up with his mother, and lay flown skulking in the straw. But Amleth had his antidote for the treachery. Afraid of being overheard by some eavesdropper, he at first resorted to his usual imbecile ways, and crowed like a noisy cock, beating his arms together to mimic the flapping of wings. Then he mounted the straw and began to swing his body and jump again and again, wishing to try if aught lurked there in hiding. Feeling a lump beneath his feet, he drove his sword into the spot, and impaled him who lay hid. Then he dragged him from his concealment and slew him. Then, cutting his body into morsels, he seethed it in boiling water, and flung it through the mouth of an open sewer for the swine to eat, bestrewing the stinking mire with his hapless limbs. Having in this wise eluded the snare, he went back to the room. Then his mother set up a great wailing, and began to lament her son's folly to his face; but he said: "Most infamous of women; dost thou seek with such lying lamentations to hide thy most heavy guilt? Wantoning like a harlot, thou hast entered a wicked and abominable state of wedlock, embracing with incestuous bosom thy husband's slayer, and wheedling with filthy lures of blandishment him who had slain the father of thy son. This, forsooth, is the way that the mares couple with the vanquishers of their mates; for brute beasts are naturally incited to pair indiscriminately; and it would seem that thou, like them, hast clean forgot thy first husband. As for me, not idly do I wear the mask of folly; for I doubt not that he who destroyed his brother will riot as ruthlessly in the blood of his kindred. Therefore it is better to choose the garb of dulness than that of sense, and to borrow some protection from a show of utter frenzy. Yet the passion to avenge my father still burns in my heart; but I am watching the chances, I await the fitting hour. There is a place for all things; against so merciless and dark spirit must be used the deeper devices of the mind. And thou, who hadst been better employed in lamenting thine own disgrace, know it is superfluity to bewail my witlessness; thou shouldst weep for the blemish in thine own mind, not for that in another's. On the rest see thou keep silence." With such reproaches he rent the heart of his mother and redeemed her to walk in the ways of virtue; teaching her to set the fires of the past above the seductions of the present.

When Feng returned, nowhere could he find the man who had

suggested the treacherous espial; he searched for him long and carefully, but none said they had seen him anywhere. Amleth, among others, was asked in jest if he had come on any trace of him, and replied that the man had gone to the sewer, but had fallen through its bottom and been stifled by the floods of filth, and that he had then been devoured by the swine that came up all about that place. This speech was flouted by those who heard; for it seemed senseless, though really it expressly avowed the truth.

Feng now suspected that his stepson was certainly full of guile, and desired to make away with him, but durst not do the deed for fear of the displeasure, not only of Amleth's grandsire Rorik, but also of his own wife. So he thought that the King of Britain should be employed to slay him, so that another could do the deed, and he be able to feign innocence. Thus, desirous to hide his cruelty, he chose rather to besmirch his friend than to bring disgrace on his own head. Amleth, on departing, gave secret orders to his mother to hang the hall with woven knots, and to perform pretended obsequies for him a year thence; promising that he would then return. Two retainers of Feng then accompanied him, bearing a letter graven on wood—a kind of writing material frequent in old times; this letter enjoined the king of the Britons to put to death the youth who was sent over to him. While they were reposing, Amleth searched their coffers, found the letter, and read the instructions therein. Whereupon he erased all the writing on the surface, substituted fresh characters, and so, changing the purport of the instructions, shifted his own doom upon his companions. Nor was he satisfied with removing from himself the sentence of death and passing the peril on to others, but added an entreaty that the King of Britain would grant his daughter in marriage to a youth of great judgment whom he was sending to him. Under this was falsely marked the signature of Feng.

Now when they had reached Britain, the envoys went to the king, and proffered him the letter which they supposed was an implement of destruction to another, but which really betokened death to themselves. The king dissembled the truth, and entreated them hospitably and kindly. Then Amleth scouted all the splendour of the royal banquet like vulgar viands, and abstaining very strangely, rejected that plenteous feast, refraining from the drink even as from the banquet. All marvelled that a youth and a foreigner should disdain the carefully cooked dainties of the royal board and the luxurious banquet provided, as if it were some peasant's relish. So, when the revel broke up, and the king was dismissing his friends to rest, he had a man sent into the sleeping-room to listen secretly, in order that he might hear the midnight conversation of his guests. Now, when Amleth's companions asked him why he had refrained from the feast of yestereve, as if it were poison, he answered that the bread was flecked with blood and tainted; that there was a tang of iron in the liquor; while the meats of the feast reeked of the stench of a human carcase, and were infected by a kind of smack of the odour of the charnel. He further said that the king had the eyes of a slave, and that the queen had in three ways shown the behaviour of a bondmaid. Thus he reviled with insulting invective not so much the feast as its givers. And presently his companions, taunting him with his old defect of wits, began to flout him with many saucy jeers, because he blamed and cavilled at seemly and worthy things, and because he attacked thus ignobly an illustrious king and a lady of so refined a behaviour, bespattering with the shamefullest abuse those who merited all praise.

All this the king heard from his retainer; and declared that he who could say such things had either more than mortal wisdom or more than mortal folly; in these few words fathoming the full depth of Amleth's penetration. Then he summoned his steward and asked him whence he had procured the bread. The steward declared that it had been made by the king's own baker. The king asked where the corn had grown of which it was made, and whether any sign was to be found there of human carnage? The other answered, that not far off was a field, covered with the ancient bones of slaughtered men, and still bearing plainly all the signs of ancient carnage; and that he had himself planted this field with grain in springtide, thinking it more fruitful than the rest, and hoping for plenteous abundance; and so, for aught he knew, the bread had caught some evil savour from this bloodshed. The king, on hearing this, surmised that Amleth had spoken truly, and took the pains to learn also what had been the source of the lard. The other declared that his hogs had, through negligence, strayed from keeping, and battened on the rotten carcase of a robber, and that perchance their pork had thus come to have something of a corrupt smack. The king, finding that Amletll's judgment was right in this thing also, asked of what liquor the steward had mixed the drink? Hearing that it had been brewed of water and meal, he had the spot of the spring pointed out to him, and set to digging deep down; and there he found, rusted away, several swords, the tang whereof it was thought had tainted the waters. Others relate that Amleth blamed the drink because, while quaffing it, he had detected some bees that had fed in the paunch of a dead man; and that the taint, which had formerly been imparted to the combs, had reappeared in the taste. The king, seeing that Amleth had rightly given the causes of the taste he had found so faulty, and learning that the ignoble eyes wherewith Amleth had reproached him concerned some stain upon his birth, had a secret interview with his mother, and asked her who his father had really been. She said she had submitted to no man but the king. But when he threatened that he would have the truth out of her by a trial, he was told that he was the offspring of a slave. By the evidence of the avowal thus extorted he understood the whole mystery of the reproach upon his origin. Abashed as he was with shame for his low estate, he was so ravished with the young man's cleverness, that he asked him why he had aspersed the queen with the reproach that she had demeaned herself like a slave? But while resenting that the courtliness of his wife had been accused in the midnight gossip of guest, he found that her mother had been a bondmaid. For Amleth said he had noted in her three blemishes showing the demeanor of a slave; first, she had muffled her head in her mantle as handmaids do; next, that she had gathered up her gown for walking; and thirdly, that she had first picked out with a splinter, and then chewed up, the remnant of food that stuck in the crevices between her teeth. Further, he mentioned that the king's mother had been brought into slavery from captivity, lest she should seem servile only in her habits, yet not in her birth.

Then the king adored the wisdom of Amleth as though it were inspired, and gave him his daughter to wife; accepting his bare word as though it were a witness from the skies. Moreover, in order to fulfil the bidding of his friend, he hanged Amleth's companions on the morrow. Amleth, feigning offence, treated this piece of kindness as a grievance, and received from the king, as compensation, some gold, which he afterwards melted in the fire, and secretly caused to be poured into some hollowed sticks.

When he had passed a whole year with the king he obtained leave to make a journey, and returned to his own land, carrying away of all his princely wealth and state only the sticks which held the gold. On reaching Jutland, he exchanged his present attire for his ancient demeanour, which he had adopted for righteous ends, purposely assuming an aspect of absurdity. Covered with filth, he entered the banquet-room where his own obsequies were being held, and struck all men utterly aghast, rumour having falsely noised abroad his death. At last terror melted into mirth, and the guests jeered and taunted one another, that he whose last rites they were celebrating as through he were dead, should appear in the flesh. When he was asked concerning his comrades, he pointed to the sticks he was carrying, and said, "Here is both the one and the other." This he observed with equal truth and pleasantry; for his speech, though most thought it idle, yet departed not from the truth; for it pointed at the weregild of the slain as though it were themselves. Thereon, wishing to bring the company into a gayer mood, he jollied the cupbearers, and diligently did the office of plying the drink. Then, to prevent his loose dress hampering his walk, he girdled his sword upon his side, and purposely drawing it several times, pricked his fingers with its point. The bystanders accordingly had both sword and scabbard riveted across with all iron nail. Then, to smooth the way more safely to his plot, he went to the lords and plied them heavily with draught upon draught, and drenched them all so deep in wine, that their feet were made feeble with drunkenness, and they turned to rest within the palace, making their bed where they had revelled. Then he saw they were in a fit state for his plots, and thought that here was a chance offered to do his purpose. So he took out of his bosom the stakes he has long ago prepared, and went into the building, where the ground lay covered with the bodies of the nobles wheezing off their sleep and their debauch. Then, cutting away its support, he brought down the hanging his mother had knitted, which covered the inner as well as the outer walls of the hall. This he flung upon the snorers, and then applying the crooked stakes, he knotted and bound them up in such insoluble intricacy, that not one of the men beneath, however hard he might struggle, could contrive to rise. After this he set fire to the palace. The flames spread, scattering the conflagration far and wide. It enveloped the whole dwelling, destroyed the palace, and burnt them all while they were either buried in deep sleep or vainly striving to arise. Then he went to the chamber of Feng, who had before this been conducted by his train into his pavilion; plucked up a sword that chanced to be hanging to the bed, and planted his own in its place. Then, awakening his uncle, he told him that his nobles were perishing in the flames, and that Amleth was here, armed with his crooks to help him, and thirsting to exact the vengeance, now long overdue, for his father's murder. Feng, on hearing this, leapt from his couch, but was cut down while deprived of his own sword, and as he strove in vain to draw the strange one. O valiant Amleth, and worthy of immortal fame, who being shrewdly armed with a feint of folly, covered a wisdom too high for human wit under a marvellous disguise of silliness! And not only found in his subtlety means to protect his own safety, but also by its guidance found opportunity to avenge his father. By this skilful defence of himself, and strenuous revenge for his parent, he has left it doubtful whether we are to think more of his wit or his bravery. (3)

ENDNOTES:

(1) Saxo now goes back to the history of Denmark. All the events hitherto related in Bk. III, after the first paragraph, are a digression in retrospect.

(2) M. conjectures that this was a certain Harald, the bastard son of Erik the Good, and a wild and dissolute man, who died in 1135, not long before the probable date of Saxo's birth.

(3) Shakespere's tragedy, "Hamlet", is derived from this story.

Swedish Nobles Bring Tribute-Money to Hother

BOOK FOUR

Amleth, when he had accomplished the slaughter of his stepfather, feared to expose his deed to the fickle judgment of his countrymen, and thought it well to lie in hiding till he had learnt what way the mob of the uncouth populace was tending. So the whole neighbourhood, who had watched the blaze during the night, and in the morning desired to know the cause of the fire they had seen, perceived the royal palace fallen in ashes; and, on searching through its ruins, which were yet warm, found only some shapeless remains of burnt corpses. For the devouring flame had consumed everything so utterly that not a single token was left to inform them of the cause of such a disaster. Also they saw the body of Feng lying pierced by the sword, amid his blood-stained raiment. Some were seized with open anger, others with grief, and some with secret delight. One party bewailed the death of their leader, the other gave thanks that the tyranny of the fratricide was now laid at rest. Thus the occurrence of the king's slaughter was greeted by the beholders with diverse minds.

Amleth, finding the people so quiet, made bold to leave his hiding. Summoning those in whom he knew the memory of his father to be fast-rooted, he went to the assembly and there made a speech after this manner:

"Nobles! Let not any who are troubled by the piteous end of Horwendil be worried by the sight of this disaster before you; be not ye, I say, distressed, who have remained loyal to your king and duteous to your father. Behold the corpse, not of a prince, but of a fratricide. Indeed, it was a sorrier sight when ye saw our prince lying lamentably butchered by a most infamous fratricide-brother, let me not call him. With your own compassionating eyes ye have beheld the mangled limbs of Horwendil; they have seen his body done to death with many wounds. Surely that most abominable butcher only deprived his king of life that he might despoil his country of freedom! The hand that slew him made you slaves. Who then so mad as to choose Feng the cruel before Horwendil the righteous? Remember how benignantly Horwendil fostered you, how justly he dealt with you, how kindly he loved you. Remember how you lost the mildest of princes and the justest of fathers, while in his place was put a tyrant and an assassin set up; how your rights were confiscated; how everything was plague-stricken; how the country was stained with infamies; how the yoke was planted on your necks, and how, your free will was forfeited! And now all this is over; for ye see the criminal stifled in his own crimes, the slayer of his kin punished for his misdoings. What man of but ordinary wit, beholding it, would account this kindness a wrong? What sane man could be sorry that the crime has recoiled upon the culprit? Who could lament the killing of a most savage executioner? Or bewail the righteous death of a most cruel despot? Ye behold the doer of the deed; he is before you. Yea, I own that I have taken vengeance for my country and my father. Your hands were equally bound to the task which mine fulfilled. What it would have beseemed you to accomplish with me, I achieved alone. Nor had I any partner in so glorious a deed, or the service of any man to help me. Not that I forget that you would have helped this work, had I asked you; for doubtless you have remained loyal to your king and loving to your prince. But I chose that the wicked should be punished without imperilling you; I thought that others need not set their shoulders to the burden when I deemed mine strong enough to bear it. Therefore I consumed all the others to ashes, and left only the trunk of Feng for your hands to burn, so that on this at least you may wreak all your longing for a righteous vengeance. Now haste up speedily, heap the pyre, burn up the body of the wicked, consume away his guilty limbs, scatter his sinful ashes, strew broadcast his ruthless dust; let no urn or barrow enclose the abominable remnants of his bones. Let no trace of his fratricide remain; let there be no spot in his own land for his tainted limbs; let no neighbourhood suck infection from him; let not sea nor soil be defiled by harboring his accursed carcase. I have done the rest; this one loyal duty is left for you. These must be the tyrant's obsequies, this the funeral procession of the fratricide. It is not seemly that he who stripped his country of her freedom should have his ashes covered by his country's earth.

"Besides, why tell again my own sorrows? Why count over my troubles? Why weave the thread of my miseries anew? Ye know them more fully than I myself. I, pursued to the death by my stepfather, scorned by my mother, spat upon by friends, have passed my years in pitiable wise, and my days in adversity; and my insecure life has teemed with fear and perils. In fine, I passed every season of my age wretchedly and in extreme calamity. Often in your secret murmurings together you have sighed over my lack of wits; there was none (you said) to avenge the father, none to punish the fratricide. And in this I found a secret testimony of your love; for I saw that the memory of the King's murder had not yet faded from your minds.

"Whose breast is so hard that it can be softened by no fellow-feeling for what I have felt? Who is so stiff and stony, that he is swayed by no compassion for my griefs? Ye whose hands are clean of the blood of Horwendil, pity your fosterling, be moved by my calamities. Pity also my stricken mother, and rejoice with me that the infamy of her who was once your queen is quenched. For this weak woman had to bear a twofold weight of ignominy, embracing one who was her husband's brother and murderer. Therefore, to hide my purpose of revenge and to veil my wit, I counterfeited a listless bearing; I feigned dulness; I planned a stratagem; and now you can see with your own eyes whether it has succeeded, whether it has achieved its purpose to the full; I am content to leave you to judge so great a matter. It is your turn; trample under foot the ashes of the murderer! Disdain the dust of him who slew his brother, and defiled his brother's queen with infamous desecration, who outraged his sovereign and treasonably assailed his majesty, who brought the sharpest tyranny upon you, stole your freedom, and crowned fratricide with incest. I have been the agent of this just vengeance; I have burned for this righteous retribution; uphold me with a high-born spirit; pay me the homage that you owe; warm me with your kindly looks. It is I who have wiped off my country's shame; I who have quenched my mother's dishonour; I who have beaten back oppression; I who have put to death the murderer; I who have baffled the artful hand of my uncle with retorted arts. Were he living, each new day would have multiplied his crimes. I resented the wrong done to father and to fatherland: I slew him who was governing you outrageously and more hardly than it beseemed men. Acknowledge my service, honour my wit, give me the throne if I have earned it; for you have in me one who has done you a mighty service, and who is no degenerate heir to his father's power; no fratricide, but the lawful successor to the throne; and a dutiful avenger of the crime of murder. It is I who have stripped you of slavery, and clothed you with freedom; I have restored your height of fortune, and given you your glory back; I have deposed the despot and triumphed over the butcher. In your hands is the reward; you know what I have done for you, and from your righteousness I ask my wage."

Every heart had been moved while the young man thus spoke; he affected some to compassion, and some even to tears. When the lamentation ceased, he was appointed king by prompt and general acclaim. For one and all rested their greatest hopes on his wisdom, since he had devised the whole of such an achievement with the deepest cunning, and accomplished it with the most astonishing contrivance. Many could have been seen marvelling how he had concealed so subtle a plan over so long a space of time.

After these deeds in Denmark, Amleth equipped three vessels, and went back to Britain to see his wife and her father. He had also enrolled in his service the flower of the warriors, and arrayed them very choicely, wishing to have everything now magnificently appointed, even as of old he had always worn contemptible gear, and to change all his old devotion to poverty for outlay on luxury. He also had a shield made for him, whereon the whole series of his exploits, beginning with his earliest youth, was painted in exquisite designs. This he bore as a record of his deeds of prowess, and gained great increase of fame thereby. Here were to be seen depicted the slaying of Horwendil; the fratricide and incest of Feng; the infamous uncle, the whimsical nephew; the shapes of the hooked stakes; the stepfather suspecting, the stepson dissembling; the various temptations offered, and the woman brought to beguile him; the gaping wolf; the finding of the rudder; the passing of the sand; the entering of the wood; the putting of the straw through the gadfly; the warning of the youth by the tokens; and the privy dealings with the maiden after the escort was eluded. And likewise could be seen the picture of the palace; the queen there with her son; the slaying of the eavesdropper; and how, after being killed, he was boiled down, and so dropped into the sewer, and so thrown out to the swine; how his limbs were strewn in the mud, and so left for the beasts to finish. Also it could be seen how Amleth surprised the secret of his sleeping attendants, how he erased the letters, and put new characters in their places; how he disdained the banquet and scorned the drink; how he condemned time face of the king and taxed the Queen with faulty behaviour. There was also represented the hanging of the envoys, and the young man's wedding; then the voyage back to Denmark; the festive celebration of the funeral rites; Amleth, in answer to questions, pointing to the sticks in place of his attendants, acting as cupbearer, and purposely drawing his sword and pricking his fingers; the sword riveted through, the swelling cheers of the banquet, the dance growing fast and furious; the hangings flung upon the sleepers, then fastened with the interlacing crooks, and wrapped tightly round them as they slumbered; the brand set to the mansion, the burning of the guests, the royal palace consumed with fire and tottering down; the visit to the sleeping-room of Feng, the theft of his sword, the useless one set in its place; and the king slain with his own sword's point by his stepson's hand. All this was there, painted upon Amleth's battle-shield by a careful craftsman in the choicest of handiwork; he copied truth in his figures, and embodied real deeds in his outlines. Moreover, Amleth's followers, to increase the splendour of their presence, wore shields which were gilt over.

The King of Britain received them very graciously, and treated them with costly and royal pomp. During the feast he asked anxiously whether Feng was alive and prosperous. His son-in-law told him that the man of whose welfare he was vainly inquiring had perished by the sword. With a flood of questions he tried to find out who had slain Feng, and learnt that the messenger of his death was likewise its author. And when the king heard this, he was secretly aghast, because he found that an old promise to avenge Feng now devolved upon himself. For Feng and he had determined of old, by a mutual compact, that one of them should act as avenger of the other. Thus the king was drawn one way by his love for his daughter and his affection for his son-in-law; another way by his regard for his friend, and moreover by his strict oath and the sanctity of their mutual declarations, which it was impious to violate. At last he slighted the ties of kinship, and sworn faith prevailed. His heart turned to vengeance, and he put the sanctity of his oath before family bonds. But since it was thought sin to wrong the holy ties of hospitality, he preferred to execrate his revenge by the hand of another, wishing to mask his secret crime with a show of innocence. So he veiled his treachery with attentions, and hid his intent to harm under a show of zealous goodwill. His queen having lately died of illness, he requested Amleth to undertake the mission of making him a fresh match, saying that he was highly delighted with his extraordinary shrewdness. He declared that there was a certain queen reigning in Scotland, whom he vehemently desired to marry. Now he knew that she was not only unwedded by reason of her chastity, but that in the cruelty of her arrogance she had always loathed her wooers, and had inflicted on her lovers the uttermost punishment, so that not one but of all the multitude was to be found who had not paid for his insolence with his life.

Perilous as this commission was Amleth started, never shrinking to obey the duty imposed upon him, but trusting partly in his own servants, and partly in the attendants of the king. He entered Scotland, and, when quite close to the abode of the queen, he went into a meadow by the wayside to rest his horses. Pleased by the look of the spot, he thought of resting—the pleasant prattle of the stream exciting a desire to sleep —and posted men to keep watch some way off. The queen on hearing of this, sent out ten warriors to spy on the approach of the foreigners and their equipment. One of these, being quick-witted, slipped past the sentries, pertinaciously made his way up, and took away the shield, which Amleth had chanced to set at his head before he slept, so gently that he did not ruffle his slumbers, though he was lying upon it, nor awaken one man of all that troop; for he wished to assure his mistress not only by report but by some token. With equal address he filched the letter entrusted to Amleth from the coffer in which it was kept. When these things were brought to the queen, she scanned the shield narrowly, and from the notes appended made out the whole argument. Then she knew that here was the man who, trusting in his own nicely calculated scheme, had avenged on his uncle the murder of his father. She also looked at the letter containing the suit for her band, and rubbed out all the writing; for wedlock with the old she utterly abhorred, and desired the embraces of young men. But she wrote in its place a commission purporting to be sent from the King of Britain to herself, signed like the other with his name and title, wherein she pretended that she was asked to marry the bearer. Moreover, she included an account of the deeds of which she had learnt from Amleth's shield, so that one would have thought the shield confirmed the letter, while the letter explained the shield. Then she told the same spies whom she had employed before to take the shield back, and put the letter in its place again; playing the very trick on Amleth which, as she had learnt, he had himself used in outwitting his companions.

Amleth, meanwhile, who found that his shield had been filched from under his head, deliberately shut his eyes and cunningly feigned sleep, hoping to regain by pretended what he had lost by real slumbers. For he thought that the success of his one attempt would incline the spy to deceive him a second time. And he was not mistaken. For as the spy came up stealthily, and wanted to put back the shield and the writing in their old place, Amleth leapt up, seized him, and detained him in bonds. Then he roused his retinue, and went to the abode of the queen. As representing his father-in-law, he greeted her, and handled her the writing, sealed with the king's seal. The queen, who was named Hermutrude, took and read it, and spoke most warmly of Amleth's diligence and shrewdness, saying, that Feng had deserved his punishment, and that the unfathomable wit of Amleth had accomplished a deed past all human estimation; seeing that not only had his impenetrable depth devised a mode of revenging his father's death and his mother's adultery, but it had further, by his notable deeds Of prowess, seized the kingdom of the man whom he had found constantly plotting against him. She marvelled therefore that a man of such instructed mind could have made the one slip of a mistaken marriage; for though his renown almost rose above mortality, he seemed to have stumbled into an obscure and ignoble match. For the parents of his wife had been slaves, though good luck had graced them with the honours of royalty. Now (said she), when looking for a wife a wise man must reckon the lustre of her birth and not of her beauty. Therefore, if he were to seek a match in a proper spirit, he should weigh the ancestry, and not be smitten by the looks; for though looks were a lure to temptation, yet their empty bedizenment had tarnished the white simplicity of many a man. Now there was a woman, as nobly born as himself, whom he could take. She herself, whose means were not poor nor her birth lowly, was worthy his embraces, since he did not surpass her in royal wealth nor outshine her in the honour of her ancestors. Indeed she was a queen, and but that her sex gainsaid it, might be deemed a king; may (and this is yet truer), whomsoever she thought worthy of her bed was at once a king, and she yielded her kingdom with herself. Thus her sceptre and her hand went together. It was no mean favour for such a woman to offer her love, who in the case of other men had always followed her refusal with the sword. Therefore she pressed him to transfer his wooing, to make over to her his marriage vows, and to learn to prefer birth to beauty. So saying, she fell upon him with a close embrace.

Amleth was overjoyed at the gracious speech of the maiden, fell to kissing back, and returned her close embrace, protesting that the maiden's wish was his own. Then a banquet was held, friends bidden, the nobles gathered, and the marriage rites performed. When they were accomplished, he went back to Britain with his bride, a strong band of Scots being told to follow close behind, that he might have its help against the diverse treacheries in his path. As he was returning, the daughter of the King of Britain, to whom he was still married, met him. Though she complained that she was slighted by the wrong of having a paramour put over her, yet, she said, it would be unworthy for her to hate him as an adulterer more than she loved him as a husband: nor would she so far shrink from her lord as to bring herself to hide in silence the guile which she knew was intended against him. For she had a son as a pledge of their marriage, and regard for him, if nothing else, must have inclined his mother to the affection of a wife. "He," she said, "may hate the supplanter of his mother, I will love her; no disaster shall put out my flame for thee; no ill-will shall quench it, or prevent me from exposing the malignant designs against thee, or from revealing the snares I have detected. Bethink thee, then, that thou must beware of thy father-in-law, for thou hast thyself reaped the harvest of thy mission, foiled the wishes of him who sent thee, and with willful trespass seized over all the fruit for thyself." By this speech she showed herself more inclined to love her husband than her father.

While she thus spoke, the King of Britain came up and embraced his son-in-law closely, but with little love, and welcomed him with a banquet, to hide his intended guile under a show of generosity. But Amleth, having learnt the deceit, dissembled his fear, took a retinue of two hundred horsemen, put on an under-shirt (of mail), and complied with the invitation, preferring the peril of falling in with the king's deceit to the shame of hanging back. So much heed for honour did he think that he must take in all things. As he rode up close, the king attacked him just under the porch of the folding doors, and would have thrust him through with his javelin, but that the hard shirt of mail threw off the blade. Amleth received a slight wound, and went to the spot where he had bidden the Scottish warriors wait on duty. He then sent back to the king his new wife's spy, whom he had captured. This man was to bear witness that he had secretly taken from the coffer where it was kept the letter which was meant for his mistress, and thus was to make the whole blame recoil on Hermutrude, by this studied excuse absolving Amleth from the charge of treachery. The king without tarrying pursued Amleth hotly as he fled, and deprived him of most of his forces. So Amleth, on the morrow, wishing to fight for dear life, and utterly despairing of his powers of resistance, tried to increase his apparent numbers. He put stakes under some of the dead bodies of his comrades to prop them up, set others on horseback like living men, and tied others to neighbouring stones, not taking off any of their armour, and dressing them in due order of line and wedge, just as if they were about to engage. The wing composed of the dead was as thick as the troop of the living. It was an amazing spectacle this, of dead men dragged out to battle, and corpses mustered to fight. The plan served him well, for the very figures of the dead men showed like a vast array as the sunbeams struck them. For those dead and senseless shapes restored the original number of the army so well, that the mass might have been unthinned by the slaughter of yesterday. The Britons, terrified at the spectacle, fled before fighting, conquered by the dead men whom they had overcome in life. I cannot tell whether to think more of the cunning or of the good fortune of this victory. The Danes came down on the king as he was tardily making off, and killed him. Amleth, triumphant, made a great plundering, seized the spoils of Britain, and went back with his wives to his own land.

Meanwhile Rorik had died, and Wiglek, who had come to the throne, had harassed Amleth's mother with all manner of insolence and stripped her of her royal wealth, complaining that her son had usurped the kingdom of Jutland and defrauded the King of Leire, who had the sole privilege of giving and taking away the rights of high offices. This treatment Amleth took with such forbearance as apparently to return kindness for slander, for he presented Wiglek with the richest of his spoils. But afterwards he seized a chance of taking vengeance, attacked him, subdued him, and from a covert became an open foe. Fialler, the governor of Skaane, he drove into exile; and the tale is that Fialler retired to a spot called Undensakre, which is unknown to our peoples. After this, Wiglek, recruited with the forces of Skaane and Zealand, sent envoys to challenge Amleth to a war. Amleth, with his marvellous shrewdness, saw that he was tossed between two difficulties, one of which involved disgrace and the other danger. For he knew that if he took up the challenge he was threatened with peril of his life, while to shrink from it would disgrace his reputation as a soldier. Yet in that spirit ever fixed on deeds of prowess the desire to save his honour won the day. Dread of disaster was blunted by more vehement thirst for glory; he would not tarnish the unblemished lustre of his fame by timidly skulking from his fate. Also he saw that there is almost as wide a gap between a mean life and a noble death as that which is acknowledged between honour and disgrace themselves.

Yet Amleth was enchained by such great love for Hermutrude, that he was more deeply concerned in his mind about her future widowhood than about his own death, and cast about very zealously how he could decide on some second husband for her before the opening of the war. Hermutrude, therefore, declared that she had the courage of a man, and promised that she would not forsake him even on the field, saying that the woman who dreaded to be united with her lord in death was abominable. But she kept this rare promise ill; for when Amleth had been slain by Wiglek in battle in Jutland, she yielded herself up unasked to be the conqueror's spoil and bride. Thus all vows of woman are loosed by change of fortune and melted by the shifting of time; the faith of their soul rests on a slippery foothold, and is weakened by casual chances; glib in promises, and as sluggish in performance, all manner of lustful promptings enslave it, and it bounds away with panting and precipitate desire, forgetful of old things in the ever hot pursuit after something fresh. So ended Amleth. Had fortune been as kind to him as nature, he would have equalled the gods in glory, and surpassed the labours of Hercules by his deeds of prowess. A plain in Jutland is to be found, famous for his name and burial-place. Wiglek's administration of the kingdom was long and peaceful, and he died of disease.

WERMUND, his son, succeeded him. The long and leisurely tranquillity of a most prosperous and quiet time flowed by and Wermund in undisturbed security maintained a prolonged and steady peace at home. He had no children during the prime of his life, but in his old age, by a belated gift of fortune, he begat a son, Uffe, though all the years which had glided by had raised him up no offspring. This Uffe surpassed all of his age in stature, but in his early youth was supposed to have so dull and foolish a spirit as to be useless for all affairs public or private. For from his first years he never used to play or make merry, but was so void of all human pleasure that he kept his lips sealed in a perennial silence, and utterly restrained his austere visage from the business of laughter. But though through the years of his youth he was reputed for an utter fool, he afterwards left that despised estate and became famous, turning out as great a pattern of wisdom and hardihood as he had been a picture of stagnation. His father, seeing him such a simpleton, got him for a wife the daughter of Frowin, the governor of the men of Sleswik; thinking that by his alliance with so famous a man Uffe would receive help which would serve him well in administering the realm. Frowin had two sons, Ket and Wig, who were youths of most brilliant parts, and their excellence, not less than that of Frowin, Wermund destined to the future advantage of his son.

At this time the King of Sweden was Athisl, a man of notable fame and energy. After defeating his neighbours far around, he was loth to leave the renown won by his prowess to be tarnished in slothful ease, and by constant and zealous practice brought many novel exercises into vogue. For one thing he had a daily habit of walking alone girt with splendid armour: in part because he knew that nothing was more excellent in warfare than the continual practice of arms; and in part that he might swell his glory by ever following this pursuit. Self-confidence claimed as large a place in this man as thirst for fame. Nothing, he thought, could be so terrible as to make him afraid that it would daunt his stout heart by its opposition. He carried his arms into Denmark, and challenged Frowin to battle near Sleswik. The armies routed one another with vast slaughter, and it happened that the generals came to engage in person, so that they conducted the affair like a duel; and, in addition to the public issues of the war, the fight was like a personal conflict. For both of them longed with equal earnestness for an issue of the combat by which they might exhibit their valour, not by the help of their respective sides, but by a trial of personal strength. The end was that, though the blows rained thick on either side, Athisl prevailed and overthrew Frowin, and won a public victory as well as a duel, breaking up and shattering the Danish ranks in all directions. When he returned to Sweden, he not only counted the slaying of Frowin among the trophies of his valour, but even bragged of it past measure, so ruining the glory of the deed by his wantonness of tongue. For it is sometimes handsomer for deeds of valour to be shrouded in the modesty of silence than to be blazoned in wanton talk.

Wermund raised the sons of Frowin to honours of the same rank as their father's, a kindness which was only due to the children of his friend who had died for the country. This prompted Athisl to carry the war again into Denmark. Emboldened therefore by his previous battle, he called back, bringing with him not only no slender and feeble force, but all the flower of the valour of Sweden, thinking he would seize the supremacy of all Denmark. Ket, the son of Frowin, sent Folk, his chief officer, to take this news to Wermund, who then chanced to be in his house Jellinge. (1) Folk found the king feasting with his friends, and did his errand, admonishing him that here was the long-wished-for chance of war at hand, and pressing itself upon the wishes of Wermund, to whom was give an immediate chance of victory and the free choice of a speedy and honourable triumph. Great and unexpected were the sweets of good fortune, so long sighed for, and now granted to him by this lucky event. For Athisl had come encompassed with countless forces of the Swedes, just as though in his firm assurance he had made sure of victory; and since the enemy who was going to fight would doubtless prefer death to flight, this chance of war gave them a fortunate opportunity to take vengeance for their late disaster.

Wermund, declaring that he had performed his mission nobly and bravely, ordered that he should take some little refreshment of the banquet, since "far-faring ever hurt fasters." When Folk said that he had no kind of leisure to take food, he begged him to take a draught to quench his thirst. This was given him; and Wermund also bade him keep the cup, which was of gold, saying that men who were weary with the heat of wayfaring found it handier to take up the water in a goblet than in the palms, and that it was better to use a cup for drinking than the hand. When the king accompanied his great gift with such gracious words, the young man, overjoyed at both, promised that, before the king should see him turn and flee, he would take a draught of his own blood to the full measure of the liquor he had drunk.

With this doughty vow Wermund accounted himself well repaid, and got somewhat more joy from giving the boon than the soldier had from gaining it. Nor did he find that Folk's talk was braver than his fighting.

For, when battle had begun, it came to pass that amidst divers charges of the troops Folk and Athisl met and fought a long while together; and that the host of the Swedes, following the fate of their captain, took to flight, and Athisl also was wounded and fled from the battle to his ships. And when Folk, dazed with wounds and toils, and moreover steeped alike in heat and toil and thirst, had ceased to follow the rout of the enemy, then, in order to refresh himself, he caught his own blood in his helmet, and put it to his lips to drain: by which deed he gloriously requited the king's gift of the cup. Wermund, who chanced to see this, praised him warmly for fulfilling his vow. Folk answered, that a noble vow ought to be strictly performed to the end: a speech wherein he showed no less approval of his own deed than Wermund.

Now, while the conquerors had laid down their arms, and, as is usual after battle, were exchanging diverse talk with one another, Ket, the governor of the men of Sleswik, declared that it was a matter of great marvel to him how it was that Athisl, though difficulties strewed his path, had contrived an opportunity to escape, especially as he had been the first and foremost in the battle, but last of all in the retreat; and though there had not been one of the enemy whose fall was so vehemently desired by the Danes. Wermund rejoined that he should know that there were four kinds of warrior to be distinguished in every army. The fighters of the first order were those who, tempering valour with forbearance, were keen to slay those who resisted, but were ashamed to bear hard on fugitives. For these were the men who had won undoubted proofs of prowess by veteran experience in arms, and who found their glory not in the flight of the conquered, but in overcoming those whom they had to conquer. Then there was a second kind of warriors, who were endowed with stout frame and spirit, but with no jot of compassion, and who raged with savage and indiscriminate carnage against the backs as

146

well as the breasts of their foes. Now of this sort were the men carried away by hot and youthful blood, and striving to grace their first campaign with good auguries of warfare. They burned as hotly with the glow of youth as with the glow for glory, and thus rushed headlong into right or wrong with equal recklessness. There was also the third kind, who, wavering betwixt shame and fear, could not go forward for terror, while shame barred retreat. Of distinguished blood, but only notable for their useless stature, they crowded the ranks with numbers and not with strength, smote the foe more with their shadows than with their arms, and were only counted among the throng of warriors as so many bodies to be seen. These men were lords of great riches, but excelled more in birth than bravery; hungry for life because owning great possessions, they were forced to yield to the sway of cowardice rather than nobleness. There were others, again, who brought show to the war, and not substance, and who, foisting themselves into the rear of their comrades, were the first to fly and the last to fight. One sure token of fear betrayed their feebleness; for they always deliberately sought excuses to shirk, and followed with timid and sluggish advance in the rear of the fighters. It must be supposed, therefore, that these were the reasons why the king had escaped safely; for when he fled he was not pursued pertinaciously by the men of the front rank; since these made it their business to preserve the victory, not to arrest the conquered, and massed their wedges, in order that the fresh-won victory might be duly and sufficiently guarded, and attain the fulness of triumph.
Now the second class of fighters, whose desire was to cut down everything in their way, had left Athisl unscathed, from lack not of will but of opportunity; for they had lacked the chance to hurt him rather than the daring. Moreover, though the men of the third kind, who frittered away the very hour of battle by wandering about in a flurried fashion, and also hampered the success of their own side, had had their chance of harming the king, they yet lacked courage to assail him. In this way Wermund satisfied the dull amazement of Ket, and declared that he had set forth and expounded the true reasons of the king's safe escape.

After this Athisl fled back to Sweden, still wantonly bragging of the slaughter of Frowin, and constantly boasting the memory of his exploit with prolix recital of his deeds; not that he bore calmly the shame of his defeat, but that he might salve the wound of his recent flight by the honours of his ancient victory. This naturally much angered Ket and Wig, and they swore a vow to unite in avenging their father. Thinking that they could hardly accomplish this in open war, they took an equipment of lighter armament, and went to Sweden alone. Then, entering a wood in which they had learnt by report that the king used to take his walks unaccompanied, they hid their weapons. Then they talked long with Athisl, giving themselves out as deserters; and when he asked them what was their native country, they said they were men of Sleswik, and had left their land "for manslaughter". The king thought that this statement referred not to their vow to commit the crime, but to the guilt of some crime already committed. For they desired by this deceit to foil his inquisitiveness, so that the truthfulness of the statement might baffle the wit of the questioner, and their true answer, being covertly shadowed forth in a fiction, might inspire in him a belief that it was false. For famous men of old thought lying a most shameful thing. Then Athisl said he would like to know whom the Danes believed to be the slayer of Frowin. Ket replied that there was a doubt as to who ought to claim so illustrious a deed, especially as the general testimony was that he had perished on the field of battle. Athisl answered that it was idle to credit others with the death of Frowin, which he, and he alone, had accomplished in mutual combat. Soon he asked whether Frowin had left any children. Ket answering that two sons of his were alive, said that he would be very glad to learn their age and stature. Ket replied that they were almost of the same size as themselves in body, alike in years, and much resembling them in tallness. Then Athisl said: "If the mind and the valour of their sire were theirs, a bitter tempest would break upon me." Then he asked whether those men constantly spoke of the slaying of their father. Ket rejoined that it was idle to go on talking and talking about a thing that could not be softened by any remedy, and declared that it was no good to harp with constant vexation on an inexpiable ill. By saying this he showed that threats ought not to anticipate vengeance.

When Ket saw that the king regularly walked apart alone in order to train his strength, he took up his arms, and with his brother followed the king as he walked in front of them. Athisl, when he saw them, stood his ground on the sand, thinking it shameful to avoid threateners. Then they said that they would take vengeance for his slaying of Frowin, especially as he avowed with so many arrogant vaunts that he alone was his slayer. But he told them to take heed lest while they sought to compass their revenge, they should be so foolhardy as to engage him with their feeble and powerless hand, and while desiring the destruction of another, should find they had fallen themselves. Thus they would cut off their goodly promise of overhasty thirst for glory. Let them then save their youth and spare their promise; let them not be seized so lightly with a desire to perish. Therefore, let them suffer him to requite with money the trespass done them in their father's death, and account it great honour that they would be credited with forcing so mighty a chief to pay a fine, and in a manner with shaking him with overmastering fear. Yet he said he advised them thus, not because he was really terrified, but because he was moved with compassion for their youth. Ket replied that it was idle to waste time in beating so much about the bush and trying to sap their righteous longing for revenge by an offer of pelf. So he bade him come forward and make trial with him in single combat of whatever strength he had. He himself would do without the aid of his brother, and would fight with his own strength, lest it should appear a shameful and unequal combat, for the ancients held it to be unfair, and also infamous, for two men to fight against one; and a victory gained by this kind of fighting they did not account honourable, but more like a disgrace than a glory. Indeed, it was considered not only a poor, but a most shameful exploit for two men to overpower one.

But Athisl was filled with such assurance that he bade them both assail him at once, declaring that if he could not cure them of the desire to fight, he would at least give them the chance of fighting more safely. But Ket shrank so much from this favour that he swore he would accept death sooner: for he thought that the terms of battle thus offered would be turned into a reproach to himself. So he engaged hotly with Athisl, who desirous to fight him in a forbearing fashion, merely thrust lightly with his blade and struck upon his shield; thus guarding his own safety with more hardihood than success. When he had done this some while, he advised him to take his brother to share in his enterprise, and not be ashamed to ask for the help of another hand, since his unaided efforts were useless. If he refused, said Athisl, he should not be spared; then making good his threats, he assailed him with all his might. But Ket received him with so sturdy a stroke of his sword, that it split the helmet and forced its way down upon the head. Stung by the wound (for a stream of blood flowed from his poll), he attacked Ket with a shower of nimble blows, and drove him to his knees. Wig, leaning more to personal love than to general usage, (2) could not bear the sight, but made affection conquer shame, and attacking Athisl, chose rather to defend the weakness of his brother than to look on at it. But he won more infamy than glory by the deed. In helping his brother he had violated the appointed conditions of the duel; and the help that he gave him was thought more useful than honourable. For on the one scale he inclined to the side of disgrace, and on the other to that of affection. Thereupon they perceived themselves that their killing of Athisl had been more swift than glorious. Yet, not to hide the deed from the common people, they cut off his head, slung his body on a horse, took it out of the wood, and handed it over to the dwellers in a village near, announcing that the sons of Frowin had taken vengeance upon Athisl, King of the Swedes, for the slaying of their father. Boasting of such a victory as this, they were received by Wermund with the highest honours; for he thought they had done a most useful deed, and he preferred to regard the glory of being rid of a rival with more attention than the infamy of committing an outrage. Nor did he judge that the killing of a tyrant was in any wise akin to shame. It passed into a proverb among foreigners, that the death of the king had broken down the ancient principle of combat.

When Wermund was losing his sight by infirmity of age, the King of Saxony, thinking that Denmark lacked a leader, sent envoys ordering him to surrender to his charge the kingdom which he held beyond the due term of life; lest, if he thirsted to hold sway too long, he should strip his country of laws and defence. For how could he be reckoned a king, whose spirit was darkened with age, and his eyes with blindness not less black and awful? If he refused, but yet had a son who would dare to accept a challenge and fight with his son, let him agree that the victor should possess the realm. But if he approved neither offer, let him learn that he must be dealt with by weapons and not by warnings; and in the end he must unwillingly surrender what he was too proud at first to yield uncompelled. Wermund, shaken by deep sighs, answered that it was too insolent to sting him with these taunts upon his years; for he had passed no timorous youth, nor shrunk from battle, that age should bring him to this extreme misery. It was equally unfitting to cast in his teeth the infirmity of his blindness: for it was common for a loss of this kind to accompany such a time of life as his, and it seemed a calamity fitter for sympathy than for taunts. It were juster to fix the blame on the impatience of the King of Saxony, whom it would have beseemed to wait for the old man's death, and not demand his throne; for it was somewhat better to succeed to the dead than to rob the living. Yet, that he might not be thought to make over the honours of his ancient freedom, like a madman, to the possession of another, he would accept the challenge with his own hand. The envoys answered that they knew that their king would shrink from the mockery of fighting a blind man, for such an absurd mode of combat was thought more shameful than honourable. It would surely be better to settle the affair by means of their offspring on either side. The Danes were in consternation, and at a sudden loss for a reply: but Uffe, who happened to be there with the rest, craved his father's leave to answer; and suddenly the dumb as it were spake. When Wermund asked who had thus begged leave to speak, and the attendants said that it was Uffe, he declared that it was enough that the insolent foreigner should jeer at the pangs of his misery, without those of his own household vexing him with the same wanton effrontery. But the courtiers persistently averred that this man was Uffe; and the king said: "He is free, whosoever he be, to say out what he thinks." Then said Uffe, "that it was idle for their king to covet a realm which could rely not only on the service of its own ruler, but also on the arms and wisdom of most valiant nobles. Moreover, the king did not lack a son nor the kingdom an heir; and they were to know that he had made up his mind to fight not only the son of their king, but also, at the same time, whatsoever man the prince should elect as his comrade out of the bravest of their nation."

The envoys laughed when they beard this, thinking it idle lip-courage. Instantly the ground for the battle was agreed on, and a fixed time appointed. But the bystanders were so amazed by the strangeness of Uffe's speaking and challenging, that one can scarce say if they were more astonished at his words or at his assurance.

But on the departure of the envoys Wermund praised him who had made the answer, because he had proved his confidence in his own valour by challenging not one only, but two; and said that he would sooner quit his kingdom for him, whoever he was, than for an insolent foe. But when one and all testified that he who with lofty self-confidence had spurned the arrogance of the envoys was his own son, he bade him come nearer to him, wishing to test with his hands what he could not with his eyes. Then he carefully felt his body, and found by the size of his limbs and by his features that he was his son; and then began to believe their assertions, and to ask him why he had taken pains to hide so sweet an eloquence with such careful dissembling, and had borne to live through so long a span of life without utterance or any intercourse of talk, so as to let men think him utterly incapable of speech, and a born mute. He replied that he had been hitherto satisfied with the protection of his father, that he had not needed the use of his own voice, until he saw the wisdom of his own land hard pressed by the glibness of a foreigner. The king also asked him why he had chosen to challenge two rather than one. He said he had desired this mode of combat in order that the death of King Athisl, which, having been caused by two men, was a standing reproach to the Danes, might be balanced by the exploit of one, and that a new ensample of valour might erase the ancient record of their disgrace. Fresh honour, he said, would thus obliterate the guilt of their old dishonour.

Wermund said that his son had judged all things rightly, and bade him first learn the use of arms, since he had been little accustomed to them. When they were offered to Uffe, he split the narrow links of the mail-coats by the mighty girth of his chest, nor could any be found large enough to hold him properly. For he was too hugely built to be able to use the arms of any other man. At last, when he was bursting even his father's coat of mail by the violent compression of his body, Wermund ordered it to be cut away on the left side and patched with a buckle; thinking it mattered little if the side guarded by the shield were exposed to the sword. He also told him to be most careful in fixing on a sword which he could use safely. Several were offered him; but Uffe, grasping the hilt, shattered them one after the other into flinders by shaking them, and not a single blade was of so hard a temper but at the first blow he broke it into many pieces. But the king had a sword of extraordinary sharpness, called "Skrep", which at a single blow of the smiter struck straight through and cleft asunder any obstacle whatsoever; nor would aught be hard enough to check its edge when driven home. The king, loth to leave this for the benefit of posterity, and greatly grudging others the use of it, had buried it deep in the earth, meaning, since he had no hopes of his son's improvement, to debar everyone else from using it. But when he was now asked whether he had a sword worthy of the strength of Uffe, he said that he had one which, if he could recognize the lie of the ground and find what he had consigned long ago to earth, he could offer him as worthy of his bodily strength. Then he bade them lead him into a field, and kept questioning his companions over all the ground. At last he recognised the tokens, found the spot where he had buried the sword, drew it out of its hole, and handed it to his son. Uffe saw it was frail with great age and rusted away; and, not daring to strike with it, asked if he must prove this one also like the rest, declaring that he must try its temper before the battle ought to be fought. Wermund replied that if this sword were shattered by mere brandishing, there was nothing left which could serve for such strength as his. He must, therefore, forbear from the act, whose issue remained so doubtful.

So they repaired to the field of battle as agreed. It is fast encompassed by the waters of the river Eider, which roll between, and forbid any approach save by ship. Hither Uffe went unattended, while the Prince of Saxony was followed by a champion famous for his strength. Dense crowds on either side, eager to see, thronged each winding bank, and all bent their eyes upon this scene. Wermund planted himself on the end of the bridge, determined to perish in the waters if defeat were the lot of his son: he would rather share the fall of his own flesh and blood than behold, with heart full of anguish, the destruction of his own country. Both the warriors assaulted Uffe; but, distrusting his sword, he parried the blows of both with his shield, being determined to wait patiently and see which of the two he must beware of most heedfully, so that he might reach that one at all events with a single stroke of his blade. Wermund, thinking that his feebleness was at fault, that he took the blows so patiently, dragged himself little by little, in his longing for death, forward to the western edge of the bridge, meaning to fling himself down and perish, should all be over with his son.

Fortune shielded the old father, for Uffe told the prince to engage with him more briskly, and to do some deed of prowess worthy of his famous race; lest the lowborn squire should seem braver than the prince. Then, in order to try the bravery of the champion, he bade him not skulk timorously at his master's heels, but requite by noble deeds of combat the trust placed in him by his prince, who had chosen him to be his single partner in the battle. The other complied, and when shame drove him to fight at close quarters, Uffe clove him through with the first stroke of his blade. The sound revived Wermund, who said that he heard the sword of his son, and asked "on what particular part he had dealt the blow?" Then the retainers answered that it had gone through no one limb, but the man's whole frame; whereat Wermund drew back from the precipice and came on the bridge, longing now as passionately to live as he had just wished to die. Then Uffe, wishing to destroy his remaining foe after the fashion of the first, incited the prince with vehement words to offer some sacrifice by way of requital to the shade of the servant slain in his cause. Drawing him by those appeals, and warily noting the right spot to plant his blow, he turned the other edge of his sword to the front, fearing that the thin side of his blade was too frail for his strength, and smote with a piercing stroke through the prince's body. When Wermund heard it, he said that the sound of his sword "Skrep" had reached his ear for the second time. Then, when the judges announced that his son had killed both enemies, he burst into tears from excess of joy. Thus gladness bedewed the cheeks which sorrow could not moisten. So while the Saxons, sad and shamefaced, bore their champions to burial with bitter shame, the Danes welcomed Uffe and bounded for joy. Then no more was heard of the disgrace of the murder of Athisl, and there was an end of the taunts of the Saxons.

Thus the realm of Saxony was transferred to the Danes, and Uffe, after his father, undertook its government; and he, who had not been thought equal to administering a single kingdom properly, was now appointed to manage both. Most men have called him Olaf, and he has won the name of "the Gentle" for his forbearing spirit. His later deeds, lost in antiquity, have lacked formal record. But it may well be supposed that when their beginnings were so notable, their sequel was glorious. I am so brief in considering his doings, because the lustre of the famous men of our nation has been lost to memory and praise by the lack of writings. But if by good luck our land had in old time been endowed with the Latin tongue, there would have been countless volumes to read of the exploits of the Danes.

Uffe was succeeded by his son DAN, who carried his arms against foreigners, and increased his sovereignty with many a trophy; but he tarnished the brightness of the glory he had won by foul and abominable presumption; falling so far away from the honour of his famous father, who surpassed all others in modesty, that he contrariwise was puffed up and proudly exalted in spirit, so that he scorned all other men. He also squandered the goods of his father on infamies, as well as his own winnings from the spoils of foreign nations;

and he devoured in expenditure on luxuries the wealth which should have ministered to his royal estate. Thus do sons sometimes, like monstrous births, degenerate from their ancestors.

After this HUGLEIK was king, who is said to have defeated in battle at sea Homod and Hogrim, the despots of Sweden.

To him succeeded FRODE, surnamed the Vigorous, who bore out his name by the strength of his body and mind. He destroyed in war ten captains of Norway, and finally approached the island which afterwards had its name from him, meaning to attack the king himself last of all. This king, Froger, was in two ways very distinguished, being notable in arms no less than in wealth; and graced his sovereignty with the deeds of a champion, being as rich in prizes for bodily feats as in the honours of rank. According to some, he was the son of Odin, and when he begged the immortal gods to grant him a boon, received the privilege that no man should conquer him, save he who at the time of the conflict could catch up in his hand the dust lying beneath Froger's feet. When Frode found that Heaven had endowed this king with such might, he challenged him to a duel, meaning to try to outwit the favour of the gods. So at first, feigning inexperience, he besought the king for a lesson in fighting, knowing (he said) his skill and experience in the same. The other, rejoicing that his enemy not only yielded to his pretensions, but even made him a request, said that he was wise to submit his youthful mind to an old man's wisdom; for his unscarred face and his brow, ploughed by no marks of battle, showed that his knowledge of such matters was but slender. So he marked off on the ground two square spaces with sides an ell long, opposite one another, meaning to begin by instructing him about the use of these plots. When they had been marked off, each took the side assigned to him. Then Frode asked Froger to exchange arms and ground with him, and the request was readily granted. For Froger was excited with the dashing of his enemy's arms, because Frode wore a gold-hilted sword, a breastplate equally bright, and a headpiece most brilliantly adorned in the same manner. So Frode caught up some dust from the ground whence Froger had gone, and thought that he had been granted an omen of victory. Nor was he deceived in his presage; for he straightway slew Froger, and by this petty trick won the greatest name for bravery; for he gained by craft what had been permitted to no man's strength before.

After him DAN came to the throne. When he was in the twelfth year of his age, he was wearied by the insolence of the embassies, which commanded him either to fight the Saxons or to pay them tribute. Ashamed, he preferred fighting to payment and was moved to die

154

stoutly rather than live a coward. So he elected to fight; and the warriors of the Danes filled the Elbe with such a throng of vessels, that the decks of the ships lashed together made it quite easy to cross, as though along a continuous bridge. The end was that the King of Saxony had to accept the very terms he was demanding from the Danes.

After Dan, FRIDLEIF, surnamed the Swift, assumed the sovereignty. During his reign, Huyrwil, the lord of Oland, made a league with the Danes and attacked Norway. No small fame was added to his deeds by the defeat of the amazon Rusila, who aspired with military ardour to prowess in battle: but he gained manly glory over a female foe. Also he took into his alliance, on account of their deeds of prowess, her five partners, the children of Finn, named Brodd, Bild, Bug, Fanning, and Gunholm. Their confederacy emboldened him to break the treaty which he made with the Danes; and the treachery of the violation made it all the more injurious, for the Danes could not believe that he could turn so suddenly from a friend into an enemy; so easily can some veer from goodwill into hate. I suppose that this man inaugurated the morals of our own day, for we do not account lying and treachery as sinful and sordid. When Huyrwil attacked the southern side of Zealand, Fridleif assailed him in the harbour which was afterwards called by Huyrwil's name. In this battle the soldiers, in their rivalry for glory, engaged with such bravery that very few fled to escape peril, and both armies were utterly destroyed; nor did the victory fall to either side, where both were enveloped in an equal ruin. So much more desirous were they all of glory than of life. So the survivors of Huyrwil's army, in order to keep united, had the remnants of their fleet lashed together at night. But, in the same night, Bild and Brodd cut the cables with which the ships were joined, and stealthily severed their own vessels from the rest, thus yielding to their own terrors by deserting their brethren, and obeying the impulses of fear rather than fraternal love. When daylight returned, Fridleif, finding that after the great massacre of their friends only Huyrwil, Gunholm, Bug, and Fanning were left, determined to fight them all single-handed, so that the mangled relics of his fleet might not again have to be imperilled. Besides his innate courage, a shirt of steel-defying mail gave him confidence; a garb which he used to wear in all public battles and in duels, as a preservative of his life. He accomplished his end with as much fortune as courage, and ended the battle successfully. For, after slaying Huyrwil, Bug, and Fanning, he killed Gunholm, who was accustomed to blunt the blade of an enemy with spells, by a shower of blows from his hilt. But while he gripped the blade too eagerly, the sinews, being cut and disabled, contracted the fingers upon the palm, and cramped them with life-long curvature.

While Fridleif was besieging Dublin, a town in Ireland, and saw from the strength of the walls that there was no chance of storming them, he imitated the shrewd wit of Hadding, and ordered fire to be shut up in wicks and fastened to the wings of swallows. When the birds got back in their own nesting-place, the dwellings suddenly flared up; and while the citizens all ran up to quench them, and paid more heed to abating the fire than to looking after the enemy, Fridleif took Dublin. After this he lost his soldiers in Britain, and, thinking that he would find it hard to get back to the coast, he set up the corpses of the slain (Amleth's device) and stationed them in line, thus producing so nearly the look of his original host that its great reverse seemed not to have lessened the show of it a whit. By this deed he not only took out of the enemy all heart for fighting, but inspired them with the desire to make their escape.

ENDNOTES:

(1) Jellinge. Lat. "Ialunga", Icel. "Jalangr".

(2) General usage. "publicus consuetudini": namely, the rule of combat that two should not fight against one.

Amleth's Last Interview with his British Wife

BOOK FIVE

After the death of Fridleif, his son FRODE, aged seven, was elected in his stead by the unanimous decision of the Danes. But they held an assembly first, and judged that the minority of the king should be taken in charge by guardians, lest the sovereignty should pass away owing to the boyishness of the ruler. For one and all paid such respect to the name and memory of Fridleif, that the royalty was bestowed on his son despite his tender years. So a selection was made, and the brothers Westmar and Koll were summoned to the charge of bringing up the king. Isulf, also, and Agg and eight other men of mark were not only entrusted with the guardianship of the king, but also granted authority to administer the realm under him. These men were rich in strength and courage, and endowed with ample gifts of mind as well as of body. Thus the state of the Danes was governed with the aid of regents until the time when the king should be a man.

The wife of Koll was Gotwar, who used to paralyse the most eloquent and fluent men by her glib and extraordinary insolence; for she was potent in wrangling, and full of resource in all kinds of disputation. Words were her weapons; and she not only trusted in questions, but was armed with stubborn answers. No man could subdue this woman, who could not fight, but who found darts in her tongue instead. Some she would argue down with a flood of impudent words, while others she seemed to entangle in the meshes of her quibbles, and strangle in the noose of her sophistries; so nimble a wit had the woman. Moreover, she was very strong, either in making or cancelling a bargain, and the sting of her tongue was the secret of her power in both. She was clever both at making and at breaking leagues; thus she had two sides to her tongue, and used it for either purpose.

Westmar had twelve sons, three of whom had the same name—Grep in common. These three men were conceived at once and delivered at one birth, and their common name declared their simultaneous origin. They were exceedingly skillful swordsmen and boxers. Frode had also given the supremacy of the sea to Odd; who was very closely related to the king. Koll rejoiced in an offspring of three sons. At this time a certain son of Frode's brother held the chief command of naval affairs for the protection of the country, Now the king had a sister, Gunwar, surnamed the Fair because of her surpassing beauty. The sons of Westmar and Koll, being ungrown in years and bold in spirit, let their courage become recklessness and devoted their guilt-stained minds to foul and degraded orgies.

Their behaviour was so outrageous and uncontrollable that they ravished other men's brides and daughters, and seemed to have outlawed chastity and banished it to the stews. Nay, they defiled the couches of matrons, and did not even refrain from the bed of virgins. A man's own chamber was no safety to him: there was scarce a spot in the land but bore traces of their lust. Husbands were vexed with fear, and wives with insult to their persons: and to these wrongs folk bowed. No ties were respected, and forced embraces became a common thing. Love was prostituted, all reverence for marriage ties died out, and lust was greedily run after. And the reason of all this was the peace; for men's bodies lacked exercise and were enervated in the ease so propitious to vices. At last the eldest of those who shared the name of Grep, wishing to regulate and steady his promiscuous wantonness, ventured to seek a haven for his vagrant amours in the love of the king's sister. Yet he did amiss. For though it was right that his vagabond and straying delights should be bridled by modesty, yet it was audacious for a man of the people to covet the child of a king. She, much fearing the impudence of her wooer, and wishing to be safer from outrage, went into a fortified building. Thirty attendants were given to her, to keep guard and constant watch over her person.

Now the comrades of Frode, sadly lacking the help of women in the matter of the wear of their garments, inasmuch as they had no means of patching or of repairing rents, advised and urged the king to marry. At first he alleged his tender years as an excuse, but in the end yielded to the persistent requests of his people. And when he carefully inquired of his advisers who would be a fit wife for him, they all praised the daughter of the King of the Huns beyond the rest. When the question was pushed, what reason Frode had for objecting to her, he replied that he had heard from his father that it was not expedient for kings to seek alliance far afield, or to demand love save from neighbours. When Gotwar heard this she knew that the king's resistance to his friends was wily. Wishing to establish his wavering spirit, and strengthen the courage of his weakling soul, she said: "Bridals are for young men, but the tomb awaits the old. The steps of youth go forward in desires and in fortune; but old age declines helpless to the sepulchre. Hope attends youth; age is bowed with hopeless decay. The fortune of young men increases; it will never leave unfinished what it begins." Respecting her words, he begged her to undertake the management of the suit. But she refused, pleading her age as her pretext, and declaring herself too stricken in years to bear so difficult a commission. The king saw that a bribe was wanted, and, proffering a golden necklace, promised it as the reward of her embassy. For the necklace had links consisting of studs, and figures of kings interspersed in bas-relief, which could be now separated and now drawn together by pulling a thread inside; a gewgaw devised more for luxury than use. Frode also ordered that Westmar and

Koll, with their sons, should be summoned to go on the same embassy, thinking that their cunning would avoid the shame of a rebuff.

They went with Gotwar, and were entertained by the King of the Huns at a three days' banquet, ere they uttered the purpose of their embassy. For it was customary of old thus to welcome guests. When the feast had been prolonged three days, the princess came forth to make herself pleasant to the envoys with a most courteous address, and her blithe presence added not a little to the festal delights of the banqueters. And as the drink went faster Westmar revealed his purpose in due course, in a very merry declaration, wishing to sound the mind of the maiden in talk of a friendly sort. And, in order not to inflict on himself a rebuff, he spoke in a mirthful vein, and broke the ground of his mission, by venturing to make up a sportive speech amid the applause of the revellers. The princess said that she disdained Frode because he lacked honour and glory. For in days of old no men were thought fit for the hand of high-born women but those who had won some great prize of glory by the lustre of their admirable deeds. Sloth was the worst of vices in a suitor, and nothing was more of a reproach in one who sought marriage than the lack of fame. A harvest of glory, and that alone, could bring wealth in everything else. Maidens admired in their wooers not so much good looks as deeds nobly done. So the envoys, flagging and despairing of their wish, left the further conduct of the affair to the wisdom of Gotwar, who tried to subdue the maiden not only with words but with love-philtres, and began to declare that Frode used his left hand as well as his right, and was a quick and skillful swimmer and fighter. Also by the drink which she gave she changed the strictness of the maiden to desire, and replaced her vanished anger with love and delight. Then she bade Westmar, Koll, and their sons go to the king and urge their mission afresh; and finally, should they find him froward, to anticipate a rebuff by a challenge to fight.

So Westmar entered the palace with his men-at-arms, and said: "Now thou must needs either consent to our entreaties, or meet in battle us who entreat thee. We would rather die nobly than go back with our mission unperformed; lest, foully repulsed and foiled of our purpose, we should take home disgrace where we hoped to will honour. If thou refuse thy daughter, consent to fight: thou must needs grant one thing or the other. We wish either to die or to have our prayers beard. Something—sorrow if not joy—we will get from thee. Frode will be better pleased to hear of our slaughter than of our repulse." Without another word, he threatened to aim a blow at the king's throat with his sword. The king replied that it was unseemly for the royal majesty to meet an inferior in rank in level combat, and unfit that those of unequal station should fight as equals. But when Westmar persisted in urging him to fight, he at last bade him find out what the real mind of the maiden was; for in old time men gave women who were to marry, free choice of a husband. For the king was embarrassed, and hung vacillating betwixt shame and fear of battle. Thus Westmar, having been referred to the thoughts of the girl's heart, and knowing that every woman is as changeable in purpose as she is fickle in soul, proceeded to fulfil his task all the more confidently because he knew how mutable the wishes of maidens were. His confidence in his charge was increased and his zeal encouraged, because she had both a maiden's simplicity, which was left to its own counsels, and a woman's freedom of choice, which must be wheedled with the most delicate and mollifying flatteries; and thus she would be not only easy to lead away, but even hasty in compliance. But her father went after the envoys, that he might see more surely into his daughter's mind. She had already been drawn by the stealthy working of the draught to love her suitor, and answered that the promise of Frode, rather than his present renown, had made her expect much of his nature: since he was sprung from so famous a father, and every nature commonly answered to its origin. The youth therefore had pleased her by her regard of his future, rather than his present, glory. These words amazed the father; but neither could he bear to revoke the freedom he had granted her, and he promised her in marriage to Frode. Then, having laid in ample stores, he took her away with the most splendid pomp, and, followed by the envoys, hastened to Denmark, knowing that a father was the best person to give away a daughter in marriage. Frode welcomed his bride most joyfully, and also bestowed the highest honours upon his future royal father-in-law; and when the marriage rites were over, dismissed him with a large gift of gold and silver.

And so with Hanund, the daughter of the King of the Huns, for his wife, he passed three years in the most prosperous peace. But idleness brought wantonness among his courtiers, and peace begot lewdness, which they displayed in the most abominable crimes. For they would draw some men up in the air on ropes, and torment them, pushing their bodies as they hung, like a ball that is tossed; or they would put a kid's hide under the feet of others as they walked, and, by stealthily pulling a rope, trip their unwary steps on the slippery skin in their path; others they would strip of their clothes, and lash with sundry tortures of stripes; others they fastened to pegs, as with a noose, and punished with mock-hanging. They scorched off the beard and hair with tapers; of others they burned the hair of the groin with a brand. Only those maidens might marry whose chastity they had first deflowered. Strangers they battered with bones; others they compelled to drunkenness with immoderate draughts, and made them burst. No man might give his daughter to wife unless he had first bought their favour and goodwill.

161

None might contract any marriage without first purchasing their consent with a bribe. Moreover, they extended their abominable and abandoned lust not only to virgins, but to the multitude of matrons indiscriminately. Thus a twofold madness incited this mixture of wantonness and frenzy. Guests and strangers were proffered not shelter but revilings. All these maddening mockeries did this insolent and wanton crew devise, and thus under a boy-king freedom fostered licence. For nothing prolongs reckless sin like the procrastination of punishment and vengeance. This unbridled impudence of the soldiers ended by making the king detested, not only by foreigners, but even by his own people, for the Danes resented such an arrogant and cruel rule. But Grep was contented with no humble loves; he broke out so outrageously that he was guilty of intercourse with the queen, and proved as false to the king as he was violent to all other men. Then by degrees the scandal grew, and the suspicion of his guilt crept on with silent step. The common people found it out before the king. For Grep, by always punishing all who alluded in the least to this circumstance, had made it dangerous to accuse him. But the rumour of his crime, which at first was kept alive in whispers, was next passed on in public reports; for it is hard for men to hide another's guilt if they are aware of it. Gunwar had many suitors; and accordingly Grep, trying to take revenge for his rebuff by stealthy wiles, demanded the right of judging the suitors, declaring that the princess ought to make the choicest match. But he disguised his anger, lest he should seem to have sought the office from hatred of the maiden. At his request the king granted him leave to examine the merits of the young men. So he first gathered all the wooers of Gunwar together on the pretence of a banquet, and then lined the customary room of the princess with their heads—a gruesome spectacle for all the rest. Yet he forfeited none of his favour with Frode, nor abated his old intimacy with him. For he decided that any opportunity of an interview with the king must be paid for, and gave out that no one should have any conversation with him who brought no presents. Access, he announced, to so great a general must be gained by no stale or usual method, but by making interest most zealously. He wished to lighten the scandal of his cruelty by the pretence of affection to his king. The people, thus tormented, vented their complaint of their trouble in silent groans. None had the spirit to lift up his voice in public against this season of misery. No one had become so bold as to complain openly of the affliction that was falling upon them. Inward resentment vexed the hearts of men, secretly indeed, but all the more bitterly.

When Gotar, the King of Norway, heard this, he assembled his soldiers, and said that the Danes were disgusted with their own king, and longed for another if they could get the opportunity; that he had himself resolved to lead an army thither, and that Denmark would be easy to seize if attacked. Frode's government of his country was as covetous as it was cruel. Then Erik rose up and gainsaid the project with contrary reasons. "We remember," he said, "how often coveters of other men's goods lose their own. He who snatches at both has oft lost both. It must be a very strong bird that can wrest the prey from the claws of another. It is idle for thee to be encouraged by the internal jealousies of the country, for these are oft blown away by the approach of an enemy. For though the Danes now seem divided in counsel, yet they will soon be of one mind to meet the foe. The wolves have often made peace between the quarrelling swine. Every man prefers a leader of his own land to a foreigner, and every province is warmer in loyalty to a native than to a stranger king. For Frode will not await thee at home, but will intercept thee abroad as thou comest. Eagles claw each other with their talons, and fowls fight fronting. Thou thyself knowest that the keen sight of the wise man must leave no cause for repentance. Thou hast an ample guard of nobles. Keep thou quiet as thou art; indeed thou wilt almost be able to find out by means of others what are thy resources for war. Let the soldiers first try the fortunes of their king. Provide in peace for thine own safety, and risk others if thou dost undertake the enterprise: better that the slave should perish than the master. Let thy servant do for thee what the tongs do for the smith, who by the aid of his iron tool guards his hand from scorching, and saves his fingers from burning. Learn thou also, by using thy men, to spare and take thought for thyself."

So spake Erik, and Gotar, who had hitherto held him a man of no parts, now marvelled that he had graced his answer with sentences so choice and weighty, and gave him the name of Shrewd-spoken, thinking that his admirable wisdom deserved some title. For the young man's reputation had been kept in the shade by the exceeding brilliancy of his brother Roller. Erik begged that some substantial gift should be added to the name, declaring that the bestowal of the title ought to be graced by a present besides. The king gave him a ship, and the oarsmen called it "Skroter." Now Erik and Roller were the sons of Ragnar, the champion, and children of one father by different mothers; Roller's mother and Erik's stepmother was named Kraka.

And so, by leave of Gotar, the task of making a raid on the Danes fell to one Hrafn. He was encountered by Odd, who had at that time the greatest prestige among the Danes as a rover, for he was such a skilled magician that he could range over the sea without a ship, and could often raise tempests by his spells, and wreck the vessels of the enemy. Accordingly, that he might not have to condescend to pit his sea-forces against the rovers, he used to ruffle the waters by enchantment, and cause them to shipwreck his foes. To traders this man was ruthless, but to tillers of the soil he was merciful, for he thought less of merchandise than of the plough-handle, but rated the clean business of the country higher than the toil for filthy lucre. When he began to fight with the Northmen he so dulled the sight of the enemy by the power of his spells that they thought the drawn swords of the Danes cast their beams from afar off, and sparkled as if aflame. Moreover, their vision was so blunted that they could not so much as look upon the sword when it was drawn from the sheath: the dazzle was too much for their eyesight, which could not endure the glittering mirage. So Hrafn and many of his men were slain, and only six vessels slipped back to Norway to teach the king that it was not so easy to crush the Danes. The survivors also spread the news that Frode trusted only in the help of his champions, and reigned against the will of his people, for his rule had become a tyranny.

In order to examine this rumour, Roller, who was a great traveller abroad, and eager to visit unknown parts, made a vow that he would get into the company of Frode. But Erik declared that, splendid as were his bodily parts, he had been rash in pronouncing the vow. At last, seeing him persisting stubbornly in his purpose, Erik bound himself under a similar vow; and the king promised them that he would give them for companions whomsoever they approved by their choice. The brethren, therefore, first resolved to visit their father and beg for the stores and the necessaries that were wanted for so long a journey. He welcomed them paternally, and on the morrow took them to the forest to inspect the herd, for the old man was wealthy in cattle. Also he revealed to them treasures which had long lain hid in caverns of the earth; and they were suffered to gather up whatsoever of these they would. The boon was accepted as heartily as it was offered: so they took the riches out of the ground, and bore away what pleased them.

Their rowers meanwhile were either refreshing themselves or exercising their skill with casting weights. Some sped leaping, some running; others tried their strength by sturdily hurling stones; others tested their archery by drawing the bow. Thus they essayed to strengthen themselves with divers exercises. Some again tried to drink themselves into a drowse. Roller was sent by his father to find out what had passed at home in the meanwhile. And when he saw smoke coming from his mother's hut he went up outside, and, stealthily applying his eye, saw through the little chink and into the house, where he perceived his mother stirring a cooked mess in an ugly-looking pot. Also he looked up at three snakes hanging from above by a thin cord, from whose mouths flowed a slaver which dribbled drops of moisture on the meal. Now two of these were pitchy of hue, while the third seemed to have whitish scales, and was hung somewhat higher than the others. This last had a fastening on its tail, while the others were held by a cord round their bellies. Roller thought the affair looked like magic, but was silent on what he had seen, that he might not be thought to charge his mother with sorcery. For he did not know that the snakes were naturally harmless, or how much strength was being brewed for that meal. Then Ragnar and Erik came up, and, when they saw the smoke issuing from the cottage, entered and went to sit at meat. When they were at table, and Kraka's son and stepson were about to eat together, she put before them a small dish containing a piebald mess, part looking pitchy, but spotted with specks of yellow, while part was whitish: the pottage having taken a different hue answering to the different appearance of the snakes. And when each had tasted a single morsel, Erik, judging the feast not by the colours but by the inward strengthening effected, turned the dish around very quickly, and transferred to himself the part which was black but compounded of stronger juices; and, putting over to Roller the whitish part which had first been set before himself, throve more on his supper. And, to avoid showing that the exchange was made on purpose, he said, "Thus does prow become stern when the sea boils up." The man had no little shrewdness, thus to use the ways of a ship to dissemble his cunning act.

So Erik, now refreshed by this lucky meal, attained by its inward working to the highest pitch of human wisdom. For the potency of the meal bred in him the fulness of all kinds of knowledge to an incredible degree, so that he had cunning to interpret even the utterances of wild beasts and cattle. For he was not only well versed in all the affairs of men, but he could interpret the particular feelings which brutes experienced from the sounds which expressed them. He was also gifted with an eloquence so courteous and graceful, that he adorned whatsoever he desired to expound with a flow of witty adages. But when Kraka came up, and found that the dish had been turned round, and that Erik had eaten the stronger share of the meal, she lamented that the good luck she had bred for her son should have passed to her stepson. Soon she began to sigh, and entreat Eric that he should never fail to help his brother, whose mother had heaped on him fortune so rich and strange: for by tasting a single savoury meal he had clearly attained sovereign wit and eloquence, besides the promise of success in combat. She added also, that Roller was almost as capable of good counsel, and that he should not utterly miss the dainty that had been intended for him. She also told him that in case of extreme and violent need, he could find speedy help by calling on her name; declaring that she trusted partially in her divine attributes, and that, consorting as she did in a manner with the gods, she wielded an innate and heavenly power. Erik said that he was naturally drawn to stand by his brother, and that the bird was infamous which fouled its own nest. But Kraka was more vexed by her own carelessness than weighed down by her son's ill-fortune: for in old time it made a craftsman bitterly ashamed to be outwitted by his own cleverness.

Then Kraka, accompanied by her husband, took away the brothers on their journey to the sea. They embarked in a single ship, but soon attached two others. They had already reached the coast of Denmark, when, reconnoitering, they learned that seven ships had come up at no great distance. Then Erik bade two men who could speak the Danish tongue well, to go to them unclothed, and, in order to spy better, to complain to Odd of their nakedness, as if Erik had caused it, and to report when they had made careful scrutiny. These men were received as friends by Odd, and hunted for every plan of the general with their sharp ears. He had determined to attack the enemy unawares at daybreak, that he might massacre them the more speedily while they were swathed in their night garments: for he said that men's bodies were wont to be most dull and heavy at that hour of dawn. He also told them, thereby hastening what was to prove his own destruction, that his ships were laden with stones fit for throwing. The spies slipped off in the first sleep of the night, reported that Odd had filled all his vessels with pebbles, and also told everything else they had heard. Erik now quite understood the case, and, when he considered the smallness of his own fleet, thought that he must call the waters to destroy the enemy, and win their aid for himself.

So he got into a boat and rowed, pulling silently, close up to the keels of the enemy; and gradually, by screwing in an auger, he bored the planks (a device practiced by Hadding and also by Frode), nearest to the water, and soon made good his return, the oar-beat being scarce audible. Now he bore himself so warily, that not one of the watchers noted his approach or departure. As he rowed off, the water got in through the chinks of Odd's vessels, and sank them, so that they were seen disappearing in the deep, as the water flooded them more and more within. The weight of the stones inside helped them mightily to sink. The billows were washing away the thwarts, and the sea was flush with the decks, when Odd, seeing the vessels almost on a level with the waves, ordered the heavy seas that had been shipped to be baled out with pitchers. And so, while the crews were toiling on to protect the sinking parts of the vessels from the flood of waters, the enemy hove close up. Thus, as they fell to their arms, the flood came upon them harder, and as they prepared to fight, they found they must swim for it. Waves, not weapons, fought for Erik, and the sea, which he had himself Enabled to approach and do harm, battled for him. Thus Erik made better use of the billow than of the steel, and by the effectual aid of the waters seemed to fight in his own absence, the ocean lending him defence. The victory was given to his craft; for a flooded ship could not endure a battle. Thus was Odd slain with all his crew; the look-outs were captured, and it was found that no man escaped to tell the tale of the disaster.

Erik, when the massacre was accomplished, made a rapid retreat, and put in at the isle Lesso. Finding nothing there to appease his hunger, he sent the spoil homeward on two ships, which were to bring back supplies for another year. He tried to go by himself to the king in a single ship. So he put in to Zealand, and the sailors ran about over the shore, and began to cut down the cattle: for they must either ease their hunger or perish of famine. So they killed the herd, skinned the carcases, and cast them on board. When the owners of the cattle found this out, they hastily pursued the free-booters with a fleet. And when Erik found that he was being attacked by the owners of the cattle, he took care that the carcases of the slaughtered cows should be tied with marked ropes and hidden under water. Then, when the Zealanders came up, he gave them leave to look about and see if any of the carcases they were seeking were in his hands; saying that a ship's corners were too narrow to hide things. Unable to find a carcase anywhere, they turned their suspicions on others, and thought the real criminals were guiltless of the plunder. Since no traces of free-booting were to be seen, they fancied that others had injured them, and pardoned the culprits. As they sailed off, Erik lifted the carcase out of the water and took it in.

Meantime Frode learnt that Odd and his men had gone down. For a widespread rumour of the massacre had got wind, though the author of the deed was unknown. There were men, however, who told how they had seen three sails putting in to shore, and departing again northwards. Then Erik went to the harbour, not far from which Frode was tarrying, and, the moment that he stepped out of the ship, tripped inadvertently, and came tumbling to the ground. He found in the slip a presage of a lucky issue, and forecast better results from this mean beginning. When Grep heard of his coming, he hastened down to the sea, intending to assail with chosen and pointed phrases the man whom he had heard was better-spoken than all other folk. Grep's eloquence was not so much excellent as impudent, for he surpassed all in stubbornness of speech. So he began the dispute with reviling, and assailed Erik as follows:

Grep: "Fool, who art thou? What idle quest is thine? Tell me, whence or whither dost thou journey? What is thy road? What thy desire? Who thy father? What thy lineage? Those have strength beyond others who have never left their own homes, and the Luck of kings is their houseluck. For the things of a vile man are acceptable unto few, and seldom are the deeds of the hated pleasing."

Erik: "Ragnar is my father; eloquence clothes my tongue; I have ever loved virtue only. Wisdom hath been my one desire; I have travelled many ways over the world, and seen the different manners of men. The mind of the fool can keep no bounds in aught: it is base and cannot control its feelings. The use of sails is better than being drawn by the oar; the gale troubles the waters, a drearier gust the land. For rowing goes through the seas and lying the lands; and it is certain that the lands are ruled with the lips, but the seas with the hand."

Grep: "Thou art thought to be as full of quibbling as a cock of dirt. Thou stinkest heavy with filth, and reekest of nought but sin. There is no need to lengthen the plea against a buffoon, whose strength is in an empty and voluble tongue."

Erik: "By Hercules, if I mistake not, the coward word is wont to come back to the utterer. The gods with righteous endeavour bring home to the speaker words cast forth without knowledge. As soon as we espy the sinister ears of the wolf, we believe that the wolf himself is near. Men think no credit due to him that hath no credit, whom report accuses of treachery."

Grep: "Shameless boy, owl astray from the path, night-owl in the darkness, thou shalt pay for thy reckless words. Thou shalt be sorry for the words thou now belchest forth madly, and shalt pay with thy death for thy unhallowed speech. Lifeless thou shalt pasture crows on thy bloodless corpse, to be a morsel for beasts, a prey to the ravenous bird."

Erik: "The boding of the coward, and the will that is trained to evil, have never kept themselves within due measure. He who betrays his lord, he who conceives foul devices, will be as great a snare to himself as to his friends. Whoso fosters a wolf in his house is thought to feed a thief and a pest for his own hearth."

Grep: "I did not, as thou thinkest, beguile the queen, but I was the guardian of her tender estate. She increased my fortunes, and her favour first brought me gifts and strength, and wealth and counsel."

Erik: "Lo, thy guilty disquiet lies heavy on thee; that man's freedom is safest whose mind remains untainted. Whoso asks a slave to be a friend, is deceived; often the henchman hurts his master."

At this Grep, shorn of his glibness of rejoinder, set spurs to his horse and rode away. Now when he reached home, he filled the palace with uproarious and vehement clamour; and shouting that he had been worsted in words, roused all his soldiers to fight, as though he would avenge by main force his luckless warfare of tongues. For he swore that he would lay the host of the foreigners under the claws of eagles. But the king warned him that he should give his frenzy pause for counsel, that blind plans were commonly hurtful; that nothing could be done both cautiously and quickly at once; that headstrong efforts were the worst obstacle; and lastly, that it was unseemly to attack a handful with a host. Also, said he, the sagacious man was he who could bridle a raging spirit, and stop his frantic empetuosity in time. Thus the king forced the headlong rage of the young man to yield to reflection. But he could not wholly recall to self-control the frenzy of his heated mind, or prevent the champion of wrangles, abashed by his hapless debate, and finding armed vengeance refused him, from asking leave at least to try his sorceries by way of revenge. He gained his request, and prepared to go back to the shore with a chosen troop of wizards. So he first put on a pole the severed head of a horse that had been sacrificed to the gods, and setting sticks beneath displayed the jaws grinning agape; hoping that he would foil the first efforts of Erik by the horror of this wild spectacle. For he supposed that the silly souls of the barbarians would give away at the bogey of a protruding neck.

Erik was already on his road to meet them, and saw the head from afar off, and, understanding the whole foul contrivance, he bade his men keep silent and behave warily; no man was to be rash or hasty of speech, lest by some careless outburst they might give some opening to the sorceries; adding that if talking happened to be needed, he would speak for all. And they were now parted by a river; when the wizards, in order to dislodge Erik from the approach to the bridge, set up close to the river, on their own side, the pole on which they had fixed the horse's head. Nevertheless Erik made dauntlessly for the bridge, and said: "On the bearer fall the ill-luck of what he bears! May a better issue attend our steps! Evil befall the evil-workers! Let the weight of the ominous burden crush the carrier! Let the better auguries bring us safety!" And it happened according to his prayer. For straightway the head was shaken off, the stick fell and crushed the bearer. And so all that array of sorceries was baffled at the bidding of a single curse, and extinguished.

Then, as Erik advanced a little, it came into his mind that strangers ought to fix on gifts for the king. So he carefully wrapped up in his robe a piece of ice which he happened to find, and managed to take it to the king by way of a present. But when they reached the palace he sought entrance first, and bade his brother follow close behind. Already the slaves of the king, in order to receive him with mockery as he entered,

169

had laid a slippery hide on the threshold; and when Erik stepped upon it, they suddenly jerked it away by dragging a rope, and would have tripped him as he stood upon it, had not Roller, following behind, caught his brother on his breast as he tottered. So Erik, having half fallen, said that "bare was the back of the brotherless." And when Gunwar said that such a trick ought not to be permitted by a king, the king condemned the folly of the messenger who took no heed against treachery. And thus he excused his flout by the heedlessness of the man he flouted.

Within the palace was blazing a fire, which the aspect of the season required: for it was now gone midwinter. By it, in different groups, sat the king on one side and the champions on the other. These latter, when Erik joined them, uttered gruesome sounds like things howling. The king stopped the clamour, telling them that the noises of wild beasts ought not to be in the breasts of men. Erik added, that it was the way of dogs, for all the others to set up barking when one started it; for all folk by their bearing betrayed their birth and revealed their race. But when Koll, who was the keeper of the gifts offered to the king, asked him whether he had brought any presents with him, he produced the ice which he had hidden in his breast. And when he had handed it to Koll across the hearth, he purposely let it go into the fire, as though it had slipped from the hand of the receiver. All present saw the shining fragment, and it seemed as though molten metal had fallen into the fire. Erik, maintaining that it had been jerked away by the carelessness of him who took it, asked what punishment was due to the loser of the gift.

The king consulted the opinion of the queen, who advised him not to relax the statute of the law which he had passed, whereby he gave warning that all who lost presents that were transmitted to him should be punished with death. Everyone else also said that the penalty by law appointed ought not to be remitted. And so the king, being counselled to allow the punishment as inevitable, gave leave for Koll to be hanged.

Then Frode began to accost Erik thus: "O thou, wantoning in insolent phrase, in boastful and bedizened speech, whence dost thou say that thou hast come hither, and why?"

Erik answered: "I came from Rennes Isle, and I took my seat by a stone."

Frode rejoined: "I ask, whither thou wentest next?"

Erik answered. "I went off from the stone riding on a beam, and often again took station by a stone."

170

Frode replied: "I ask thee whither thou next didst bend thy course, or where the evening found thee?"

Then said Erik: "Leaving a crag, I came to a rock, and likewise lay by a stone."

Frode said: "The boulders lay thick in those parts."
Erik answered: "Yet thicker lies the sand, plain to see."

Frode said: "Tell what thy business was, and whither thou struckest off thence."

Then said Erik: "Leaving the rock, as my ship ran on, I found a dolphin."

Frode said: "Now thou hast said something fresh, though both these things are common in the sea: but I would know what path took thee after that?"

Erik answered: "After a dolphin I went to a dolphin."

Frode said: "The herd of dolphins is somewhat common."

Then said Erik: "It does swim somewhat commonly on the waters."

Frode said: "I would fain blow whither thou wert borne on thy toilsome journey after leaving the dolphins?"

Erik answered: "I soon came upon the trunk of a tree."

Frode rejoined: "Whither didst thou next pass on thy journey?"

Then said Erik: "From a trunk I passed on to a log."

Frode said: "That spot must be thick with trees, since thou art always calling the abodes of thy hosts by the name of trunks."

Erik replied: "There is a thicker place in the woods."

Frode went on: "Relate whither thou next didst bear thy steps."

Erik answered: "Oft again I made my way to the lopped timbers of the woods; but, as I rested there, wolves that were sated on human carcases licked the points of the spears. There a lance-head was shaken from the shaft of the king, and it was the grandson of Fridleif."

Frode said: "I am bewildered, and know not what to think about the dispute: for thou hast beguiled my mind with very dark riddling."

Erik answered: "Thou owest me the prize for this contest that is finished: for under a veil I have declared to thee certain things thou hast ill understood. For under the name I gave before of `spear-point' I signified Odd, whom my hand had slain."

And when the queen also had awarded him the palm of eloquence and the prize for flow of speech, the king straightway took a bracelet from his arm, and gave it to him as the appointed reward, adding: "I would fain learn from thyself thy debate with Grep, wherein he was not ashamed openly to avow himself vanquished."

Then said Erik: "He was smitten with shame for the adultery wherewith he was taxed; for since he could bring no defence, he confessed that he had committed it with thy wife."

The king turned to Hanund and asked her in what spirit she received the charge; and she not only confessed her guilt by a cry, but also put forth in her face a blushing signal of her sin, and gave manifest token of her fault. The king, observing not only her words, but also the signs of her countenance, but doubting with what sentence he should punish the criminal, let the queen settle by her own choice the punishment which her crime deserved. When she learnt that the sentence committed to her concerned her own guilt, she wavered awhile as she pondered how to appraise her transgression; but Grep sprang up and ran forward to transfix Erik with a spear, wishing to buy off his own death by slaying the accuser. But Roller fell on him with drawn sword, and dealt him first the doom he had himself purposed.

Erik said: "The service of kin is best for the helpless."

And Roller said: "In sore needs good men should be dutifully summoned."

Then Frode said: "I think it will happen to you according to the common saying, `that the striker sometimes has short joy of his stroke', and `that the hand is seldom long glad of the smiting'."

Erik answered: "The man must not be impeached whose deed justice excuses. For my work is as far as from that of Grep, as an act of self-defence is from an attack upon another."

Then the brethren of Grep began to spring up and clamour and swear that they would either bring avengers upon the whole fleet of Erik, or would fight him and ten champions with him.

Erik said to them: "Sick men have to devise by craft some provision for their journey. He whose sword-point is dull should only probe things that are soft and tender. He who has a blunt knife must search out the ways to cut joint by joint. Since, therefore, it is best for a man in distress to delay the evil, and nothing is more fortunate in trouble than to stave off hard necessity, I ask three days' space to get ready, provided that I may obtain from the king the skill of a freshly slain ox."

Frode answered: "He who fell on a hide deserves a hide"; thus openly taunting the asker with his previous fall. But Erik, when the hide was given him, made some sandals, which he smeared with a mixture of tar and sand, in order to plant his steps the more firmly, and fitted them on to the feet of himself and his people. At last, having meditated what spot he should choose for the fight—for he said that he was unskilled in combat by land and in all warfare—he demanded it should be on the frozen sea. To this both sides agreed. The king granted a truce for preparations, and bade the sons of Westmar withdraw, saying that it was amiss that a guest, even if he had deserved ill should be driven from his lodging. Then he went back to examine into the manner of the punishment, which he had left to the queen's own choice to exact. For she forebore to give judgment, and begged pardon for her slip. Erik added, that woman's errors must often be forgiven, and that punishment ought not to be inflicted, unless amendment were unable to get rid of her fault. So the king pardoned Hanund. As twilight drew near, Erik said: "With Gotar, not only are rooms provided when the soldiers are coming to feast at the banquet, but each is appointed a separate place and seat where he is to lie." Then the king gave up for their occupation the places where his own champions had sat; and next the servants brought the banquet. But Erik, knowing well the courtesy of the king, which made him forbid them to use up any of the meal that was left, cast away the piece of which he had tasted very little, calling whole portions broken bits of food. And so, as the dishes dwindled, the servants brought up fresh ones to the lacking and shamefaced guests, thus spending on a little supper what might have served for a great banquet.

So the king said: "Are the soldiers of Gotar wont to squander the meat after once touching it, as if it were so many pared-off crusts? And to spurn the first dishes as if they were the last morsels?"

Erik said: "Uncouthness claims no place in the manners of Gotar, neither does any disorderly habit feign there."

173

But Frode said: "Then thy manners are not those of thy lord, and thou hast proved that thou hast not taken all wisdom to heart. For he who goes against the example of his elders shows himself a deserter and a renegade."

Then said Erik: "The wise man must be taught by the wiser. For knowledge grows by learning, and instruction is advanced by doctrine."

Frode rejoined: "This affectation of thine of superfluous words, what exemplary lesson will it teach me?"

Erik said: "A loyal few are a safer defence for a king than many traitors."

Frode said to him: "Wilt thou then show us closer allegiance than the rest?"

Erik answered: "No man ties the unborn (horse) to the crib, or the unbegotten to the stall. For thou hast not yet experienced all things. Besides, with Gotar there is always a mixture of drinking with feasting; liquor, over and above, and as well as meat, is the joy of the reveller."

Frode said: "Never have I found a more shameless beggar of meat and drink."

Erik replied: "Few reckon the need of the silent, or measure the wants of him who holds his peace."

Then the king bade his sister bring forth the drink in a great goblet. Erik caught hold of her right hand and of the goblet she offered at the same time, and said: "Noblest of kings, hath thy benignity granted me this present? Dost thou assure me that what I hold shall be mine as an irrevocable gift?"

The king, thinking that he was only asking for the cup, declared it was a gift. But Erik drew the maiden to him, as if she was given with the cup. When the king saw it, he said: "A fool is shown by his deed; with us freedom of maidens is ever held inviolate."
Then Erik, feigning that he would cut off the girl's hand with his sword, as though it had been granted under the name of the cup, said: "If I have taken more than thou gavest, or if I am rash to keep the whole, let me at least get some." The king saw his mistake in his promise, and gave him the maiden, being loth to undo his heedlessness by fickleness, and that the weight of his pledge might seem the greater; though it is held an act more of ripe judgment than of unsteadfastness

174

to take back a foolish promise.

Then, taking from Erik security that he would return, he sent him to the ships; for the time appointed for the battle was at hand. Erik and his men went on to the sea, then covered near with ice; and, thanks to the stability of their sandals, felled the enemy, whose footing was slippery and unsteady. For Frode had decreed that no man should help either side if it wavered or were distressed. Then he went back in triumph to the king. So Gotwar, sorrowing at the destruction of her children who had miserably perished, and eager to avenge them, announced that it would please her to have a flyting with Erik, on condition that she should gage a heavy necklace and he his life; so that if he conquered he should win gold, but if he gave in, death. Erik agreed to the contest, and the gage was deposited with Gunwar. So Gotwar began thus:

"Quando tuam limas admissa cote bipennem,
Nonne terit tremulas mentula quassa nates?"

Erik rejoined:

"Ut cuivis natura pilos in corpore sevit,
Omnis nempe suo barba ferenda loco est.
Re Veneris homines artus agitare necesse est;
Motus quippe suos nam labor omnis habet.
Cum natis excipitur nate, vel cum subdita penem
Vulva capit, quid ad haec addere mas renuit?"

Powerless to answer this, Gotwar had to give the gold to the man whom she had meant to kill, and thus wasted a lordly gift instead of punishing the slayer of her son. For her ill fate was crowned, instead of her ill-will being avenged. First bereaved, and then silenced by furious words, she lost at once her wealth and all reward of her eloquence. She made the man blest who had taken away her children, and enriched her bereaver with a present: and took away nothing to make up the slaughter of her sons save the reproach of ignorance and the loss of goods. Westmar, when he saw this, determined to attack the man by force, since he was the stronger of tongue, and laid down the condition that the reward of the conqueror should be the death of the conquered, so that the life of both parties was plainly at stake. Erik, unwilling to be thought quicker of tongue than of hand, did not refuse the terms.

Now the manner of combat was as follows. A ring, plaited of withy or rope, used to be offered to the combatants for them to drag away by wrenching it with a great effort of foot and hand; and the prize went to the stronger, for if either of the combatants could wrench it from the

175

other, he was awarded the victory. Erik struggled in this manner, and, grasping the rope sharply, wrested it out of the hands of his opponent. When Erode saw this, he said: "I think it is hard to tug at a rope with a strong man."

And Erik said: "Hard, at any rate, when a tumour is in the body or a hunch sits on the back."

And straightway, thrusting his foot forth, he broke the infirm neck and back of the old man, and crushed him. And so Westmar failed to compass his revenge: zealous to retaliate, he fell into the portion of those who need revenging; being smitten down even as those whose slaughter he had desired to punish.

Now Frode intended to pierce Erik by throwing a dagger at him. But Gunwar knew her brother's purpose, and said, in order to warn her betrothed of his peril, that no man could be wise who took no forethought for himself. This speech warned Erik to ward off the treachery, and he shrewdly understood the counsel of caution. For at once he sprang up and said that the glory of the wise man would be victorious, but that guile was its own punishment; thus censuring his treacherous intent in very gentle terms. But the king suddenly flung his knife at him, yet was too late to hit him; for he sprang aside, and the steel missed its mark and ran into the wall opposite. Then said Erik: "Gifts should be handed to friends, and not thrown; thou hadst made the present acceptable if thou hadst given the sheath to keep the blade company."

On this request the king at once took the sheath from his girdle and gave it to him, being forced to abate his hatred by the self-control of his foe. Thus he was mollified by the prudent feigning of the other, and with goodwill gave him for his own the weapon which he had cast with ill will. And thus Erik, by taking the wrong done him in a dissembling manner, turned it into a favour, accepting as a splendid gift the steel which had been meant to slay him. For he put a generous complexion on what Frode had done with intent to harm. Then they gave themselves up to rest. In the night Gunwar awoke Erik silently, and pointed out to him that they ought to fly, saying that it was very expedient to return with safe chariot ere harm was done. He went with her to the shore, where he happened to find the king's fleet beached: so, cutting away part of the sides, he made it unseaworthy, and by again replacing some laths he patched it so that the damage might be unnoticed by those who looked at it. Then he caused the vessel whither he and his company had retired to put off a little from the shore.

The king prepared to give them chase with his mutilated ships, but soon the waves broke through; and though he was very heavily laden with his armour, he began to swim off among the rest, having become more anxious to save his own life than to attack that of others. The bows plunged over into the sea, the tide flooded in and swept the rowers from their seats. When Erik and Roller saw this they instantly flung themselves into the deep water, spurning danger, and by swimming picked up the king, who was tossing about. Thrice the waves had poured over him and borne him down when Erik caught him by the hair, and lifted him out of the sea. The remaining crowd of the wrecked either sank in the waters, or got with trouble to the land. The king was stripped of his dripping attire and swathed round with dry garments, and the water poured in floods from his chest as he kept belching it; his voice also seemed to fail under the exhaustion of continual pantings. At last heat was restored to his limbs, which were numbed with cold, and his breathing became quicker. He had not fully got back his strength, and could sit but not rise. Gradually his native force returned. But when he was asked at last whether he sued for life and grace, he put his hand to his eyes, and strove to lift up their downcast gaze. But as, little by little, power came back to his body, and as his voice became more assured, he said:

"By this light, which I am loth to look on, by this heaven which I behold and drink in with little joy, I beseech and conjure you not to persuade me to use either any more. I wished to die; ye have saved me in vain. I was not allowed to perish in the waters; at least I will die by the sword. I was unconquered before; thine, Erik, was the first wit to which I yielded: I was all the more unhappy, because I had never been beaten by men of note, and now I let a low-born man defeat me. This is great cause for a king to be ashamed. This is a good and sufficient reason for a general to die; it is right that he should care for nothing so much as glory. If he want that, then take it that he lacks all else. For nothing about a king is more on men's lips than his repute. I was credited with the height of understanding and eloquence. But I have been stripped of both the things wherein I was thought to excel, and am all the more miserable because I, the conqueror of kings, am seen conquered by a peasant. Why grant life to him whom thou hast robbed of honour? I have lost sister, realm, treasure, household gear, and, what is greater than them all, renown: I am luckless in all chances, and in all thy good fortune is confessed. Why am I to be kept to live on for all this ignominy? What freedom can be so happy for me that it can wipe out all the shame of captivity? What will all the following time bring for me? It can beget nothing but long remorse in my mind, and will savour only of past woes. What will prolonging of life avail, if it only brings back the memory of sorrow? To the stricken nought is pleasanter than death, and that

177

decease is happy which comes at a man's wish, for it cuts not short any sweetness of his days, but annihilates his disgust at all things. Life in prosperity, but death in adversity, is best to seek. No hope of better things tempts me to long for life. What hap can quite repair my shattered fortunes? And by now, had ye not rescued me in my peril, I should have forgotten even these. What though thou shouldst give me back my realm, restore my sister, and renew my treasure? Thou canst never repair my renown. Nothing that is patched up can have the lustre of the unimpaired, and rumour will recount for ages that Frode was taken captive. Moreover, if ye reckon the calamities I have inflicted on you, I have deserved to die at your hands; if ye recall the harms I have done, ye will repent your kindness. Ye will be ashamed of having aided a foe, if ye consider how savagely he treated you. Why do ye spare the guilty? Why do ye stay your hand from the throat of your persecutor? It is fitting that the lot which I had prepared for you should come home to myself. I own that if I had happened to have you in my power as ye now have me, I should have paid no heed to compassion. But if I am innocent before you in act, I am guilty at least in will. I pray you, let my wrongful intention, which sometimes is counted to stand for the deed, recoil upon me. If ye refuse me death by the sword I will take care to kill myself with my own hand."

Erik rejoined thus: "I pray that the gods may turn thee from the folly of thy purpose; turn thee, I say, that thou mayst not try to end a most glorious life abominably. Why, surely the gods themselves have forbidden that a man who is kind to others should commit unnatural self-murder. Fortune has tried thee to find out with what spirit thou wouldst meet adversity. Destiny has proved thee, not brought thee low. No sorrow has been inflicted on thee which a happier lot cannot efface. Thy prosperity has not been changed; only a warning has been given thee. No man behaves with self-control in prosperity who has not learnt to endure adversity. Besides, the whole use of blessings is reaped after misfortunes have been graciously acknowledged. Sweeter is the joy which follows on the bitterness of fate. Wilt thou shun thy life because thou hast once had a drenching, and the waters closed over thee? But if the waters can crush thy spirit, when wilt thou with calm courage bear the sword? Who would not reckon swimming away in his armour more to his glory than to his shame? How many men would think themselves happy were they unhappy with thy fortune? The sovereignty is still thine; thy courage is in its prime; thy years are ripening; thou canst hope to compass more than thou hast yet achieved. I would not find thee fickle enough to wish, not only to shun hardships, but also to fling away thy life, because thou couldst not bear them. None is so unmanly as he who from fear of adversity loses heart to live. No wise man makes up for his calamities by dying. Wrath against another is foolish, but against a man's self it is foolhardy; and it is a coward frenzy which dooms its owner. But if thou go without need to thy death for some wrong suffered, or for some petty perturbation of spirit, whom dost thou leave behind to avenge thee? Who is so mad that he would wish to punish the fickleness of fortune by destroying himself? What man has lived so prosperously but that ill fate has sometimes stricken him? Hast thou enjoyed felicity unbroken and passed thy days without a shock, and now, upon a slight cloud of sadness, dost thou prepare to quit thy life, only to save thy anguish? If thou bear trifles so ill, how shalt thou endure the heavier frowns of fortune? Callow is the man who has never tasted of the cup of sorrow; and no man who has not suffered hardships is temperate in enjoying ease. Wilt thou, who shouldst have been a pillar of courage, show a sign of a palsied spirit? Born of a brave sire, wilt thou display utter impotence? Wilt thou fall so far from thy ancestors as to turn softer than women? Hast thou not yet begun thy prime, and art thou already taken with weariness of life? Whoever set such an example before? Shall the grandson of a famous man, and the child of the unvanquished, be too weak to endure a slight gust of adversity? Thy nature portrays the courage of thy sires; none has conquered thee, only thine own heedlessness has hurt thee. We snatched thee from peril, we did not subdue thee; wilt thou give us hatred for love, and set our friendship down as wrongdoing? Our service should have appeased thee, and not troubled thee. May the gods never desire thee to go so far in frenzy, as to persist in branding thy preserver as a traitor! Shall we be guilty before thee in a matter wherein we do thee good? Shall we draw anger on us for our service? Wilt thou account him thy foe whom thou hast to thank for thy life? For thou wert not free when we took thee, but in distress, and we came in time to help thee. And, behold, I restore thy treasure, thy wealth, thy goods. If thou thinkest thy sister was betrothed to me over-hastily, let her marry the man whom thou commandest; for her chastity remains inviolate. Moreover, if thou wilt accept me, I wish to fight for thee. Beware lest thou wrongfully steel thy mind in anger. No loss of power has shattered thee, none of thy freedom has been forfeited. Thou shalt see that I am obeying, not commanding thee. I agree to any sentence thou mayst pronounce against my life. Be assured that thou art as strong here as-in thy palace; thou hast the same power to rule here as in thy court. Enact concerning us here whatsoever would have been thy will in the palace: we are ready to obey." Thus much said Erik.

Now this speech softened the king towards himself as much as towards his foe. Then, everything being arranged and made friendly, they returned to the shore. The king ordered that Erik and his sailors should be taken in carriages. But when they reached the palace he had an assembly summoned, to which he called Erik, and under the pledge of

179

betrothal gave him his sister and command over a hundred men. Then he added that the queen would be a weariness to him, and that the daughter of Gotar had taken his liking. He must, therefore, have a fresh embassy, and the business could best be done by Erik, for whose efforts nothing seemed too hard. He also said that he would stone Gotwar to death for her complicity in concealing the crime; but Hanund he would restore to her father, that he might not have a traitress against his life dwelling amongst the Danes. Erik approved his plans, and promised his help to carry out his bidding; except that he declared that it would be better to marry the queen, when she had been put away, to Roller, of whom his sovereignty need have no fears. This opinion Frode received reverentially, as though it were some lesson vouchsafed from above. The queen also, that she might not seem to be driven by compulsion, complied, as women will, and declared that there was no natural necessity to grieve, and that all distress of spirit was a creature of fancy: and, moreover, that one ought not to bewail the punishment that befell one's deserts. And so the brethren celebrated their marriages together, one wedding the sister of the king, and the other his divorced queen.

Then they sailed back to Norway, taking their wives with them. For the women could not be torn from the side of their husbands, either by distance of journey or by dread of peril, but declared that they would stick to their lords like a feather to something shaggy. They found that Ragnar was dead, and that Kraka had already married one Brak. Then they remembered the father's treasure, dug up the money, and bore it off. But Erik's fame had gone before him, and Gotar had learnt all his good fortune. Now when Gotar learnt that he had come himself, he feared that his immense self-confidence would lead him to plan the worst against the Norwegians, and was anxious to take his wife from him and marry him to his own daughter in her place: for his queen had just died, and he was anxious to marry the sister of Frode more than anyone. Erik, when he learnt of his purpose, called his men together, and told them that his fortune had not yet got off from the reefs. Also he said that he saw, that as a bundle that was not tied by a band fell to pieces, so likewise the heaviest punishment that was not constrained on a man by his own fault suddenly collapsed. They had experienced this of late with Frode; for they saw how at the hardest pass their innocence had been protected by the help of the gods; and if they continued to preserve it they should hope for like aid in their adversity. Next, they must pretend flight for a little while, if they were attacked by Gotar, for so they would have a juster plea for fighting. For they had every right to thrust out the hand in order to shield the head from peril. Seldom could a man carry to a successful end a battle he had begun against the innocent; so, to give them a better plea for assaulting the enemy, he must be provoked to attack them first.

Erik then turned to Gunwar, and asked her, in order to test her fidelity, whether she had any love for Gotar, telling her it was unworthy that a maid of royal lineage should be bound to the bed of a man of the people. Then she began to conjure him earnestly by the power of heaven to tell her whether his purpose was true or reigned? He said that he had spoken seriously, and she cried: "And so thou art prepared to bring on me the worst of shame by leaving me a widow, whom thou lovedst dearly as a maid! Common rumour often speaks false, but I have been wrong in my opinion of thee. I thought I had married a steadfast man; I hoped his loyalty was past question; but now I find him to be more fickle than the winds." Saying this, she wept abundantly.

Dear to Erik was his wife's fears; presently he embraced her and said: "I wished to know how loyal thou wert to me. Nought but death has the right to sever us, but Gotar means to steal thee away, seeking thy love by robbery. When he has committed the theft, pretend it is done with thy goodwill; yet put off the wedding till he has given me his daughter in thy place. When she has been granted, Gotar and I will hold our marriage on the same day. And take care that thou prepare rooms for our banqueting which have a common party-wall, yet are separate: lest perchance, if I were before thine eyes, thou shouldst ruffle the king with thy lukewarm looks at him. For this will be a most effective trick to baffle the wish of the ravisher." Then he bade Brak (one of his men), to lie in ambush not far from the palace with a chosen band of his quickest men, that he might help him at need.

Then he summoned Roller, and fled in his ship with his wife and all his goods, in order to tempt the king out, pretending panic: So, when he saw that the fleet of Gotar was pressing him hard, he said: "Behold how the bow of guile shooteth the shaft of treachery;" and instantly rousing his sailors with the war-shout, he steered the ship about. Gotar came close up to him and asked who was the pilot of the ship, and he was told that it was Erik. He also shouted a question whether he was the same man who by his marvellous speaking could silence the eloquence of all other men. Erik, when he heard this, replied that he had long since received the surname of the "Shrewd-spoken", and that he had not won the auspicious title for nothing. Then both went back to the nearest shore, where Gotar, when he learnt the mission of Erik, said that he wished for the sister of Frode, but would rather offer his own daughter to Frode's envoy, that Erik might not repent the passing of his own wife to another man. Thus it would not be unfitting for the fruit of the mission to fall to the ambassador.

Erik, he said, was delightful to him as a son-in-law, if only he could win alliance with Frode through Gunwar.

Erik lauded the kindness of the king and approved his judgment, declaring he could not have expected a greater thing from the immortal gods than what was now offered him unasked. Still, he said, the king must first discover Gunwar's own mind and choice. She accepted the flatteries of the king with feigned goodwill, and seemed to consent readily to his suit, but besought him to suffer Erik's nuptials to precede hers; because, if Erik's were accomplished first, there would be a better opportunity for the king's; but chiefly on this account, that, if she were to marry again, she might not be disgusted at her new marriage troth by the memory of the old recurring. She also declared it inexpedient for two sets of preparations to be confounded in one ceremony. The king was prevailed upon by her answers, and highly approved her requests.

Gotar's constant talks with Erik furnished him with a store of most fairshapen maxims, wherewith to rejoice and refresh his mind. So, not satisfied with giving him his daughter in marriage he also made over to him the district of Lither, thinking that their connection deserved some kindness. Now Kraka, whom Erik, because of her cunning in witchcraft, had brought with him on his travels, feigned weakness of the eyes, and muffled up her face in her cloak, so that not a single particle of her head was visible for recognition. When people asked her who she was, she said that she was Gunwar's sister, child of the same mother but a different father.

Now when they came to the dwelling of Gotar, the wedding-feast of Alfhild (this was his daughter's name) was being held. Erik and the king sat at meat in different rooms, with a party-wall in common, and also entirely covered on the inside with hanging tapestries. Gunwar sat by Gotar, but Erik sat close between Kraka on the one side and Alfhild on the other. Amid the merrymaking, he gradually drew a lath out of the wall, and made an opening large enough to allow the passage of a human body; and thus, without the knowledge of the guests, he made a space wide enough to go through. Then, in the course of the feast, he began to question his betrothed closely whether she would rather marry himself or Frode: especially since, if due heed were paid to matches, the daughter of a king ought to go to the arms of one as noble as herself, so that the lowliness of one of the pair might not impair the lordliness of the other. She said that she would never marry against the permission of her father; but he turned her aversion into compliance by promises that she should be queen, and that she should be richer than all other women, for she was captivated by the promise of wealth quite as much as of glory. There is also a tradition that Kraka turned the maiden's inclinations to Frode by a drink which she mixed and gave to her.

Now Gotar, after the feast, in order to make the marriage-mirth go fast and furious, went to the revel of Erik. As he passed out, Gunwar, as she had been previously bidden, went through the hole in the party-wall where the lath had been removed, and took the seat next to Erik. Gotar marvelled that she was sitting there by his side, and began to ask eagerly how and why she had come there. She said that she was Gunwar's sister, and that the king was deceived by the likeness of their looks. And when the king, in order to look into the matter, hurried back to the royal room, Gunwar returned through the back door by which she had come and sat in her old place in the sight of all. Gotar, when he saw her, could scarcely believe his eyes, and in the utmost doubt whether he had recognized her aright, he retraced his steps to Erik; and there he saw before him Gunwar, who had got back in her own fashion. And so, as often as he changed to go from one hall to the other, he found her whom he sought in either place. By this time the king was tormented by great wonder at what was no mere likeness, but the very same face in both places. For it seemed flatly impossible that different people should look exactly and undistinguishably alike. At last, when the revel broke up, he courteously escorted his daughter and Erik as far as their room, as the manner is at weddings, and went back himself to bed elsewhere.

But Erik suffered Alfhild, who was destined for Frode, to lie apart, and embraced Gunwar as usual, thus outwitting the king. So Gotar passed a sleepless night, revolving how he had been apparently deluded with a dazed and wandering mind: for it seemed to him no mere likeness of looks, but sameness. Thus he was filled with such wavering and doubtful judgment, that though he really discerned the truth he thought he must have been mistaken. At last it flashed across his mind that the wall might have been tampered with. He gave orders that it should be carefully surveyed and examined, but found no traces of a breakage: in fact, the entire room seemed to be whole and unimpaired. For Erik, early in the night, had patched up the damage of the broken wall, that his trick might not be detected. Then the king sent two men privily into the bedroom of Erik to learn the truth, and bade them stand behind the hangings and note all things carefully. They further received orders to kill Erik if they found him with Gunwar. They went secretly into the room, and, concealing themselves in the curtained corners, beheld Erik and Gunwar in bed together with arms entwined. Thinking them only drowsy, they waited for their deeper sleep, wishing to stay until a heavier slumber gave them a chance to commit their crime. Erik snored lustily, and they knew it was a sure sign that he slept soundly; so they straightway came forth with drawn blades in order to butcher him. Erik was awakened by their treacherous onset, and seeing their swords hanging over his head, called out the name of his stepmother, (Kraka), to which long ago he had been bidden to appeal when in peril, and he found a speedy help in his need. For his shield, which hung aloft from the rafter, instantly fell and covered his unarmed body, and, as if on purpose, covered it from impalement by the cutthroats. He did not fail to make use of his luck, but, snatching his sword, lopped off both feet of the nearest of them. Gunwar, with equal energy, ran a spear through the other: she had the body of a woman, but the spirit of a man.

Thus Erik escaped the trap; whereupon he went back to the sea and made ready to sail off by night. But Roller sounded on his horn the signal for those who had been bidden to watch close by, to break into the palace. When the king heard this, he thought it meant that the enemy was upon them, and made off hastily in a ship. Meanwhile Brak, and those who had broken in with him, snatched up the goods of the king, and got them on board Erik's ships. Almost half the night was spent in pillaging. In the morning, when the king found that they had fled, he prepared to pursue them, but was advised by one of his friends not to plan anything on a sudden or do it in haste. His friend, indeed, tried to convince him that he needed a larger equipment, and that it was ill-advised to pursue the fugitives to Denmark with a handful. But neither could this curb the king's impetuous spirit; it could not bear the loss; for nothing had stung him more than this, that his preparations to slay another should have recoiled on his own men. So he sailed to the harbour which is now called Omi. Here the weather began to be bad, provision failed, and they thought it better, since die they must, to die by the sword than by famine. And so the sailors turned their hand against one another, and hastened their end by mutual blows. The king with a few men took to the cliffs and escaped. Lofty barrows still mark the scene of the slaughter. Meanwhile Erik ended his voyage fairly, and the wedding of Alfhild and Frode was kept.

Then came tidings of an inroad of the Sclavs, and Erik was commissioned to suppress it with eight ships, since Frode as yet seemed inexperienced in war. Erik, loth ever to flinch from any manly undertaking, gladly undertook the business and did it bravely. Learning that the pirates had seven ships, he sailed up to them with only one of his own, ordering the rest to be girt with timber parapets, and covered over with pruned boughs of trees. Then he advanced to observe the number of the enemy more fully, but when the Sclavs pursued closely, he beat a quick retreat to his men. But the enemy, blind to the trap, and as eager to take the fugitives, rowed smiting the waters fast and incessantly. For the ships of Erik could not be clearly distinguished,

184

looking like a leafy wood. The enemy, after venturing into a winding strait, suddenly saw themselves surrounded by the fleet of Erik. First, confounded by the strange sight, they thought that a wood was sailing; and then they saw that guile lurked under the leaves. Therefore, tardily repenting their rashness, they tried to retrace their incautious voyage: but while they were trying to steer about, they saw the enemy boarding them; Erik, however, put his ship ashore, and slung stones against the enemy from afar. Thus most of the Sclavs were killed, and forty taken, who afterwards under stress of bonds and famine, and in strait of divers torments, gave up the ghost.

Meantime Frode, in order to cross on an expedition into Sclavia, had mustered a mighty fleet from the Danes, as well as from neighbouring peoples. The smallest boat of this fleet could carry twelve sailors, and be rowed by as many oars. Then Erik, bidding his men await him patiently went to tell Frode the tidings of the defeat he had inflicted. As he sailed along he happened to see a pirate ship aground on some shallows; and being wont to utter weighty words upon chance occurrences, he said, "Obscure is the lot of the base-born, and mean is the fortune of the lowly." Then he brought his ship up close and destroyed the pirates, who were trying to get off their own vessel with poles, and busily engrossed in saving her. This accomplished, he made his way back to the king's fleet; and wishing to cheer Frode with a greeting that heralded his victory, he said, "Hail to the maker of a most prosperous peace!" The king prayed that his word might come true, and declared that the spirit of the wise man was prophetic. Erik answered that he spoke truly, and that the petty victory brought an omen of a greater one; declaring that a presage of great matters could often be got from trifles. Then the king counselled him to scatter his force, and ordered the horsemen of Jutland to go by the land way, while the rest of the army went by the short sea-passage. But the sea was covered with such a throng of vessels, that there were not enough harbours to take them in, nor shores for them to encamp on, nor money for their provisions; while the land army is said to have been so great that, in order to shorten the way, it levelled mountains, made marshes passable, filled up pits with material, and the hugest chasms by casting in great boulders.

Meanwhile Strunik the King of the Sclavs sent envoys to ask for a truce; but Frode refused him time to equip himself, saying that an enemy ought not to be furnished with a truce. Moreover, he said, he had hitherto passed his life without experience of war, and now he ought not to delay its beginning by waiting in doubt; for the man that conducted his first campaign successfully might hope for as good fortune in the rest. For each side would take the augury afforded by the first engagements as a presage of the combat; since the preliminary successes of war were often a prophecy of the sequel. Erik commended the wisdom of the reply, declaring that the game ought to be played abroad just as it had been begun at home: meaning that the Danes had been challenged by the Sclavs. After these words he fought a furious battle, slew Strunik with the bravest of his race, and received the surrender of the rest. Then Frode called the Sclavs together, and proclaimed by a herald that any man among them who had been trained to theft or plunder should be speedily given up; promising that he would reward the character of such men with the highest honours. He also ordered that all of them, who were versed in evil arts should come forth to have their reward. This offer pleased the Sclavs: and some of them, tempted by their hopes of the gift, betrayed themselves with more avarice than judgment, before the others could make them known. These were misled by such great covetousness, that they thought less of shame than lucre, and accounted as their glory what was really their guilt. When these had given themselves up of their own will, he said: "Sclavs! This is the pest from which you must clear your land yourselves." And straightway he ordered the executioners to seize them, and had them fixed upon the highest gallows by the hand of their own countrymen. The punishers looked fewer than the punished. And thus the shrewd king, by refusing to those who owned their guilt the pardon which he granted to the conquered foe, destroyed almost the entire stock of the Sclavic race. Thus the longing for an undeserved reward was visited with a deserved penalty, and the thirst for an undue wage justly punished. I should think that these men were rightly delivered to their doom, who brought the peril on their own heads by speaking, when they could have saved their lives by the protection of silence.

The king, exalted by the honours of his fresh victory, and loth to seem less strong in justice than in battle, resolved to remodel his army by some new laws, some of which are retained by present usage, while others men have chosen to abolish for new ones. (a) For he decreed, when the spoil was divided, that each of the vanguard should receive a greater share than the rest of the soldiery: while he granted all gold that was taken to the generals (before whom the standards were always borne in battle) on account of their rank; wishing the common soldiers to be content with silver. He ordered that the arms should go to the champions, but the captured ships should pass to the common people, as the due of those who had the right of building and equipping vessels. (b) Also he forbade that anyone should venture to lock up his household goods, as he would receive double the value of any losses from the treasury of the king; but if anyone thought fit to keep it in locked coffers, he must pay the king a gold mark. He also laid down that anyone who spared a thief should be punished as a thief. (d) Further, that the first man to flee in battle should forfeit all common rights. (e) But when he had returned into Denmark he wished to amend by good measures any corruption caused by the evil practices of Grep; and therefore granted women free choice in marriage, so that there might be no compulsory wedlock. And so he provided by law that women should be held duly married to those whom they had wedded without consulting their fathers. (f) But if a free woman agreed to marry a slave, she must fall to his rank, lose the blessing of freedom, and adopt the standing of a slave. (g) He also imposed on men the statute that they must marry any woman whom they had seduced. (h) He ordained that adulterers should be deprived of a member by the lawful husbands, so that continence might not be destroyed by shameful sins. (I) Also he ordained that if a Dane plundered another Dane, he should repay double, and be held guilty of a breach of the peace. (k) And if any man were to take to the house of another anything which he had got by thieving, his host, if he shut the door of his house behind the man, should incur forfeiture of all his goods, and should be beaten in full assembly, being regarded as having made himself guilty of the same crime. (l) Also, whatsoever exile should turn enemy to his country, or bear a shield against his countrymen, should be punished with the loss of life and goods. (m) But if any man, from a contumacious spirit, were slack in fulfilling the orders of the king, he should be punished with exile. For, on all occasion of any sudden and urgent war, an arrow of wood, looking like iron, used to be passed on everywhere from man to man as a messenger. (n) But if any one of the commons went in front of the vanguard in battle, he was to rise from a slave into a freeman, and from a peasant into a nobleman; but if he were nobly-born already, he should be created a governor. So great a guerdon did valiant men earn of old; and thus did the ancients think noble rank the due of bravery. For it was thought that the luck a man had should be set down to his valour, and not his valour to his luck. (o) He also enacted that no dispute should be entered on with a promise made under oath and a gage deposited; but whosoever requested another man to deposit a gage against him should pay that man half a gold mark, on pain of severe bodily chastisement. For the king had foreseen that the greatest occasions of strife might arise from the depositing of gages. (p) But he decided that any quarrel whatsoever should be decided by the sword, thinking a combat of weapons more honourable than one of words. But if either of the combatants drew back his foot, and stepped out of the ring of the circle previously marked, he was to consider himself conquered, and suffer the loss of his case. But a man of the people, if he attacked a champion on any score, should be armed to meet him; but the champion should only fight with a truncheon an ell long. (q) Further, he appointed that if an alien killed a Dane, his death should be redressed by the slaying of two foreigners.

Meanwhile, Gotar, in order to punish Erik, equipped his army for war: and Frode, on the other side, equipped a great fleet to go against Norway. When both alike had put into Rennes-Isle, Gotar, terrified by the greatness of Frode's name, sent ambassadors to pray for peace. Erik said to them, "Shameless is the robber who is the first to seek peace, or ventures to offer it to the good. He who longs to win must struggle: blow must counter blow, malice repel malice."

Gotar listened attentively to this from a distance, and then said, as loudly as he could: "Each man fights for valour according as he remembers kindness." Erik said to him: "I have requited thy kindness by giving thee back counsel." By this speech he meant that his excellent advice was worth more than all manner of gifts. And, in order to show that Gotar was ungrateful for the counsel he had received, he said: "When thou desiredst to take my life and my wife, thou didst mar the look of thy fair example. Only the sword has the right to decide between us." Then Gotar attacked the fleet of the Danes; he was unsuccessful in the engagement, and slain.

Afterwards Roller received his realm from Frode as a gift; it stretched over seven provinces. Erik likewise presented Roller with the province which Gotar had once bestowed upon him. After these exploits Frode passed three years in complete and tranquil peace.

Meanwhile the King of the Huns, when he heard that his daughter had been put away, allied himself with Olmar, King of the Easterlings, and in two years equipped an armament against the Danes. So Frode levied an army not only of native Danes, but also of Norwegians and Sclavs. Erik, whom he had sent to spy out the array of the enemy, found Olmar, who had received the command of the fleet, not far from Russia; while the King of the Huns led the land forces. He addressed Olmar thus:

"What means, prithee, this strong equipment of war? Or whither dost thou speed, King Olmar, mighty in thy fleet?"

Olmar. "We are minded to attack the son of Fridleif. And who art thou, whose bold lips ask such questions?"

Erik. "Vain hope of conquering the unconquered hath filled thy heart; over Frode no man can prevail."

Olmar. "Whatsoever befalls, must once happen for the first time; and often enough the unexpected comes to pass."

By this saying he let him know that no man must put too much trust in fortune. Then Erik rode up to inspect the army of the Huns. As it passed by him, and he in turn by it, it showed its vanguard to the rising and its rear to the setting sun. So he asked those whom he met, who had the command of all those thousands. Hun, the King of the Huns, happened to see him, and heard that he had undertaken to reconnoitre, and asked what was the name of the questioner. Erik said he was the man who came everywhere and was found nowhere. Then the king, when an interpreter was brought, asked what work Frode was about. Erik replied, "Frode never waits at home for a hostile army, nor tarries in his house for his foe. For he who covets the pinnacle of another's power must watch and wake all night. No man has ever won a victory by snoring, and no wolf has ever found a carcase by lying asleep."

The king, perceiving that he was a cunning speaker of choice maxims, said: "Here, perchance, is that Erik who, as I have heard, accused my daughter falsely."

But Erik, when they were bidden to seize him instantly, said that it was unseemly for one man to be dragged off by really; and by this saying he not only appeased the mind of the king, but even inclined him to be willing to pardon him. But it was clear that this impunity came more from cunning than kindness; for the chief reason why he was let go was that he might terrify Frode by the report of their vast numbers. When he returned, Frode bad him relate what he had discovered, and he said that he had seen six kings each with his fleet; and that each of these fleets contained five thousand ships, each ship being known to hold three hundred rowers. Each millenary of the whole total he said consisted of four wings; now, since the full number of a wing is three hundred, he meant that a millenary should be understood to contain twelve hundred men. When Frode wavered in doubt what he could do against so many, and looked eagerly round for reinforcements, Erik said: "Boldness helps the righteous; a valiant dog must attack the bear; we want wolf-hounds, and not little unwarlike birds." This said, he advised Frode to muster his fleet. When it was drawn up they sailed off against the enemy; and so they fought and subdued the islands lying between Denmark and the East; and as they advanced thence, met some ships of the Ruthenian fleet. Frode thought it shameful to attack such a handful, but Erik said: "We must seek food from the gaunt and lean. He who falls shall seldom fatten, nor has that man the power to bite whom the huge sack has devoured." By this warning he cured the king of all shame about making an assault, and presently induced him to attack a small number with a throng; for he showed him that advantage must be counted before honour.

After this they went on to meet Olmar, who because of the slowness of his multitude preferred awaiting the enemy to attacking it; for the vessels of the Ruthenians seemed disorganized, and, owing to their size, not so well able to row. But not even did the force of his multitudes avail him. For the extraordinary masses of the Ruthenians were stronger in numbers than in bravery, and yielded the victory to the stout handful of the Danes.

When Frode tried to return home, his voyage encountered an unheard-of difficulty. For the crowds of dead bodies, and likewise the fragments of shields and spears, bestrewed the entire gulf of the sea, and tossed on the tide, so that the harbours were not only straitened, but stank. The vessels stuck, hampered amid the corpses. They could neither thrust off with oars, nor drive away with poles, the rotting carcases that floated around, or prevent, when they had put one away, another rolling up and driving against the fleet. You would have thought that a war had arisen with the dead, and there was a strange combat with the lifeless.

So Frode summoned the nations which he had conquered, and enacted (a) that any father of a family who had fallen in that war should be buried with his horse and all his arms and decorations. And if any body-snatcher, in his abominable covetousness, made an attempt on him, he was to suffer for it, not only with his life, but also with the loss of burial for his own body; he should have no barrow and no funeral. For he thought it just that he who despoiled another's ashes should be granted no burial, but should repeat in his own person the fate he had inflicted on another. He appointed that the body of a centurion or governor should receive funeral on a pyre built of his own ship. He ordered that the bodies of every ten pilots should be burnt together with a single ship, but that every earl or king that was killed should be put on his own ship and burnt with it. He wished this nice attention to be paid in conducting the funerals of the slain, because he wished to prevent indiscriminate obsequies. By this time all the kings of the Russians except Olmar and Dag had fallen in battle. (b) He also ordered the Russians to conduct their warfare in imitation of the Danes, and never to marry a wife without buying her. He thought that bought marriages would have more security, believing that the troth which was sealed with a price was the safest. (d) Moreover, anyone who durst attempt the violation of a virgin was to be punished with the severance of his bodily parts, or else to requite the wrong of his intercourse with a thousand talents. (e) He also enacted that any man that applied himself to war, who aspired to the title of tried soldier, should attack a single man, should stand the attack of two, should only withdraw his foot a little to avoid three, but should not blush to flee from four. (f) He also

190

proclaimed that a new custom concerning the pay of the soldiers should be observed by the princes under his sway. He ordered that each native soldier and housecarl should be presented in the winter season with three marks of silver, a common or hired soldier with two, a private soldier who had finished his service with only one. By this law he did injustice to valour, reckoning the rank of the soldiers and not their courage; and he was open to the charge of error in the matter, because he set familiar acquaintance above desert.

After this the king asked Erik whether the army of the Huns was as large as the forces of Olmar, and Erik answered in the following song:

"By Hercules, I came on a countless throng, a throng that neither earth nor wave could hold. Thick flared all their camp-fires, and the whole wood blazed up; the flame betokened a numberless array. The earth sank under the fraying of the horse-hoofs; creaking waggons rattled swiftly. The wheels rumbled, the driver rode upon the winds, so that the chariots sounded like thunder. The earth hardly bore the throngs of men-at-arms, speeding on confusedly; they trod it, but it could not bear their weight. I thought that the air crashed and the earth was shaken, so mighty was the motion of the stranger army. For I saw fifteen standards flickering at once; each of them had a hundred lesser standards, and after each of these could have been seen twenty; and the captains in their order were equal in number to the standards."

Now when Frode asked wherewithal he was to resist so many, Erik instructed him that he must return home and suffer the enemy first to perish of their own hugeness. His counsel was obeyed, the advice being approved as heartily as it was uttered. But the Huns went on through pathless deserts, and, finding provisions nowhere, began to run the risk of general starvation; for it was a huge and swampy district, and nothing could be found to relieve their want. At last, when the beasts of burden had been cut down and eaten, they began to scatter, lacking carriages as much as food. Now their straying from the road was as perilous to them as their hunger. Neither horses nor asses were spared, nor did they refrain from filthy garbage. At last they did not even spare dogs: to dying men every abomination was lawful; for there is nothing too hard for the bidding of extreme need. At last when they were worn out with hunger, there came a general mortality. Bodies were carried out for burial without end, for all feared to perish, and none pitied the perishing. Fear indeed had cast out humanity. So first the divisions deserted from the king little by little; and then the army melted away by companies. He was also deserted by the prophet Ygg, a man of unknown age, which was prolonged beyond the human span; this man went as a deserter to Frode, and told him of all the preparations of the

Huns.

Meanwhile Hedin, prince of a considerable tribe of the Norwegians, approached the fleet of Frode with a hundred and fifty vessels. Choosing twelve out of these, he proceeded to cruise nearer, signalling the approach of friends by a shield raised on the mast. He thus greatly augmented the forces of the king, and was received into his closest friendship. A mutual love afterwards arose between this man and Hilda, the daughter of Hogni, a chieftain of the Jutes, and a maiden of most eminent renown. For, though they had not yet seen one another, each had been kindled by the other's glory. But when they had a chance of beholding one another, neither could look away; so steadfast was the love that made their eyes linger.

Meanwhile, Frode distributed his soldiers through the towns, and carefully gathered in the materials needed for the winter supplies; but even so he could not maintain his army, with its burden of expense: and plague fell on him almost as great as the destruction that met the Huns. Therefore, to prevent the influx of foreigners, he sent a fleet to the Elbe to take care that nothing should cross; the admirals were Revil and Mevil. When the winter broke up, Hedin and Hogni resolved to make a roving-raid together; for Hogni did not know that his partner was in love with his daughter. Now Hogni was of unusual stature, and stiff in temper; while Hedin was very comely, but short. Also, when Frode saw that the cost of keeping up his army grew daily harder to bear, he sent Roller to Norway, Olmar to Sweden, King Onef and Glomer, a rover captain, to the Orkneys for supplies, each with his own forces. Thirty kings followed Frode, and were his friends or vassals. But when Hun heard that Frode had sent away his forces he mustered another and a fresh army. But Hogni betrothed his daughter to Hedin, after they had sworn to one another that whichever of them should perish by the sword should be avenged by the other.

In the autumn, the men in search of supplies came back, but they were richer in trophies than in food. For Roller had made tributary the provinces Sundmor and Nordmor, after slaying Arthor their king. But Olmar conquered Thor the Long, the King of the Jemts and the Helsings, with two other captains of no less power, and also took Esthonia and Kurland, with Oland, and the isles that fringe Sweden; thus he was a most renowned conqueror of savage lands. So he brought back 700 ships, thus doubling the numbers of those previously taken out. Onef and Glomer, Hedin and Hogni, won victories over the Orkneys, and returned with 900 ships. And by this time revenues had been got in from far and wide, and there were ample materials gathered by plunder to recruit their resources. They had also added twenty kingdoms to the sway of Frode, whose kings, added to the thirty named before, fought on the side of the Danes.

Trusting in their strength, they engaged with the Huns. Such a carnage broke out on the first day of this combat that the three chief rivers of Russia were bestrewn with a kind of bridge of corpses, and could be crossed and passed over. Also the traces of the massacre spread so wide that for the space of three days' ride the ground was to be seen covered with human carcases. So, when the battle had been seven days prolonged, King Hun fell; and his brother of the same name, when he saw the line of the Huns giving way, without delay surrendered himself and his company. In that war 170 kings, who were either Huns or fighting amongst the Huns, surrendered to the king. This great number Erik had comprised in his previous description of the standards, when he was giving an account of the multitude of the Huns in answer to the questions of Frode. So Frode summoned the kings to assembly, and imposed a rule upon them that they should all live under one and the same law. Now he set Olmar over Holmgard; Onef over Conogard; and he bestowed Saxony on Hun, his prisoner, and gave Revil the Orkneys. To one Dimar he allotted the management of the provinces of the Helsings, of the Jarnbers, and the Jemts, as well as both Laplands; while on Dag he bestowed the government of Esthonia. Each of these men he burdened with fixed conditions of tribute, thus making allegiance a condition of his kindness. So the realms of Frode embraced Russia on the east, and on the west were bounded by the Rhine.

Meantime, certain slanderous tongues accused Hedin to Hogni of having tempted and defiled his daughter before the rites of betrothal; which was then accounted an enormous crime by all nations. So the credulous ears of Hogni drank in this lying report, and with his fleet he attacked Hedin, who was collecting the king's dues among the Slavs; there was an engagement, and Hogni was beaten, and went to Jutland. And thus the peace instituted by Frode was disturbed by intestine war, and natives were the first to disobey the king's law. Frode, therefore, sent men to summon them both at once, and inquired closely what was the reason of their feud. When he had heard it, he gave judgment according to the terms of the law he had enacted; but when he saw that even this could not reconcile them (for the father obstinately demanded his daughter back), he decreed that the quarrel should be settled by the sword—it seemed the only remedy for ending the dispute. The fight began, and Hedin was grievously wounded; but when he began to lose blood and bodily strength, he received unexpected mercy from his enemy. For though Hogni had an easy chance of killing him, yet, pitying youth and beauty, he constrained his cruelty to give way to clemency.

And so, loth to cut off a stripling who was panting at his last gasp, he refrained his sword. For of old it was accounted shameful to deprive of his life one who was ungrown or a weakling; so closely did the antique bravery of champions take heed of all that could incline them to modesty. So Hedin, with the help of his men, was taken back to his ship, saved by the kindness of his foe.

In the seventh year after, these same men began to fight on Hedin's isle, and wounded each other so that they died. Hogni would have been lucky if he had shown severity rather than compassion to Hedin when he had once conquered him. They say that Hilda longed so ardently for her husband, that she is believed to have conjured up the spirits of the combatants by her spells in the night in order to renew the war.

At the same time came to pass a savage war between Alrik, king of the Swedes, and Gestiblind, king of the Goths. The latter, being the weaker, approached Frode as a suppliant, willing, if he might get his aid, to surrender his kingdom and himself. He soon received the aid of Skalk, the Skanian, and Erik, and came back with reinforcements. He had determined to let loose his attack on Alrik, but Erik thought that he should first assail his son Gunthion, governor of the men of Wermland and Solongs, declaring that the storm-weary mariner ought to make for the nearest shore, and moreover that the rootless trunk seldom burgeoned. So he made an attack, wherein perished Gunthion, whose tomb records his name. Alrik, when he heard of the destruction of his son, hastened to avenge him, and when he had observed his enemies, he summoned Erik, and, in a secret interview, recounted the leagues of their fathers, imploring him to refuse to fight for Gestiblind. This Erik steadfastly declined, and Alrik then asked leave to fight Gestiblind, thinking that a duel was better than a general engagement. But Erik said that Gestiblind was unfit for arms by reason of old age, pleading his bad health, and above all his years; but offered himself to fight in his place, explaining that it would be shameful to decline a duel on behalf of the man for whom he had come to make a war. Then they fought without delay: Alrik was killed, and Erik was most severely wounded; it was hard to find remedies, and he did not for long time recover health. Now a false report had come to Frode that Erik had fallen, and was tormenting the king's mind with sore grief; but Erik dispelled this sadness with his welcome return; indeed, he reported to Frode that by his efforts Sweden, Wermland, Helsingland, and the islands of the Sun (Soleyar) had been added to his realm. Frode straightway made him king of the nations he had subdued, and also granted to him Helsingland with the two Laplands, Finland and Esthonia, under a yearly tribute. None of the Swedish kings before him was called by the name of Erik, but the title passed from him to the rest.

At the same time Alf was king in Hethmark, and he had a son Asmund. Biorn ruled in the province of Wik, and had a son Aswid. Asmund was engaged on an unsuccessful hunt, and while he was proceeding either to stalk the game with dogs or to catch it in nets, a mist happened to come on. By this he was separated from his sharers on a lonely track, wandered over the dreary ridges, and at last, destitute of horse and clothing, ate fungi and mushrooms, and wandered on aimlessly till he came to the dwelling of King Biorn. Moreover, the son of the king and he, when they had lived together a short while, swore by every vow, in order to ratify the friendship which they observed to one another, that whichever of them lived longest should be buried with him who died. For their fellowship and love were so strong, that each determined he would not prolong his days when the other was cut off by death.

After this Frode gathered together a host of all his subject nations, and attacked Norway with his fleet, Erik being bidden to lead the land force. For, after the fashion of human greed, the more he gained the more he wanted, and would not suffer even the dreariest and most rugged region of the world to escape this kind of attack; so much is increase of wealth wont to encourage covetousness. So the Norwegians, casting away all hope of self-defence, and losing all confidence in their power to revolt, began to flee for the most part to Halogaland. The maiden Stikla also withdrew from her country to save her chastity, proferring the occupations of war to those of wedlock.

Meanwhile Aswid died of an illness, and was consigned with his horse and dog to a cavern in the earth. And Asmund, because of his oath of friendship, had the courage to be buried with him, food being put in for him to eat.

Now just at this time Erik, who had crossed the uplands with his army, happened to draw near the barrow of Aswid; and the Swedes, thinking that treasures were in it, broke the hill open with mattocks, and saw disclosed a cave deeper than they had thought. To examine it, a man was wanted, who would lower himself on a hanging rope tied around him. One of the quickest of the youths was chosen by lot; and Asmund, when he saw him let down in a basket following a rope, straightway cast him out and climbed into the basket. Then he gave the signal to draw him up to those above who were standing by and controlling the rope. They drew in the basket in the hopes of great treasure; but when they saw the unknown figure of the man they had taken out, they were scared by his extraordinary look, and, thinking that the dead had come to life, flung down the rope and fled all ways. For Asmund looked ghastly and seemed to be covered as with the corruption of the charnel.

He tried to recall the fugitives, and began to clamour that they were wrongfully afraid of a living man. And when Erik saw him, he marvelled most at the aspect of his bloody face: the blood flowing forth and spurting over it. For Aswid had come to life in the nights, and in his continual struggles had wrenched off his left ear; and there was to be seen the horrid sight of a raw and unhealed scar. And when the bystanders bade him tell how he had got such a wound, he began to speak thus:—

"Why stand ye aghast, who see me colourless? Surely every live man fades among the dead. Evil to the lonely man, and burdensome to the single, remains every dwelling in the world. Hapless are they whom chance hath bereft of human help. The listless night of the cavern, the darkness of the ancient den, have taken all joy from my eyes and soul. The ghastly ground, the crumbling barrow, and the heavy tide of filthy things have marred the grace of my youthful countenance, and sapped my wonted pith and force. Besides all this, I have fought with the dead, enduring the heavy burden and grievous peril of the wrestle; Aswid rose again and fell on me with rending nails, by hellish might renewing ghastly warfare after he was ashes.

"Why stand ye aghast, who see me colourless? Surely every live man fades among the dead.

"By some strange enterprise of the power of hell the spirit of Aswid was sent up from the nether world, and with cruel tooth eats the fleet-footed (horse), and has given his dog to his abominable jaws. Not sated with devouring the horse or hound, he soon turned his swift nails upon me, tearing my cheek and taking off my ear. Hence the hideous sight of my slashed countenance, the blood-spurts in the ugly wound. Yet the bringer of horrors did it not unscathed; for soon I cut off his head with my steel, and impaled his guilty carcase with a stake.

"Why stand ye aghast who see me colourless? Surely every live man fades among the dead."

Frode had by this taken his fleet over to Halogaland; and here, in order to learn the numbers of his host, which seemed to surpass all bounds and measure that could be counted, he ordered his soldiers to pile up a hill, one stone being cast upon the heap for each man. The enemy also pursued the same method of numbering their host, and the hills are still to be seen to convince the visitor. Here Frode joined battle with the Norwegians, and the day was bloody. At nightfall both sides determined to retreat. As daybreak drew near, Erik, who had come across the land, came up and advised the king to renew the battle. In this war the Danes suffered such slaughter that out of 3,000 ships only 170 are supposed to have survived. The Northmen, however, were exterminated in such a mighty massacre, that (so the story goes) there were not men left to till even a fifth of their villages.

Frode, now triumphant, wished to renew peace among all nations, that he might ensure each man's property from the inroads of thieves and now ensure peace to his realms after war. So he hung one bracelet on a crag which is called Frode's Rock, and another in the district of Wik, after he had addressed the assembled Norwegians; threatening that these necklaces should serve to test the honesty which he had decreed, and threatening that if they were filched punishment should fall on all the governors of the district. And thus, sorely imperilling the officers, there was the gold unguarded, hanging up full in the parting of the roads, and the booty, so easy to plunder, a temptation to all covetous spirits. (a) Frode also enacted that seafarers should freely use oars wherever they found them; while to those who wished to cross a river he granted free use of the horse which they found nearest to the ford. He decreed that they must dismount from this horse when its fore feet only touched land and its hind feet were still washed by the waters. For he thought that services such as these should rather be accounted kindness than wrongdoing. Moreover, he ordained that whosoever durst try and make further use of the horse after he had crossed the river should be condemned to death. (b) He also ordered that no man should hold his house or his coffer under lock and key, or should keep anything guarded by bolts, promising that all losses should be made good threefold. Also, he appointed that it was lawful to claim as much of another man's food for provision as would suffice for a single supper. If anyone exceeded this measure in his takings, he was to be held guilty of theft. Now, a thief (so he enacted) was to be hung up with a sword passed through his sinews, with a wolf fastened by his side, so that the wicked man might look like the savage beast, both being punished alike. He also had the same penalty extended to accomplices in thefts. Here he passed seven most happy years of peace, begetting a son Alf and a daughter Eyfura.

It chanced that in these days Arngrim, a champion of Sweden, who had challenged, attacked, and slain Skalk the Skanian because he had once robbed him of a vessel, came to Frode. Elated beyond measure with his deed, he ventured to sue for Frode's daughter; but, finding the king deaf to him, he asked Erik, who was ruling Sweden, to help him. Erik advised him to win Frode's goodwill by some illustrious service, and to fight against Egther, the King of Permland, and Thengil, the King of Finmark, since they alone seemed to repudiate the Danish rule, while all men else submitted. Without delay he led his army to that country. Now, the

Finns are the uttermost peoples of the North, who have taken a portion of the world that is barely habitable to till and dwell in. They are very keen spearmen, and no nation has a readier skill in throwing the javelin. They fight with large, broad arrows; they are addicted to the study of spells; they are skilled hunters. Their habitation is not fixed, and their dwellings are migratory; they pitch and settle wherever they have caught game. Riding on curved boards (skees or snow-skates), they run over ridges thick with snow. These men Arngrim attacked, in order to win renown, and he crushed them. They fought with ill success; but, as they were scattering in flight, they cast three pebbles behind them, which they caused to appear to the eyes of the enemy like three mountains. Arngrim's eyes were dazzled and deluded, and he called back his men from the pursuit of the enemy, fancying that he was checked by a barrier of mighty rocks. Again, when they engaged and were beaten on the morrow, the Finns cast snow upon the ground and made it look like a mighty river. So the Swedes, whose eyes were utterly deluded, were deceived by their misjudgment, for it seemed the roaring of an extraordinary mass of waters. Thus, the conqueror dreading the unsubstantial phantom of the waters, the Finns managed to escape. They renewed the war again on the third day; but there was no effective means of escape left any longer, for when they saw that their lines were falling back, they surrendered to the conqueror. Arngrim imposed on them the following terms of tribute: that the number of the Finns should be counted, and that, after the lapse of (every) three years, every ten of them should pay a carriage-full of deer-skins by way of assessment. Then he challenged and slew in single combat Egther, the captain of the men of Permland, imposing on the men of Permland the condition that each of them should pay one skin. Enriched with these spoils and trophies, he returned to Erik, who went with him into Denmark, and poured loud praises of the young warrior into the ear of Frode, declaring that he who had added the ends of the world to his realms deserved his daughter. Then Frode, considering his splendid deserts, thought it was not amiss to take for a son-in-law a man who had won wide-resounding fame by such a roll of noble deeds.

Arngrim had twelve sons by Eyfura, whose names I here subjoin: Brand, Biarbe, Brodd, Hiarrande; Tand, Tyrfing, two Haddings; Hiortuar, Hiartuar, Hrane, Anganty. These followed the business of sea-roving from their youth up; and they chanced to sail all in one ship to the island Samso, where they found lying off the coast two ships belonging to Hialmar and Arvarodd (Arrow-Odd) the rovers. These ships they attacked and cleared of rowers; but, not knowing whether they had cut down the captains, they fitted the bodies of the slain to their several thwarts, and found that those whom they sought were missing. At this they were sad, knowing that the victory they had won was not worth a straw, and that their safety would run much greater risk in the battle that was to come. In fact, Hialmar and Arvarodd, whose ships had been damaged by a storm, which had torn off their rudders, went into a wood to hew another; and, going round the trunk with their axes, pared down the shapeless timber until the huge stock assumed the form of a marine implement. This they shouldered, and were bearing it down to the beach, ignorant of the disaster of their friends, when the sons of Eyfura, reeking with the fresh blood of the slain, attacked them, so that they two had to fight many; the contest was not even equal, for it was a band of twelve against two. But the victory did not go according to the numbers. For all the sons of Eyfura were killed; Hialmar was slain by them, but Arvarodd gained the honours of victory, being the only survivor left by fate out of all that band of comrades. He, with an incredible effort, poised the still shapeless hulk of the rudder, and drove it so strongly against the bodies of his foes that, with a single thrust of it, he battered and crushed all twelve. And, so, though they were rid of the general storm of war, the band of rovers did not yet quit the ocean.

This it was that chiefly led Frode to attack the West, for his one desire was the spread of peace. So he summoned Erik, and mustered a fleet of all the kingdoms that bid him allegiance, and sailed to Britain with numberless ships. But the king of that island, perceiving that he was unequal in force (for the ships seemed to cover the sea), went to Frode, affecting to surrender, and not only began to flatter his greatness, but also promised to the Danes, the conquerors of nations, the submission of himself and of his country; proffering taxes, assessment, tribute, what they would. Finally, he gave them a hospitable invitation. Frode was pleased with the courtesy of the Briton, though his suspicions of treachery were kept by so ready and unconstrained a promise of everything, so speedy a surrender of the enemy before fighting; such offers being seldom made in good faith. They were also troubled with alarm about the banquet, fearing that as drunkenness came on their sober wits might be entangled in it, and attacked by hidden treachery. So few guests were bidden, moreover, that it seemed unsafe for them to accept the invitation; and it was further thought foolish to trust their lives to the good faith of an enemy whom they did not know.

When the king found their minds thus wavering he again approached Frode, and invited him to the banquet with 2,400 men; having before bidden him to come to the feast with 1,200 nobles. Frode was encouraged by the increase in the number of guests, and was able to go to the banquet with greater inward confidence; but he could not yet lay aside his suspicions, and privily caused men to scour the interior and let him know quickly of any treachery which they might espy. On this errand they went into the forest, and, coming upon the array of an armed encampment belonging to the forces of the Britons, they halted in doubt, but hastily retraced their steps when the truth was apparent. For the tents were dusky in colour, and muffled in a sort of pitchy coverings, that they might not catch the eye of anyone who came near. When Frode learned this, he arranged a counter-ambuscade with a strong force of nobles, that he might not go heedlessly to the banquet, and be cheated of timely aid. They went into hiding, and he warned them that the note of the trumpet was the signal for them to bring assistance. Then with a select band, lightly armed, he went to the banquet. The hall was decked with regal splendour; it was covered all round with crimson hangings of marvellous rich handiwork. A curtain of purple dye adorned the propelled walls. The flooring was bestrewn with bright mantles, which a man would fear to trample on. Up above was to be seen the twinkle of many lanterns, the gleam of lamps lit with oil, and the censers poured forth fragrance whose sweet vapour was laden with the choicest perfumes. The whole way was blocked by the tables loaded with good things; and the places for reclining were decked with gold-embroidered couches; the seats were full of pillows. The majestic hall seemed to smile upon the guests, and nothing could be noticed in all that pomp either inharmonious to the eye or offensive to the smell. In the midst of the hall stood a great butt ready for refilling the goblets, and holding an enormous amount of liquor; enough could be drawn from it for the huge revel to drink its fill. Servants, dressed in purple, bore golden cups, and courteously did the office of serving the drink, pacing in ordered ranks. Nor did they fail to offer the draught in the horns of the wild ox.

The feast glittered with golden bowls, and was laden with shining goblets, many of them studded with flashing jewels. The place was filled with an immense luxury; the tables groaned with the dishes, and the bowls brimmed over with divers liquors. Nor did they use wine pure and simple, but, with juices sought far and wide, composed a nectar of many flavours. The dishes glistened with delicious foods, being filled mostly with the spoils of the chase; though the flesh of tame animals was not lacking either. The natives took care to drink more sparingly than the guests; for the latter felt safe, and were tempted to make an orgy; while the others, meditating treachery, had lost all temptations to be drunken. So the Danes, who, if I may say so with my country's leave, were seasoned to drain the bowl against each other, took quantities of wine. The Britons, when they saw that the Danes were very drunk, began gradually to slip away from the banquet, and, leaving their guests within the hall, made immense efforts, first to block the doors of the palace by applying bars and all kinds of obstacles, and then to set fire to the house. The Danes were penned inside the hall, and when the fire began to spread, battered vainly at the doors; but they could not get out, and soon attempted to make a sally by assaulting the wall. And the Angles, when they saw that it was tottering under the stout attack of the Danes, began to shove against it on their side, and to prop the staggering pile by the application of large blocks on the outside, to prevent the wall being shattered and releasing the prisoners. But at last it yielded to the stronger hand of the Danes, whose efforts increased with their peril; and those pent within could sally out with ease. Then Frode bade the trumpet strike in, to summon the band that had been posted in ambush; and these, roused by the note of the clanging bugle, caught the enemy in their own trap; for the King of the Britons, with countless hosts of his men, was utterly destroyed. Thus the band helped Frode doubly, being both the salvation of his men and the destruction of his enemies.

Meantime the renown of the Danish bravery spread far, and moved the Irish to strew iron calthrops on the ground, in order to make their land harder to invade, and forbid access to their shores. Now the Irish use armour which is light and easy to procure. They crop the hair close with razors, and shave all the hair off the back of the head, that they may not be seized by it when they run away. They also turn the points of their spears towards the assailant, and deliberately point their sword against the pursuer; and they generally fling their lances behind their back, being more skilled at conquering by flight than by fighting. Hence, when you fancy that the victory is yours, then is the moment of danger. But Frode was wary and not rash in his pursuit of the foe who fled so treacherously, and he routed Kerwil (Cearbal), the leader of the nation, in battle. Kerwil's brother survived, but lost heart for resistance, and surrendered his country to the king (Frode), who distributed among his soldiers the booty he had won, to show himself free from all covetousness and excessive love of wealth, and only ambitious to gain honour.

After the triumphs in Britain and the spoiling of the Irish they went back to Denmark; and for thirty years there was a pause from all warfare. At this time the Danish name became famous over the whole world almost for its extraordinary valour. Frode, therefore, desired to prolong and establish for ever the lustre of his empire, and made it his first object to inflict severe treatment upon thefts and brigandage, feeling these were domestic evils and intestine plagues, and that if the nations were rid of them they would come to enjoy a more tranquil life; so that no ill-will should mar and hinder the continual extention of peace. He also took care that the land should not be devoured by any plague at home when the enemy was at rest, and that intestine wickedness should not encroach when there was peace abroad. At last he ordered that in Jutland, the chief district of his realm, a golden bracelet, very heavy, should be set up on the highways (as he had done before in the district of Wik), wishing by this magnificent price to test the honesty which he had enacted. Now, though the minds of the dishonest were vexed with the provocation it furnished, and the souls of the evil tempted, yet the unquestioned dread of danger prevailed. For so potent was the majesty of Frode, that it guarded even gold that was thus exposed to pillage, as though it were fast with bolts and bars. The strange device brought great glory upon its inventor. After dealing destruction everywhere, and gaining famous victories far and wide, he resolved to bestow quiet on all men, that the cheer of peace should follow the horrors of war, and the end of slaughter might be the beginning of safety. He further thought that for the same reason all men's property should be secured to them by a protective decree, so that what had been saved from a foreign enemy might not find a plunderer at home.

About the same time, the Author of our general salvation, coming to the earth in order to save mortals, bore to put on the garb of mortality; at which time the fires of war were quenched, and all the lands were enjoying the calmest and most tranquil peace. It has been thought that the peace then shed abroad so widely, so even and uninterrupted over the whole world, attended not so much an earthly rule as that divine birth; and that it was a heavenly provision that this extraordinary gift of time should be a witness to the presence of Him who created all times.

Meantime a certain matron, skilled in sorcery, who trusted in her art more than she feared the severity of the king, tempted the covetousness of her son to make a secret effort for the prize; promising him impunity, since Frode was almost at death's door, his body failing, and the remnant of his doting spirit feeble. To his mother's counsels he objected the greatness of the peril; but she bade him take hope, declaring, that either a sea-cow should have a calf, or that the king's vengeance should be baulked by some other chance. By this speech she banished her son's fears, and made him obey her advice. When the deed was done,

Frode, stung by the affront, rushed with the utmost heat and fury to raze the house of the matron, sending men on to arrest her and bring her with her children. This the woman foreknew, and deluded her enemies by a trick, changing from the shape of a woman into that of a mare. When Frode came up she took the shape of a sea-cow, and seemed to be straying and grazing about the shore; and she also made her sons look like calves of smaller size. This portent amazed the king, and he ordered that they should be surrounded and cut off from returning to the waters. Then he left the carriage, which he used because of the feebleness of his aged body, and sat on the ground marvelling. But the mother, who had taken the shape of the larger beast, charged at the king with outstretched tusk, and pierced one of his sides. The wound killed him; and his end was unworthy of such majesty as his. His soldiers, thirsting to avenge his death, threw their spears and transfixed the monsters, and saw, when they were killed, that they were the corpses of human beings with the heads of wild beasts: a circumstance which exposed the trick more than anything.

So ended Frode, the most famous king in the whole world. The nobles, when he had been disembowelled, had his body kept embalmed for three years, for they feared the provinces would rise if the king's end were published. They wished his death to be concealed above all from foreigners, so that by the pretence that he was alive they might preserve the boundaries of the empire, which had been extended for so long; and that, on the strength of the ancient authority of their general, they might exact the usual tribute from their subjects. So, the lifeless corpse was carried away by them in such a way that it seemed to be taken, not in a funeral bier, but in a royal carriage, as if it were a due and proper tribute from the soldiers to an infirm old man not in full possession of his forces. Such splendour did his friends bestow on him even in death. But when his limbs rotted, and were seized with extreme decay, and when the corruption could not be arrested, they buried his body with a royal funeral in a barrow near Waere, a bridge of Zealand; declaring that Frode had desired to die and be buried in what was thought the chief province of his kingdom.

Frode Humbles Himself Before Erik

BOOK SIX

After the death of Frode, the Danes wrongly supposed that Fridleif, who was being reared in Russia, had perished; and, thinking that the sovereignty halted for lack of an heir, and that it could no longer be kept on in the hands of the royal line, they considered that the sceptre would be best deserved by the man who should affix to the yet fresh grave of Frode a song of praise in his glorification, and commit the renown of the dead king to after ages by a splendid memorial. Then one HIARN, very skilled in writing Danish poetry, wishing to give the fame of the hero some notable record of words, and tempted by the enormous prize, composed, after his own fashion, a barbarous stave. Its purport, expressed in four lines, I have transcribed as follows:

"Frode, whom the Danes would have wished to live long, they bore long through their lands when he was dead. The great chief's body, with this turf heaped above it, bare earth covers under the lucid sky."

When the composer of this song had uttered it, the Danes rewarded him with the crown. Thus they gave a kingdom for an epitaph, and the weight of a whole empire was presented to a little string of letters. Slender expense for so vast a guerdon! This huge payment for a little poem exceeded the glory of Caesar's recompense; for it was enough for the divine Julius to pension with a township the writer and glorifier of those conquests which he had achieved over the whole world. But now the spendthrift kindness of the populace squandered a kingdom on a churl. Nay, not even Africanus, when he rewarded the records of his deed, rose to the munificence of the Danes. For there the wage of that laborious volume was in mere gold, while here a few callow verses won a sceptre for a peasant.

At the same time Erik, who held the governorship of Sweden, died of disease; and his son Halfdan, who governed in his father's stead, alarmed by the many attacks of twelve brothers of Norwegian birth, and powerless to punish their violence, fled, hoping for reinforcements, to ask aid of Fridleif, then sojourning in Russia. Approaching him with a suppliant face, he lamented that he was himself shattered and bruised by a foreign foe, and brought a dismal plaint of his wrongs. From him Fridleif heard the tidings of his father's death, and granting the aid he sought, went to Norway in armed array. At this time the aforesaid brothers, their allies forsaking them, built a very high rampart within an island surrounded by a swift stream, also extending their earthworks along the level. Trusting to this refuge, they harried the neighborhood with continual raids. For they built a bridge on which they used to get to the mainland when they left the island. This bridge was fastened to the gate of the stronghold; and they worked it by the guidance of ropes, in such a way that it turned as if on some revolving hinge, and at one time let them pass across the river; while at another, drawn back from above by unseen cords, it helped to defend the entrance.

These warriors were of valiant temper, young and stalwart, of splendid bodily presence, renowned for victories over giants, full of trophies of conquered nations, and wealthy with spoil. I record the names of some of them—for the rest have perished in antiquity—Gerbiorn, Gunbiorn, Arinbiorn, Stenbiorn, Esbiorn, Thorbiorn, and Biorn. Biorn is said to have had a horse which was splendid and of exceeding speed, so that when all the rest were powerless to cross the river it alone stemmed the roaring eddy without weariness. This rapid comes down in so swift and sheer a volume that animals often lose all power of swimming in it, and perish. For, trickling from the topmost crests of the hills, it comes down the steep sides, catches on the rocks, and is shattered, falling into the deep valleys with a manifold clamour of waters; but, being straightway rebuffed by the rocks that bar the way, it keeps the speed of its current ever at the same even pace. And so, along the whole length of the channel, the waves are one turbid mass, and the white foam brims over everywhere. But, after rolling out of the narrows between the rocks, it spreads abroad in a slacker and stiller flood, and turns into an island a rock that lies in its course. On either side of the rock juts out a sheer ridge, thick with divers trees, which screen the river from distant view. Biorn had also a dog of extraordinary fierceness, a terribly vicious brute, dangerous for people to live with, which had often singly destroyed twelve men. But, since the tale is hearsay rather than certainty, let good judges weigh its credit. This dog, as I have heard, was the favourite of the giant Offot (Un-foot), and used to watch his herd amid the pastures.

Now the warriors, who were always pillaging the neighbourhood, used often to commit great slaughters. Plundering houses, cutting down cattle, sacking everything, making great hauls of booty, rifling houses, then burning them, massacring male and female promiscuously—these, and not honest dealings, were their occupations. Fridleif surprised them while on a reckless raid, and drove them all back for refuge to the stronghold; he also seized the immensely powerful horse, whose rider, in the haste of his panic, had left it on the hither side of the river in order to fly betimes; for he durst not take it with him over the bridge. Then Fridleif proclaimed that he would pay the weight of the dead body in gold to any man who slew one of those brothers. The hope of the prize stimulated some of the champions of the king; and yet they were fired not so much with covetousness as with valour; so, going secretly to Fridleif, they promised to attempt the task, vowing to sacrifice their lives if they did not bring home the severed heads of the robbers. Fridleif praised their valour and their vows, but bidding the onlookers wait, went in the night to the river, satisfied with a single companion. For, not to seem better provided with other men's valour than with his own, he determined to forestall their aid by his own courage. Thereupon he crushed and killed his companion with a shower of flints, and flung his bloodless corpse into the waves, having dressed it in his own clothes; which he stripped off, borrowing the cast-off garb of the other, so that when the corpse was seen it might look as if the king had perished. He further deliberately drew blood from the beast on which he had ridden, and bespattered it, so that when it came back into camp he might make them think he himself was dead. Then he set spur to his horse and drove it into the midst of the eddies, crossed the river and alighted, and tried to climb over the rampart that screened the stronghold by steps set up against the mound. When he got over the top and could grasp the battlements with his hand, he quietly put his foot inside, and, without the knowledge of the watch, went lightly on tiptoe to the house into which the bandits had gone to carouse. And when he had reached its hall, he sat down under the porch overhanging the door. Now the strength of their fastness made the warriors feel so safe that they were tempted to a debauch; for they thought that the swiftly rushing river made their garrison inaccessible, since it seemed impossible either to swim over or to cross in boats. For no part of the river allowed of fording.

Biorn, moved by the revel, said that in his sleep he had seen a beast come out of the waters, which spouted ghastly fire from its mouth, enveloping everything in a sheet of flame. Therefore the holes and corners of the island should, he said, be searched; nor ought they to trust so much to their position, as rashly to let overweening confidence bring them to utter ruin. No situation was so strong that the mere protection of nature was enough for it without human effort. Moreover they must take great care that the warning of his slumbers was not followed by a yet more gloomy and disastrous fulfilment. So they all sallied forth from the stronghold, and narrowly scanned the whole circuit of the island; and finding the horse they surmised that Fridleif had been drowned in the waters of the river. They received the horse within the gates with rejoicing, supposing that it had flung off its rider and swum over. But Biorn, still scared with the memory of the visions of the night, advised them to keep watch, since it was not safe for them yet to put aside suspicion of danger. Then he went to his room to rest, with the memory of his vision deeply stored in his heart.

Meanwhile the horse, which Fridleif, in order to spread a belief in his death, had been loosed and besprinkled with blood (though only with that which lies between flesh and skin), burst all bedabbled into the camp of his soldiers. They went straight to the river, and finding the carcase of the slave, took it for the body of the king; the hissing eddies having cast it on the bank, dressed in brave attire. Nothing helped their mistake so much as the swelling of the battered body; inasmuch as the skin was torn and bruised with the flints, so that all the features were blotted out, bloodless and wan. This exasperated the champions who had just promised Fridleif to see that the robbers were extirpated: and they approached the perilous torrent, that they might not seem to tarnish the honour of their promise by a craven neglect of their vow. The rest imitated their boldness, and with equal ardour went to the river, ready to avenge their king or to endure the worst. When Fridleif saw them he hastened to lower the bridge to the mainland; and when he had got the champions he cut down the watch at the first attack. Thus he went on to attack the rest and put them to the sword, all save Biorn; whom he tended very carefully and cured of his wounds; whereupon, under pledge of solemn oath, he made him his colleague, thinking it better to use his services than to boast of his death. He also declared it would be shameful if such a flower of bravery were plucked in his first youth and perished by an untimely death.

Now the Danes had long ago had false tidings of Fridleif's death, and when they found that he was approaching, they sent men to fetch him, and ordered Hiarn to quit the sovereignty, because he was thought to be holding it only on sufferance and carelessly. But he could not bring himself to resign such an honour, and chose sooner to spend his life for glory than pass into the dim lot of common men. Therefore he resolved to fight for his present estate, that he might not have to resume his former one stripped of his royal honours. Thus the land was estranged and vexed with the hasty commotion of civil strife; some were of Hiarn's party, while others agreed to the claims of Fridleif, because of the vast services of Frode; and the voice of the commons was perplexed and divided, some of them respecting things as they were, others the memory of the past. But regard for the memory of Frode weighed most, and its sweetness gave Fridleif the balance of popularity.

Many wise men thought that a person of peasant rank should be removed from the sovereignty; since, contrary to the rights of birth, and only by the favour of fortune, he had reached an unhoped-for eminence; and in order that the unlawful occupant might not debar the rightful heir to the office, Fridleif told the envoys of the Danes to return, and request Hiarn either to resign the kingdom or to meet him in battle. Hiarn thought it more grievous than death to set lust of life before honour, and to seek safety at the cost of glory. So he met Fridleif in the field, was crushed, and fled into Jutland, where, rallying a band, he again attacked his conqueror. But his men were all consumed with the sword, and he fled unattended, as the island testifies which has taken its name from his (Hiarno). And so, feeling his lowly fortune, and seeing himself almost stripped of his forces by the double defeat, he turned his mind to craft, and went to Fridleif with his face disguised, meaning to become intimate, and find an occasion to slay him treacherously.

Hiarn was received by the king, hiding his purpose under the pretence of servitude. For, giving himself out as a salt-distiller, he performed base offices among the servants who did the filthiest work. He used also to take the last place at meal-time, and he refrained from the baths, lest his multitude of scars should betray him if he stripped. The king, in order to ease his own suspicions, made him wash; and when he knew his enemy by the scars, he said: "Tell me now, thou shameless bandit, how wouldst thou have dealt with me, if thou hadst found out plainly that I wished to murder thee?" Hiarn, stupefied, said: "Had I caught thee I would have first challenged thee, and then fought thee, to give thee a better chance of wiping out thy reproach." Fridleif presently took him at his word, challenged him and slew him, and buried his body in a barrow that bears the dead man's name.

Soon after FRIDLEIF was admonished by his people to think about marrying, that he might prolong his line; but he maintained that the unmarried life was best, quoting his father Frode, on whom his wife's wantonness had brought great dishonour. At last, yielding to the persistent entreaties of all, he proceeded to send ambassadors to ask for the daughter of Amund, King of Norway. One of these, named Frok, was swallowed by the waves in mid-voyage, and showed a strange portent at his death. For when the closing flood of billows encompassed him, blood arose in the midst of the eddy, and the whole face of the sea was steeped with an alien redness, so that the ocean, which a moment before was foaming and white with tempest, was presently swollen with crimson waves, and was seen to wear a colour foreign to its nature.

Around implacably declined to consent to the wishes of the king, and treated the legates shamefully, declaring that he spurned the embassy because the tyranny of Frode had of old borne so heavily upon Norway. But Amund's daughter, Frogertha, not only looking to the birth of Fridleif, but also honouring the glory of his deeds, began to upbraid her father, because he scorned a son-in-law whose nobility was perfect, being both sufficient in valour and flawless in birth. She added that the portentous aspect of the sea, when the waves were suddenly turned into blood, simply and solely signified the defeat of Norway, and was a plain presage of the victory of Denmark. And when Fridleif sent a further embassy to ask for her, wishing to vanquish the refusal by persistency, Amund was indignant that a petition he had once denied should be obstinately pressed, and hurried the envoys to death, wishing to offer a brutal check to the zeal of this brazen wooer. Fridleif heard news of this outrage, and summoning Halfdan and Biorn, sailed round Norway. Amund, equipped with his native defences, put out his fleet against him. The firth into which both fleets had mustered is called Frokasund. Here Fridleif left the camp at night to reconnoitre; and, hearing an unusual kind of sound close to him as of brass being beaten, he stood still and looked up, and heard the following song of three swans, who were crying above him:

"While Hythin sweeps the sea and cleaves the ravening tide, his serf drinks out of gold and licks the cups of milk. Best is the estate of the slave on whom waits the heir, the king's son, for their lots are rashly interchanged." Next, after the birds had sung, a belt fell from on high, which showed writing to interpret the song. For while the son of Hythin, the King of Tellemark, was at his boyish play, a giant, assuming the usual appearance of men, had carried him off, and using him as an oarsman (having taken his skiff over to the neighbouring shore), was then sailing past Fridleif while he was occupied reconnoitering. But the king would not suffer him to use the service of the captive youth, and longed to rob the spoiler of his prey. The youth warned him that he must first use sharp reviling against the giant, promising that he would prove easy to attack, if only he were assailed with biting verse. Then Fridleif began thus:

"Since thou art a giant of three bodies, invincible, and almost reachest heaven with thy crest, why does this silly sword bind thy thigh? Why doth a broken spear gird thy huge side? Why, perchance, dost thou defend thy stalwart breast with a feeble sword, and forget the likeness of thy bodily stature, trusting in a short dagger, a petty weapon? Soon, soon will I balk thy bold onset, when with blunted blade thou attemptest war. Since thou art thyself a timid beast, a lump lacking proper pith, thou art swept headlong like a flying shadow, having with a fair and famous body got a heart that is unwarlike and unstable with fear, and a spirit quite unmatched to thy limbs. Hence thy frame totters, for thy goodly presence is faulty through the overthrow of thy soul, and thy nature in all her parts is at strife. Hence shall all tribute of praise quit thee, nor shalt thou be accounted famous among the brave, but shalt be reckoned among ranks obscure."

When he had said this he lopped off a hand and foot of the giant, made him fly, and set his prisoner free. Then he went straightway to the giant's headland, took the treasure out of his cave, and carried it away. Rejoicing in these trophies, and employing the kidnapped youth to row him over the sea, he composed with cheery voice the following strain:

"In the slaying of the swift monster we wielded our blood-stained swords and our crimsoned blade, whilst thou, Amund, lord of the Norwegian ruin, wert in deep slumber; and since blind night covers thee, without any light of soul, thy valour has melted away and beguiled thee. But we crushed a giant who lost use of his limbs and wealth, and we pierced into the disorder of his dreary den. There we seized and plundered his piles of gold. And now with oars we sweep the wave-wandering main, and joyously return, rowing back to the shore our booty-laden ship; we fleet over the waves in a skiff that travels the sea; gaily let us furrow those open waters, lest the dawn come and betray us to the foe. Lightly therefore, and pulling our hardest, let us scour the sea, making for our camp and fleet ere Titan raise his rosy head out of the clear waters; that when fame noises the deed about, and Frogertha knows that the spoil has been won with a gallant struggle, her heart may be stirred to be more gentle to our prayer."

On the morrow there was a great muster of the forces, and Fridleif had a bloody battle with Amund, fought partly by sea and partly by land. For not only were the lines drawn up in the open country, but the warriors also made an attack with their fleet. The battle which followed cost much blood. So Biorn, when his ranks gave back, unloosed his hound and sent it against the enemy; wishing to win with the biting of a dog the victory which he could not achieve with the sword. The enemy were by this means shamefully routed, for a square of the warriors ran away when attacked with its teeth.

There is no saying whether their flight was more dismal or more disgraceful. Indeed, the army of the Northmen was a thing to blush for; for an enemy crushed it by borrowing the aid of a brute. Nor was it treacherous of Fridleif to recruit the failing valour of his men with the aid of a dog. In this war Amund fell; and his servant Ane, surnamed the Archer, challenged Fridleif to fight him; but Biorn, being a man of meaner estate, not suffering the king to engage with a common fellow, attacked him himself. And when Biorn had bent his bow and was fitting the arrow to the string, suddenly a dart sent by Ane pierced the top of the cord. Soon another arrow came after it and struck amid the joints of his fingers. A third followed, and fell on the arrow as it was laid to the string. For Ane, who was most dexterous at shooting arrows from a distance, had purposely only struck the weapon of his opponent, in order that, by showing it was in his power to do likewise to his person, he might recall the champion from his purpose. But Biorn abated none of his valour for this, and, scorning bodily danger, entered the fray with heart and face so steadfast, that he seemed neither to yield anything to the skill of Ane, nor lay aside aught of his wonted courage. Thus he would in nowise be made to swerve from his purpose, and dauntlessly ventured on the battle. Both of them left it wounded; and fought another also on Agdar Ness with an emulous thirst for glory.

By the death of Amund, Fridleif was freed from a most bitter foe, and obtained a deep and tranquil peace; whereupon he forced his savage temper to the service of delight; and, transferring his ardour to love, equipped a fleet in order to seek the marriage which had once been denied him. At last he set forth on his voyage; and his fleet being becalmed, he invaded some villages to look for food; where, being received hospitably by a certain Grubb, and at last winning his daughter in marriage, he begat a son named Olaf. After some time had passed he also won Frogertha; but, while going back to his own country, he had a bad voyage, and was driven on the shores of an unknown island. A certain man appeared to him in a vision, and instructed him to dig up a treasure that was buried in the ground, and also to attack the dragon that guarded it, covering himself in an ox-hide to escape the poison; teaching him also to meet the envenomed fangs with a hide stretched over his shield. Therefore, to test the vision, he attacked the snake as it rose out of the waves, and for a long time cast spears against its scaly side; in vain, for its hard and shelly body foiled the darts flung at it. But the snake, shaking its mass of coils, uprooted the trees which it brushed past by winding its tail about them. Moreover, by constantly dragging its body, it hollowed the ground down to the solid rock, and had made a sheer bank on either hand, just as in some places we see hills parted by an intervening valley. So Fridleif, seeing that the upper part of the creature was proof against attack, assailed the lower side with his sword, and piercing the groin, drew blood from the quivering beast. When it was dead, he unearthed the money from the underground chamber and had it taken off in his ships.

When the year had come to an end, he took great pains to reconcile Biorn and Ane, who had often challenged and fought one another, and made them exchange their hatred for friendship; and even entrusted to them his three-year-old son, Olaf, to rear. But his mistress, Juritha, the mother of Olaf, he gave in marriage to Ane, whom he made one of his warriors; thinking that she would endure more calmly to be put away, if she wedded such a champion, and received his robust embrace instead of a king's.

The ancients were wont to consult the oracles of the Fates concerning the destinies of their children. In this way Fridleif desired to search into the fate of his son Olaf; and, after solemnly offering up his vows, he went to the house of the gods in entreaty; where, looking into the chapel, he saw three maidens, sitting on three seats. The first of them was of a benignant temper, and bestowed upon the boy abundant beauty and ample store of favour in the eyes of men. The second granted him the gift of surpassing generosity. But the third, a woman of more mischievous temper and malignant disposition, scorning the unanimous kindness of her sisters, and likewise wishing to mar their gifts, marked the future character of the boy with the slur of niggardliness. Thus the benefits of the others were spoilt by the poison of a lamentable doom; and hence, by virtue of the twofold nature of these gifts Olaf got his surname from the meanness which was mingled with his bounty. So it came about that this blemish which found its way into the gift marred the whole sweetness of its first benignity.

When Fridleif had returned from Norway, and was traveling through Sweden, he took on himself to act as ambassador, and sued successfully for Hythin's daughter, whom he had once rescued from a monster, to be the wife of Halfdan, he being still unwedded. Meantime his wife Frogertha bore a son FRODE, who afterwards got his surname from his noble munificence. And thus Frode, because of the memory of his grandsire's prosperity, which he recalled by his name, became from his very cradle and earliest childhood such a darling of all men, that he was not suffered even to step or stand on the ground, but was continually cherished in people's laps and kissed. Thus he was not assigned to one upbringer only, but was in a manner everybody's fosterling. And, after his father's death, while he was in his twelfth year, Swerting and Hanef, the kings of Saxony, disowned his sway, and tried to rebel openly. He overcame them in battle, and imposed on the conquered peoples a poll-tax of a coin, which they were to pay as his slaves. For he showed himself so generous that he doubled the ancient pay of the soldiers: a fashion of bounty which then was novel. For he did not, as despots do, expose himself to the vulgar allurements of vice, but strove to covet ardently whatsoever he saw was nearest honour; to make his wealth public property; to surpass all other men in bounty, to forestall them all in offices of kindness; and, hardest of all, to conquer envy by virtue. By this means the youth soon won such favour with all men, that he not only equalled in renown the honours of his forefathers, but surpassed the most ancient records of kings.

At the same time one Starkad, the son of Storwerk, escaped alone, either by force or fortune, from a wreck in which his friends perished, and was received by Frode as his guest for his incredible excellence both of mind and body. And, after being for some little time his comrade, he was dressed in a better and more comely fashion every day, and was at last given a noble vessel, and bidden to ply the calling of a rover, with the charge of guarding the sea. For nature had gifted him with a body of superhuman excellence; and his greatness of spirit equalled it, so that folk thought him behind no man in valour. So far did his glory spread, that the renown of his name and deeds continues famous even yet. He shone out among our own countrymen by his glorious roll of exploits, and he had also won a most splendid record among all the provinces of the Swedes and Saxons. Tradition says that he was born originally in the country which borders Sweden on the east, where barbarous hordes of Esthonians and other nations now dwell far and wide. But a fabulous yet common rumour has invented tales about his birth which are contrary to reason and flatly incredible. For some relate that he was sprung from giants, and betrayed his monstrous birth by an extraordinary number of hands, four of which, engendered by the superfluity of his nature, they declare that the god Thor tore off, shattering the framework of the sinews and wrenching from his whole body the monstrous bunches of fingers; so that he had but two left, and that his body, which had before swollen to the size of a giant's, and, by reason of its shapeless crowd of limbs looked gigantic, was thenceforth chastened to a better appearance, and kept within the bounds of human shortness.

For there were of old certain men versed in sorcery, Thor, namely, and Odin, and many others, who were cunning in contriving marvellous sleights; and they, winning the minds of the simple, began to claim the rank of gods. For, in particular, they ensnared Norway, Sweden and Denmark in the vainest credulity, and by prompting these lands to worship them, infected them with their imposture. The effects of their deceit spread so far, that all other men adored a sort of divine power in them, and, thinking them either gods or in league with gods, offered up solemn prayers to these inventors of sorceries, and gave to blasphemous error the honour due to religion. Hence it has come about that the holy days, in their regular course, are called among us by the names of these men; for the ancient Latins are known to have named these days severally, either after the titles of their own gods, or after the planets, seven in number. But it can be plainly inferred from the mere names of the holy days that the objects worshipped by our countrymen were not the same as those whom the most ancient of the Romans called Jove and Mercury, nor those to whom Greece and Latium paid idolatrous homage. For the days, called among our countrymen Thors-day or Odins-day, the ancients termed severally the holy day of Jove or of Mercury. If, therefore, according to the distinction implied in the interpretation I have quoted, we take it that Thor is Jove and Odin Mercury, it follows that Jove was the son of Mercury; that is, if the assertion of our countrymen holds, among whom it is told as a matter of common belief, that Thor was Odin's son. Therefore, when the Latins, believing to the contrary effect, declare that Mercury was sprung from Jove, then, if their declaration is to stand, we are driven to consider that Thor was not the same as Jove, and that Odin was also different from

Mercury. Some say that the gods, whom our countrymen worshipped, shared only the title with those honoured by Greece or Latium, but that, being in a manner nearly equal to them in dignity, they borrowed from them the worship as well as the name. This must be sufficient discourse upon the deities of Danish antiquity. I have expounded this briefly for the general profit, that my readers may know clearly to what worship in its heathen superstition our country has bowed the knee. Now I will go back to my subject where I left it.

Ancient tradition says that Starkad, whom I mentioned above, offered the first-fruits of his deeds to the favour of the gods by slaying Wikar, the king of the Norwegians. The affair, according to the version of some people, happened as follows:—

Odin once wished to slay Wikar by a grievous death; but, loth to do the deed openly, he graced Starkad, who was already remarkable for his extraordinary size, not only with bravery, but also with skill in the composing of spells, that he might the more readily use his services to accomplish the destruction of the king. For that was how he hoped that Starkad would show himself grateful for the honour he paid him. For the same reason he also endowed him with three spans of mortal life, that he might be able to commit in them as many abominable deeds. So Odin resolved that Starkad's days should be prolonged by the following crime: Starkad presently went to Wikar and dwelt awhile in his company, hiding treachery under homage. At last he went with him sea-roving. And in a certain place they were troubled with prolonged and bitter storms; and when the winds checked their voyage so much that they had to lie still most of the year, they thought that the gods must be appeased with human blood. When the lots were cast into the urn it so fell that the king was required for death as a victim. Then Starkad made a noose of withies and bound the king in it; saying that for a brief instant he should pay the mere semblance of a penalty. But the tightness of the knot acted according to its nature, and cut off his last breath as he hung. And while he was still quivering Starkad rent away with his steel the remnant of his life; thus disclosing his treachery when he ought to have brought aid. I do not think that I need examine the version which relates that the pliant withies, hardened with the sudden grip, acted like a noose of iron.

When Starkad had thus treacherously acted he took Wikar's ship and went to one Bemon, the most courageous of all the rovers of Denmark, in order to take up the life of a pirate. For Bemon's partner, named Frakk, weary of the toil of sea-roving, had lately withdrawn from partnership with him, after first making a money-bargain. Now Starkad and Bemon were so careful to keep temperate, that they are said never

215

to have indulged in intoxicating drink, for fear that continence, the greatest bond of bravery, might be expelled by the power of wantonness. So when, after overthrowing provinces far and wide, they invaded Russia also in their lust for empire, the natives, trusting little in their walls or arms, began to bar the advance of the enemy with nails of uncommon sharpness, that they might check their inroad, though they could not curb their onset in battle; and that the ground might secretly wound the soles of the men whom their army shrank from confronting in the field. But not even such a barrier could serve to keep off the foe. The Danes were cunning enough to foil the pains of the Russians. For they straightway shod themselves with wooden clogs, and trod with unhurt steps upon the points that lay beneath their soles. Now this iron thing is divided into four spikes, which are so arranged that on whatsoever side chance may cast it, it stands steadily on three equal feet. Then they struck into the pathless glades, where the woods were thickets, and expelled Flokk, the chief of the Russians, from the mountain hiding-places into which he had crept. And here they got so much booty, that there was not one of them but went back to the fleet laden with gold and silver.

Now when Bemon was dead, Starkad was summoned because of his valour by the champions of Permland. And when he had done many noteworthy deeds among them, he went into the land of the Swedes, where he lived at leisure for seven years' space with the sons of Frey. At last he left them and betook himself to Hakon, the tyrant of Denmark, because when stationed at Upsala, at the time of the sacrifices, he was disgusted by the effeminate gestures and the clapping of the mimes on the stage, and by the unmanly clatter of the bells. Hence it is clear how far he kept his soul from lasciviousness, not even enduring to look upon it. Thus does virtue withstand wantonness.

Starkad took his fleet to the shore of Ireland with Hakon, in order that even the furthest kingdoms of the world might not be untouched by the Danish arms. The king of the island at this time was Hugleik, who, though he had a well-filled treasury, was yet so prone to avarice, that once, when he gave a pair of shoes which had been adorned by the hand of a careful craftsman, he took off the ties, and by thus removing the latches turned his present into a slight. This unhandsome act blemished his gift so much that he seemed to reap hatred for it instead of thanks. Thus he used never to be generous to any respectable man, but to spend all his bounty upon mimes and jugglers. For so base a fellow was bound to keep friendly company with the base, and such a slough of vices to wheedle his partners in sin with pandering endearments.

Still Hugleik had the friendship of Geigad and Swipdag, nobles of tried valour, who, by the lustre of their warlike deeds, shone out among their unmanly companions like jewels embedded in ordure; these alone were found to defend the riches of the king. When a battle began between Hugleik and Hakon, the hordes of mimes, whose light-mindedness unsteadied their bodies, broke their ranks and scurried off in panic; and this shameful flight was their sole requital for all their king's benefits. Then Geigad and Swipdag faced all those thousands of the enemy single-handed, and fought with such incredible courage, that they seemed to do the part not merely of two warriors, but of a whole army. Geigad, moreover, dealt Hakon, who pressed him hard, such a wound in the breast that he exposed the upper part of his liver. It was here that Starkad, while he was attacking Geigad with his sword, received a very sore wound on the head; wherefore he afterwards related in a certain song that a ghastlier wound had never befallen him at any time; for, though the divisions of his gashed head were bound up by the surrounding outer skin, yet the livid unseen wound concealed a foul gangrene below.

Starkad conquered, killed Hugleik and routed the Irish; and had the actors beaten whom chance made prisoner; thinking it better to order a pack of buffoons to be ludicrously punished by the loss of their skins than to command a more deadly punishment and take their lives. Thus he visited with a disgraceful chastisement the baseborn throng of professional jugglers, and was content to punish them with the disgusting flouts of the lash. Then the Danes ordered that the wealth of the king should be brought out of the treasury in the city of Dublin and publicly pillaged. For so vast a treasure had been found that none took much pains to divide it strictly.

After this, Starkad was commissioned, together with Win, the chief of the Sclavs, to check the revolt of the East. They, having fought against the armies of the Kurlanders, the Sembs, the Sangals, and, finally, all the Easterlings, won splendid victories everywhere.
A champion of great repute, named Wisin, settled upon a rock in Russia named Ana-fial, and harried both neighbouring and distant provinces with all kinds of outrage. This man used to blunt the edge of every weapon by merely looking at it. He was made so bold in consequence, by having lost all fear of wounds, that he used to carry off the wives of distinguished men and drag them to outrage before the eyes of their husbands. Starkad was roused by the tale of this villainy, and went to Russia to destroy the criminal; thinking nothing too hard to overcome, he challenged Wisin, attacked him, made even his tricks useless to him, and slew him. For Starkad covered his blade with a very fine skin, that it might not met the eye of the sorcerer; and neither the power of his

217

sleights nor his great strength were any help to Wisin, for he had to yield to Starkad. Then Starkad, trusting in his bodily strength, fought with and overcame a giant at Byzantium, reputed invincible, named Tanne, and drove him to fly an outlaw to unknown quarters of the earth. Therefore, finding that he was too mighty for any hard fate to overcome him, he went to the country of Poland, and conquered in a duel a champion whom our countrymen name Wasce; but the Teutons, arranging the letters differently, call him Wilzce.

Meanwhile the Saxons began to attempt a revolt, and to consider particularly how they could destroy Frode, who was unconquered in war, by some other way than an open conflict. Thinking that it would be best done by a duel, they sent men to provoke the king with a challenge, knowing that he was always ready to court any hazard, and that his high spirit would not yield to any admonition whatever. They fancied that this was the best time to attack him, because they knew that Starkad, whose valour most men dreaded, was away on business. But while Frode hesitated, and said that he would talk with his friends about the answer to be given, Starkad, who had just returned from his sea-roving, appeared, and blamed such a challenge, principally (he said) because it was fitting for kings to fight only with their equals, and because they should not take up arms against men of the people; but it was more fitting for himself, who was born in a lowlier station, to manage the battle.

The Saxons approached Hame, who was accounted their most famous champion, with many offers, and promised him that, if he would lend his services for the duel they would pay him his own weight in gold. The fighter was tempted by the money, and, with all the ovation of a military procession, they attended him to the ground appointed for the combat. Thereupon the Danes, decked in warlike array, led Starkad, who was to represent his king, out to the duelling-ground. Hame, in his youthful assurance, despised him as withered with age, and chose to grapple rather than fight with an outworn old man. Attacking Starkad, he would have flung him tottering to the earth, but that fortune, who would not suffer the old man to be conquered, prevented him from being hurt. For he is said to have been so crushed by the fist of Hame, as he dashed on him, that he touched the earth with his chin, supporting himself on his knees. But he made up nobly for his tottering; for, as soon as he could raise his knee and free his hand to draw his sword, he clove Hame through the middle of the body. Many lands and sixty bondmen apiece were the reward of the victory.

After Hame was killed in this manner the sway of the Danes over the Saxons grew so insolent, that they were forced to pay every year a small tax for each of their limbs that was a cubit (ell) long, in token of their slavery. This Hanef could not bear, and he meditated war in his desire to remove the tribute. Steadfast love of his country filled his heart every day with greater compassion for the oppressed; and, longing to spend his life for the freedom of his countrymen, he openly showed a disposition to rebel. Frode took his forces over the Elbe, and killed him near the village of Hanofra (Hanover), so named after Hanef. But Swerting, though he was equally moved by the distress of his countrymen, said nothing about the ills of his land, and revolved a plan for freedom with a spirit yet more dogged than Hanef's. Men often doubt whether this zeal was liker to vice or to virtue; but I certainly censure it as criminal, because it was produced by a treacherous desire to revolt. It may have seemed most expedient to seek the freedom of the country, but it was not lawful to strive after this freedom by craft and treachery. Therefore, since the deed of Swerting was far from honourable, neither will it be called expedient; for it is nobler to attack openly him whom you mean to attack, and to exhibit hatred in the light of day, than to disguise a real wish to do harm under a spurious show of friendship. But the gains of crime are inglorious, its fruits are brief and fading. For even as that soul is slippery, which hides its insolent treachery by stealthy arts, so is it right that whatsoever is akin to guilt should be frail and fleeting. For guilt has been usually found to come home to its author; and rumour relates that such was the fate of Swerting. For he had resolved to surprise the king under the pretence of a banquet, and burn him to death; but the king forestalled and slew him, though slain by him in return. Hence the crime of one proved the destruction of both; and thus, though the trick succeeded against the foe, it did not bestow immunity on its author.

Frode was succeeded by his son Ingild, whose soul was perverted from honour. He forsook the examples of his forefathers, and utterly enthralled himself to the lures of the most wanton profligacy. Thus he had not a shadow of goodness and righteousness, but embraced vices instead of virtue; he cut the sinews of self-control, neglected the duties of his kingly station, and sank into a filthy slave of riot. Indeed, he fostered everything that was adverse or ill-fitted to an orderly life. He tainted the glories of his father and grandfather by practising the foulest lusts, and bedimmed the brightest honours of his ancestors by most shameful deeds. For he was so prone to gluttony, that he had no desire to avenge his father, or repel the aggressions of his foes; and so, could he but gratify his gullet, he thought that decency and self-control need be observed in nothing. By idleness and sloth he stained his glorious lineage, living a loose and sensual life; and his soul, so degenerate, so far perverted and astray from the steps of his fathers, he loved to plunge into most abominable gulfs of foulness. Fowl-fatteners, scullions, frying-pans, countless cook-houses, different cooks to roast or spice the banquet—the choosing of these stood to him for glory. As to arms, soldiering, and wars, he could endure neither to train himself to them, nor to let others practise them. Thus he cast away all the ambitions of a man and aspired to those of women; for his incontinent itching of palate stirred in him love of every kitchen-stench. Ever breathing of his debauch, and stripped of every rag of soberness, with his foul breath he belched the undigested filth in his belly. He was as infamous in wantonness as Frode was illustrious in war. So utterly had his spirit been enfeebled by the untimely seductions of gluttony. Starkad was so disgusted at the excess of Ingild, that he forsook his friendship, and sought the fellowship of Halfdan, the King of Swedes, preferring work to idleness. Thus he could not bear so much as to countenance excessive indulgence. Now the sons of Swerting, fearing that they would have to pay to Ingild the penalty of their father's crime, were fain to forestall his vengeance by a gift, and gave him their sister in marriage. Antiquity relates that she bore him sons, Frode, Fridleif, Ingild, and Olaf (whom some say was the son of Ingild's sister).

Ingild's sister Helga had been led by amorous wooing to return the flame of a certain low-born goldsmith, who was apt for soft words, and furnished with divers of the little gifts which best charm a woman's wishes. For since the death of the king there had been none to honour the virtues of the father by attention to the child; she had lacked protection, and had no guardians. When Starkad had learnt this from the repeated tales of travellers, he could not bear to let the wantonness of the smith pass unpunished. For he was always heedful to bear kindness in mind, and as ready to punish arrogance. So he hastened to chastise such bold and enormous insolence, wishing to repay the orphan ward the benefits he had of old received from Frode. Then he travelled through Sweden, went into the house of the smith, and posted himself near the threshold muffling his face in a cap to avoid discovery. The smith, who had not learnt the lesson that "strong hands are sometimes found under a mean garment", reviled him, and bade him quickly leave the house, saying that he should have the last broken victuals among the crowd of paupers. But the old man, whose ingrained self-control lent him patience, was nevertheless fain to rest there, and gradually study the wantonness of his host. For his reason was stronger than his impetuosity, and curbed his increasing rage. Then the smith approached the girl with open shamelessness, and cast himself in her lap, offering the hair of his head to be combed out by her maidenly hands.

Also he thrust forward his loin cloth, and required her help in picking out the fleas; and exacted from this woman of lordly lineage that she should not blush to put her sweet fingers in a foul apron. Then, believing that he was free to have his pleasure, he ventured to put his longing palms within her gown and to set his unsteady hands close to her breast. But she, looking narrowly, was aware of the presence of the old man whom she once had known, and felt ashamed. She spurned the wanton and libidinous fingering, and repulsed the unchaste hands, telling the man also that he had need of arms, and urging him to cease his lewd sport.

Starkad, who had sat down by the door, with the hat muffling his head, had already become so deeply enraged at this sight, that he could not find patience to hold his hand any longer, but put away his covering and clapped his right hand to his sword to draw it. Then the smith, whose only skill was in lewdness, faltered with sudden alarm, and finding that it had come to fighting, gave up all hope of defending himself, and saw in flight the only remedy for his need. Thus it was as hard to break out of the door, of which the enemy held the approach, as it was grievous to await the smiter within the house. At last necessity forced him to put an end to his delay, and he judged that a hazard wherein there lay but the smallest chance of safety was more desirable than sure and manifest danger. Also, hard as it was to fly, the danger being so close, yet he desired flight because it seemed to bring him aid, and to be the nearer way to safety; and he cast aside delay, which seemed to be an evil bringing not the smallest help, but perhaps irretrievable ruin. But just as he gained the threshold, the old man watching at the door smote him through the hams, and there, half dead, he tottered and fell. For the smiter thought he ought carefully to avoid lending his illustrious hands to the death of a vile cinder-blower, and considered that ignominy would punish his shameless passion worse than death. Thus some men think that he who suffers misfortune is worse punished than he who is slain outright. Thus it was brought about, that the maiden, who had never had parents to tend her, came to behave like a woman of well-trained nature, and did the part, as it were, of a zealous guardian to herself. And when Starkad, looking round, saw that the household sorrowed over the late loss of their master, he heaped shame on the wounded man with more invective, and thus began to mock:

"Why is the house silent and aghast? What makes this new grief? Or where now rest that doting husband whom the steel has just punished for his shameful love? Keeps he still aught of his pride and lazy wantonness? Holds he to his quest, glows his lust as hot as before? Let him while away an hour with me in converse, and allay with friendly words my hatred of yesterday. Let your visage come forth with better cheer; let not lamentation resound in the house, or suffer the faces to become dulled with sorrow.

"Wishing to know who burned with love for the maiden, and was deeply enamoured of my beloved ward, I put on a cap, lest my familiar face might betray me. Then comes in that wanton smith, with lewd steps, bending his thighs this way and that with studied gesture, and likewise making eyes as he ducked all ways. His covering was a mantle fringed with beaver, his sandals were inlaid with gems, his cloak was decked with gold. Gorgeous ribbons bound his plaited hair, and a many-coloured band drew tight his straying locks. Hence grew a sluggish and puffed-up temper; he fancied that wealth was birth, and money forefathers, and reckoned his fortune more by riches than by blood. Hence came pride unto him, and arrogance led to fine attire. For the wretch began to think that his dress made him equal to the high-born; he, the cinder-blower, who hunts the winds with hides, and puffs with constant draught, who rakes the ashes with his fingers, and often by drawing back the bellows takes in the air, and with a little fan makes a breath and kindles the smouldering fires! Then he goes to the lap of the girl, and leaning close, says, `Maiden, comb my hair and catch the skipping fleas, and remove what stings my skin.' Then he sat and spread his arms that sweated under the gold, lolling on the smooth cushion and leaning back on his elbow, wishing to flaunt his adornment, just as a barking brute unfolds the gathered coils of its twisted tail. But she knew me, and began to check her lover and rebuff his wanton hands; and, declaring that it was I, she said, `Refrain thy fingers, check thy promptings, take heed to appease the old man sitting close by the doors. The sport will turn to sorrow. I think Starkad is here, and his slow gaze scans thy doings.' The smith answered: `Turn not pale at the peaceful raven and the ragged old man; never has that mighty one whom thou fearest stooped to such common and base attire. The strong man loves shining raiment, and looks for clothes to match his courage.' Then I uncovered and drew my sword, and as the smith fled I clove his privy parts; his hams were laid open, cut away from the bone; they showed his entrails. Presently I rise and crush the girl's mouth with my fist, and draw blood from her bruised nostril. Then her lips, used to evil laughter, were wet with tears mingled with blood, and foolish love paid for all the sins it committed with soft eyes. Over is the sport of the hapless woman who rushed on, blind with desire, like a maddened mare, and makes her lust the grave of her beauty. Thou deservest to be sold for a price to foreign peoples and to grind at the mill, unless blood pressed from thy breasts prove thee falsely accused, and thy nipple's lack of milk clear thee of the crime. Howbeit, I think thee free from this fault; yet bear not tokens of suspicion, nor lay thyself open to lying tongues, nor give thyself to the chattering populace to gird at. Rumour hurts many, and a lying slander often harms. A little word deceives the thoughts of common men. Respect thy grandsires, honour thy fathers, forget not thy parents, value thy forefathers; let thy flesh and blood keep its fame. What madness came on thee? And thou, shameless smith, what fate drove thee in thy lust to attempt a high-born race? Or who sped thee, maiden, worthy of the lordliest pillows, to loves obscure? Tell me, how durst thou taste with thy rosy lips a mouth reeking of ashes, or endure on thy breast hands filthy with charcoal, or bring close to thy side the arms that turn the live coals over, and put the palms hardened with the use of the tongs to thy pure cheeks, and embrace the head sprinkled with embers, taking it to thy bright arms?

"I remember how smiths differ from one another, for once they smote me. All share alike the name of their calling, but the hearts beneath are different in temper. I judge those best who weld warriors' swords and spears for the battle, whose temper shows their courage, who betoken their hearts by the sternness of their calling, whose work declares their prowess. There are also some to whom the hollow mould yields bronze, as they make the likeness of divers things in molten gold, who smelt the veins and recast the metal. But Nature has fashioned these of a softer temper, and has crushed with cowardice the hands which she has gifted with rare skill. Often such men, while the heat of the blast melts the bronze that is poured in the mould, craftily filch flakes of gold from the lumps, when the vessel thirsts after the metal they have stolen."

So speaking, Starkad got as much pleasure from his words as from his works, and went back to Halfdan, embracing his service with the closest friendship, and never ceasing from the exercise of war; so that he weaned his mind from delights, and vexed it with incessant application to arms.

Now Ingild had two sisters, Helga and Asa; Helga was of full age to marry, while Asa was younger and unripe for wedlock. Then Helge the Norwegian was moved with desire to ask for Helga for his wife, and embarked. Now he had equipped his vessel so luxuriously that he had lordly sails decked with gold, held up also on gilded masts, and tied with crimson ropes. When he arrived Ingild promised to grant him his wish if, to test his reputation publicly, he would first venture to meet in battle the champions pitted against him. Helge did not flinch at the terms; he answered that he would most gladly abide by the compact. And so the troth-plight of the future marriage was most ceremoniously solemnized.

A story is remembered that there had grown up at the same time, on the Isle of Zealand, the nine sons of a certain prince, all highly gifted with strength and valour, the eldest of whom was Anganty. This last was a rival suitor for the same maiden; and when he saw that the match which he had been denied was promised to Helge, he challenged him to a struggle, wishing to fight away his vexation. Helge agreed to the proposed combat. The hour of the fight was appointed for the wedding-day by the common wish of both. For any man who, being challenged, refused to fight, used to be covered with disgrace in the sight of all men. Thus Helge was tortured on the one side by the shame of refusing the battle, on the other by the dread of waging it. For he thought himself attacked unfairly and counter to the universal laws of combat, as he had apparently undertaken to fight nine men single-handed. While he was thus reflecting his betrothed told him that he would need help, and counselled him to refrain from the battle, wherein it seemed he would encounter only death and disgrace, especially as he had not stipulated for any definite limit to the number of those who were to be his opponents. He should therefore avoid the peril, and consult his safety by appealing to Starkad, who was sojourning among the Swedes; since it was his way to help the distressed, and often to interpose successfully to retrieve some dismal mischance.

Then Helge, who liked the counsel thus given very well, took a small escort and went into Sweden; and when he reached its most famous city, Upsala, he forbore to enter, but sent in a messenger who was to invite Starkad to the wedding of Frode's daughter, after first greeting him respectfully to try him. This courtesy stung Starkad like an insult. He looked sternly on the youth, and said, "That had he not had his beloved Frode named in his instructions, he should have paid dearly for his senseless mission. He must think that Starkad, like some buffoon or trencherman, was accustomed to rush off to the reek of a distant kitchen for the sake of a richer diet." Helge, when his servant had told him this, greeted the old man in the name of Frode's daughter, and asked him to share a battle which he had accepted upon being challenged, saying that he was not equal to it by himself, the terms of the agreement being such as to leave the number of his adversaries uncertain. Starkad, when he had heard the time and place of the combat, not only received the suppliant well, but also encouraged him with the offer of aid, and told him to go back to Denmark with his companions, telling him that he would find his way to him by a short and secret path. Helge departed, and if we may trust report, Starkad, by sheer speed of foot, travelled in one day's journeying over as great a space as those who went before him are said to have accomplished in twelve; so that both parties, by a chance meeting, reached their journey's end, the palace of Ingild, at the very same time. Here Starkad passed, just as the servants did, along the tables filled with guests; and the aforementioned nine, howling horribly with repulsive gestures, and running about as if they were on the stage, encouraged one another to the battle. Some say that they barked like furious dogs at the champion as he approached. Starkad rebuked them for making themselves look ridiculous with such an unnatural visage, and for clowning with wide grinning cheeks; for from this, he declared, soft and effeminate profligates derived their wanton incontinence. When Starkad was asked banteringly by the nine whether he had valour enough to fight, he answered that doubtless he was strong enough to meet, not merely one, but any number that might come against him. And when the nine heard this they understood that this was the man whom they had heard would come to the succour of Helge from afar. Starkad also, to protect the bride-chamber with a more diligent guard, voluntarily took charge of the watch; and, drawing back the doors of the bedroom, barred them with a sword instead of a bolt, meaning to post himself so as to give undisturbed quiet to their bridal.

When Helge woke, and, shaking off the torpor of sleep, remembered his pledge, he thought of buckling on his armour. But, seeing that a little of the darkness of night yet remained, and wishing to wait for the hour of dawn, he began to ponder the perilous business at hand, when sleep stole on him and sweetly seized him, so that he took himself back to bed laden with slumber. Starkad, coming in on him at daybreak, saw him locked asleep in the arms of his wife, and would not suffer him to be vexed with a sudden shock, or summoned from his quiet slumbers; lest he should seem to usurp the duty of wakening him and breaking upon the sweetness of so new a union, all because of cowardice. He thought it, therefore, more handsome to meet the peril alone than to gain a comrade by disturbing the pleasure of another. So he quietly retraced his steps, and scorning his enemies, entered the field which in our tongue is called Roliung, and finding a seat under the slope of a certain hill, he exposed himself to wind and snow. Then, as though the gentle airs of spring weather were breathing upon him, he put off his cloak, and set to picking out the fleas. He also cast on the briars a purple mantle which Helga had lately given him, that no clothing might seem to lend him shelter against the raging shafts of hail. Then the champions came and climbed the hill on the opposite side; and, seeking a spot sheltered from the winds wherein to sit, they lit a fire and drove off the cold. At last, not seeing Starkad, they sent a man to the crest of the hill, to watch his coming more clearly, as from a watch-tower. This man climbed to the top of the lofty mountain, and saw, on its sloping side, an old man covered shoulder-high with the snow that showered down. He asked him if he was the man who was to fight according to the promise. Starkad declared that he was. Then the rest came up and asked him whether he had resolved to meet them all at once or one by one. But he said, "Whenever a surly pack of curs yelps at me, I commonly send them flying all at once, and not in turn." Thus he let them know that he would rather fight with-them all together than one by one, thinking that his enemies should be spurned with words first and deeds afterwards.

225

The fight began furiously almost immediately, and he felled six of them without receiving any wound in return; and though the remaining three wounded him so hard in seventeen places that most of his bowels gushed out of his belly, he slew them notwithstanding, like their brethren. Disembowelled, with failing strength, he suffered from dreadful straits of thirst, and, crawling on his knees in his desire to find a draught, he longed for water from the streamlet that ran close by. But when he saw it was tainted with gore he was disgusted at the look of the water, and refrained from its infected draught. For Anganty had been struck down in the waves of the river, and had dyed its course so deep with his red blood that it seemed now to flow not with water, but with some ruddy liquid. So Starkad thought it nobler that his bodily strength should fail than that he should borrow strength from so foul a beverage. Therefore, his force being all but spent, he wriggled on his knees, up to a rock that happened to be lying near, and for some little while lay leaning against it. A hollow in its surface is still to be seen, just as if his weight as he lay had marked it with a distinct impression of his body. But I think this appearance is due to human handiwork, for it seems to pass all belief that the hard and uncleavable rock should so imitate the softness of wax, as, merely by the contact of a man leaning on it, to present the appearance of a man having sat there, and assume concavity for ever.

A certain man, who chanced to be passing by in a cart, saw Starkad wounded almost all over his body. Equally aghast and amazed, he turned and drove closer, asking what reward he should have if he were to tend and heal his wounds. But Starkad would rather be tortured by grievous wounds than use the service of a man of base estate, and first asked his birth and calling. The man said that his profession was that of a sergeant. Starkad, not content with despising him, also spurned him with revilings, because, neglecting all honourable business, he followed the calling of a hanger-on; and because he had tarnished his whole career with ill repute, thinking the losses of the poor his own gains; suffering none to be innocent, ready to inflict wrongful accusation upon all men, most delighted at any lamentable turn in the fortunes of another; and toiling most at his own design, namely of treacherously spying out all men's doings, and seeking some traitorous occasion to censure the character of the innocent.

As this first man departed, another came up, promising aid and remedies. Like the last comer, he was bidden to declare his condition; and he said that he had a certain man's handmaid to wife, and was doing peasant service to her master in order to set her free. Starkad refused to accept his help, because he had married in a shameful way by taking a slave to his embrace. Had he had a shred of virtue he should at least have disdained to be intimate with the slave of another, but should have enjoyed some freeborn partner of his bed. What a mighty man, then, must we deem Starkad, who, when enveloped in the most deadly perils, showed himself as great in refusing aid as in receiving wounds!

When this man departed a woman chanced to approach and walk past the old man. She came up to him in order to wipe his wounds, but was first bidden to declare what was her birth and calling. She said that she was a handmaid used to grinding at the mill. Starkad then asked her if she had children; and when he was told that she had a female child, he told her to go home and give the breast to her squalling daughter; for he thought it most uncomely that he should borrow help from a woman of the lowest degree. Moreover, he knew that she could nourish her own flesh and blood with milk better than she could minister to the wounds of a stranger.

As the woman was departing, a young man came riding up in a cart. He saw the old man, and drew near to minister to his wounds. On being asked who he was, he said his father was a labourer, and added that he was used to the labours of a peasant. Starkad praised his origin, and pronounced that his calling was also most worthy of honour; for, he said, such men sought a livelihood by honourable traffic in their labour, inasmuch as they knew not of any gain, save what they had earned by the sweat of their brow. He also thought that a country life was justly to be preferred even to the most splendid riches; for the most wholesome fruits of it seemed to be born and reared in the shelter of a middle estate, halfway between magnificence and squalor. But he did not wish to pass the kindness of the youth unrequited, and rewarded the esteem he had shown him with the mantle he had cast among the thorns. So the peasant's son approached, replaced the parts of his belly that had been torn away, and bound up with a plait of withies the mass of intestines that had fallen out. Then he took the old man to his car, and with the most zealous respect carried him away to the palace.

Meantime Helga, in language betokening the greatest wariness, began to instruct her husband, saying that she knew that Starkad, as soon as he came back from conquering the champions, would punish him for his absence, thinking that he had inclined more to sloth and lust than to his promise to fight as appointed. Therefore he must withstand Starkad boldly, because he always spared the brave but loathed the coward. Helge respected equally her prophecy and her counsel, and braced his soul and body with a glow of valorous enterprise. Starkad, when he had been driven to the palace, heedless of the pain of his wounds, leaped

227

swiftly out of the cart, and just like a man who was well from top to toe, burst into the bridal-chamber, shattering the doors with his fist. Then Helge leapt from his bed, and, as he had been taught by the counsel of his wife, plunged his blade full at Starkad's forehead. And since he seemed to be meditating a second blow, and to be about to make another thrust with his sword, Helga flew quickly from the couch, caught up a shield, and, by interposing it, saved the old man from impending destruction; for, notwithstanding, Helge with a stronger stroke of his blade smote the shield right through to the boss. Thus the praiseworthy wit of the woman aided her friend, and her hand saved him whom her counsel had injured; for she protected the old man by her deed, as well as her husband by her warning. Starkad was induced by this to let Helge go scot-free; saying that a man whose ready and assured courage so surely betokened manliness, ought to be spared; for he vowed that a man ill deserved death whose brave spirit was graced with such a dogged will to resist.

Starkad went back to Sweden before his wounds had been treated with medicine, or covered with a single scar. Halfdan had been killed by his rivals; and Starkad, after quelling certain rebels, set up Siward as the heir to his father's sovereignty. With him he sojourned a long time; but when he heard—for the rumour spread—that Ingild, the son of Frode (who had been treacherously slain), was perversely minded, and instead of punishing his father's murderers, bestowed upon them kindness and friendship, he was vexed with stinging wrath at so dreadful a crime. And, resenting that a youth of such great parts should have renounced his descent from his glorious father, he hung on his shoulders a mighty mass of charcoal, as though it were some costly burden, and made his way to Denmark. When asked by those he met why he was taking along so unusual a load, he said that he would sharpen the dull wits of King Ingild to a point by bits of charcoal. So he accomplished a swift and headlong journey, as though at a single breath, by a short and speedy track; and at last, becoming the guest of Ingild, he went up, as his custom was, in to the seat appointed for the great men; for he had been used to occupy the highest post of distinction with the kings of the last generation.

When the queen came in, and saw him covered over with filth and clad in the mean, patched clothes of a peasant, the ugliness of her guest's dress made her judge him with little heed; and, measuring the man by the clothes, she reproached him with crassness of wit, because he had gone before greater men in taking his place at table, and had assumed a seat that was too good for his boorish attire. She bade him quit the place, that he might not touch the cushions with his dress, which was fouler than it should have been. For she put down to crassness and

228

brazenness what Starkad only did from proper pride; she knew not that on a high seat of honour the mind sometimes shines brighter than the raiment. The spirited old man obeyed, though vexed at the rebuff, and with marvellous self-control choked down the insult which his bravery so ill deserved; uttering at this disgrace he had received neither word nor groan. But he could not long bear to hide the bitterness of his anger in silence. Rising, and retreating to the furthest end of the palace, he flung his body against the walls; and strong as they were, he so battered them with the shock, that the beams quaked mightily; and he nearly brought the house down in a crash. Thus, stung not only with his rebuff, but with the shame of having poverty cast in his teeth, he unsheathed his wrath against the insulting speech of the queen with inexorable sternness.

Ingild, on his return from hunting, scanned him closely, and, when he noticed that he neither looked cheerfully about, nor paid him the respect of rising, saw by the sternness written on his brow that it was Starkad. For when he noted his hands horny with fighting, his scars in front, the force and fire of his eye, he perceived that a man whose body was seamed with so many traces of wounds had no weakling soul. He therefore rebuked his wife, and charged her roundly to put away her haughty tempers, and to soothe and soften with kind words and gentle offices the man she had reviled; to comfort him with food and drink, and refresh him with kindly converse; saying, that this man had been appointed his tutor by his father long ago, and had been a most tender guardian of his childhood. Then, learning too late the temper of the old man, she turned her harshness into gentleness, and respectfully waited on him whom she had rebuffed and railed at with bitter revilings. The angry hostess changed her part, and became the most fawning of flatterers. She wished to check his anger with her attentiveness; and her fault was the less, inasmuch as she was so quick in ministering to him after she had been chidden. But she paid dearly for it, for she presently beheld stained with the blood of her brethren the place where she had flouted and rebuffed the brave old man from his seat.

Now, in the evening, Ingild took his meal with the sons of Swerting, and fell to a magnificent feast, loading the tables with the profusest dishes. With friendly invitation he kept the old man back from leaving the revel too early; as though the delights of elaborate dainties could have undermined that staunch and sturdy virtue! But when Starkad had set eyes on these things, he scorned so wanton a use of them; and, not to give way a whit to foreign fashions, he steeled his appetite against these tempting delicacies with the self-restraint which was his greatest strength. He would not suffer his repute as a soldier to be impaired by the allurements of an orgy. For his valour loved thrift, and was a stranger to all superfluity of food, and averse to feasting in excess. For his was a courage which never at any moment had time to make luxury of aught account, and always forewent pleasure to pay due heed to virtue. So, when he saw that the antique character of self-restraint, and all good old customs, were being corrupted by new-fangled luxury and sumptuosity, he wished to be provided with a morsel fitter for a peasant, and scorned the costly and lavish feast.

Spurning profuse indulgence in food, Starkad took some smoky and rather rancid fare, appeasing his hunger with a bitter relish because more simply; and being unwilling to enfeeble his true valour with the tainted sweetness of sophisticated foreign dainties, or break the rule of antique plainness by such strange idolatries of the belly. He was also very wroth that they should go, to the extravagance of having the same meat both roasted and boiled at the same meal; for he considered an eatable which was steeped in the vapours of the kitchen, and which the skill of the cook rubbed over with many kinds of flavours, in the light of a monstrosity.

Unlike Starkad Ingild flung the example of his ancestors to the winds, and gave himself freer licence of innovation in the fashions of the table than the custom of his fathers allowed. For when he had once abandoned himself to the manners of Teutonland, he did not blush to yield to its unmanly wantonness. No slight incentives to debauchery have flowed down our country's throat from that sink of a land. Hence came magnificent dishes, sumptuous kitchens, the base service of cooks, and all sorts of abominable sausages. Hence came our adoption, wandering from the ways of our fathers, of a more dissolute dress. Thus our country, which cherished self-restraint as its native quality, has gone begging to our neighbours for luxury; whose allurements so charmed Ingild, that he did not think it shameful to requite wrongs with kindness; nor did the grievous murder of his father make him heave one sigh of bitterness when it crossed his mind.

But the queen would not depart without effecting her purpose. Thinking that presents would be the best way to banish the old man's anger, she took off her own head a band of marvellous handiwork, and put it in his lap as he supped: desiring to buy his favour since she could not blunt his courage. But Starkad, whose bitter resentment was not yet abated, flung it back in the face of the giver, thinking that in such a gift there was more scorn than respect. And he was wise not to put this strange ornament of female dress upon the head that was all bescarred and used to the helmet; for he knew that the locks of a man ought not to wear a woman's head-band. Thus he avenged slight with slight, and repaid with retorted scorn the disdain he had received; thereby bearing himself well-nigh as nobly in avenging his disgrace as he had borne himself in enduring it.

To the soul of Starkad reverence for Frode was grappled with hooks of love. Drawn to him by deeds of bounty, countless kindnesses, he could not be wheedled into giving up his purpose of revenge by any sort of alluring complaisance. Even now, when Frode was no more, he was eager to pay the gratitude due to his benefits, and to requite the kindness of the dead, whose loving disposition and generous friendship he had experienced while he lived. For he bore graven so deeply in his heart the grievous picture of Frode's murder, that his honour for that most famous captain could never be plucked from the inmost chamber of his soul; and therefore he did not hesitate to rank his ancient friendship before the present kindness. Besides, when he recalled the previous affront, he could not thank the complaisance that followed; he could not put aside the disgraceful wound to his self-respect. For the memory of benefits or injuries ever sticks more firmly in the minds of brave men than in those of weaklings. For he had not the habits of those who follow their friends in prosperity and quit them in adversity, who pay more regard to fortune than to looks, and sit closer to their own gain than to charity toward others.

But the woman held to her purpose, seeing that even so she could not win the old man to convivial mirth. Continuing with yet more lavish courtesy her efforts to soothe him, and to heap more honours on the guest, she bade a piper strike up, and started music to melt his unbending rage. For she wanted to unnerve his stubborn nature by means of cunning sounds. But the cajolery of pipe or string was just as powerless to enfeeble that dogged warrior. When he heard it, he felt that the respect paid him savoured more of pretence than of love. Hence the crestfallen performer seemed to be playing to a statue rather than a man, and learnt that it is vain for buffoons to assail with, their tricks a settled and weighty sternness, and that a mighty mass cannot be shaken with the idle puffing of the lips. For Starkad had set his face so firmly in his stubborn wrath, that he seemed not a whit easier to move than ever. For the inflexibility which he owed his vows was not softened either by the strain of the lute or the enticements of the palate; and he thought that more respect should be paid to his strenuous and manly purpose than to the tickling of the ears or the lures of the feast. Accordingly he flung the bone, which he had stripped in eating the meat, in the face of the harlequin, and drove the wind violently out of his puffed cheeks, so that they collapsed. By this he showed how his austerity loathed the clatter of the stage; for his ears were stopped with anger and open to no influence of delight. This reward, befitting an actor, punished an unseemly performance with a shameful wage. For

Starkad excellently judged the man's deserts, and bestowed a shankbone for the piper to pipe on, requiting his soft service with a hard fee. None could say whether the actor piped or wept the louder; he showed by his bitter flood of tears how little place bravery has in the breasts of the dissolute. For the fellow was a mere minion of pleasure, and had never learnt to bear the assaults of calamity. This man's hurt was ominous of the carnage that was to follow at the feast. Right well did Starkad's spirit, heedful of sternness, hold with stubborn gravity to steadfast revenge; for he was as much disgusted at the lute as others were delighted, and repaid the unwelcome service by insultingly flinging a bone; thus avowing that he owed a greater debt to the glorious dust of his mighty friend than to his shameless and infamous ward.

But when Starkad saw that the slayers of Frode were in high favour with the king, his stern glances expressed the mighty wrath which he harboured, and his face betrayed what he felt. The visible fury of his gaze betokened the secret tempest in his heart. At last, when Ingild tried to appease him with royal fare, he spurned the dainty. Satisfied with cheap and common food, he utterly spurned outlandish delicacies; he was used to plain diet, and would not pamper his palate with any delightful flavour. When he was asked why he had refused the generous attention of the king with such a clouded brow, he said that he had come to Denmark to find the son of Frode, not a man who crammed his proud and gluttonous stomach with rich elaborate feasts. For the Teuton extravagance which the king favoured had led him, in his longing for the pleasures of abundance, to set to the fire again, for roasting, dishes which had been already boiled. Thereupon he could not forbear from attacking Ingild's character, but poured out the whole bitterness of his reproaches on his head. He condemned his unfilial spirit, because he gaped with repletion and vented his squeamishness in filthy hawkings; because, following the lures of the Saxons, he strayed and departed far from soberness; because he was so lacking in manhood as not to pursue even the faintest shadow of it. But, declared Starkad, he bore the heaviest load of infamy, because, even when he first began to see service, he forgot to avenge his father, to whose butchers, forsaking the law of nature, he was kind and attentive. Men whose deserts were most vile he welcomed with loving affection; and not only did he let those go scot-free, whom he should have punished most sharply, but he even judged them fit persons to live with and entertain at his table, whereas he should rather have put them to death. Hereupon Starkad is also said to have sung as follows:

"Let the unwarlike youth yield to the aged, let him honour all the years of him that is old. When a man is brave, let none reproach the number of his days.

232

"Though the hair of the ancient whiten with age, their valour stays still the same; nor shall the lapse of time have power to weaken their manly heart.

"I am elbowed away by the offensive guest, who taints with vice his outward show of goodness, whilst he is the slave of his belly and prefers his daily dainties to anything.

"When I was counted as a comrade of Frode, I ever sat in the midst of warriors on a high seat in the hall, and I was the first of the princes to take my meal.

"Now, the lot of a nobler age is reversed; I am shut in a corner, I am like the fish that seeks shelter as it wanders to and fro hidden in the waters.

"I, who used surely in the former age to lie back on a couch handsomely spread, am now thrust among the hindmost and driven from the crowded hall.

"Perchance I had been driven on my back at the doors, had not the wall struck my side and turned me back, and had not the beam, in the way made it hard for me to fly when I was thrust forth.

"I am baited with the jeers of the court-folk; I am not received as a guest should be; I am girded at with harsh gibing, and stung with babbling taunts.

"I am a stranger, and would gladly know what news are spread abroad by busy rumour; what is the course of events; what the order of the land; what is doing in your country.

"Thou, Ingild, buried in sin, why dost thou tarry in the task of avenging thy father? Wilt thou think tranquilly of the slaughter of thy righteous sire?

"Why dost thou, sluggard, think only of feasting, and lean thy belly back in ease, more effeminate than harlots? Is the avenging of thy slaughtered father a little thing to thee?

"When last I left thee, Frode, I learned by my prophetic soul that thou, mightiest of kings, wouldst surely perish by the sword of enemies.

"And while I travelled long in the land, a warning groan rose in my soul, which augured that thereafter I was never to see thee more.

233

"Wo is me, that then I was far away, harrying the farthest peoples of the earth, when the traitorous guest aimed craftily at the throat of his king.

"Else I would either have shown myself the avenger of my lord, or have shared his fate and fallen where he fell, and would joyfully have followed the blessed king in one and the same death.

"I have not come to indulge in gluttonous feasting, the sin whereof I will strive to chastise; nor will I take mine ease, nor the delights of the fat belly.

"No famous king has ever set me before in the middle by the strangers. I have been wont to sit in the highest seats among friends.

"I have come from Sweden, travelling over wide lands, thinking that I should be rewarded, if only I had the joy to find the son of my beloved Frode.

"But I sought a brave man, and I have come to a glutton, a king who is the slave of his belly and of vice, whose liking has been turned back towards wantonness by filthy pleasure.

"Famous is the speech men think that Halfdan spoke: he warned us it would soon come to pass that an understanding father should beget a witless son.

"Though the heir be deemed degenerate, I will not suffer the wealth of mighty Frode to profit strangers or to be made public like plunder."

At these words the queen trembled, and she took from her head the ribbon with which she happened, in woman's fashion, to be adorning her hair, and proffered it to the enraged old man, as though she could avert his anger with a gift. Starkad in anger flung it back most ignominiously in the face of the giver, and began again in a loud voice:

"Take hence, I pray thee, thy woman's gift, and set back thy headgear on thy head; no brave man assumes the chaplets that befit Love only.

"For it is amiss that the hair of men that are ready for battle should be bound back with wreathed gold; such attire is right for the throngs of the soft and effeminate.

"But take this gift to thy husband, who loves luxury, whose finger itches, while he turns over the rump and handles the flesh of the bird roasted brown.

"The flighty and skittish wife of Ingild longs to observe the fashions of the Teutons; she prepares the orgy and makes ready the artificial dainties.

"For she tickles the palate with a new-fangled feast; she pursues the zest of an unknown flavour, raging to load all the tables with dishes yet more richly than before.

"She gives her lord wine to drink in bowls, pondering all things with zealous preparation; she bids the cooked meats be roasted, and intends them for a second fire.

"Wantonly she feeds her husband like a hog; a shameless whore, trusting....

"She roasts the boiled, and recooks the roasted meats, planning the meal with spendthrift extravagance, careless of right and wrong, practising sin, a foul woman.

"Wanton in arrogance, a soldier of Love, longing for dainties, she abjures the fair ways of self-control, and also provides devices for gluttony.

"With craving stomach she desires turnip strained in a smooth pan, cakes with thin juice, and shellfish in rows.

"I do not remember the Great Frode putting his hand to the sinews of birds, or tearing the rump of a cooked fowl with crooked thumb.

"What former king could have been so gluttonous as to stir the stinking filthy flesh, or rummage in the foul back of a bird with plucking fingers?

"The food of valiant men is raw; no need, methinks, of sumptuous tables for those whose stubborn souls are bent on warfare.

"It had been fitter for thee to have torn the stiff beard, biting hard with thy teeth, than greedily to have drained the bowl of milk with thy wide mouth.

"We fled from the offence of the sumptuous kitchen; we stayed our stomach with rancid fare; few in the old days loved cooked juices.

"A dish with no sauce of herbs gave us the flesh of rams and swine. We

235

partook temperately, tainting nothing with bold excess.

"Thou who now lickest the milk-white fat, put on, prithee, the spirit of a man; remember Frode, and avenge thy father's death.

"The worthless and cowardly heart shall perish, and shall not parry the thrust of death by flight, though it bury itself in a valley, or crouch in darkling dens.

"Once we were eleven princes, devoted followers of King Hakon, and here Geigad sat above Helge in the order of the meal.

"Geigad used to appease the first pangs of hunger with a dry rump of ham; and plenty of hard crust quelled the craving of his stomach.

"No one asked for a sickly morsel; all took their food in common; the meal of mighty men cost but slight display.

"The commons shunned foreign victual, and the greatest lusted not for a feast; even the king remembered to live temperately at little cost.

"Scorning to look at the mead, he drank the fermented juice of Ceres; he shrank not from the use of undercooked meats, and hated the roast.

"The board used to stand with slight display, a modest salt-cellar showed the measure of its cost; lest the wise ways of antiquity should in any wise be changed by foreign usage.

"Of old, no man put flagons or mixing-bowls on the tables; the steward filled the cup from the butt, and there was no abundance of adorned vessels.

"No one who honoured past ages put the smooth wine-jars beside the tankards, and of old no bedizened lackey heaped the platter with dainties.

"Nor did the vainglorious host deck the meal with little salt-shell or smooth cup; but all has been now abolished in shameful wise by the new-fangled manners.

"Who would ever have borne to take money in ransom for the death of a lost parent, or to have asked a foe for a gift to atone for the murder of a father?

"What strong heir or well-starred son would have sat side by side with such as these, letting a shameful bargain utterly unnerve the warrior?

"Wherefore, when the honours of kings are sung, and bards relate the victories of captains, I hide my face for shame in my mantle, sick at heart.

"For nothing shines in thy trophies, worthy to be recorded by the pen; no heir of Frode is named in the roll of the honourable.

"Why dost thou vex me with insolent gaze, thou who honourest the foe guilty of thy father's blood, and art thought only to take thy vengeance with loaves and warm soup?

"When men speak well of the avengers of crimes, then long thou to lose thy quick power of hearing, that thy impious spirit may not be ashamed.

"For oft has the virtue of another vexed a heart that knows its guilt, and the malice in the breast is abashed by the fair report of the good.

"Though thou go to the East, or live sequestered in the countries of the West, or whether, driven thence, thou seek the midmost place of the earth;

"Whether thou revisit the cold quarter of the heaven where the pole is to be seen, and carries on the sphere with its swift spin, and looks down upon the neighbouring Bear;

"Shame shall accompany thee far, and shall smite thy countenance with heavy disgrace, when the united assembly of the great kings is taking pastime.

"Since everlasting dishonour awaits thee, thou canst not come amidst the ranks of the famous; and in every clime thou shalt pass thy days in infamy.

"The fates have given Frode an offspring born into the world when gods were adverse, whose desires have been enthralled by crime and ignoble lust.

"Even as in a ship all things foul gather to the filthy hollow of the bilge, even so hath a flood of vices poured into Ingild.

"Therefore, in terror of thy shame being published, thou shalt lie crushed in the corners of the land, sluggish on thy foul hearth, and never to be seen in the array of the famous.

"Then shalt thou shake thy beard at thine evil fate, kept down by the taunts of thy mistresses, when thy paramour galls thy ear with her querulous cries.

"Since chill fear retards thy soul, and thou dreadest to become the avenger of thy sire, thou art utterly degenerate, and thy ways are like a slave's.

"It would have needed scant preparation to destroy thee; even as if a man should catch and cut the throat of a kid, or slit the weazand of a soft sheep and butcher it.

"Behold, a son of the tyrant Swerting shall take the inheritance of Denmark after thee; he whose slothful sister thou keepest in infamous union.

"Whilst thou delightest to honour thy bride, laden with gems and shining in gold apparel, we burn with all indignation that is linked with shame, lamenting thy infamies.

"When thou art stirred by furious lust, our mind is troubled, and recalls the fashion of ancient times, and bids us grieve sorely.

"For we rate otherwise than thou the crime of the foes whom now thou holdest in honour; wherefore the face of this age is a burden to me, remembering the ancient ways.

"I would crave no greater blessing, O Frode, if I might see those guilty of thy murder duly punished for such a crime."

Now he prevailed so well by this stirring counsel, that his reproach served like a flint wherewith to strike a blazing flame of valour in the soul that had been chill and slack. For the king had at first heard the song inattentively; but, stirred by the earnest admonition of his guardian, he conceived in his heart a tardy fire of revenge; and, forgetting the reveller, he changed into the foeman. At last he leapt up from where he lay, and poured the whole flood of his anger on those at table with him; insomuch that he unsheathed his sword upon the sons of Swerting with bloody ruthlessness, and aimed with drawn blade at the throats of those whose gullets he had pampered with the pleasures of the table. These men he forthwith slew; and by so doing he drowned the holy rites of the table in blood. He sundered the feeble bond of their league, and exchanged a shameful revel for enormous cruelty; the host became the foe, and that vilest slave of excess the bloodthirsty agent of revenge. For the vigorous pleading of his counsellor bred a breath of courage in his soft and unmanly youth; it drew out his valour from its lurking-place, and renewed it, and so fashioned it that the authors of a most grievous murder were punished even as they deserved. For the young man's valour had been not quenched, but only in exile, and the aid of an old man had drawn it out into the light; and it accomplished a deed which was all the greater for its tardiness; for it was somewhat nobler to steep the cups in blood than in wine. What a spirit, then, must we think that old man had, who by his eloquent adjuration expelled from that king's mind its infinite sin, and who, bursting the bonds of iniquity, implanted a most effectual seed of virtue. Starkad aided the king with equal achievements; and not only showed the most complete courage in his own person, but summoned back that which had been rooted out of the heart of another. When the deed was done, he thus begun:

"King Ingild, farewell; thy heart, full of valour, hath now shown a deed of daring. The spirit that reigns in thy body is revealed by its fair beginning; nor did there lack deep counsel in thy heart, though thou wert silent till this hour; for thou dost redress by thy bravery what delay had lost, and redeemest the sloth of thy spirit by mighty valour. Come now, let us rout the rest, and let none escape the peril which all alike deserve. Let the crime come home to the culprit; let the sin return and crush its contriver.

"Let the servants take up in a car the bodies of the slain, and let the attendant quickly bear out the carcases. Justly shall they lack the last rites; they are unworthy to be covered with a mound; let no funeral procession or pyre suffer them the holy honour of a barrow; let them be scattered to rot in the fields, to be consumed by the beaks of birds; let them taint the country all about with their deadly corruption.

"Do thou too, king, if thou hast any wit, flee thy savage bride, lest the she-wolf bring forth a litter like herself, and a beast spring from thee that shall hurt its own father.

"Tell me, Rote, continual derider of cowards, thinkest thou that we have avenged Frode enough, when we have spent seven deaths on the vengeance of one? Lo, those are borne out dead who paid homage not to thy sway in deed, but only in show, and though obsequious they planned treachery. But I always cherished this hope, that noble fathers have noble offspring, who will follow in their character the lot which they received by their birth. Therefore, Ingild, better now than in time past dost thou deserve to be called lord of Leire and of Denmark.

"When, O King Hakon, I was a beardless youth, and followed thy leading and command in warfare, I hated luxury and wanton souls, and practiced only wars. Training body and mind together, I banished every unholy thing from my soul, and shunned the pleasures of the belly, loving deeds of prowess. For those that followed the calling of arms had rough clothing and common gear and short slumbers and scanty rest. Toil drove ease far away, and the time ran by at scanty cost. Not as with some men now, the light of whose reason is obscured by insatiate greed with its blind maw. Some one of these clad in a covering of curiously wrought raiment effeminately guides the fleet-footed (steed), and unknots his dishevelled locks, and lets his hair fly abroad loosely.

"He loves to plead often in the court, and to covet a base pittance, and with this pursuit he comforts his sluggish life, doing with venal tongue the business entrusted to him.

"He outrages the laws by force, he makes armed assault upon men's rights, he tramples on the innocent, he feeds on the wealth of others, he practices debauchery and gluttony, he vexes good fellowship with biting jeers, and goes after harlots as a hoe after the grass.

"The coward falls when battles are lulled in peace. Though he who fears death lie in the heart of the valley, no mantlet shall shelter him. His final fate carries off every living man; doom is not to be averted by skulking. But I, who have shaken the whole world with my slaughters, shall I enjoy a peaceful death? Shall I be taken up to the stars in a quiet end? Shall I die in my bed without a wound?"

Duel Between Hame and Starkad

BOOK SEVEN

We are told by historians of old, that Ingild had four sons, of whom three perished in war, while OLAF alone reigned after his father; but some say that Olaf was the son of Ingild's sister, though this opinion is doubtful. Posterity has but an uncertain knowledge of his deeds, which are dim with the dust of antiquity; nothing but the last counsel of his wisdom has been rescued by tradition. For when he was in the last grip of death he took thought for his sons FRODE and HARALD, and bade them have royal sway, one over the land and the other over the sea, and receive these several powers, not in prolonged possession, but in yearly rotation. Thus their share in the rule was made equal; but Frode, who was the first to have control of the affairs of the sea, earned disgrace from his continual defeats in roving. His calamity was due to his sailors being newly married, and preferring nuptial joys at home to the toils of foreign warfare. After a time Harald, the younger son, received the rule of the sea, and chose soldiers who were unmarried, fearing to be baffled like his brother. Fortune favoured his choice; for he was as glorious a rover as his brother was inglorious; and this earned him his brother's hatred. Moreover, their queens, Signe and Ulfhild, one of whom was the daughter of Siward, King of Sweden, the other of Karl, the governor of Gothland, were continually wrangling as to which was the nobler, and broke up the mutual fellowship of their husbands. Hence Harald and Frode, when their common household was thus shattered, divided up the goods they held in common, and gave more heed to the wrangling altercations of the women than to the duties of brotherly affection.

Moreover, Frode, judging that his brother's glory was a disgrace to himself and brought him into contempt, ordered one of his household to put him to death secretly; for he saw that the man of whom he had the advantage in years was surpassing him in courage. When the deed was done, he had the agent of his treachery privily slain, lest the accomplice should betray the crime. Then, in order to gain the credit of innocence and escape the brand of crime, he ordered a full inquiry to be made into the mischance that had cut off his brother so suddenly. But he could not manage, by all his arts, to escape silent condemnation in the thoughts of the common people. He afterwards asked Karl, "Who had killed Harald?" and Karl replied that it was deceitful in him to ask a question about something which he knew quite well. These words earned him his death; for Frode thought that he had reproached him covertly with fratricide.

After this, the lives of Harald and Halfdan, the sons of Harald by Signe the daughter of Karl, were attempted by their uncle. But the guardians devised a cunning method of saving their wards. For they cut off the claws of wolves and tied them to the soles of their feet; and then made them run along many times so as to harrow up the mud near their dwelling, as well as the ground (then covered with, snow), and give the appearance of an attack by wild beasts. Then they killed the children of some bond-women, tore their bodies into little pieces, and scattered their mangled limbs all about. So when the youths were looked for in vain, the scattered limbs were found, the tracks of the beasts were pointed out, and the ground was seen besmeared with blood. It was believed that the boys had been devoured by ravening wolves; and hardly anyone was suffered to doubt so plain a proof that they were mangled. The belief in this spectacle served to protect the wards. They were presently shut up by their guardians in a hollow oak, so that no trace of their being alive should get abroad, and were fed for a long time under pretence that they were dogs; and were even called by hounds' names, to prevent any belief getting abroad that they were hiding. (1)

Frode alone refused to believe in their death; and he went and inquired of a woman skilled in divination where they were hid. So potent were her spells, that she seemed able, at any distance, to perceive anything, however intricately locked away, and to summon it out to light. She declared that one Ragnar had secretly undertaken to rear them, and had called them by the names of dogs to cover the matter. When the young men found themselves dragged from their hiding by the awful force of her spells, and brought before the eyes of the enchantress, loth to be betrayed by this terrible and imperious compulsion, they flung into her lap a shower of gold which they had received from their guardians. When she had taken the gift, she suddenly feigned death, and fell like one lifeless. Her servants asked the reason why she fell so suddenly; and she declared that the refuge of the sons of Harald was inscrutable; for their wondrous might qualified even the most awful effects of her spells. Thus she was content with a slight benefit, and could not bear to await a greater reward at the king's hands. After this Ragnar, finding that the belief concerning himself and his wards was becoming rife in common talk, took them, both away into Funen. Here he was taken by Frode, and confessed that he had put the young men in safe keeping; and he prayed the king to spare the wards whom he had made fatherless, and not to think it a piece of good fortune to be guilty of two unnatural murders. By this speech he changed the king's cruelty into shame; and he promised that if they attempted any plots in their own land, he would give information to the king. Thus he gained safety for his wards, and lived many years in freedom from terror.

When the boys grew up, they went to Zealand, and were bidden by their friends to avenge their father. They vowed that they and their uncle should not both live out the year. When Ragnar found this out, he went by night to the palace, prompted by the recollection of his covenant, and announced that he was come privily to tell the king something he had promised. But the king was asleep, and he would not suffer them to wake him up, because Frode had been used to punish any disturbance of his rest with the sword. So mighty a matter was it thought of old to break the slumbers of a king by untimely intrusion. Frode heard this from the sentries in the morning; and when he perceived that Ragnar had come to tell him of the treachery, he gathered together his soldiers, and resolved to forestall deceit by ruthless measures. Harald's sons had no help for it but to feign madness. For when they found themselves suddenly attacked, they began to behave like maniacs, as if they were distraught. And when Frode thought that they were possessed, he gave up his purpose, thinking it shameful to attack with the sword those who seemed to be turning the sword against themselves. But he was burned to death by them on the following night, and was punished as befitted a fratricide. For they attacked the palace, and first crushing the queen with a mass of stones and then, having set fire to the house, they forced Frode to crawl into a narrow cave that had been cut out long before, and into the dark recesses of tunnels. Here he lurked in hiding and perished, stifled by the reek and smoke.

After Frode was killed, HALFDAN reigned over his country about three years, and then, handing over his sovereignty to his brother Harald as deputy, went roving, and attacked and ravaged Oland and the neighbouring isles, which are severed from contact with Sweden by a winding sound. Here in the winter he beached and entrenched his ships, and spent three years on the expedition. After this he attacked Sweden, and destroyed its king in the field. Afterwards he prepared to meet the king's grandson Erik, the son of his own uncle Frode, in battle; and when he heard that Erik's champion, Hakon, was skillful in blunting swords with his spells, he fashioned, to use for clubbing, a huge mace studded with iron knobs, as if he would prevail by the strength of wood over the power of sorcery. Then—for he was conspicuous beyond all others for his bravery—amid the hottest charges of the enemy, he covered his head with his helmet, and, without a shield, poised his club, and with the help of both hands whirled it against the bulwark of shields before him. No obstacle was so stout but it was crushed to pieces by the blow of the mass that smote it. Thus he overthrew the champion, who ran against him in the battle, with a violent stroke of his weapon. But he was conquered notwithstanding, and fled away into Helsingland, where he went to one Witolf (who had served of old with Harald), to seek tendance for his wounds. This man had spent most of his life in camp; but at last, after the grievous end of his general, he had retreated into this lonely district, where he lived the life of a peasant, and rested from the pursuits of war. Often struck himself by the missiles of the enemy, he had gained no slight skill in leechcraft by constantly tending his own wounds. But if anyone came with flatteries to seek his aid, instead of curing him he was accustomed to give him something that would secretly injure him, thinking it somewhat nobler to threaten than to wheedle for benefits. When the soldiers of Erik menaced his house, in their desire to take Halfdan, he so robbed them of the power of sight that they could neither perceive the house nor trace it with certainty, though it was close to them. So utterly had their eyesight been dulled by a decisive mist.

When Halfdan had by this man's help regained his full strength, he summoned Thore, a champion of notable capacity, and proclaimed war against Erik. But when the forces were led out on the other side, and he saw that Erik was superior in numbers, he hid a part of his army, and instructed it to lie in ambush among the bushes by the wayside, in order to destroy the enemy by an ambuscade as he marched through the narrow part of the path. Erik foresaw this, having reconnoitred his means of advancing, and thought he must withdraw for fear, if he advanced along the track he had intended, of being hard-pressed by the tricks of the enemy among the steep windings of the hills. They therefore joined battle, force against force, in a deep valley, inclosed all round by lofty mountain ridges. Here Halfdan, when he saw the line of his men wavering, climbed with Thore up a crag covered with stones and, uprooting boulders, rolled them down upon the enemy below; and the weight of these as they fell crushed the line that was drawn up in the lower position. Thus he regained with stones the victory which he had lost with arms. For this deed of prowess he received the name of Biargramm ("rock strong"), a word which seems to have been compounded from the name of his fierceness and of the mountains. He soon gained so much esteem for this among the Swedes that he was thought to be the son of the great Thor, and the people bestowed divine honours upon him, and judged him worthy of public libation.

But the souls of the conquered find it hard to rest, and the insolence of the beaten ever struggles towards the forbidden thing. So it came to pass that Erik, in his desire to repair the losses incurred in flight, attacked the districts subject to Halfdan. Even Denmark he did not exempt from this harsh treatment; for he thought it a most worthy deed to assail the country of the man who had caused him to be driven from his own. And so, being more anxious to inflict injury than to repel it, he set Sweden free from the arms of the enemy. When Halfdan heard that his brother Harald had been beaten by Erik in three battles, and slain in the fourth, he was afraid of losing his empire; he had to quit the land of the Swedes and go back to his own country. Thus Erik regained the kingdom of Sweden all the more quickly, that he quitted it so lightly. Had fortune wished to favour him in keeping his kingdom as much as she had in regaining it, she would in nowise have given him into the hand of Halfdan. This capture was made in the following way: When Halfdan had gone back into Sweden, he hid his fleet craftily, and went to meet Erik with two vessels. Erik attacked him with ten; and Halfdan, sailing through sundry winding channels, stole back to his concealed forces. Erik pursued him too far, and the Danish fleet came out on the sea. Thus Erik was surrounded; but he rejected the life, which was offered him under condition of thraldom. He could not bear to think more of the light of day than liberty, and chose to die rather than serve; lest he should seem to love life so well as to turn from a slave into a freeman; and that he might not court with new-born obeisance the man whom fortune had just before made only his equal. So little knows virtue how to buy life with dishonour. Wherefore he was put in chains, and banished to a place haunted by wild beasts; an end unworthy of that lofty spirit.

Halfdan had thus become sovereign of both kingdoms, and graced his fame with a triple degree of honour. For he was skillful and eloquent in composing poems in the fashion of his country; and he was no less notable as a valorous champion than as a powerful king. But when he heard that two active rovers, Toke and Anund, were threatening the surrounding districts, he attacked and routed them in a sea-fight. For the ancients thought that nothing was more desirable than glory which was gained, not by brilliancy of wealth, but by address in arms. Accordingly, the most famous men of old were so minded as to love seditions, to renew quarrels, to loathe ease, to prefer fighting to peace, to be rated by their valour and not by their wealth, to find their greatest delight in battles, and their least in banquetings.

But Halfdan was not long to seek for a rival. A certain Siwald, of most illustrious birth, related with lamentation in the assembly of the Swedes the death of Frode and his queen; and inspired in almost all of them such a hatred of Halfdan, that the vote of the majority granted him permission to revolt. Nor was he content with the mere goodwill of their voices, but so won the heart of the commons by his crafty canvassing that he induced almost all of them to set with their hands the royal emblem on his head. Siwald had seven sons, who were such clever sorcerers that often, inspired with the force of sudden frenzy, they would roar savagely, bite their shields, swallow hot coals, and go through any fire that could be piled up; and their frantic passion could only be checked by the rigour of chains, or propitiated by slaughter of men. With such a frenzy did their own sanguinary temper, or else the fury of demons, inspire them.

When Halfdan had heard of these things while busy roving, he said it was right that his soldiers, who had hitherto spent their rage upon foreigners, should now smite with the steel the flesh of their own countrymen, and that they who had been used to labour to extend their realm should now avenge its wrongful seizure. On Halfdan approaching, Siwald sent him ambassadors and requested him, if he was as great in act as in renown, to meet himself and his sons in single combat, and save the general peril by his own. When the other answered, that a combat could not lawfully be fought by more than two men, Siwald said, that it was no wonder that a childless bachelor should refuse the proffered conflict, since his nature was void of heat, and had struck a disgraceful frost into his soul and body. Children, he added, were not different from the man who begot them, since they drew from him their common principle of birth. Thus he and his sons were to be accounted as one person, for nature seemed in a manner to have bestowed on them a single body. Halfdan, stung with this shameful affront, accepted the challenge; meaning to wipe out with noble deeds of valour such an insulting taunt upon his celibacy. And while he chanced to be walking through a shady woodland, he plucked up by the roots all oak that stuck in his path, and, by simply stripping it of its branches, made it look like a stout club. Having this trusty weapon, he composed a short song as follows:

"Behold! The rough burden which I bear with straining crest, shall unto crests bring wounds and destruction. Never shall any weapon of leafy wood crush the Goths with direr augury. It shall shatter the towering strength of the knotty neck, and shall bruise the hollow temples with the mass of timber. The club which shall quell the wild madness of the land shall be no less fatal to the Swedes. Breaking bones, and brandished about the mangled limbs of warriors, the stock I have wrenched off shall crush the backs of the wicked, crush the hearths of our kindred, shed the blood of our countrymen, and be a destructive pest upon our land."

When he had said this, he attacked Siwald and his seven sons, and destroyed them, their force and bravery being useless against the enormous mass of his club.

At this time one Hardbeen, who came from Helsingland, gloried in kidnapping and ravishing princesses, and used to kill any man who hindered him in his lusts. He preferred high matches to those that were lowly; and the more illustrious the victims he could violate, the more noble he thought himself. No man escaped unpunished who durst measure himself with Hardbeen in valour. He was so huge, that his stature reached the measure of nine ells. He had twelve champions dwelling with him, whose business it was to rise up and to restrain his fury with the aid of bonds, whenever the rage came on him that foreboded of battle. These men asked Halfdan to attack Hardbeen and his champions man by man; and he not only promised to fight, but assured himself the victory with most confident words. When Hardbeen heard this, a demoniacal frenzy suddenly took him; he furiously bit and devoured the edges of his shield; he kept gulping down fiery coals; he snatched live embers in his mouth and let them pass down into his entrails; he rushed through the perils of crackling fires; and at last, when he had raved through every sort of madness, he turned his sword with raging hand against the hearts of six of his champions. It is doubtful whether this madness came from thirst for battle or natural ferocity. Then with the remaining band of his champions he attacked Halfdan, who crushed him with a hammer of wondrous size, so that he lost both victory and life; paying the penalty both to Halfdan, whom he had challenged, and to the kings whose offspring he had violently ravished.

Fortune never seemed satisfied with the trying of Halfdan's strength, and used to offer him unexpected occasions for fighting. It so happened that Egther, a Finlander, was harrying the Swedes on a roving raid. Halfdan, having found that he had three ships, attacked him with the same number. Night closed the battle, so that he could not conquer him; but he challenged Egther next day, fought with and overthrew him. He next heard that Grim, a champion of immense strength, was suing, under threats of a duel, for Thorhild, the daughter of the chief Hather, and that her father had proclaimed that he who put the champion out of the way should have her. Halfdan, though he had reached old age a bachelor, was stirred by the promise of the chief as much as by the insolence of the champion, and went to Norway. When he entered it, he blotted out every mark by which he could be recognized, disguising his face with splashes of dirt; and when he came to the spot of the battle, drew his sword first. And when he knew that it had been blunted by the glance of the enemy, he cast it on the ground, drew another from the sheath, with which he attacked Grim, cutting through the meshes on the edge of his cuirass, as well as the lower part of his shield. Grim wondered at the deed, and said, "I cannot remember an old man who fought more keenly;" and, instantly drawing his sword, he pierced through and shattered the target that was opposed to his blade. But as his right arm tarried on the stroke, Halfdan, without wavering, met and smote it swiftly with his sword. The other, notwithstanding, clasped his sword with his left hand, and cut through the thigh of the striker, revenging the mangling of his own body with a slight wound. Halfdan, now conqueror, allowed the conquered man to ransom the remnant of his life with a sum of money; he would not be thought shamefully to rob a maimed man, who could not fight, of the pitiful remainder of his days.

By this deed he showed himself almost as great in saving as in conquering his enemy. As a prize for this victory he won Thorhild in marriage, and had by her a son Asmund, from whom the kings of Norway treasure the honour of being descended; retracing the regular succession of their line down from Halfdan.

After this, Ebbe, a rover of common birth, was so confident of his valour, that he was moved to aspire to a splendid marriage. He was a suitor for Sigrid, the daughter of Yngwin, King of the Goths, and moreover demanded half the Gothic kingdom for her dowry. Halfdan was consulted whether the match should be entertained, and advised that a feigned consent should be given, promising that he would baulk the marriage. He also gave instructions that a seat should be allotted to himself among the places of the guests at table. Yngwin approved the advice; and Halfdan, utterly defacing the dignity of his royal presence with an unsightly and alien disguise, and coming by night on the wedding feast, alarmed those who met him; for they marvelled at the coming of a man of such superhuman stature.

When Halfdan entered the palace, he looked round on all and asked, who was he that had taken the place next to the king? Upon Ebbe replying that the future son-in-law of the king was next to his side, Halfdan asked him, in the most passionate language, what madness, or what demons, had brought him to such wantonness, as to make bold to unite his contemptible and filthy race with a splendid and illustrious line, or to dare to lay his peasant finger upon the royal family: and, not content even with such a claim, to aspire, as it seemed, to a share even in the kingdom of another. Then he bade Ebbe fight him, saying that he must get the victory before he got his wish. The other answered that the night was the time to fight with monsters, but the day the time with men; but Halfdan, to prevent him shirking the battle by pleading the hour, declared that the moon was shining with the brightness of daylight. Thus he forced Ebbe to fight, and felled him, turning the banquet into a spectacle, and the wedding into a funeral.

Some years passed, and Halfdan went back to his own country, and being childless he bequeathed the royal wealth by will to Yngwin, and appointed him king. YNGWIN was afterwards overthrown in war by a rival named Ragnald, and he left a son SIWALD.

Siwald's daughter, Sigrid, was of such excellent modesty, that though a great concourse of suitors wooed her for her beauty, it seemed as if she could not be brought to look at one of them. Confident in this power of self-restraint, she asked her father for a husband who by the sweetness of his blandishments should be able to get a look back from her. For in old time among us the self-restraint of the maidens was a great subduer of wanton looks, lest the soundness of the soul should be infected by the licence of the eyes; and women desired to avouch the purity of their hearts by the modesty of their faces. Then one Ottar, the son of Ebb, kindled with confidence in the greatness either of his own achievements, or of his courtesy and eloquent address, stubbornly and ardently desired to woo the maiden. And though he strove with all the force of his wit to soften her gaze, no device whatever could move her downcast eyes; and, marvelling at her persistence in her indomitable rigour, he departed.

A giant desired the same thing, but, finding himself equally foiled, he suborned a woman; and she, pretending friendship for the girl, served her for a while as her handmaid, and at last enticed her far from her father's house, by cunningly going out of the way; then the giant rushed upon her and bore her off into the closest fastnesses of a ledge on the mountain. Others think that he disguised himself as a woman, treacherously continued his devices so as to draw the girl away from her own house, and in the end carried her off. When Ottar heard of this, he ransacked the recesses of the mountain in search of the maiden, found her, slew the giant, and bore her off. But the assiduous giant had bound back the locks of the maiden, tightly twisting her hair in such a way that the matted mass of tresses was held in a kind of curled bundle; nor was it easy for anyone to unravel their plaited tangle, without using the steel. Again, he tried with divers allurements to provoke the maiden to look at him; and when he had long laid vain siege to her listless eyes, he abandoned his quest, since his purpose turned out so little to his liking. But he could not bring himself to violate the girl, loth to defile with ignoble intercourse one of illustrious birth. She then wandered long, and sped through divers desert and circuitous paths, and happened to come to the hut of a certain huge woman of the woods, who set her to the task of pasturing her goats. Again Ottar granted her his aid to set her free, and again he tried to move her, addressing her in this fashion: "Wouldst thou rather hearken to my counsels, and embrace me even as I desire, than be here and tend the flock of rank goats?

"Spurn the hand of thy wicked mistress, and flee hastily from thy cruel taskmistress, that thou mayst go back with me to the ships of thy friends and live in freedom.

"Quit the care of the sheep entrusted to thee; scorn to drive the steps of the goats; share my bed, and fitly reward my prayers.

"O thou whom I have sought with such pains, turn again thy listless

250

beams; for a little while—it is an easy gesture—lift thy modest face.

"I will take thee hence, and set thee by the house of thy father, and unite thee joyfully with thy loving mother, if but once thou wilt show me thine eyes stirred with soft desires.

"Thou, whom I have borne so oft from the prisons of the giants, pay thou some due favour to my toil of old; pity my hard endeavours, and be stern no more.

"For why art thou become so distraught and brainsick, that thou wilt choose to tend the flock of another, and be counted among the servants of monsters, sooner than encourage our marriage-troth with fitting and equal consent?"

But she, that she might not suffer the constancy of her chaste mind to falter by looking at the world without, restrained her gaze, keeping her lids immovably rigid. How modest, then, must we think, were the women of that age, when, under the strongest provocations of their lovers, they could not be brought to make the slightest motion of their eyes! So when Ottar found that even by the merits of his double service he could not stir the maiden's gaze towards him, he went back to the fleet, wearied out with shame and chagrin. Sigrid, in her old fashion, ran far away over the rocks, and chanced to stray in her wanderings to the abode of Ebb; where, ashamed of her nakedness and distress, she pretended to be a daughter of paupers. The mother of Ottar saw that this woman, though bestained and faded, and covered with a meagre cloak, was the scion of some noble stock; and took her, and with honourable courtesy kept her by her side in a distinguished seat. For the beauty of the maiden was a sign that betrayed her birth, and her telltale features echoed her lineage. Ottar saw her, and asked why she hid her face in her robe. Also, in order to test her mind more surely, he feigned that a woman was about to become his wife, and, as he went up into the bride-bed, gave Sigrid the torch to hold. The lights had almost burnt down, and she was hard put to it by the flame coming closer; but she showed such an example of endurance that she was seen to hold her hand motionless, and might have been thought to feel no annoyance from the heat. For the fire within mastered the fire without, and the glow of her longing soul deadened the burn of her scorched skin. At last Ottar bade her look to her hand. Then, modestly lifting her eyes, she turned her calm gaze upon him; and straightway, the pretended marriage being put away, went up unto the bride-bed to be his wife. Siwald afterwards seized Ottar, and thought that he ought to be hanged for defiling his daughter.

But Sigrid at once explained how she had happened to be carried away, and not only brought Ottar back into the king's favour, but also induced her father himself to marry Ottar's sister. After this a battle was fought between Siwald and Ragnald in Zealand, warriors of picked valour being chosen on both sides. For three days they slaughtered one another; but so great was the bravery of both sides, that it was doubtful how the victory would go. Then Ottar, whether seized with weariness at the prolonged battle, or with desire of glory, broke, despising death, through the thickest of the foe, cut down Ragnald among the bravest of his soldiers, and won the Danes a sudden victory. This battle was notable for the cowardice of the greatest nobles. For the whole mass fell into such a panic, that forty of the bravest of the Swedes are said to have turned and fled. The chief of these, Starkad, had been used to tremble at no fortune, however cruel, and no danger, however great. But some strange terror stole upon him, and he chose to follow the flight of his friends rather than to despise it. I should think that he was filled with this alarm by the power of heaven, that he might not think himself courageous beyond the measure of human valour. Thus the prosperity of mankind is wont ever to be incomplete. Then all these warriors embraced the service of King Hakon, the mightiest of the rovers, like remnants of the war drifting to him.

After this Siwald was succeeded by his son SIGAR, who had sons Siwald, Alf, and Alger, and a daughter Signe. All excelled the rest in spirit and beauty, and devoted himself to the business of a rover. Such a grace was shed on his hair, which had a wonderful dazzling glow, that his locks seemed to shine silvery. At the same time Siward, the king of the Goths, is said to have had two sons, Wemund and Osten, and a daughter Alfhild, who showed almost from her cradle such faithfulness to modesty that she continually kept her face muffled in her robe, lest she should cause her beauty to provoke the passion of another. Her father banished her into very close keeping, and gave her a viper and a snake to rear, wishing to defend her chastity by the protection of these reptiles when they came to grow up. For it would have been hard to pry into her chamber when it was barred by so dangerous a bolt. He also enacted that if any man tried to enter it, and failed, he must straightway yield his head to be taken off and impaled on a stake. The terror which was thus attached to wantonness chastened the heated spirits of the young men.

Alf, the son of Sigar, thinking that peril of the attempt only made it nobler, declared himself a wooer, and went to subdue the beasts that kept watch beside the room of the maiden; inasmuch as, according to the decree, the embraces of the maiden were the prize of their subduer. Alf covered his body with a blood-stained hide in order to make them more frantic against him. Girt with this, as soon as he had entered the doors of the enclosure, he took a piece of red-hot steel in the tongs, and plunged it into the yawning throat of the viper, which he laid dead. Then he flung his spear full into the gaping mouth of the snake as it wound and writhed forward, and destroyed it. And when he demanded the gage which was attached to victory by the terms of the covenant, Siward answered that he would accept that man only for his daughter's husband of whom she made a free and decided choice. None but the girl's mother was stiff against the wooer's suit; and she privately spoke to her daughter in order to search her mind. The daughter warmly praised her suitor for his valour; whereon the mother upbraided her sharply, that her chastity should be unstrung, and she be captivated by charming looks; and because, forgetting to judge his virtue, she cast the gaze of a wanton mind upon the flattering lures of beauty. Thus Alfhild was led to despise the young Dane; whereupon she exchanged woman's for man's attire, and, no longer the most modest of maidens, began the life of a warlike rover.

Enrolling in her service many maidens who were of the same mind, she happened to come to a spot where a band of rovers were lamenting the death of their captain, who had been lost in war; they made her their rover captain for her beauty, and she did deeds beyond the valour of woman. Alf made many toilsome voyages in pursuit of her, and in winter happened to come on a fleet of the Blacmen. The waters were at this time frozen hard, and the ships were caught in such a mass of ice that they could not get on by the most violent rowing. But the continued frost promised the prisoners a safer way of advance; and Alf ordered his men to try the frozen surface of the sea in their brogues, after they had taken off their slippery shoes, so that they could run over the level ice more steadily. The Blacmen supposed that they were taking to flight with all the nimbleness of their heels, and began to fight them, but their steps tottered exceedingly and they gave back, the slippery surface under their soles making their footing uncertain. But the Danes crossed the frozen sea with safer steps, and foiled the feeble advance of the enemy, whom they conquered, and then turned and sailed to Finland. Here they chanced to enter a rather narrow gulf, and, on sending a few men to reconnoitre, they learnt that the harbour was being held by a few ships. For Alfhild had gone before them with her fleet into the same narrows. And when she saw the strange ships afar off, she rowed in swift haste forward to encounter them, thinking it better to attack the foe than to await them. Alf's men were against attacking so many ships with so few; but he replied that it would be shameful if anyone should report to Alfhild that his desire to advance could be checked by a few ships in the path; for he said that their record of honours ought not to be tarnished by such a trifle.

The Danes wondered whence their enemies got such grace of bodily beauty and such supple limbs. So, when they began the sea-fight, the young man Alf leapt on Alfhild's prow, and advanced towards the stern, slaughtering all that withstood him. His comrade Borgar struck off Alfhild's helmet, and, seeing the smoothness of her chin, saw that he must fight with kisses and not with arms; that the cruel spears must be put away, and the enemy handled with gentler dealings. So Alf rejoiced that the woman whom he had sought over land and sea in the face of so many dangers was now beyond all expectation in his power; whereupon he took hold of her eagerly, and made her change her man's apparel for a woman's; and afterwards begot on her a daughter, Gurid. Also Borgar wedded the attendant of Alfhild, Groa, and had by her a son, Harald, to whom the following age gave the surname Hyldeland.

And that no one may wonder that this sex laboured at warfare, I will make a brief digression, in order to give a short account of the estate and character of such women. There were once women among the Danes who dressed themselves to look like men, and devoted almost every instant of their lives to the pursuit of war, that they might not suffer their valour to be unstrung or dulled by the infection of luxury. For they abhorred all dainty living, and used to harden their minds and bodies with toil and endurance. They put away all the softness and lightmindedness of women, and inured their womanish spirit to masculine ruthlessness. They sought, moreover, so zealously to be skilled in warfare, that they might have been thought to have unsexed themselves. Those especially, who had either force of character or tall and comely persons, used to enter on this kind of life. These women, therefore (just as if they had forgotten their natural estate, and preferred sternness to soft words), offered war rather than kisses, and would rather taste blood than busses, and went about the business of arms more than that of amours. They devoted those hands to the lance which they should rather have applied to the loom. They assailed men with their spears whom they could have melted with their looks, they thought of death and not of dalliance. Now I will cease to wander, and will go back to my theme.

In the early spring, Alf and Alger, who had gone back to sea-roving, were exploring the sea in various directions, when they lighted with a hundred ships upon Helwin, Hagbard, and Hamund, sons of the kinglet Hamund. These they attacked and only the twilight stayed their blood-wearied hands; and in the night the soldiers were ordered to keep truce. On the morrow this was ratified for good by a mutual oath; for such loss had been suffered on both sides in the battle of the day before that they had no force left to fight again. Thus, exhausted bye quality of valour, they were driven perforce to make peace. About the same time Hildigisl, a Teuton Of noble birth, relying on his looks and his rank, sued for Signe, the daughter of Sigar. But she scorned him, chiefly for his insignificance, inasmuch as he was not brave, but wished to adorn his fortunes with the courage of other people. But this woman was inclined to love Hakon, chiefly for the high renown of his great deeds. For she thought more of the brave than the feeble; she admired notable deeds more than looks, knowing that every allurement of beauty is mere dross when reckoned against simple valour, and cannot weigh equal with it in the balance. For there are maids that are more charmed by the fame than by the face of their lovers; who go not by the looks, but by the mind, and whom naught but regard for a man's spirit can kindle to pledge their own troth. Now Hagbard, going to Denmark with the sons of Sigar, gained speech of their sister without their knowledge, and in the end induced her to pledge her word to him that she would secretly become his mistress. Afterwards, when the waiting-women happened to be comparing the honourable deeds of the nobles, she preferred Hakon to Hildigisl, declaring that the latter had nothing to praise but his looks, while in the case of the other a wrinkled visage was outweighed by a choice spirit. Not content with this plain kind of praise, she is said to have sung as follows:

"This man lacks fairness, but shines with foremost courage, measuring his features by his force.

"For the lofty soul redeems the shortcoming of harsh looks, and conquers the body's blemish.

"His look flashes with spirit, his face, notable in its very harshness, delights in fierceness.

"He who strictly judges character praises not the mind for the fair hue, but rather the complexion for the mind.

"This man is not prized for beauty, but for brave daring and war-won honour.

"While the other is commended by his comely head and radiant countenance and crest of lustrous locks.

"Vile is the empty grace of beauty, self-confounded the deceptive pride of comeliness.

"Valour and looks are swayed by different inclinations: one lasts on, the other perishes.

"Empty red and white brings in vice, and is frittered away little by little by the lightly gliding years;

"But courage plants firmer the hearts devoted to it, and does not slip and straightway fall.

"The voice of the multitude is beguiled by outward good, and forsakes the rule of right;

"But I praise virtue at a higher rate, and scorn the grace of comeliness."

This utterance fell on the ears of the bystanders in such a way, that they thought she praised Hagbard under the name of Hakon. And Hildigisl, vexed that she preferred Hagbard to himself, bribed a certain blind man, Bolwis, to bring the sons of Sigar and the sons of Hamund to turn their friendship into hatred. For King Sigar had been used to transact almost all affairs by the advice of two old men, one of whom was Bolwis. The temper of these two men was so different, that one used to reconcile folk who were at feud, while the other loved to sunder in hatred those who were bound by friendship, and by estranging folk to fan pestilent quarrels.

So Bolwis began by reviling the sons of Hamund to the sons of Sigar, in lying slanders, declaring that they never used to preserve the bonds of fellowship loyally, and that they must be restrained by war rather than by league. Thus the alliance of the young men was broken through; and while Hagbard was far away, the sons of Sigar, Alf and Alger, made an attack, and Helwin and Hamund were destroyed by the harbour which is called Hamund's Bay. Hagbard then came up with fresh forces to avenge his brothers, and destroyed them in battle. Hildigisl slunk off with a spear through both buttocks, which was the occasion for a jeer at the Teutons, since the ugliness of the blow did not fail to brand it with disgrace.

Afterwards Hagbard dressed himself in woman's attire, and, as though he had not wronged Sigar's daughter by slaying her brothers, went back to her alone, trusting in the promise he had from her, and feeling more safe in her loyalty than alarmed by reason of his own misdeed. Thus does lust despise peril. And, not to lack a pretext for his journey, he gave himself out as a fighting-maid of Hakon, saying that he took an embassy from him to Sigar. And when he was taken to bed at night among the handmaids, and the woman who washed his feet were wiping them, they asked him why he had such hairy legs, and why his

256

hands were not at all soft to touch, he answered:

"What wonder that the soft hollow of my foot should harden, and that long hairs should stay on my shaggy leg, when the sand has so often smitten my soles beneath, and the briars have caught me in mid-step?

"Now I scour the forest with leaping, now the waters with running. Now the sea, now the earth, now the wave is my path.

"Nor could my breast, shut in bonds of steel, and wont to be beaten with lance and missile, ever have been soft to the touch, as with you who are covered by the mantle or the smooth gown.

"Not the distaff or the wool-frails, but spears dripping from the slaughter, have served for our handling."

Signe did not hesitate to back up his words with like dissembling, and replied that it was natural that hands which dealt more in wounds than wools, and in battle than in tasks of the house should show the hardness that befitted their service; and that, unenfeebled with the pliable softness of women, they should not feel smooth to the touch of others. For they were hardened partly by the toils of war, partly by the habit of seafaring. For, said she, the warlike handmaid of Hakon did not deal in woman's business, but had been wont to bring her right hand blood-stained with hurling spears and flinging missiles. It was no wonder, therefore, if her soles were hardened by the immense journeys she had gone; and that, when the shores she had scoured so often had bruised them with their rough and broken shingle, they should toughen in a horny stiffness, and should not feel soft to the touch like theirs, whose steps never strayed, but who were forever cooped within the confines of the palace. Hagbard received her as his bedfellow, under plea that he was to have the couch of honour; and, amid their converse of mutual delight, he addressed her slowly in such words as these:

"If thy father takes me and gives me to bitter death, wilt thou ever, when I am dead, forget so strong a troth, and again seek the marriage-plight?

"For if the chance should fall that way, I can hope for no room for pardon; nor will the father who is to avenge his sons spare or have pity.

"For I stripped thy brothers of their power on the sea and slew them; and now, unknown to thy father, as though I had done naught before counter to his will, I hold thee in the couch we share.

"Say, then, my one love, what manner of wish wilt thou show when thou

257

lackest the accustomed embrace?"

Signe answered:

"Trust me, dear; I wish to die with thee, if fate brings thy turn to perish first, and not to prolong my span of life at all, when once dismal death has cast thee to the tomb.

"For if thou chance to close thy eyes for ever, a victim to the maddened attack of the men-at-arms;—by whatsoever doom thy breath be cut off, by sword or disease, by sea or soil, I forswear every wanton and corrupt flame, and vow myself to a death like thine; that they who were bound by one marriage-union may be embraced in one and the same punishment. Nor will I quit this man, though I am to feel the pains of death; I have resolved he is worthy of my love who gathered the first kisses of my mouth, and had the first fruits of my delicate youth. I think that no vow will be surer than this, if speech of woman have any loyalty at all."

This speech so quickened the spirit of Hagbard, that he found more pleasure in her promise than peril in his own going away (to his death). The serving-women betrayed him; and when Sigar's men-at-arms attacked him, he defended himself long and stubbornly, and slew many of them in the doorway. But at last he was taken, and brought before the assembly, and found the voices of the people divided over him. For very many said that he should be punished for so great an offence; but Bilwis, the brother of Bolwis, and others, conceived a better judgment, and advised that it would be better to use his stout service than to deal with him too ruthlessly. Then Bolwis came forward and declared that it was evil advice which urged the king to pardon when he ought to take vengeance, and to soften with unworthy compassion his righteous impulse to anger. For how could Sigar, in the case of this man, feel any desire to spare or pity him, when he had not only robbed him of the double comfort of his sons, but had also bestained him with the insult of deflowering his daughter? The greater part of the assembly voted for this opinion; Hagbard was condemned, and a gallows-tree planted to receive him. Hence it came about that he who at first had hardly one sinister voice against him was punished with general harshness. Soon after the queen handed him a cup, and, bidding him assuage his thirst, vexed him with threats after this manner:

"Now, insolent Hagbard, whom the whole assembly has pronounced worthy of death, now to quench thy thirst thou shalt give thy lips liquor to drink in a cup of horn.

"Wherefore cast away fear, and, at this last hour of thy life, taste with bold lips the deadly goblet;

"That, having drunk it, thou mayst presently land by the dwellings of those below, passing into the sequestered palace of stern Dis, giving thy body to the gibbet and thy spirit to Orcus."

Then the young man took the cup offered him, and is said to have made answer as follows:

"With this hand, wherewith I cut off thy twin sons, I will take my last taste, yea the draught of the last drink.

"Now not unavenged shall I go to the Elysian regions, not unchastising to the stern ghosts. For these men have first been shut in the dens of Tartarus by a slaughter wrought by my endeavours. This right hand was wet with blood that was yours, this hand robbed thy children of the years of their youth, children whom thy womb brought to light; but the deadly sword spared it not then. Infamous woman, raving in spirit, hapless, childless mother, no years shall restore to thee the lost, no time and no day whatsoever shall save thy child from the starkness of death, or redeem him!"

Thus he avenged the queen's threats of death by taunting her with the youths whom he had slain; and, flinging back the cup at her, drenched her face with the sprinkled wine.

Meantime Signe asked her weeping women whether they could endure to bear her company in the things which she purposed. They promised that they would carry out and perform themselves whatsoever their mistress should come to wish, and their promise was loyally kept. Then, drowned in tears, she said that she wished to follow in death the only partner of her bed that she had ever had; and ordered that, as soon as the signal had been given from a place of watch, torches should be put to the room, then that halters should be made out of their robes; and to these they should proffer their throats to be strangled, thrusting away the support to the feet. They agreed, and that they might blench the less at death, she gave them a draught of wine. After this Hagbard was led to the hill, which afterwards took its name from him, to be hanged. Then, to test the loyalty of his true love, he told the executioners to hang up his mantle, saying that it would be a pleasure to him if he could see the likeness of his approaching death rehearsed in some way. The request was granted; and the watcher on the outlook, thinking that the thing was being done to Hagbard, reported what she saw to the maidens who were shut within the palace. They quickly fired the house, and thrusting away the wooden support under their feet, gave their necks to the noose to be writhen. So Hagbard, when he saw the palace wrapped in fire, and the familiar chamber blazing, said that he felt more joy from the loyalty of his mistress than sorrow at his approaching death. He also charged the bystanders to do him to death, witnessing how little he made of his doom by a song like this:

"Swiftly, O warriors! Let me be caught and lifted into the air. Sweet, O my bride! Is it for me to die when thou hast gone.

"I perceive the crackling and the house ruddy with flames; and the love, long-promised, declares our troth.

"Behold, thy covenant is fulfilled with no doubtful vows, since thou sharest my life and my destruction.

"We shall have one end, one bond after our troth, and somewhere our first love will live on.

"Happy am I, that have deserved to have joy of such a consort, and not to go basely alone to the gods of Tartarus!

"Then let the knot gripe the midst of the throat; nought but pleasure the last doom shall bring,

"Since there remains a sure hope of the renewal of love, and a death which will soon have joys of its own.

"Either country is sweet; in both worlds shall be held in honour the repose of our souls together, our equal truth in love,

"For, see now, I welcome the doom before me; since not even among the shades does very love suffer the embrace of its partner to perish." And as he spoke the executioners strangled him. And, that none may think that all traces of antiquity have utterly disappeared, a proof of the aforesaid event is afforded by local marks yet existing; for the killing of Hagbard gave his name to the stead; and not far from the town of Sigar there is a place to be seen, where a mound a little above the level, with the appearance of a swelling in the ground, looks like an ancient homestead. Moreover, a man told Absalon that he had seen a beam found in the spot, which a countryman struck with his ploughshare as he burrowed into the clods.

Hakon, the son of Hamund, heard of this; but when he was seen to be on the point of turning his arms from the Irish against the Danes in order to avenge his brother, Hakon the Zealander, the son of Wigar, and Starkad deserted him. They had been his allies from the death of Ragnald up to that hour: one, because he was moved by regard for friendship, the other by regard for his birth; so that different reasons made both desire the same thing.

Now patriotism diverted Hakon (of Zealand) from attacking his country; for it was apparent that he was going to fight his own people, while all the rest warred with foreigners. But Starkad forbore to become the foe of the aged Sigar, whose hospitality he had enjoyed, lest he should be thought to wrong one who deserved well of him. For some men pay such respect to hospitality that, if they can remember ever to have experienced kindly offices from folk, they cannot be thought to inflict any annoyance on them. But Hakon thought the death of his brother a worse loss than the defection of his champions; and, gathering his fleet into the haven called Herwig in Danish, and in Latin Hosts' Bight, he drew up his men, and posted his line of foot-soldiers in the spot where the town built by Esbern now defends with its fortifications those who dwell hard by, and repels the approach of barbarous savages. Then he divided his forces in three, and sent on two-thirds of his ships, appointing a few men to row to the river Susa. This force was to advance on a dangerous voyage along its winding reaches, and to help those on foot if necessary. He marched in person by land with the remainder, advancing chiefly over wooded country to escape notice. Part of this path, which was once closed up with thick woods, is now land ready for the plough, and fringed with a scanty scrub. And, in order that when they got out into the plain they might not lack the shelter of trees, he told them to cut and carry branches. Also, that nothing might burden their rapid march, he bade them cast away some of their clothes, as well as their scabbards; and carry their swords naked. In memory of this event he left the mountain and the ford a perpetual name. Thus by his night march he eluded two pickets of sentries; but when he came upon the third, a scout, observing the marvellous event, went to the sleeping-room of Sigar, saying that he brought news of a portentous thing; for he saw leaves and shrubs like men walking. Then the king asked him how far off was the advancing forest; and when he heard that it was near, he added that this prodigy boded his own death. Hence the marsh where the shrubs were cut down was styled in common parlance Deadly Marsh. Therefore, fearing the narrow passages, he left the town, and went to a level spot which was more open, there to meet the enemy in battle. Sigar fought unsuccessfully, and was crushed and slain at the spot that is called in common speech Walbrunna, but in Latin the Spring of Corpses or Carnage. Then Hakon used his conquest to cruel purpose, and followed up his good fortune so wickedly, that he lusted for an indiscriminate massacre, and thought no forbearance should be shown to rank or sex. Nor did he yield to any regard for compassion or shame, but stained his sword in the blood of women, and attacked mothers and children in one general and ruthless slaughter.

SIWALD, the son of Sigar, had thus far stayed under his father's roof. But when he heard of this, he mustered an army in order to have his vengeance. So Hakon, alarmed at the gathering of such numbers, went back with a third of his army to his fleet at Herwig, and planned to depart by sea. But his colleague, Hakon, surnamed the Proud, thought that he ought himself to feel more confidence at the late victory than fear at the absence of Hakon; and, preferring death to flight, tried to defend the remainder of the army. So he drew back his camp for a little, and for a long time waited near the town of Axelsted, for the arrival of the fleet, blaming his friends for their tardy coming. For the fleet that had been sent into the river had not yet come to anchor in the appointed harbour. Now the killing of Sigar and the love of Siwald were stirring the temper of the people one and all, so that both sexes devoted themselves to war, and you would have thought that the battle did not lack the aid of women.

On the morrow Hakon and Siwald met in an encounter and fought two whole days. The combat was most frightful; both generals fell; and victory graced the remnants of the Danes. But, in the night after the battle, the fleet, having penetrated the Susa, reached the appointed haven. It was once possible to row along this river; but its bed is now choked with solid substances, and is so narrowed by its straits that few vessels can get in, being prevented by its sluggishness and contractedness. At daybreak, when the sailors saw the corpses of their friends, they heaped up, in order to bury the general, a barrow of notable size, which is famous to this day, and is commonly named Hakon's Howe.

But Borgar, with Skanian chivalry suddenly came up and slaughtered a multitude of them. When the enemy were destroyed, he manned their ships, which now lacked their rowers, and hastily, with breathless speed, pursued the son of Hamund. He encountered him, and ill-fortune befell Hakon, who fled in hasty panic with three ships to the country of the Scots, where, after two years had gone by, he died.

All these perilous wars and fortunes had so exhausted the royal line among the Danes, that it was found to be reduced to GURID alone, the daughter of Alf, and granddaughter of Sigar. And when the Danes saw themselves deprived of their usual high-born sovereigns, they committed the kingdom to men of the people, and appointed rulers out of the commons, assigning to Ostmar the regency of Skaane, and that of Zealand to Hunding; on Hane they conferred the lordship of Funen; while in the hands of Rorik and Hather they put the supreme power of Jutland, the authority being divided. Therefore, that it may not be unknown from what father sprang the succeeding line of kings, some matters come to my mind which must be glanced at for a while in a needful digression.

They say that Gunnar, the bravest of the Swedes, was once at feud with Norway for the most weighty reasons, and that he was granted liberty to attack it, but that he turned this liberty into licence by the greatest perils, and fell, in the first of the raids he planned, upon the district of Jather, which he put partly to the sword and partly to the flames. Forbearing to plunder, he rejoiced only in passing through the paths that were covered with corpses, and the blood-stained ways. Other men used to abstain from bloodshed, and love pillage more than slaughter; but he preferred bloodthirstiness to booty, and liked best to wreak his deadly pleasure by slaughtering men. His cruelty drove the islanders to forestall the impending danger by a public submission. Moreover, Ragnald, the King of the Northmen, now in extreme age, when he heard how the tyrant busied himself, had a cave made and shut up in it his daughter Drota, giving her due attendance, and providing her maintenance for a long time. Also he committed to the cave some swords which had been adorned with the choicest smith-craft, besides the royal household gear; so that he might not leave the enemy to capture and use the sword, which he saw that he could not wield himself. And, to prevent the cave being noticed by its height, he levelled the hump down to the firmer ground. Then he set out to war; but being unable with his aged limbs to go down into battle, he leaned on the shoulders of his escort and walked forth propped by the steps of others. So he perished in the battle, where he fought with more ardour than success, and left his country a sore matter for shame.

For Gunnar, in order to punish the cowardice of the conquered race by terms of extraordinary baseness, had a dog set over them as a governor. What can we suppose to have been his object in this action, unless it were to make a haughty nation feel that their arrogance was being more signally punished when they bowed their stubborn heads before a yapping hound? To let no insult be lacking, he appointed governors to look after public and private affairs in its name; and he appointed separate ranks of nobles to keep continual and steadfast watch over it. He also enacted that if any one of the courtiers thought it contemptible to do allegiance to their chief, and omitted offering most respectful homage to its various goings and comings as it ran hither and thither, he should be punished with loss of his limbs. Also Gunnar

263

imposed on the nation a double tribute, one to be paid out of the autumn harvest, the other in the spring. Thus he burst the bubble conceit of the Norwegians, to make them feel clearly how their pride was gone, when they saw it forced to do homage to a dog.

When he heard that the king's daughter was shut up in some distant hiding-place, Gunnar strained his wits in every nerve to track her out. Hence, while he was himself conducting the search with others, his doubtful ear caught the distant sound of a subterranean hum. Then he went on slowly, and recognized a human voice with greater certainty. He ordered the ground underfoot to be dug down to the solid rock; and when the cave was suddenly laid open, he saw the winding tunnels. The servants were slain as they tried to guard the now uncovered entrance to the cave, and the girl was dragged out of the hole, together with the booty therein concealed. With great foresight, she had consigned at any rate her father's swords to the protection of a more secret place. Gunnar forced her to submit to his will, and she bore a son Hildiger. This man was such a rival to his father in cruelty, that he was ever thirsting to kill, and was bent on nothing but the destruction of men, panting with a boundless lust for bloodshed. Outlawed by his father on account of his unbearable ruthlessness, and soon after presented by Alver with a government, he spent his whole life in arms, visiting his neighbours with wars and slaughters; nor did he, in his estate of banishment, relax his accustomed savagery a whir, but would not change his spirit with his habitation.

Meanwhile Borgar, finding that Gunnar had married Drota, the daughter of Ragnald, by violence, took from him both life and wife, and wedded Drota himself. She was not an unwilling bride; she thought it right for her to embrace the avenger of her parent. For the daughter mourned her father, and could never bring herself to submit with any pleasure to his murderer. This woman and Borgar had a son Halfdan, who through all his early youth was believed to be stupid, but whose later years proved illustrious for the most glorious deeds, and famous for the highest qualities that can grace life. Once, when a stripling, he mocked in boyish fashion at a champion of noble repute, who smote him with a buffet; whereupon Halfdan attacked him with the staff he was carrying and killed him. This deed was an omen of his future honours; he had hitherto been held in scorn, but henceforth throughout his life he had the highest honour and glory. The affair, indeed, was a prophecy of the greatness of his deeds in war.

At this period, Rothe, a Ruthenian rover, almost destroyed our country with his rapine and cruelty. His harshness was so notable that, while other men spared their prisoners utter nakedness, he did not think it

264

uncomely to strip of their coverings even the privy parts of their bodies; wherefore we are wont to this day to call all severe and monstrous acts of rapine Rothe-Ran (Rothe's Robbery). He used also sometimes to inflict the following kind of torture: Fastening the men's right feet firmly to the earth, he tied the left feet to boughs for the purpose that when these should spring back the body would be rent asunder. Hane, Prince of Funen, wishing to win honour and glory, tried to attack this man with his sea-forces, but took to flight with one attendant. It was in reproach of him that the proverb arose: "The cock (Hane) fights better on its own dunghill." Then Borgar, who could not bear to see his countrymen perishing any longer, encountered Rothe. Together they fought and together they perished. It is said that in this battle Halfdan was sorely stricken, and was for some time feeble with the wounds he had received. One of these was inflicted conspicuously on his mouth, and its scar was so manifest that it remained as an open blotch when all the other wounds were healed; for the crushed portion of the lip was so ulcerated by the swelling, that the flesh would not grow out again and mend the noisome gash. This circumstance fixed on him a most insulting nickname,... although wounds in the front of the body commonly bring praise and not ignominy. So spiteful a colour does the belief of the vulgar sometimes put upon men's virtues.

Meanwhile Gurid, the daughter of Alf, seeing that the royal line was reduced to herself alone, and having no equal in birth whom she could marry, proclaimed a vow imposing chastity on herself, thinking it better to have no husband than to take one from the commons. Moreover, to escape outrage, she guarded her room with a chosen band of champions. Once Halfdan happened to come to see her. The champions, whose brother he had himself slain in his boyhood, were away. He told her that she ought to loose her virgin zone, and exchange her austere chastity for deeds of love; that she ought not to give in so much to her inclination for modesty as to be too proud to make a match, and so by her service repair the fallen monarchy. So he bade her look on himself, who was of eminently illustrious birth, in the light of a husband, since it appeared that she would only admit pleasure for the reason he had named. Gurid answered that she could not bring her mind to ally the remnants of the royal line to a man of meaner rank. Not content with reproaching his obscure birth, she also taunted his unsightly countenance. Halfdan rejoined that she brought against him two faults: one that his blood was not illustrious enough; another, that he was blemished with a cracked lip whose scar had never healed. Therefore he would not come back to ask for her before he had wiped away both marks of shame by winning glory in war.

Halfdan entreated her to suffer no man to be privy to her bed until she

265

heard certain tidings either of his return or his death. The champions, whom he had bereaved of their brother long ago, were angry that he had spoken to Gurid, and tried to ride after him as he went away. When he saw it, he told his comrades to go into ambush, and said he would encounter the champions alone. His followers lingered, and thought it shameful to obey his orders, but he drove them off with threats, saying that Gurid should not find that fear had made him refuse to fight. Presently he cut down an oak-tree and fashioned it into a club, fought the twelve single-handed, and killed them. After their destruction, not content with the honours of so splendid an action, and meaning to do one yet greater, he got from his mother the swords of his grandfather, one of which was called Lyusing.... and the other Hwyting, after the sheen of its well-whetted point. But when he heard that war was raging between Alver, the King of Sweden, and the Ruthenians (Russians), he instantly went to Russia, offered help to the natives, and was received by all with the utmost honour. Alver was not far off, there being only a little ground to cross to cover the distance between the two. Alver's soldier Hildiger, the son of Gunnar, challenged the champions of the Ruthenians to fight him; but when he saw that Halfdan was put up against him, though knowing well that he was Halfdan's brother, he let natural feeling prevail over courage, and said that he, who was famous for the destruction of seventy champions, would not fight with an untried man. Therefore he told him to measure himself in enterprises of lesser moment, and thenceforth to follow pursuits fitted to his strength. He made this announcement not from distrust in his own courage, but in order to preserve his uprightness; for he was not only very valiant, but also skilled at blunting the sword with spells. For when he remembered that Halfdan's father had slain his own, he was moved by two feelings— the desire to avenge his father, and his love for his brother. He therefore thought it better to retire from the challenge than to be guilty of a very great crime. Halfdan demanded another champion in his place, slew him when he appeared, and was soon awarded the palm of valour even by the voice of the enemy, being accounted by public acclamation the bravest of all. On the next day he asked for two men to fight with, and slew them both. On the third day he subdued three; on the fourth he overcame four who met him; and on the fifth he asked for five.

When Halfdan conquered these, and when the eighth day had been reached with an equal increase in the combatants and in the victory, he laid low eleven who attacked him at once. Hildiger, seeing that his own record of honours was equalled by the greatness of Halfdan's deeds could not bear to decline to meet him any longer. And when he felt that Halfdan had dealt him a deadly wound with a sword wrapped in rags, he threw away his arms, and, lying on the earth, addressed his brother as follows:

"It is pleasing to pass an hour away in mutual talk; and, while the sword rests, to sit a little on the ground and while away the time by speaking in turn, and keep ourselves in good heart. Time is left for our purpose; our two destinies have a different lot; one is surely doomed to die by a fatal weird, while triumph and glory and all the good of living await the other in better years. Thus our omens differ, and our portions are distinguished. Thou art a son of the Danish land, I of the country of Sweden. Once, Drota thy mother had her breast swell for thee; she bore me, and by her I am thy foster-brother. Lo now, there perishes a righteous offspring, who had the heart to fight with savage spears; brothers born of a shining race charge and bring death on one another; while they long for the height of power, they lose their days, and, having now received a fatal mischief in their desire for a sceptre, they will go to Styx in a common death. Fast by my head stands my Swedish shield, which is adorned with (as) a fresh mirror of diverse chasing, and ringed with layers of marvellous fretwork. There a picture of really hues shows slain nobles and conquered champions, and the wars also and the notable deed of my right hand. In the midst is to be seen, painted in bright relief, the figure of my son, whom this hand bereft of his span of life. He was our only heir, the only thought of his father's mind, and given to his mother with comfort from above. An evil lot, which heaps years of ill-fortune on the joyous, chokes mirth in mourning, and troubles our destiny. For it is lamentable and wretched to drag out a downcast life, to draw breath through dismal days and to chafe at foreboding. But whatsoever things are bound by the prophetic order of the fates, whatsoever are shadowed in the secrets of the divine plan, whatsoever are foreseen and fixed in the course of the destinies, no change of what is transient shall cancel these things."

When he had thus spoken, Halfdan condemned Hildiger for sloth in avowing so late their bond of brotherhood; he declared he had kept silence that he might not be thought a coward for refusing to fight, or a villain if he fought; and while intent on these words of excuse, he died. But report had given out among the Danes that Hildiger had overthrown Halfdan. After this, Siwar, a Saxon of very high birth, began to be a suitor for Gurid, the only survivor of the royal blood among the Danes. Secretly she preferred Halfdan to him, and imposed on her wooer the condition that he should not ask her in marriage till he had united into one body the kingdom of the Danes, which was now torn limb from limb, and restored by arms what had been wrongfully taken from her. Siwar made a vain attempt to do this; but as he bribed all the guardians, she was at last granted to him in betrothal. Halfdan heard of this in Russia through traders, and voyaged so hard that he arrived before the time of the wedding-rites. On their first day, before he went to the palace, he gave orders that his men should not stir from the watches appointed them till their ears caught the clash of the steel in the distance. Unknown to the guests, he came and stood before the maiden, and, that he might not reveal his meaning to too many by bare and common speech, he composed a dark and ambiguous song as follows:

"As I left my father's sceptre, I had no fear of the wiles of woman's device nor of female subtlety.

"When I overthrew, one and two, three and four, and soon five, and next six, then seven, and also eight, yea eleven single-handed, triumphant in battle.

"But neither did I then think that I was to be shamed with the taint of disgrace, with thy frailness to thy word and thy beguiling pledges."

Gurid answered: "My soul wavered in suspense, with slender power over events, and shifted about with restless fickleness. The report of thee was so fleeting, so doubtful, borne on uncertain stories, and parched by doubting heart. I feared that the years of thy youth had perished by the sword. Could I withstand singly my elders and governors, when they forbade me to refuse that thing, and pressed me to become a wife? My love and my flame are both yet unchanged, they shall be mate and match to thine; nor has my troth been disturbed, but shall have faithful approach to thee.

"For my promise has not yet beguiled thee at all, though I, being alone, could not reject the counsel of such manifold persuasion, nor oppose their stern bidding in the matter of my consent to the marriage bond."

Before the maiden had finished her answer, Halfdan had already run his sword through the bridegroom. Not content with having killed one man, he massacred most of the guests. Staggering tipsily backwards, the Saxons ran at him, but his servants came up and slaughtered them. After this HALFDAN took Gurid to wife. But finding in her the fault of barrenness, and desiring much to have offspring, he went to Upsala in order to procure fruitfulness for her; and being told in answer, that he must make atonement to the shades of his brother if he would raise up children, he obeyed the oracle, and was comforted by gaining his desire. For he had a son by Gurid, to whom he gave the name of Harald. Under his title Halfdan tried to restore the kingdom of the Danes to its ancient estate, as it was torn asunder by the injuries of the chiefs; but, while fighting in Zealand, he attacked Wesete, a very famous champion, in battle, and was slain. Gurid was at the battle in man's attire, from love for her son. She saw the event; the young man fought hotly, but his companions fled; and she took him on her shoulders to a neighbouring wood. Weariness, more than anything else, kept the enemy from pursuing him; but one of them shot him as he hung, with an arrow, through the hinder parts, and Harald thought that his mother's care brought him more shame than help.

HARALD, being of great beauty and unusual size, and surpassing those of his age in strength and stature, received such favour from Odin (whose oracle was thought to have been the cause of his birth), that steel could not injure his perfect soundness. The result was, that shafts which wounded others were disabled from doing him any harm. Nor was the boon unrequited; for he is reported to have promised to Odin all the souls which his sword cast out of their bodies. He also had his father's deeds recorded for a memorial by craftsmen on a rock in Bleking, whereof I have made mention.

After this, hearing that Wesete was to hold his wedding in Skaane, he went to the feast disguised as a beggar; and when all were sunken in wine and sleep, he battered the bride-chamber with a beam. But Wesete, without inflicting a wound, so beat his mouth with a cudgel, that he took out two teeth; but two grinders unexpectedly broke out afterwards and repaired their loss: an event which earned him the name of Hyldetand, which some declare he obtained on account of a prominent row of teeth. Here he slew Wesete, and got the sovereignty of Skaane. Next he attacked and killed Hather in Jutland; and his fall is marked by the lasting name of the town. After this he overthrew Hunding and Rorik, seized Leire, and reunited the dismembered realm of Denmark into its original shape. Then he found that Asmund, the King of the Wikars, had been deprived of his throne by his elder sister; and, angered by such presumption on the part of a woman, went to Norway with a single ship, while the war was still undecided, to help him. The battle began; and, clothed in a purple cloak, with a coif broidered with gold, and with his hair bound up, he went against the enemy trusting not in arms, but in his silent certainty of his luck, insomuch that he seemed dressed more for a feast than a fray. But his spirit did not match his attire. For, though unarmed and only adorned with his emblems of royalty, he outstripped the rest who bore arms, and exposed himself, lightly-armed as he was, to the hottest perils of the battle. For the shafts aimed against him lost all power to hurt, as if their points had been blunted. When the other side saw him fighting unarmed, they made an attack, and were forced for very shame into assailing him more hotly. But Harald, whole in body, either put them to the sword, or made them take to flight; and thus he overthrew the sister of Asmund, and restored him his kingdom. When Asmund offered him the prizes of victory, he said that the reward of glory was enough by itself; and demeaned himself as greatly in refusing the gifts as he had in earning them. By this he made all men admire his self-restraint as much as his valour; and declared that the victory should give him a harvest not of gold but glory.

Meantime Alver, the King of the Swedes, died leaving sons Olaf, Ing, and Ingild. One of these, Ing, dissatisfied with the honours his father bequeathed him, declared war with the Danes in order to extend his empire. And when Harald wished to inquire of oracles how this war would end, an old man of great height, but lacking one eye, and clad also in a hairy mantle, appeared before him, and declared that he was called Odin, and was versed in the practice of warfare; and he gave him the most useful instruction how to divide up his army in the field. Now he told him, whenever he was going to make war with his land-forces, to divide his whole army into three squadrons, each of which he was to pack into twenty ranks; the centre squadron, however, he was to extend further than the rest by the number of twenty men. This squadron he was also to arrange in the form of the point of a cone or pyramid, and to make the wings on either side slant off obliquely from it. He was to compose the successive ranks of each squadron in the following way: the front should begin with two men, and the number in each succeeding rank should only increase by one; he was, in fact, to post a rank of three in the second line, four in the third, and so on behind. And thus, when the men mustered, all the succeeding ranks were to be manned at the same rate of proportion, until the end of (the edge that made) the junction of men came down to the wings; each wing was to be drawn up in ten lines from that point. Likewise after these squadrons he was to put the young men, equipped with lances, and behind these to set the company of aged men, who would support their comrades with what one might call a veteran valour if they faltered; next, a skilful reckoner should attach wings of slingers to stand behind the ranks of their fellows and attack the enemy from a distance with missiles. After these he was to enroll men of any age or rank indiscriminately, without heed of their estate. Moreover, he was to draw up the rear like the vanguard, in three separated divisions, and arranged in ranks similarly proportioned. The back of this, joining on to the body in front would protect it by facing in the opposite direction. But if a sea-battle happened to occur, he should withdraw a portion of his fleet, which when he began the intended engagement, was to cruise round that of the enemy, wheeling to and fro continually. Equipped with this system of warfare, he forestalled matters in Sweden, and killed Ing and Olaf as they were making ready to fight. Their brother Ingild sent messengers to beg a truce, on pretence of his ill-health. Harald granted his request, that his own valour, which had learnt to spare distress, might not triumph over a man in the hour of lowliness and dejection. When Ingild afterwards provoked Harald by wrongfully ravishing his sister, Harald vexed him with long and indecisive war, but then took him into his friendship, thinking it better to have him for ally than for enemy.

After this he heard that Olaf, King of the Thronds, had to fight with the maidens Stikla and Rusila for the kingdom. Much angered at this arrogance on the part of women, he went to Olaf unobserved, put on dress which concealed the length of his teeth, and attacked the maidens. He overthrew them both, leaving to two harbours a name akin to theirs. It was then that he gave a notable exhibition of valour; for defended only by a shirt under his shoulders, he fronted the spears with unarmed breast.

When Olaf offered Harald the prize of victory, he rejected the gift, thus leaving it a question whether he had shown a greater example of bravery or self-control. Then he attacked a champion of the Frisian nation, named Ubbe, who was ravaging the borders of Jutland and destroying numbers of the common people; and when Harald could not subdue him to his arms, he charged his soldiers to grip him with their hands, throw him on the ground, and to bind him while thus overpowered. Thus he only overcame the man and mastered him by a shameful kind of attack, though a little before he thought he would inflict a heavy defeat on him. But Harald gave him his sister in marriage, and thus gained him for his soldier.

Harald made tributaries of the nations that lay along the Rhine, levying troops from the bravest of that race. With these forces he conquered Sclavonia in war, and caused its generals, Duk and Dal, because of their bravery, to be captured, and not killed. These men he took to serve with him, and, after overcoming Aquitania, soon went to Britain, where he overthrew the King of the Humbrians, and enrolled the smartest of the warriors he had conquered, the chief of whom was esteemed to be Orm, surnamed the Briton. The fame of these deeds brought champions from divers parts of the world, whom he formed into a band of mercenaries. Strengthened by their numbers, he kept down insurrections in all kingdoms by the terror of his name, so that he took out of their rulers all courage to fight with one another. Moreover, no man durst assume any sovereignty on the sea without his consent; for of old the state of the Danes had the joint lordship of land and sea.

Meantime Ingild died in Sweden, leaving only a very little son, Ring, whom he had by the sister of Harald. Harald gave the boy guardians, and put him over his father's kingdom. Thus, when he had overcome princes and provinces, he passed fifty years in peace. To save the minds of his soldiers from being melted into sloth by this inaction, he

271

decreed that they should assiduously learn from the champions the way of parrying and dealing blows. Some of these were skilled in a remarkable manner of fighting, and used to smite the eyebrow on the enemy's forehead with an infallible stroke; but if any man, on receiving the blow, blinked for fear, twitching his eyebrow, he was at once expelled the court and dismissed the service.

At this time Ole, the son of Siward and of Harald's sister, came to Denmark from the land of Norway in the desire to see his uncle. Since it is known that he had the first place among the followers of Harald, and that after the Swedish war he came to the throne of Denmark, it bears somewhat on the subject to relate the traditions of his deeds. Ole, then, when he had passed his tenth to his fifteenth year with his father, showed incredible proofs of his brilliant gifts both of mind and body. Moreover, he was so savage of countenance that his eyes were like the arms of other men against the enemy, and he terrified the bravest with his stern and flashing glance. He heard the tidings that Gunn, ruler of Tellemark, with his son Grim, was haunting as a robber the forest of Etha-scog, which was thick with underbrush and full of gloomy glens. The offence moved his anger; then he asked his father for a horse, a dog, and such armour as could be got, and cursed his youth, which was suffering the right season for valour to slip sluggishly away. He got what he asked, and explored the aforesaid wood very narrowly. He saw the footsteps of a man printed deep on the snow; for the rime was blemished by the steps, and betrayed the robber's progress. Thus guided, he went over a hill, and came on a very great river. This effaced the human tracks he had seen before, and he determined that he must cross. But the mere mass of water, whose waves ran down in a headlong torrent, seemed to forbid all crossing; for it was full of hidden reefs, and the whole length of its channel was turbid with a kind of whirl of foam. Yet all fear of danger was banished from Ole's mind by his impatience to make haste. So valour conquered fear, and rashness scorned peril; thinking nothing hard to do if it were only to his mind, he crossed the hissing eddies on horseback. When he had passed these, he came upon defiles surrounded on all sides with swamps, the interior of which was barred from easy approach by the pinnacle of a bank in front. He took his horse over this, and saw an enclosure with a number of stalls. Out of this he turned many horses, and was minded to put in his own, when a certain Tok, a servant of Gunn, angry that a stranger should wax so insolent, attacked him fiercely; but Ole foiled his assailant by simply opposing his shield. Thinking it a shame to slay the fellow with the sword, he seized him, shattered him limb by limb, and flung him across into the house whence he had issued in his haste. This insult quickly aroused Gunn and Grim: they ran out by different side-doors, and charged Ole both at once, despising his age and strength.

272

He wounded them fatally; and, when their bodily powers were quite spent, Grim, who could scarce muster a final gasp, and whose force was almost utterly gone, with his last pants composed this song:

"Though we be weak in frame, and the loss of blood has drained our strength; since the life-breath, now drawn out by my wound, scarce quivers softly in my pierced breast:

"I counsel that we should make the battle of our last hour glorious with dauntless deeds, that none may say that a combat has anywhere been bravelier waged or harder fought;

"And that our wild strife while we bore arms may, when our weary flesh has found rest in the tomb, win us the wage of immortal fame.

"Let our first stroke crush the shoulder-blades of the foe, let our steel cut off both his hands; so that, when Stygian Pluto has taken us, a like doom may fall on Ole also, and a common death tremble over three, and one urn cover the ashes of three."

Here Grim ended. But his father, rivalling his indomitable spirit, and wishing to give some exhortation in answer to his son's valiant speech, thus began:

"What though our veins be wholly bloodless, and in our frail body the life be brief, yet our last fight be so strong and strenuous that it suffer not the praise of us to be brief also.

"Therefore aim the javelin first at the shoulders and arms of the foe, so that the work of his hands may be weakened; and thus when we are gone three shall receive a common sepulchre, and one urn alike for three shall cover our united dust."

When he had said this, both of them, resting on their knees (for the approach of death had drained their strength), made a desperate effort to fight Ole hand to hand, in order that, before they perished, they might slay their enemy also; counting death as nothing if only they might envelope their slayer in a common fall. Ole slew one of them with his sword, the other with his hound. But even he gained no bloodless victory; for though he had been hitherto unscathed, now at last he received a wound in front. His dog diligently licked him over, and he regained his bodily strength: and soon, to publish sure news of his victory, he hung the bodies of the robbers upon gibbets in wide view. Moreover, he took the stronghold, and put in secret keeping all the booty he found there, in reserve for future use.

At this time the arrogant wantonness of the brothers Skate and Hiale waxed so high that they would take virgins of notable beauty from their parents and ravish them. Hence it came about that they formed the purpose of seizing Esa, the daughter of Olaf, prince of the Werms; and bade her father, if he would not have her serve the passion of a stranger, fight either in person, or by some deputy, in defence of his child. When Ole had news of this, he rejoiced in the chance of a battle, and borrowing the attire of a peasant, went to the dwelling of Olaf. He received one of the lowest places at table; and when he saw the household of the king in sorrow, he called the king's son closer to him, and asked why they all wore so lamentable a face. The other answered, that unless someone quickly interposed to protect them, his sister's chastity would soon be outraged by some ferocious champions. Ole next asked him what reward would be received by the man who devoted his life for the maiden. Olaf, on his son asking him about this matter, said that his daughter should go to the man who fought for her: and these words, more than anything, made Ole long to encounter the danger.

Now the maiden was wont to go from one guest to another in order to scan their faces narrowly, holding out a light that she might have a surer view of the dress and character of those who were entertained. It is also believed that she divined their lineage from the lines and features of the face, and could discern any man's birth by sheer shrewdness of vision. When she stood and fixed the scrutiny of her gaze upon Olaf, she was stricken with the strange awfulness of his eyes, and fell almost lifeless. But when her strength came slowly back, and her breath went and came more freely, she again tried to look at the young man, but suddenly slipped and fell forward, as though distraught. A third time also she strove to lift her closed and downcast gaze, but suddenly tottered and fell, unable not only to move her eyes, but even to control her feet; so much can strength be palsied by amazement. When Olaf saw it, he asked her why she had fallen so often. She averred that she was stricken by the savage gaze of the guest; that he was born of kings; and she declared that if he could baulk the will of the ravishers, he was well worthy of her arms. Then all of them asked Ole, who was keeping his face muffled in a hat, to fling off his covering, and let them see something by which to learn his features. Then, bidding them all lay aside their grief, and keep their heart far from sorrow, he uncovered his brow; and he drew the eyes of all upon him in marvel at his great beauty. For his locks were golden and the hair of his head was radiant; but he kept the lids close over his pupils, that they might not terrify the beholders.

274

All were heartened with the hope of better things; the guests seemed to dance and the courtiers to leap for joy; the deepest melancholy seemed to be scattered by an outburst of cheerfulness. Thus hope relieved their fears; the banquet wore a new face, and nothing was the same, or like what it had been before. So the kindly promise of a single guest dispelled the universal terror. Meanwhile Hiale and Skate came up with ten servants, meaning to carry off the maiden then and there, and disturbed all the place with their noisy shouts. They called on the king to give battle, unless he produced his daughter instantly. Ole at once met their frenzy with the promise to fight, adding the condition that no one should stealthily attack an opponent in the rear, but should only combat in the battle face to face. Then, with his sword called Logthi, he felled them all, single-handed—an achievement beyond his years. The ground for the battle was found on an isle in the middle of a swamp, not far from which is a stead that serves to memorise this slaughter, bearing the names of the brothers Hiale and Skate together.

So the girl was given him as prize of the combat, and bore him a son Omund. Then he gained his father-in-law's leave to revisit his father. But when he heard that his country was being attacked by Thore, with the help of Toste Sacrificer, and Leotar, surnamed.... he went to fight them, content with a single servant, who was dressed as a woman. When he was near the house of Thore, he concealed his own and his attendant's swords in hollowed staves. And when he entered the palace, he disguised his true countenance, and feigned to be a man broken with age. He said that with Siward he had been king of the beggars, but that he was now in exile, having been stubbornly driven forth by the hatred of the king's son Ole. Presently many of the courtiers greeted him with the name of king, and began to kneel and offer him their hands in mockery. He told them to bear out in deeds what they had done in jest; and, plucking out the swords which he and his man kept shut in their staves, attacked the king. So some aided Ole, taking it more as jest than earnest, and would not be false to the loyalty which they mockingly yielded him; but most of them, breaking their idle vow, took the side of Thore. Thus arose an internecine and undecided fray. At last Thore was overwhelmed and slain by the arms of his own folk, as much as by these of his guests; and Leotar, wounded to the death, and judging that his conqueror, Ole, was as keen in mind as he was valorous in deeds, gave him the name of the Vigorous, and prophesied that he should perish by the same kind of trick as he had used with Thore; for, without question he should fall by the treachery of his own house. And, as he spoke, he suddenly passed away. Thus we can see that the last speech of the dying man expressed by its shrewd divination the end that should come upon his conqueror.

After these deeds Ole did not go back to his father till he had restored peace to his house. His father gave him the command of the sea, and he destroyed seventy sea-kings in a naval battle. The most distinguished among these were Birwil and Hwirwil, Thorwil, Nef and Onef, Redward (?), Rand and Erand (?). By the honour and glory of this exploit he excited many champions, whose whole heart's desire was for bravery, to join in alliance with him. He also enrolled into a bodyguard the wild young warriors who were kindled with a passion for glory. Among these he received Starkad with the greatest honour, and cherished him with more friendship than profit. Thus fortified, he checked, by the greatness of his name, the wantonness of the neighbouring kings, in that he took from them all their forces and all liking and heart for mutual warfare.

After this he went to Harald, who made him commander of the sea; and at last he was transferred to the service of Ring. At this time one Brun was the sole partner and confidant of all Harald's councils. To this man both Harald and Ring, whenever they needed a secret messenger, used to entrust their commissions. This degree of intimacy he obtained because he had been reared and fostered with them. But Brun, amid the toils of his constant journeys to and fro, was drowned in a certain river; and Odin, disguised under his name and looks, shook the close union of the kings by his treacherous embassage; and he sowed strife so guilefully that he engendered in men, who were bound by friendship and blood, a bitter mutual hate, which seemed unappeasable except by war. Their dissensions first grew up silently; at last both sides betrayed their leanings, and their secret malice burst into the light of day. So they declared their feuds, and seven years passed in collecting the materials of war. Some say that Harald secretly sought occasions to destroy himself, not being moved by malice or jealousy for the crown, but by a deliberate and voluntary effort. His old age and his cruelty made him a burden to his subjects; he preferred the sword to the pangs of disease, and liked better to lay down his life in the battle-field than in his bed, that he might have an end in harmony with the deeds of his past life. Thus, to make his death more illustrious, and go to the nether world in a larger company, he longed to summon many men to share his end; and he therefore of his own will prepared for war, in order to make food for future slaughter. For these reasons, being seized with as great a thirst to die himself as to kill others, and wishing the massacre on both sides to be equal, he furnished both sides with equal resources; but let Ring have a somewhat stronger force, preferring he should conquer and survive him.

ENDNOTES:

(1) A parallel is the Lionel-Lancelot story of children saved by being turned into dogs.

BOOK EIGHT

STARKAD was the first to set in order in Danish speech the history of the Swedish war, a conflict whereof he was himself a mighty pillar; the said history being rather an oral than a written tradition. He set forth and arranged the course of this war in the mother tongue according to the fashion of our country; but I purpose to put it into Latin, and will first recount the most illustrious princes on either side. For I have felt no desire to include the multitude, which are even past exact numbering. And my pen shall relate first those on the side of Harald, and presently those who served under Ring.

Now the most famous of the captains that mustered to Harald are acknowledged to have been Sweyn and Sambar (Sam?), Ambar and Elli; Rati of Funen, Salgard and Roe (Hrothgar), whom his long beard distinguished by a nickname. Besides these, Skalk the Scanian, and Alf the son of Agg; to whom are joined Olwir the Broad, and Gnepie the Old. Besides these there was Gardh, founder of the town Stang. To these are added the kinsfolk or bound followers of Harald: Blend (Blaeng?), the dweller in furthest Thule, (1) and Brand, whose surname was Crumb (Bitling?). Allied with these were Thorguy, with Thorwig, Tatar (Teit), and Hialte. These men voyaged to Leire with bodies armed for war; but they were also mighty in excellence of wit, and their trained courage matched their great stature; for they had skill in discharging arrows both from bow and catapult, and at fighting their foe as they commonly did, man to man; and also at readily stringing together verse in the speech of their country: so zealously had they trained mind and body alike. Now out of Leire came Hortar (Hjort) and Borrhy (Borgar or Borgny), and also Belgi and Beigad, to whom were added Bari and Toli. Now out of the town of Sle, under the captains Hetha (Heid) and Wisna, with Hakon Cut-cheek came Tummi the Sailmaker. On these captains, who had the bodies of women, nature bestowed the souls of men. Webiorg was also inspired with the same spirit, and was attended by Bo (Bui) Bramason and Brat the Jute, thirsting for war. In the same throng came Orm of England, Ubbe the Frisian, Ari the One-eyed, and Alf Gotar. Next in the count came Dal the Fat and Duk the Sclav; Wisna, a woman, filled with sternness, and a skilled warrior, was guarded by a band of Sclavs: her chief followers were Barri and Gnizli. But the rest of the same company had their bodies covered by little shields, and used very long swords and targets of skiey hue, which, in time of war, they either cast behind their backs or gave over to the baggage-bearers; while they cast away all protection to their breasts, and exposed their bodies to every peril, offering battle with drawn swords. The most illustrious of these were Tolkar and Ymi. After these, Toki of the province of Wohin was conspicuous together with Otrit surnamed the Young. Hetha, guarded by a retinue of very active men, brought an armed company to the war, the chiefs of whom were Grim and Grenzli; next to whom are named Geir the Livonian, Hame also and Hunger, Humbli and Biari, bravest of the princes. These men often fought duels successfully, and won famous victories far and wide.

The maidens I have named, in fighting as well as courteous array, led their land-forces to the battle-field. Thus the Danish army mustered company by company. There were seven kings, equal in spirit but differing in allegiance, some defending Harald, and some Ring. Moreover, the following went to the side of Harald: Homi and Hosathul (Eysothul?), Him...., Hastin and Hythin (Hedin) the Slight, also Dahar (Dag), named Grenski, and Harald Olafsson also. From the province of Aland came Har and Herlewar (Herleif), with Hothbrodd, surnamed the Furious; these fought in the Danish camp. But from Imisland arrived Humnehy (?) and Harald. They were joined by Haki and by Sigmund and Serker the sons of Bemon, all coming from the North. All these were retainers of the king, who befriended them most generously; for they were held in the highest distinction by him, receiving swords adorned with gold, and the choicest spoils of war. There came also.... the sons of Gandal the old, who were in the intimate favour of Harald by reason of ancient allegiance. Thus the sea was studded with the Danish fleet, and seemed to interpose a bridge, uniting Zealand to Skaane. To those that wished to pass between those provinces, the sea offered a short road on foot over the dense mass of ships. But Harald would not have the Swedes unprepared in their arrangements for war, and sent men to Ring to carry his public declaration of hostilities, and notify the rupture of the mediating peace. The same men were directed to prescribe the place of combat. These then whom I have named were the fighters for Harald.

Now, on the side of Ring were numbered Ulf, Aggi (Aki?), Windar (Eywind?), Egil the One-eyed; Gotar, Hildi, Guti Alfsson; Styr the Stout, and (Tolo-) Stein, who lived by the Wienic Mere. To these were joined Gerd the Glad and Gromer (Glum?) from Wermland. After these are reckoned the dwellers north on the Elbe, Saxo the Splitter, Sali the Goth; Thord the Stumbler, Throndar Big-nose; Grundi, Oddi, Grindir, Tovi; Koll, Biarki, Hogni the Clever, Rokar the Swart. Now these scorned fellowship with the common soldiers, and had formed themselves into a separate rank apart from the rest of the company. Besides these are numbered Hrani Hildisson and Lyuth Guthi (Hljot Godi), Svein the Topshorn, (Soknarsoti?), Rethyr (Hreidar?) Hawk, and Rolf the Uxorious (Woman-lover). Massed with these were Ring Adilsson and Harald who came from Thotn district. Joined to these were Walstein of Wick, Thorolf the Thick, Thengel the Tall, Hun, Solwe, Birwil the Pale, Borgar and Skumbar (Skum). But from, Tellemark came the bravest of all, who had most courage but least arrogance—Thorleif the Stubborn, Thorkill the Gute (Gothlander), Grettir the Wicked and the Lover of Invasions. Next to these came Hadd the Hard and Rolder (Hroald) Toe-joint.

From Norway we have the names of Thrand of Throndhjem, Thoke (Thore) of More, Hrafn the White, Haf (war), Biarni, Blihar (Blig?) surnamed Snub-nosed; Biorn from the district of Sogni; Findar (Finn) born in the Firth; Bersi born in the town F(I)alu; Siward Boarhead, Erik the Story-teller, Holmstein the White, Hrut Rawi (or Vafi, the Doubter), Erling surnamed Snake. Now from the province of Jather came Odd the Englishman, Alf the Far-wanderer, Enar the Paunched, and Ywar surnamed Thriug. Now from Thule (Iceland) came Mar the Red, born and bred in the district called Midfirth; Grombar the Aged, Gram Brundeluk (Bryndalk?) Grim from the town of Skier (um) born in Skagafiord. Next came Berg the Seer, accompanied by Bragi and Rafnkel.

Now the bravest of the Swedes were these: Arwakki, Keklu-Karl (Kelke-Karl), Krok the Peasant, (from Akr), Gudfast and Gummi from Gislamark. These were kindred of the god Frey, and most faithful witnesses to the gods. Ingi (Yngwe) also, and Oly, Alver, Folki, all sons of Elrik (Alrek), embraced the service of Ring; they were men ready of hand, quick in counsel, and very close friends of Ring. They likewise held the god Frey to be the founder of their race. Amongst these from the town of Sigtun also came Sigmund, a champion advocate, versed in making contracts of sale and purchase; besides him Frosti surnamed Bowl: allied with him was Alf the Lofty (Proud?) from the district of Upsala; this man was a swift spear-thrower, and used to go in the front of the battle.

Ole had a body-guard in which were seven kings, very ready of hand and of counsel; namely, Holti, Hendil, Holmar, Lewy (Leif), and Hame; with these was enrolled Regnald the Russian, the grandson of Radbard; and Siwald also furrowed the sea with eleven light ships. Lesy (Laesi), the conqueror of the Pannonians (Huns), fitted with a sail his swift galley ringed with gold. Thririkar (Erik Helsing) sailed in a ship whose prows were twisted like a dragon. Also Thrygir (Tryggve) and Torwil sailed and brought twelve ships jointly. In the entire fleet of Ring there were 2,500 ships.

The fleet of Gotland was waiting for the Swedish fleet in the harbour named Garnum. So Ring led the land-force, while Ole was instructed to command the fleet. Now the Goths were appointed a time and a place between Wik and Werund for the conflict with the Swedes. Then was the sea to be seen furrowed up with prows, and the canvas unfurled upon the masts cut off the view over the ocean. The Danes had so far been distressed with bad weather; but the Swedish fleet had a fair voyage, and had reached the scene of battle earlier. Here Ring disembarked his forces from his fleet, and then massed and prepared to draw up in line both these and the army he had himself conducted overland. When these forces were at first loosely drawn up over the open country, it was found that one wing reached all the way to Werund. The multitude was confused in its places and ranks; but the king rode round it, and posted in the van all the smartest and most excellently-armed men, led by Ole, Regnald, and Wivil; then he massed the rest of the army on the two wings in a kind of curve. Ung, with the sons of Alrek, and Trig, he ordered to protect the right wing, while the left was put under the command of Laesi. Moreover, the wings and the masses were composed mainly of a close squadron of Kurlanders and of Esthonians. Last stood the line of slingers.

Meantime the Danish fleet, favoured by kindly winds, sailed, without stopping, for twelve days, and came to the town (stead) of Kalmar. The wind-blown sails covering the waters were a marvel; and the canvas stretched upon the yards blotted out the sight of the heavens. For the fleet was augmented by the Sclavs and the Livonians and 7,000 Saxons. But the Skanians, knowing the country, were appointed as guides and scouts to those who were going over the dry land. So when the Danish army came upon the Swedes, who stood awaiting them, Ring told his men to stand quietly until Harald had drawn up his line of battle; bidding them not to sound the signal before they saw the king settled in his chariot beside the standards; for he said he should hope that an army would soon come to grief which trusted in the leading of a blind man. Harald, moreover, he said, had been seized in extreme age with the desire of foreign empire, and was as witless as he was sightless; wealth could not satisfy a man who, if he looked to his years, ought to be well-nigh contented with a grave. The Swedes therefore were bound to fight for their freedom, their country, and their children, while the enemy had undertaken the war in rashness and arrogance. Moreover, on the other side, there were very few Danes, but a mass of Saxons and other unmanly peoples stood arrayed. Swedes and Norwegians should therefore consider, how far the multitudes of the North had always surpassed the Germans and the Sclavs. They should therefore despise an army which seemed to be composed more of a mass of fickle offscourings than of a firm and stout soldiery.

By this harangue of King Ring he kindled high the hearts of the soldiers. Now Brun, being instructed to form the line on Harald's behalf, made the front in a wedge, posting Hetha on the right flank, putting Hakon in command of the left, and making Wisna standard-bearer. Harald stood up in his chariot and complained, in as loud a voice as he could, that Ring was requiting his benefits with wrongs; that the man who had got his kingdom by Harald's own gift was now attacking him; so that Ring neither pitied an old man nor spared an uncle, but set his own ambitions before any regard for Harald's kinship or kindness. So he bade the Danes remember how they had always won glory by foreign conquest, and how they were more wont to command their neighbours than to obey them. He adjured them not to let such glory as theirs to be shaken by the insolence of a conquered nation, nor to suffer the empire, which he had won in the flower of his youth, to be taken from him in his outworn age.

Then the trumpets sounded, and both sides engaged in battle with all their strength. The sky seemed to fall suddenly on the earth, fields and woods to sink into the ground; all things were confounded, and old Chaos come again; heaven and earth mingling in one tempestuous turmoil, and the world rushing to universal ruin. For, when the spear-throwing began, the intolerable clash of arms filled the air with an incredible thunder. The steam of the wounds suddenly hung a mist over the sky, the daylight was hidden under the hail of spears. The help of the slingers was of great use in the battle. But when the missiles had all been flung from hand or engines, they fought with swords or iron-shod maces; and it was now at close quarters that most blood was spilt. Then the sweat streamed down their weary bodies, and the clash of the swords could be heard afar.

Starkad, who was the first to set forth the history of this war in the telling, fought foremost in the fray, and relates that he overthrew the nobles of Harald, Hun and Elli, Hort and Burgha, and cut off the right hand of Wisna. He also relates that one Roa, with two others, Gnepie and Gardar, fell wounded by him in the field. To these he adds the father of Skalk, whose name is not given. He also declares that he cast Hakon, the bravest of the Danes, to the earth, but received from him such a wound in return that he had to leave the war with his lung protruding from his chest, his neck cleft to the centre, and his hand deprived of one finger; so that he long had a gaping wound, which seemed as if it would never either scar over or be curable. The same man witnesses that the maiden Weghbiorg (Webiorg) fought against the

281

enemy and felled Soth the champion. While she was threatening to slay more champions, she was pierced through by an arrow from the bowstring of Thorkill, a native of Tellemark. For the skilled archers of the Gotlanders strung their bows so hard that the shafts pierced through even the shields; nothing proved more murderous; for the arrow-points made their way through hauberk and helmet as if they were men's defenceless bodies.

Meanwhile Ubbe the Frisian, who was the readiest of Harald's soldiers, and of notable bodily stature, slew twenty-five picked champions, besides eleven whom he had wounded in the field. All these were of Swedish or Gothic blood. Then he attacked the vanguard and burst into the thickest of the enemy, driving the Swedes struggling in a panic every way with spear and sword. It had all but come to a flight, when Hagder (Hadd), Rolder (Hroald), and Grettir attacked the champion, emulating his valour, and resolving at their own risk to retrieve the general ruin. But, fearing to assault him at close quarters, they accomplished their end with arrows from afar; and thus Ubbe was riddled by a shower of arrows, no one daring to fight him hand to hand. A hundred and forty-four arrows had pierced the breast of the warrior before his bodily strength failed and he bent his knee to the earth. Then at last the Danes suffered a great defeat, owing to the Thronds and the dwellers in the province of Dala. For the battle began afresh by reason of the vast mass of the archers, and nothing damaged our men more.

But when Harald, being now blind with age, heard the lamentable murmur of his men, he perceived that fortune had smiled on his enemies. So, as he was riding in a chariot armed with scythes, he told Brun, who was treacherously acting as charioteer, to find out in what manner Ring had his line drawn up. Brun's face relaxed into something of a smile, and he answered that he was fighting with a line in the form of a wedge. When the king heard this he began to be alarmed, and to ask in great astonishment from whom Ring could have learnt this method of disposing his line, especially as Odin was the discoverer and imparter of this teaching, and none but himself had ever learnt from him this new pattern of warfare. At this Brun was silent, and it came into the king's mind that here was Odin, and that the god whom he had once known so well was now disguised in a changeful shape, in order either to give help or withhold it. Presently he began to beseech him earnestly to grant the final victory to the Danes, since he had helped them so graciously before, and to fill up his last kindness to the measure of the first; promising to dedicate to him as a gift the spirits of all who fell. But Brun, utterly unmoved by his entreaties, suddenly jerked the king out of the chariot, battered him to the earth, plucked the club from him as he fell, whirled it upon his head, and slew him with his own weapon.

Countless corpses lay round the king's chariot, and the horrid heap overtopped the wheels; the pile of carcases rose as high as the pole. For about 12,000 of the nobles of Ring fell upon the field. But on the side of Harald about 30,000 nobles fell, not to name the slaughter of the commons.

When Ring heard that Harald was dead, he gave the signal to his men to break up their line and cease fighting. Then under cover of truce he made treaty with the enemy, telling them that it was vain to prolong the fray without their captain. Next he told the Swedes to look everywhere among the confused piles of carcases for the body of Harald, that the corpse of the king might not wrongfully lack its due rights. So the populace set eagerly to the task of turning over the bodies of the slain, and over this work half the day was spent. At last the body was found with the club, and he thought that propitiation should be made to the shade of Harald. So he harnessed the horse on which he rode to the chariot of the king, decked it honourably with a golden saddle, and hallowed it in his honour. Then he proclaimed his vows, and added his prayer that Harald would ride on this and outstrip those who shared his death in their journey to Tartarus; and that he would pray Pluto, the lord of Orcus, to grant a calm abode there for friend and foe. Then he raised a pyre, and bade the Danes fling on the gilded chariot of their king as fuel to the fire. And while the flames were burning the body cast upon them, he went round the mourning nobles and earnestly charged them that they should freely give arms, gold, and every precious thing to feed the pyre in honour of so great a king, who had deserved so nobly of them all. He also ordered that the ashes of his body, when it was quite burnt, should be transferred to an urn, taken to Leire, and there, together with the horse and armour, receive a royal funeral. By paying these due rites of honour to his uncle's shade, he won the favour of the Danes, and turned the hate of his enemies into goodwill. Then the Danes besought him to appoint Hetha over the remainder of the realm; but, that the fallen strength of the enemy might not suddenly rally, he severed Skaane from the mass of Denmark, and put it separately under the governorship of Ole, ordering that only Zealand and the other lands of the realm should be subject to Hetha. Thus the changes of fortune brought the empire of Denmark under the Swedish rule. So ended the Bravic war.

But the Zealanders, who had had Harald for their captain, and still had the picture of their former fortune hovering before their minds, thought it shameful to obey the rule of a woman, and appealed to OLE not to suffer men that had been used to serve under a famous king to be kept under a woman's yoke. They also promised to revolt to him if he would take up arms to remove their ignominious lot. Ole, tempted as much by the memory of his ancestral glory as by the homage of the soldiers, was not slow to answer their entreaties. So he summoned Hetha, and forced her by threats rather than by arms to quit every region under her control except Jutland; and even Jutland he made a tributary state, so as not to allow a woman the free control of a kingdom. He also begot a son whom he named Omund. But he was given to cruelty, and showed himself such an unrighteous king, that all who had found it a shameful thing to be ruled by a queen now repented of their former scorn.

Twelve generals, whether moved by the disasters of their country, or hating Ole for some other reason, began to plot against his life. Among these were Hlenni, Atyl, Thott, and Withne, the last of whom was a Dane by birth, though he held a government among the Sclavs. Moreover, not trusting in their strength and their cunning to accomplish their deed, they bribed Starkad to join them. He was prevailed to do the deed with the sword; he undertook the bloody work, and resolved to attack the king while at the bath. In he went while the king was washing, but was straightway stricken by the keenness of his gaze and by the restless and quivering glare of his eyes. His limbs were palsied with sudden dread; he paused, stepped back, and stayed his hand and his purpose. Thus he who had shattered the arms of so many captains and champions could not bear the gaze of a single unarmed man. But Ole, who well knew about his own countenance, covered his face, and asked him to come closer and tell him what his message was; for old fellowship and long-tried friendship made him the last to suspect treachery. But Starkad drew his sword, leapt forward, thrust the king through, and struck him in the throat as he tried to rise. One hundred and twenty marks of gold were kept for his reward. Soon afterwards he was smitten with remorse and shame, and lamented his crime so bitterly, that he could not refrain from tears if it happened to be named. Thus his soul, when he came to his senses, blushed for his abominable sin. Moreover, to atone for the crime he had committed, he slew some of those who had inspired him to it, thus avenging the act to which he had lent his hand.

Now the Danes made OMUND, the son of Ole, king, thinking that more heed should be paid to his father's birth than to his deserts. Omund, when he had grown up, fell in nowise behind the exploits of his father; for he made it his aim to equal or surpass the deeds of Ole.

At this time a considerable tribe of the Northmen (Norwegians) was governed by Ring, and his daughter Esa's great fame commended her to Omund, who was looking out for a wife.
But his hopes of wooing her were lessened by the peculiar inclination of Ring, who desired no son-in-law but one of tried valour; for he found as

much honour in arms as others think lies in wealth. Omund therefore, wishing to become famous in that fashion, and to win the praise of valour, endeavoured to gain his desire by force, and sailed to Norway with a fleet, to make an attempt on the throne of Ring under plea of hereditary right. Odd, the chief of Jather, who declared that Ring had assuredly seized his inheritance, and lamented that he harried him with continual wrongs, received Omund kindly. Ring, in the meantime, was on a roving raid in Ireland, so that Omund attacked a province without a defender. Sparing the goods of the common people, he gave the private property of Ring over to be plundered, and slew his kinsfolk; Odd also having joined his forces to Omund. Now, among all his divers and manifold deeds, he could never bring himself to attack an inferior force, remembering that he was the son of a most valiant father, and that he was bound to fight armed with courage, and not with numbers.

Meanwhile Ring had returned from roving; and when Omund heard he was back, he set to and built a vast ship, whence, as from a fortress, he could rain his missiles on the enemy. To manage this ship he enlisted Homod and Thole the rowers, the soils of Atyl the Skanian, one of whom was instructed to act as steersman, while the other was to command at the prow. Ring lacked neither skill nor dexterity to encounter them. For he showed only a small part of his forces, and caused the enemy to be attacked on the rear. Omund, when told of his strategy by Odd, sent men to overpower those posted in ambush, telling Atyl the Skanian to encounter Ring. The order was executed with more rashness than success; and Atyl, with his power defeated and shattered, fled beaten to Skaane. Then Omund recruited his forces with the help of Odd, and drew up his fleet to fight on the open sea.

Atyl at this time had true visions of the Norwegian war in his dreams, and started on his voyage in order to make up for his flight as quickly as possible, and delighted Omund by joining him on the eve of battle. Trusting in his help, Omund began to fight with equal confidence and success. For, by fighting himself, he retrieved the victory which he had lost when his servants were engaged. Ring, wounded to the death, gazed at him with faint eyes, and, beckoning to him with his hand, as well as he could—for his voice failed him—he besought him to be his son-in-law, saying that he would gladly meet his end if he left his daughter to such a husband. Before he could receive an answer he died. Omund wept for his death, and gave Homod, whose trusty help he had received in the war, in marriage to one of the daughters of Ring, taking the other himself.

At the same time the amazon Rusla, whose prowess in warfare exceeded the spirit of a woman, had many fights in Norway with her brother, Thrond, for the sovereignty. She could not endure that Omund rule over the Norwegians, and she had declared war against all the subjects of the Danes. Omund, when he heard of this, commissioned his most active men to suppress the rising. Rusla conquered them, and, waxing haughty on her triumph, was seized with overweening hopes, and bent her mind upon actually acquiring the sovereignty of Denmark. She began her attack on the region of Halland, but was met by Homod and Thode, whom the king had sent over. Beaten, she retreated to her fleet, of which only thirty ships managed to escape, the rest being taken by the enemy. Thrond encountered his sister as she was eluding the Danes, but was conquered by her and stripped of his entire army; he fled over the Dovrefjeld without a single companion. Thus she, who had first yielded before the Danes, soon overcame her brother, and turned her flight into a victory. When Omund heard of this, he went back to Norway with a great fleet, first sending Homod and Thole by a short and secret way to rouse the people of Tellemark against the rule of Rusla. The end was that she was driven out of her kingdom by the commons, fled to the isles for safety, and turned her back, without a blow, upon the Danes as they came up. The king pursued her hotly, caught up her fleet on the sea, and utterly destroyed it, the enemy suffered mightily, and he won a bloodless victory and splendid spoils. But Rusla escaped with a very few ships, and rowed ploughing the waves furiously; but, while she was avoiding the Danes, she met her brother and was killed. So much more effectual for harm are dangers unsurmised; and chance sometimes makes the less alarming evil worse than that which threatens. The king gave Thrond a governorship for slaying his sister, put the rest under tribute, and returned home.

At this time Thorias (?) and Ber (Biorn), the most active of the soldiers of Rusla, were roving in Ireland; but when they heard of the death of their mistress, whom they had long ago sworn to avenge, they hotly attacked Omund, and challenged him to a duel, which it used to be accounted shameful for a king to refuse; for the fame of princes of old was reckoned more by arms than by riches. So Homod and Thole came forward, offering to meet in battle the men who had challenged the king. Omund praised them warmly, but at first declined for very shame to allow their help. At last, hard besought by his people, he brought himself to try his fortune by the hand of another. We are told that Ber fell in this combat, while Thorias left the battle severely wounded. The king, having first cured him of his wounds, took him into his service, and made him prince (earl) over Norway. Then he sent ambassadors to exact the usual tribute from the Sclavs; these were killed, and he was even attacked in Jutland by a Sclavish force; but he overcame seven kings in a single combat, and ratified by conquest his accustomed right to tribute.

Meantime, Starkad, who was now worn out with extreme age, and who seemed to be past military service and the calling of a champion, was loth to lose his ancient glory through the fault of eld, and thought it would be a noble thing if he could make a voluntary end, and hasten his death by his own free will. Having so often fought nobly, he thought it would be mean to die a bloodless death; and, wishing to enhance the glory of his past life by the lustre of his end, he preferred to be slain by some man of gallant birth rather than await the tardy shaft of nature. So shameful was it thought that men devoted to war should die by disease. His body was weak, and his eyes could not see clearly, so that he hated to linger any more in life. In order to buy himself an executioner, he wore hanging on his neck the gold which he had earned for the murder of Ole; thinking there was no fitter way of atoning for the treason he had done than to make the price of Ole's death that of his own also, and to spend on the loss of his own life what he had earned by the slaying of another. This, he thought, would be the noblest use he could make of that shameful price. So he girded him with two swords, and guided his powerless steps leaning on two staves.

One of the common people, seeing him, thinking two swords superfluous for the use of an old man, mockingly asked him to make him a present of one of them. Starkad, holding out hopes of consent, bade him come nearer, drew the sword from his side, and ran him through. This was seen by a certain Hather, whose father Hlenne Starkad had once killed in repentance for his own impious crime. Hatfier was hunting game with his dogs, but now gave over the chase, and bade two of his companions spur their horses hard and charge at the old man to frighten him. They galloped forward, and tried to make off, but were stopped by the staves of Starkad, and paid for it with their lives. Hather, terrified by the sight, galloped up closer, and saw who the old man was, but without being recognized by him in turn; and asked him if he would like to exchange his sword for a carriage. Starkad replied that he used in old days to chastise jeerers, and that the insolent had never insulted him unpunished. But his sightless eyes could not recognize the features of the youth; so he composed a song, wherein he should declare the greatness of his anger, as follows:

"As the unreturning waters sweep down the channel; so, as the years run by, the life of man flows on never to come back; fast gallops the cycle of doom, child of old age who shall make an end of all. Old age smites alike the eyes and the steps of men, robs the warrior of his speech and soul, tarnishes his fame by slow degrees, and wipes out his deeds of honour. It seizes his failing limbs, chokes his panting utterance, and numbs his nimble wit. When a cough is taken, when the skin itches with the scab, and the teeth are numb and hollow, and the stomach turns squeamish,—then old age banishes the grace of youth, covers the complexion with decay, and sows many a wrinkle in the dusky skin. Old age crushes noble arts, brings down the memorials of men of old, and scorches ancient glories up; shatters wealth, hungrily gnaws away the worth and good of virtue, turns athwart and disorders all things.

"I myself have felt the hurtful power of injurious age, I, dim-sighted, and hoarse in my tones and in my chest; and all helpful things have turned to my hurt. Now my body is less nimble, and I prop it up, leaning my faint limbs on the support of staves. Sightless I guide my steps with two sticks, and follow the short path which the rod shows me, trusting more in the leading of a stock than in my eyes. None takes any charge of me, and no man in the ranks brings comfort to the veteran, unless, perchance, Hather is here, and succours his shattered friend. Whomsoever Hather once thinks worthy of his duteous love, that man he attends continually with even zeal, constant to his purpose, and fearing to break his early ties. He also often pays fit rewards to those that have deserved well in war, and fosters their courage; he bestows dignities on the brave, and honours his famous friends with gifts. Free with his wealth, he is fain to increase with bounty the brightness of his name, and to surpass many of the mighty. Nor is he less in war: his strength is equal to his goodness; he is swift in the fray, slow to waver, ready to give battle; and he cannot turn his back when the foe bears him hard. But for me, if I remember right, fate appointed at my birth that wars I should follow and in war I should die, that I should mix in broils, watch in arms, and pass a life of bloodshed. I was a man of camps, and rested not; hating peace, I grew old under thy standard, O War-god, in utmost peril; conquering fear, I thought it comely to fight, shameful to loiter, and noble to kill and kill again, to be for ever slaughtering! Oft have I seen the stern kings meet in war, seen shield and helmet bruised, and the fields redden with blood, and the cuirass broken by the spear-point, and the corselets all around giving at the thrust of the steel, and the wild beasts battening on the unburied soldier. Here, as it chanced, one that attempted a mighty thing, a strong-handed warrior, fighting against the press of the foe, smote through the mail that covered my head, pierced my helmet, and plunged his blade into my crest. This sword also hath often been driven by my right hand in war, and, once unsheathed, hath cleft the skin and bitten into the skull."

Hather, in answer, sang as follows:

"Whence comest thou, who art used to write the poems of thy land, leaning thy wavering steps on a frail staff? Or whither dost thou speed, who art the readiest bard of the Danish muse? All the glory of thy great strength is faded and lost; the hue is banished from thy face, the joy is gone out of thy soul; the voice has left thy throat, and is hoarse and dull; thy body has lost its former stature; the decay of death begins, and has wasted thy features and thy force. As a ship wearies, buffeted by continual billows, even so old age, gendered by a long course of years, brings forth bitter death; and the life falls when its strength is done, and suffers the loss of its ancient lot. Famous old man, who has told thee that thou mayst not duly follow the sports of youth, or fling balls, or bite and eat the nut? I think it were better for thee now to sell thy sword, and buy a carriage wherein to ride often, or a horse easy on the bit, or at the same cost to purchase a light cart. It will be more fitting for beasts of burden to carry weak old men, when their steps fail them; the wheel, driving round and round, serves for him whose foot totters feebly. But if perchance thou art loth to sell the useless steel, thy sword, if it be not for sale, shall be taken from thee and shall slay thee."

Starkad answered: "Wretch, thy glib lips scatter idle words, unfit for the ears of the good. Why seek the gifts to reward that guidance, which thou shouldst have offered for naught? Surely I will walk afoot, and will not basely give up my sword and buy the help of a stranger; nature has given me the right of passage, and hath bidden me trust in my own feet. Why mock and jeer with insolent speech at him whom thou shouldst have offered to guide upon his way? Why give to dishonour my deeds of old, which deserve the memorial of fame? Why requite my service with reproach? Why pursue with jeers the old man mighty in battle, and put to shame my unsurpassed honours and illustrious deeds, belittling my glories and girding at my prowess? For what valour of thine dost thou demand my sword, which thy strength does not deserve? It befits not the right hand or the unwarlike side of a herdsman, who is wont to make his peasant-music on the pipe, to see to the flock, to keep the herds in the fields. Surely among the henchmen, close to the greasy pot, thou dippest thy crust in the bubbles of the foaming pan, drenching a meagre slice in the rich, oily fat, and stealthily, with thirsty finger, licking the warm juice; more skilled to spread thy accustomed cloak on the ashes, to sleep on the hearth, and slumber all day long, and go busily about the work of the reeking kitchen, than to make the brave blood flow with thy shafts in war. Men think thee a hater of the light and a lover of a filthy hole, a wretched slave of thy belly, like a whelp who licks the coarse grain, husk and all.

"By heaven, thou didst not try to rob me of my sword when thrice at great peril I fought (for?) the son of Ole. For truly, in that array, my hand either broke the sword or shattered the obstacle, so heavy was the blow of the smiter. What of the day when I first taught them, to run with wood-shod feet over the shore of the Kurlanders, and the path bestrewn with countless points? For when I was going to the fields studded with calthrops, I guarded their wounded feet with clogs below them. After this I slew Hame, who fought me mightily; and soon, with the captain Rin the son of Flebak, I crushed the Kurlanders, yea, or all the tribes Esthonia breeds, and thy peoples, O Semgala! Then I attacked the men of Tellemark, and took thence my head bloody with bruises, shattered with mallets, and smitten with the welded weapons. Here first I learnt how strong was the iron wrought on the anvil, or what valour the common people had. Also it was my doing that the Teutons were punished, when, in avenging my lord, I laid low over their cups thy sons, O Swerting, who were guilty of the wicked slaughter of Frode.

"Not less was the deed when, for the sake of a beloved maiden, I slew nine brethren in one fray;—witness the spot, which was consumed by the bowels that left me, and brings not forth the grain anew on its scorched sod. And soon, when Ker the captain made ready a war by sea, with a noble army we beat his serried ships. Then I put Waske to death, and punished the insolent smith by slashing his hinder parts; and with the sword I slew Wisin, who from the snowy rocks blunted the spears. Then I slew the four sons of Ler, and the champions of Permland; and then having taken the chief of the Irish race, I rifled the wealth of Dublin; and our courage shall ever remain manifest by the trophies of Bravalla. Why do I linger? Countless are the deeds of my bravery, and when I review the works of my hands I fail to number them to the full. The whole is greater than I can tell. My work is too great for fame, and speech serves not for my doings."

So sang Starkad. At last, when he found by their talk that Hather was the son of Hlenne, and saw that the youth was of illustrious birth, he offered him his throat to smite, bidding him not to shrink from punishing the slayer of his father. He promised him that if he did so he should possess the gold which he had himself received from Hlenne. And to enrage his heart more vehemently against him, he is said to have harangued him as follows:

"Moreover, Hather, I robbed thee of thy father Hlenne; requite me this, I pray, and strike down the old man who longs to die; aim at my throat with the avenging steel. For my soul chooses the service of a noble smiter, and shrinks to ask its doom at a coward's hand. Righteously may a man choose to forstall the ordinance of doom. What cannot be escaped it will be lawful also to anticipate. The fresh tree must be fostered, the old one hewn down. He is nature's instrument who destroys what is near its doom and strikes down what cannot stand. Death is best when it is sought: and when the end is loved, life is wearisome. Let not the troubles of age prolong a miserable lot."

So saying, he took money from his pouch and gave it him. But Hather, desiring as much to enjoy the gold as to accomplish vengeance for his father, promised that he would comply with his prayer, and would not refuse the reward. Starkad eagerly handed him the sword, and at once stooped his neck beneath it, counselling him not to do the smiter's work timidly, or use the sword like a woman; and telling him that if, when he had killed him, he could spring between the head and the trunk before the corpse fell, he would be rendered proof against arms. It is not known whether he said this in order to instruct his executioner or to punish him, for perhaps, as he leapt, the bulk of the huge body would have crushed him. So Hather smote sharply with the sword and hacked off the head of the old man. When the severed head struck the ground, it is said to have bitten the earth; thus the fury of the dying lips declared the fierceness of the soul. But the smiter, thinking that the promise hid some treachery, warily refrained from leaping. Had he done so rashly, perhaps he would have been crushed by the corpse as it fell, and have paid with his own life for the old man's murder. But he would not allow so great a champion to lie unsepulchred, and had his body buried in the field that is commonly called Rolung.

Now Omund, as I have heard, died most tranquilly, while peace was unbroken, leaving two sons and two daughters. The eldest of these, SIWARD, came to the throne by right of birth, while his brother Budle was still of tender years. At this time Gotar, King of the Swedes, conceived boundless love for one of the daughters of Omund, because of the report of her extraordinary beauty, and entrusted one Ebb, the son of Sibb, with the commission of asking for the maiden. Ebb did his work skilfully, and brought back the good news that the girl had consented. Nothing was now lacking to Gotar's wishes but the wedding; but, as he feared to hold this among strangers, he demanded that his betrothed should be sent to him in charge of Ebb, whom he had before used as envoy.

Ebb was crossing Halland with a very small escort, and went for a night's lodging to a country farm, where the dwellings of two brothers faced one another on the two sides of a river. Now these men used to receive folk hospitably and then murder them, but were skilful to hide their brigandage under a show of generosity. For they had hung on certain hidden chains, in a lofty part of the house, an oblong beam like a press, and furnished it with a steel point; they used to lower this in the night by letting down the fastenings, and cut off the heads of those that lay below. Many had they beheaded in this way with the hanging mass. So when Ebb and his men had been feasted abundantly, the servants laid them out a bed near the hearth, so that by the swing of the treacherous beam they might mow off their heads, which faced the fire. When they departed, Ebb, suspecting the contrivance slung overhead, told his men to feign slumber and shift their bodies, saying that it would be very wholesome for them to change their place.

Now among these were some who despised the orders which the others obeyed, and lay unmoved, each in the spot where he had chanced to lie down. Then towards the mirk of night the heavy hanging machine was set in motion by the doers of the treachery. Loosened from the knots of its fastening, it fell violently on the ground, and slew those beneath it. Thereupon those who had the charge of committing the crime brought in a light, that they might learn clearly what had happened, and saw that Ebb, on whose especial account they had undertaken the affair, had wisely been equal to the danger. He straightway set on them and punished them with death; and also, after losing his men in the mutual slaughter, he happened to find a vessel, crossed a river full of blocks of ice, and announced to Gotar the result, not so much of his mission as of his mishap.

Gotar judged that this affair had been inspired by Siward, and prepared to avenge his wrongs by arms. Siward, defeated by him in Halland, retreated into Jutland, the enemy having taken his sister. Here he conquered the common people of the Sclavs, who ventured to fight without a leader; and he won as much honour from this victory as he had got disgrace by his flight. But a little afterwards, the men whom he had subdued when they were ungeneraled, found a general and defeated Siward in Funen. Several times he fought them in Jutland, but with ill-success. The result was that he lost both Skaane and Jutland, and only retained the middle of his realm without the head, like the fragments of some body that had been consumed away. His son Jarmerik (Eormunrec), with his child-sisters, fell into the hands of the enemy; one of these was sold to the Germans, the other to the Norwegians; for in old time marriages were matters of purchase. Thus the kingdom of the Danes, which had been enlarged with such valour, made famous by such ancestral honours, and enriched by so many conquests, fell, all by the sloth of one man, from the most illustrious fortune and prosperity into such disgrace that it paid the tribute which it used to exact. But Siward, too often defeated and guilty of shameful flights, could not endure, after that glorious past, to hold the troubled helm of state any longer in this shameful condition of his land; and, fearing that living longer might strip him of his last shred of glory, he hastened to win an honourable death in battle. For his soul could not forget his calamity, it was fain to cast off its sickness, and was racked with weariness of life. So much did he abhor the light of life in his longing to wipe out his shame. So he mustered his army for battle, and openly declared war with one Simon, who was governor of Skaane under Gotar. This war he pursued with stubborn rashness; he slew Simon, and ended his own life amid a great slaughter of his foes. Yet his country could not be freed from the burden of the tribute.

Jarmerik, meantime, with his foster-brother of the same age as himself, Gunn, was living in prison, in charge of Ismar, the King of the Sclavs. At last he was taken out and put to agriculture, doing the work of a peasant. So actively did he manage this matter that he was transferred and made master of the royal slaves. As he likewise did this business most uprightly, he was enrolled in the band of the king's retainers. Here he bore himself most pleasantly as courtiers use, and was soon taken into the number of the king's friends and obtained the first place in his intimacy; thus, on the strength of a series of great services, he passed from the lowest estate to the most distinguished height of honour. Also, loth to live a slack and enfeebled youth, he trained himself to the pursuits of war, enriching his natural gifts by diligence. All men loved Jarmerik, and only the queen mistrusted the young man's temper. A sudden report told them that the king's brother had died. Ismar, wishing to give his body a splendid funeral, prepared a banquet of royal bounty to increase the splendour of the obsequies.

But Jarmerik, who used at other times to look after the household affairs together with the queen, began to cast about for means of escape; for a chance seemed to be offered by the absence of the king. For he saw that even in the lap of riches he would be the wretched thrall of a king, and that he would draw, as it were, his very breath on sufferance and at the gift of another. Moreover, though he held the highest offices with the king, he thought that freedom was better than delights, and burned with a mighty desire to visit his country and learn his lineage. But, knowing that the queen had provided sufficient guards to see that no prisoner escaped, he saw that he must approach by craft where he could not arrive by force. So he plaited one of those baskets of rushes and withies, shaped like a man, with which countrymen used to scare the birds from the corn, and put a live dog in it; then he took off his own clothes, and dressed it in them, to give a more plausible likeness to a human being. Then he broke into the private treasury of the king, took out the money, and hid himself in places of which he alone knew.

Meantime Gunn, whom he had told to conceal the absence of his friend, took the basket into the palace and stirred up the dog to bark; and when the queen asked what this was, he answered that Jarmerik was out of his mind and howling. She, beholding the effigy, was deceived by the likeness, and ordered that the madman should be cast out of the house.

293

Then Gunn took the effigy out and put it to bed, as though it were his distraught friend. But towards night he plied the watch bountifully with wine and festal mirth, cut off their heads as they slept, and set them at their groins, in order to make their slaying more shameful. The queen, roused by the din, and wishing to learn the reason of it, hastily rushed to the doors. But while she unwarily put forth her head, the sword of Gunn suddenly pierced her through. Feeling a mortal wound, she sank, turned her eyes on her murderer, and said, "Had it been granted me to live unscathed, no screen or treachery should have let thee leave this land unpunished." A flood of such threats against her slayer poured from her dying lips.

Then Jarmerik, with Gunn, the partner of his noble deed, secretly set fire to the tent wherein the king was celebrating with a banquet the obsequies of his brother; all the company were overcome with liquor. The fire filled the tent and spread all about; and some of them, shaking off the torpor of drink, took horse and pursued those who had endangered them. But the young men fled at first on the beasts they had taken; and at last, when these were exhausted with their long gallop, took to flight on foot. They were all but caught, when a river saved them. For they crossed a bridge, of which, in order to delay the pursuer, they first cut the timbers down to the middle, thus making it not only unequal to a burden, but ready to come down; then they retreated into a dense morass.

The Sclavs pressed on them hard and, not forseeing the danger, unwarily put the weight of their horses on the bridge; the flooring sank, and they were shaken off and flung into the river. But, as they swam up to the bank, they were met by Gunn and Jarmerik, and either drowned or slain. Thus the young men showed great cunning, and did a deed beyond their years, being more like sagacious old men than runaway slaves, and successfully achieving their shrewd design. When they reached the strand they seized a vessel chance threw in their way, and made for the deep. The barbarians who pursued them, tried, when they saw them sailing off, to bring them back by shouting promises after them that they should be kings if they returned; "for, by the public statute of the ancients, the succession was appointed to the slayers of the kings." As they retreated, their ears were long deafened by the Sclavs obstinately shouting their treacherous promises.

At this time BUDLE, the brother of Siward, was Regent over the Danes, who forced him to make over the kingdom to JARMERIK when he came; so that Budle fell from a king into a common man. At the same time Gotar charged Sibb with debauching his sister, and slew him. Sibb's kindred, much angered by his death, came wailing to Jarmerik, and promised to attack Gotar with him, in order to avenge their kinsman. They kept their promise well, for Jarmerik, having overthrown Gotar by their help, gained Sweden. Thus, holding the sovereignty of both nations, he was encouraged by his increased power to attack the Sclavs, forty of whom he took and hung with a wolf tied to each of them. This kind of punishment was assigned of old to those who slew their own kindred; but he chose to inflict it upon enemies, that all might see plainly, just from their fellowship with ruthless beasts, how grasping they had shown themselves towards the Danes.

When Jarmerik had conquered the country, he posted garrisons in all the fitting places, and departing thence, he made a slaughter of the Sembs and the Kurlanders, and many nations of the East. The Sclavs, thinking that this employment of the king gave them a chance of revolting, killed the governors whom he had appointed, and ravaged Denmark. Jarmerik, on his way back from roving, chanced to intercept their fleet, and destroyed it, a deed which added honour to his roll of conquests. He also put their nobles to death in a way that one would weep to see; namely, by first passing thongs through their legs, and then tying them to the hoofs of savage bulls; then hounds set on them and dragged them into miry swamps. This deed took the edge off the valour of the Sclavs, and they obeyed the authority of the king in fear and trembling.

Jarmerik, enriched with great spoils, wished to provide a safe storehouse for his booty, and built on a lofty hill a treasure-house of marvellous handiwork. Gathering sods, he raised a mound, laying a mass of rocks for the foundation, and girt the lower part with a rampart, the centre with rooms, and the top with battlements. All round he posted a line of sentries without a break. Four huge gates gave free access on the four sides; and into this lordly mansion he heaped all his splendid riches. Having thus settled his affairs at home, he again turned his ambition abroad. He began to voyage, and speedily fought a naval battle with four brothers whom he met on the high seas, Hellespontines by race, and veteran rovers. After this battle had lasted three days, he ceased fighting, having bargained for their sister and half the tribute which they had imposed on those they had conquered.

After this, Bikk, the son of the King of the Livonians, escaped from the captivity in which he lay under these said brothers, and went to Jarmerik. But he did not forget his wrongs, Jarmerik having long before deprived him of his own brothers. He was received kindly by the king, in all whose secret counsels he soon came to have a notable voice; and, as soon as he found the king pliable to his advice in all things, he led him, when his counsel was asked, into the most abominable acts, and drove him to commit crimes and infamies. Thus he sought some device to injure the king by a feint of loyalty, and tried above all to steel him against his nearest of blood; attempting to accomplish the revenge of his brother by guile, since he could not by force. So it came to pass that the king embraced filthy vices instead of virtues, and made himself generally hated by the cruel deeds which he committed at the instance of his treacherous adviser. Even the Sclavs began to rise against him; and, as a means of quelling them, he captured their leaders, passed a rope through their shanks, and delivered them to be torn asunder by horses pulling different ways. So perished their chief men, punished for their stubbornness of spirit by having their bodies rent apart. This kept the Sclavs duly obedient in unbroken and steady subjugation.

Meantime, the sons of Jarmerik's sister, who had all been born and bred in Germany, took up arms, on the strength of their grandsire's title, against their uncle, contending that they had as good a right to the throne as he. The king demolished their strongholds in Germany with engines, blockaded or took several towns, and returned home with a bloodless victory. The Hellespontines came to meet him, proffering their sister for the promised marriage. After this had been celebrated, at Bikk's prompting he again went to Germany, took his nephews in war, and incontinently hanged them. He also got together the chief men under the pretence of a banquet and had them put to death in the same fashion.

Meantime, the king appointed Broder, his son by another marriage, to have charge over his stepmother, a duty which he fulfilled with full vigilance and integrity. But Bikk accused this man to his father of incest; and, to conceal the falsehood of the charge, suborned witnesses against him. When the plea of the accusation had been fully declared, Broder could not bring any support for his defence, and his father bade his friends pass sentence upon the convicted man, thinking it less impious to commit the punishment proper for his son to the judgment of others. All thought that he deserved outlawry except Bikk, who did not shrink from giving a more terrible vote against his life, and declaring that the perpetrator of an infamous seduction ought to be punished with hanging. But lest any should think that this punishment was due to the cruelty of his father, Bikk judged that, when he had been put in the noose, the servants should hold him up on a beam put beneath him, so that, when weariness made them take their hands from the burden, they might be as good as guilty of the young man's death, and by their own fault exonerate the king from an unnatural murder. He also pretended that, unless the accused were punished, he would plot against his father's life. The adulteress Swanhild, he said, ought to suffer a shameful end, trampled under the hoofs of beasts.

The king yielded to Bikk; and, when his son was to be hanged, he made the bystanders hold him up by means of a plank, that he might not be choked. Thus his throat was only a little squeezed, the knot was harmless, and it was but a punishment in show. But the king had the queen tied very tight on the ground, and delivered her to be crushed under the hoofs of horses. The story goes that she was so beautiful, that even the beasts shrank from mangling limbs so lovely with their filthy feet. The king, divining that this proclaimed the innocence of his wife, began to repent of his error, and hastened to release the slandered lady. But meantime Bikk rushed up, declaring that when she was on her back she held off the beasts by awful charms, and could only be crushed if she lay on her face; for he knew that her beauty saved her. When the body of the queen was placed in this manner, the herd of beasts was driven upon it, and trod it down deep with their multitude of feet. Such was the end of Swanhild.

Meantime, the favourite dog of Broder came creeping to the king making a sort of moan, and seemed to bewail its master's punishment; and his hawk, when it was brought in, began to pluck out its breast-feathers with its beak. The king took its nakedness as an omen of his bereavement, to frustrate which he quickly sent men to take his son down from the noose: for he divined by the featherless bird that he would be childless unless he took good heed. Thus Broder was freed from death, and Bikk, fearing he would pay the penalty of an informer, went and told the men of the Hellespont that Swanhild had been abominably slain by her husband. When they set sail to avenge their sister, he came back to Jarmerik, and told him that the Hellespontines were preparing war.

The king thought that it would be safer to fight with walls than in the field, and retreated into the stronghold which he had built. To stand the siege, he filled its inner parts with stores, and its battlements with men-at-arms. Targets and shields flashing with gold were hung round and adorned the topmost circle of the building.

It happened that the Hellespontines, before sharing their booty, accused a great band of their men of embezzling, and put them to death. Having now destroyed so large a part of their forces by internecine slaughter, they thought that their strength was not equal to storming the palace, and consulted a sorceress named Gudrun. She brought it to pass that the defenders of the king's side were suddenly blinded and turned their arms against one another. When the Hellespontines saw this, they brought up a shield-mantlet, and seized the approaches of the gates. Then they tore up the posts, burst into the building, and hewed down the blinded ranks of the enemy. In this uproar Odin appeared, and, making for the thick of the ranks of the fighters, restored by his divine power to the Danes that vision which they had lost by sleights; for he ever cherished them with fatherly love. He instructed them to shower stones to batter the Hellespontines, who used spells to harden their bodies against weapons. Thus both companies slew one another and perished. Jarmerik lost both feet and both hands, and his trunk was rolled among the dead. BRODER, little fit for it, followed him as king.

The next king was SIWALD. His son SNIO took vigorously to roving in his father's old age, and not only preserved the fortunes of his country, but even restored them, lessened as they were, to their former estate. Likewise, when he came to the sovereignty, he crushed the insolence of the champions Eskil and Alkil, and by this conquest reunited to his country Skaane, which had been severed from the general jurisdiction of Denmark. At last he conceived a passion for the daughter of the King of the Goths; it was returned, and he sent secret messengers to seek a chance of meeting her. These men were intercepted by the father of the damsel and hanged: thus paying dearly for their rash mission. Snio, wishing to avenge their death, invaded Gothland. Its king met him with his forces, and the aforesaid champions challenged him to send strong men to fight. Snio laid down as condition of the duel, that each of the two kings should either lose his own empire or gain that of the other, according to the fortune of the champions, and that the kingdom of the conquered should be staked as the prize of the victory. The result was that the King of the Goths was beaten by reason of the ill-success of his defenders, and had to quit his kingdom for the Danes. Snio, learning that this king's daughter had been taken away at the instance of her father to wed the King of the Swedes, sent a man clad in ragged attire, who used to ask alms on the public roads, to try her mind. And while he lay, as beggars do, by the threshold, he chanced to see the queen, and whined in a weak voice, "Snio loves thee." She feigned not to have heard the sound that stole on her ears, and neither looked nor stepped back, but went on to the palace, then returned straightway, and said in a low whisper, which scarcely reached his ears, "I love him who loves me"; and having said this she walked away.

The beggar rejoiced that she had returned a word of love, and, as he sat on the next day at the gate, when the queen came up, he said, briefly as ever, "Wishes should have a tryst." Again she shrewdly caught his cunning speech, and passed on, dissembling wholly. A little later she passed by her questioner, and said that she would shortly go to Bocheror; for this was the spot to which she meant to flee. And when the beggar heard this, he insisted, with his wonted shrewd questions, upon being told a fitting time for the tryst. The woman was as cunning

298

as he, and as little clear of speech, and named as quickly as she could the beginning of the winter.

Her train, who had caught a flying word of this love-message, took her great cleverness for the raving of utter folly. And when Snio had been told all this by the beggar, he contrived to carry the queen off in a vessel; for she got away under pretence of bathing, and took her husband's treasures. After this there were constant wars between Snio and the King of Sweden, whereof the issue was doubtful and the victory changeful; the one king seeking to regain his lawful, the other to keep his unlawful love.

At this time the yield of crops was ruined by most inclement weather, and a mighty dearth of corn befell. Victuals began to be scarce, and the commons were distressed with famine, so that the king, anxiously pondering how to relieve the hardness of the times, and seeing that the thirsty spent somewhat more than the hungry, introduced thrift among the people. He abolished drinking-bouts, and decreed that no drink should be prepared from gram, thinking that the bitter famine should be got rid of by prohibiting needless drinking, and that plentiful food could be levied as a loan on thirst.

Then a certain wanton slave of his belly, lamenting the prohibition against drink, adopted a deep kind of knavery, and found a new way to indulge his desires. He broke the public law of temperance by his own excess, contriving to get at what he loved by a device both cunning and absurd. For he sipped the forbidden liquor drop by drop, and so satisfied his longing to be tipsy. When he was summoned for this by the king, he declared that there was no stricter observer of sobriety than he, inasmuch as he mortified his longing to quaff deep by this device for moderate drinking. He persisted in the fault with which he was taxed, saying that he only sucked. At last he was also menaced with threats, and forbidden not only to drink, but even to sip; yet he could not check his habits. For in order to enjoy the unlawful thing in a lawful way, and not to have his throat subject to the command of another, he sopped morsels of bread in liquor, and fed on the pieces thus soaked with drink; tasting slowly, so as to prolong the desired debauch, and attaining, though in no unlawful manner, the forbidden measure of satiety.

Thus his stubborn and frantic intemperance risked his life, all for luxury; and, undeterred even by the threats of the king, he fortified his rash appetite to despise every peril. A second time he was summoned by the king on the charge of disobeying his regulation. Yet he did not even theft cease to defend his act, but maintained that he had in no wise contravened the royal decree, and that the temperance prescribed by the ordinance had been in no way violated by that which allured him; especially as the thrift ordered in the law of plain living was so described, that it was apparently forbidden to drink liquor, but not to eat it. Then the king called heaven to witness, and swore by the general good, that if he ventured on any such thing hereafter he would punish him with death. But the man thought that death was not so bad as temperance, and that it was easier to quit life than luxury; and he again boiled the grain in water, and then fermented the liquor; whereupon, despairing of any further plea to excuse his appetite, he openly indulged in drink, and turned to his cups again unabashed. Giving up cunning for effrontery, he chose rather to await the punishment of the king than to turn sober. Therefore, when the king asked him why he had so often made free to use the forbidden thing, he said:

"O king, this craving is begotten, not so much of my thirst, as of my goodwill towards thee! For I remembered that the funeral rites of a king must be paid with a drinking-bout. Therefore, led by good judgment more than the desire to swill, I have, by mixing the forbidden liquid, taken care that the feast whereat thy obsequies are performed should not, by reason of the scarcity of corn, lack the due and customary drinking. Now I do not doubt that thou wilt perish of famine before the rest, and be the first to need a tomb; for thou hast passed this strange law of thrift in fear that thou wilt be thyself the first to lack food. Thou art thinking for thyself, and not for others, when thou bringest thyself to start such strange miserly ways."

This witty quibbling turned the anger of the king into shame; and when he saw that his ordinance for the general good came home in mockery to himself, he thought no more of the public profit, but revoked the edict, relaxing his purpose sooner than anger his subjects.

Whether it was that the soil had too little rain, or that it was too hard baked, the crops, as I have said, were slack, and the fields gave but little produce; so that the land lacked victual, and was worn with a weary famine. The stock of food began to fail, and no help was left to stave off hunger. Then, at the proposal of Agg and of Ebb, it was provided by a decree of the people that the old men and the tiny children should be slain; that all who were too young to bear arms should be taken out of the land, and only the strong should be vouchsafed their own country; that none but able-bodied soldiers and husbandmen should continue to abide under their own roofs and in the houses of their fathers. When Agg and Ebb brought news of this to their mother Gambaruk, she saw that the authors of this infamous decree had found safety in crime. Condemning the decision of the assembly, she said that it was wrong to relieve distress by murder of kindred, and declared that a plan both more honourable and more desirable for the good of their souls and bodies would be, to preserve respect towards their parents and children, and choose by lot men who should quit the country. And if the lot fell on old men and weak, then the stronger should offer to go into exile in their place, and should of their own free will undertake to bear the burden of it for the feeble. But those men who had the heart to save their lives by crime and impiety, and to prosecute their parents and their children by so abominable a decree, did not deserve life; for they would be doing a work of cruelty and not of love. Finally, all those whose own lives were dearer to them than the love of their parents or their children, deserved but ill of their country. These words were reported to the assembly, and assented to by the vote of the majority. So the fortunes of all were staked upon the lot and those upon whom it fell were doomed to be banished. Thus those who had been loth to obey necessity of their own accord had now to accept the award of chance. So they sailed first to Bleking, and then, sailing past Moring, they came to anchor at Gothland; where, according to Paulus, they are said to have been prompted by the goddess Frigg to take the name of the Longobardi (Lombards), whose nation they afterwards founded. In the end they landed at Rugen, and, abandoning their ships, began to march overland. They crossed and wasted a great portion of the world; and at last, finding an abode in Italy, changed the ancient name of the nation for their own.

Meanwhile, the land of the Danes, where the tillers laboured less and less, and all traces of the furrows were covered with overgrowth, began to look like a forest. Almost stripped of its pleasant native turf, it bristled with the dense unshapely woods that grew up. Traces of this are yet seen in the aspect of its fields. What were once acres fertile in grain are now seen to be dotted with trunks of trees; and where of old the tillers turned the earth up deep and scattered the huge clods there has now sprung up a forest covering the fields, which still bear the tracks of ancient tillage. Had not these lands remained untilled and desolate with long overgrowth, the tenacious roots of trees could never have shared the soil of one and the same land with the furrows made by the plough. Moreover, the mounds which men laboriously built up of old on the level ground for the burial of the dead are now covered by a mass of woodland. Many piles of stones are also to be seen interspersed among the forest glades. These were once scattered over the whole country, but the peasants carefully gathered the boulders and piled them into a heap that they might not prevent furrows being cut in all directions; for they would sooner sacrifice a little of the land than find the whole of it stubborn. From this work, done by the toil of the peasants for the easier working of the fields, it is judged that the population in ancient times was greater than the present one, which is satisfied with small fields, and keeps its agriculture within narrower limits than those of the ancient tillage. Thus the present generation is amazed to behold that it has exchanged a soil which could once produce grain for one only fit to grow acorns, and the plough-handle and the cornstalks for a landscape studded with trees. Let this account of Snio, which I have put together as truly as I could, suffice.

Snio was succeeded by BIORN; and after him HARALD became sovereign. Harald's son GORM won no mean place of honour among the ancient generals of the Danes by his record of doughty deeds. For he ventured into fresh fields, preferring to practise his inherited valour, not in war, but in searching the secrets of nature; and, just as other kings are stirred by warlike ardour, so his heart thirsted to look into marvels; either what he could experience himself, or what were merely matters of report. And being desirous to go and see all things foreign and extraordinary, he thought that he must above all test a report which he had heard from the men of Thule concerning the abode of a certain Geirrod. For they boasted past belief of the mighty piles of treasure in that country, but said that the way was beset with peril, and hardly passable by mortal man. For those who had tried it declared that it was needful to sail over the ocean that goes round the lands, to leave the sun and stars behind, to journey down into chaos, and at last to pass into a land where no light was and where darkness reigned eternally.

But the warrior trampled down in his soul all fear of the dangers that beset him. Not that he desired booty, but glory; for he hoped for a great increase of renown if he ventured on a wholly unattempted quest. Three hundred men announced that they had the same desire as the king; and he resolved that Thorkill, who had brought the news, should be chosen to guide them on the journey, as he knew the ground and was versed in the approaches to that country. Thorkill did not refuse the task, and advised that, to meet the extraordinary fury of the sea they had to cross, strongly-made vessels should be built, fitted with many knotted cords and close-set nails, filled with great store of provision, and covered above with ox-hides to protect the inner spaces of the ships from the spray of the waves breaking in. Then they sailed off in only three galleys, each containing a hundred chosen men.

Now when they had come to Halogaland (Helgeland), they lost their favouring breezes, and were driven and tossed divers ways over the seas in perilous voyage. At last, in extreme want of food, and lacking even bread, they staved off hunger with a little pottage. Some days passed, and they heard the thunder of a storm brawling in the distance, as if it were deluging the rocks. By this perceiving that land was near, they bade a youth of great nimbleness climb to the masthead and look out; and he reported that a precipitous island was in sight. All were overjoyed, and gazed with thirsty eyes at the country at which he pointed, eagerly awaiting the refuge of the promised shore. At last they managed to reach it, and made their way out over the heights that blocked their way, along very steep paths, into the higher ground. Then Thorkill told them to take no more of the herds that were running about in numbers on the coast, than would serve once to appease their hunger. If they disobeyed, the guardian gods of the spot would not let them depart. But the seamen, more anxious to go on filling their bellies than to obey orders, postponed counsels of safety to the temptations of gluttony, and loaded the now emptied holds of their ships with the carcases of slaughtered cattle. These beasts were very easy to capture, because they gathered in amazement at the unwonted sight of men, their fears being made bold. On the following night monsters dashed down upon the shore, filled the forest with clamour, and beleaguered and beset the ships. One of them, huger than the rest, strode over the waters, armed with a mighty club. Coming close up to them, he bellowed out that they should never sail away till they had atoned for the crime they had committed in slaughtering the flock, and had made good the losses of the herd of the gods by giving up one man for each of their ships. Thorkill yielded to these threats; and, in order to preserve the safety of all by imperilling a few, singled out three men by lot and gave them up.

This done, a favouring wind took them, and they sailed to further Permland. It is a region of eternal cold, covered with very deep snows, and not sensible to the force even of the summer heats; full of pathless forests, not fertile in grain and haunted by beasts uncommon elsewhere. Its many rivers pour onwards in a hissing, foaming flood, because of the reefs imbedded in their channels.

Here Thorkill drew up his ships ashore, and bade them pitch their tents on the beach, declaring that they had come to a spot whence the passage to Geirrod would be short. Moreover, he forbade them to exchange any speech with those that came up to them, declaring that nothing enabled the monsters to injure strangers so much as uncivil words on their part: it would be therefore safer for his companions to keep silence; none but he, who had seen all the manners and customs of this nation before, could speak safely. As twilight approached, a man of extraordinary bigness greeted the sailors by their names, and came among them. All were aghast, but Thorkill told them to greet his arrival cheerfully, telling them that this was Gudmund, the brother of Geirrod, and the most faithful guardian in perils of all men who landed in that spot. When the man asked why all the rest thus kept silence, he answered that they were very unskilled in his language, and were ashamed to use a speech they did not know. Then Gudmund invited them to be his guests, and took them up in carriages. As they went forward, they saw a river which could be crossed by a bridge of gold. They wished to go over it, but Gudmund restrained them, telling them that by this channel nature had divided the world of men from the world of monsters, and that no mortal track might go further. Then they reached the dwelling of their guide; and here Thorkill took his companions apart and warned them to behave like men of good counsel amidst the divers temptations chance might throw in their way; to abstain from the food of the stranger, and nourish their bodies only on their own; and to seek a seat apart from the natives, and have no contact with any of them as they lay at meat. For if they partook of that food they would lose recollection of all things, and must live for ever in filthy intercourse amongst ghastly hordes of monsters. Likewise he told them that they must keep their hands off the servants and the cups of the people.

Round the table stood twelve noble sons of Gudmund, and as many daughters of notable beauty. When Gudmund saw that the king barely tasted what his servants brought, he reproached him with repulsing his kindness, and complained that it was a slight on the host. But Thorkill was not at a loss for a fitting excuse. He reminded him that men who took unaccustomed food often suffered from it seriously, and that the king was not ungrateful for the service rendered by another, but was merely taking care of his health, when he refreshed himself as he was wont, and furnished his supper with his own viands. An act, therefore, that was only done in the healthy desire to escape some bane, ought in no wise to be put down to scorn. Now when Gudmund saw that the temperance of his guest had baffled his treacherous preparations, he determined to sap their chastity, if he could not weaken their abstinence, and eagerly strained every nerve of his wit to enfeeble their self-control. For he offered the king his daughter in marriage, and promised the rest that they should have whatever women of his household they desired. Most of them inclined to his offer: but Thorkill by his healthy admonitions prevented them, as he had done before, from falling into temptation.

With wonderful management Thorkill divided his heed between the suspicious host and the delighted guests. Four of the Danes, to whom lust was more than their salvation, accepted the offer; the infection maddened them, distraught their wits, and blotted out their recollection: for they are said never to have been in their right mind after this. If these men had kept themselves within the rightful bounds of temperance, they would have equalled the glories of Hercules, surpassed with their spirit the bravery of giants, and been ennobled for ever by their wondrous services to their country.

Gudmund, stubborn to his purpose, and still spreading his nets, extolled the delights of his garden, and tried to lure the king thither to gather fruits, desiring to break down his constant wariness by the lust of the eye and the baits of the palate. The king, as before, was strengthened against these treacheries by Thorkill, and rejected this feint of kindly service; he excused himself from accepting it on the plea that he must hasten on his journey. Gudmund perceived that Thorkill was shrewder than he at every point; so, despairing to accomplish his treachery, he carried them all across the further side of the river, and let them finish their journey.

They went on; and saw, not far off, a gloomy, neglected town, looking more like a cloud exhaling vapour. Stakes interspersed among the battlements showed the severed heads of warriors and dogs of great ferocity were seen watching before the doors to guard the entrance. Thorkill threw them a horn smeared with fat to lick, and so, at slight cost, appeased their most furious rage. High up the gates lay open to enter, and they climbed to their level with ladders, entering with difficulty. Inside the town was crowded with murky and misshapen phantoms, and it was hard to say whether their shrieking figures were more ghastly to the eye or to the ear; everything was foul, and the reeking mire afflicted the nostrils of the visitors with its unbearable stench. Then they found the rocky dwelling which Geirrod was rumoured to inhabit for his palace. They resolved to visit its narrow and horrible ledge, but stayed their steps and halted in panic at the very entrance. Then Thorkill, seeing that they were of two minds, dispelled their hesitation to enter by manful encouragement, counselling them, to restrain themselves, and not to touch any piece of gear in the house they were about to enter, albeit it seemed delightful to have or pleasant to behold; to keep their hearts as far from all covetousness as from fear; neither to desire what was pleasant to take, nor dread what was awful to look upon, though they should find themselves amidst abundance of both these things. If they did, their greedy hands would suddenly be bound fast, unable to tear themselves away from the thing they touched, and knotted up with it as by inextricable bonds. Moreover, they should enter in order, four by four.

Broder and Buchi (Buk?) were the first to show courage to attempt to enter the vile palace; Thorkill with the king followed them, and the rest advanced behind these in ordered ranks.

Inside, the house was seen to be ruinous throughout, and filled with a violent and abominable reek. And it also teemed with everything that could disgust the eye or the mind: the door-posts were begrimed with the soot of ages, the wall was plastered with filth, the roof was made up of spear-heads, the flooring was covered with snakes and bespattered with all manner of uncleanliness. Such an unwonted sight struck terror into the strangers, and, over all, the acrid and incessant stench assailed their afflicted nostrils. Also bloodless phantasmal monsters huddled on the iron seats, and the places for sitting were railed off by leaden trellises; and hideous doorkeepers stood at watch on the thresholds. Some of these, armed with clubs lashed together, yelled, while others played a gruesome game, tossing a goat's hide from one to the other with mutual motion of goatish backs.

Here Thorkill again warned the men, and forbade them to stretch forth their covetous hands rashly to the forbidden things. Going on through the breach in the crag, they beheld an old man with his body pierced through, sitting not far off, on a lofty seat facing the side of the rock that had been rent away. Moreover, three women, whose bodies were covered with tumours, and who seemed to have lost the strength of their back-bones, filled adjoining seats. Thorkill's companions were very curious; and he, who well knew the reason of the matter, told them that long ago the god Thor had been provoked by the insolence of the giants to drive red-hot irons through the vitals of Geirrod, who strove with him, and that the iron had slid further, torn up the mountain, and battered through its side; while the women had been stricken by the might of his thunderbolts, and had been punished (so he declared) for their attempt on the same deity, by having their bodies broken.

As the men were about to depart thence, there were disclosed to them seven butts hooped round with belts of gold; and from these hung circlets of silver entwined with them in manifold links. Near these was found the tusk of a strange beast, tipped at both ends with gold. Close by was a vast stag-horn, laboriously decked with choice and flashing gems, and this also did not lack chasing. Hard by was to be seen a very heavy bracelet. One man was kindled with an inordinate desire for this bracelet, and laid covetous hands upon the gold, not knowing that the glorious metal covered deadly mischief, and that a fatal bane lay hid under the shining spoil. A second also, unable to restrain his covetousness, reached out his quivering hands to the horn. A third, matching the confidence of the others, and having no control over his fingers, ventured to shoulder the tusk. The spoil seemed alike lovely to look upon and desirable to enjoy, for all that met the eye was fair and tempting to behold. But the bracelet suddenly took the form of a snake, and attacked him who was carrying it with its poisoned tooth; the horn lengthened out into a serpent, and took the life of the man who bore it; the tusk wrought itself into a sword, and plunged into the vitals of its bearer.

The rest dreaded the fate of perishing with their friends, and thought that the guiltless would be destroyed like the guilty; they durst not hope that even innocence would be safe. Then the side-door of another room showed them a narrow alcove: and a privy chamber with a yet richer treasure was revealed, wherein arms were laid out too great for those of human stature. Among these were seen a royal mantle, a handsome hat, and a belt marvellously wrought. Thorkill, struck with amazement at these things, gave rein to his covetousness, and cast off all his purposed self-restraint. He who so oft had trained others could not so much as conquer his own cravings. For he laid his hand upon the mantle, and his rash example tempted the rest to join in his enterprise of plunder. Thereupon the recess shook from its lowest foundations, and began suddenly to reel and totter. Straightway the women raised a shriek that the wicked robbers were being endured too long. Then they, who were before supposed to be half-dead or lifeless phantoms, seemed to obey the cries of the women, and, leaping suddenly up from their seats, attacked the strangers with furious onset. The other creatures bellowed hoarsely.

But Broder and Buchi fell to their old and familiar arts, and attacked the witches, who ran at them, with a shower of spears from every side; and with the missiles from their bows and slings they crushed the array of monsters. There could be no stronger or more successful way to repulse them; but only twenty men out of all the king's company were rescued by the intervention of this archery; the rest were torn in pieces by the monsters. The survivors returned to the river, and were ferried over by Gudmund, who entertained them at his house. Long and often as he besought them, he could not keep them back; so at last he gave them presents and let them go.

Buchi relaxed his watch upon himself; his self-control became unstrung, and he forsook the virtue in which he hitherto rejoiced. For he conceived an incurable love for one of the daughters of Gudmund, and embraced her; but he obtained a bride to his undoing, for soon his brain suddenly began to whirl, and he lost his recollection. Thus the hero who had subdued all the monsters and overcome all the perils was mastered by passion for one girl; his soul strayed far from temperance, and he lay under a wretched sensual yoke. For the sake of respect, he started to accompany the departing king; but as he was about to ford the river in his carriage, his wheels sank deep, he was caught up in the violent eddies and destroyed.

The king bewailed his friend's disaster and departed hastening on his voyage. This was at first prosperous, but afterwards he was tossed by bad weather; his men perished of hunger, and but few survived, so that he began to feel awe in his heart, and fell to making vows to heaven, thinking the gods alone could help him in his extreme need. At last the others besought sundry powers among the gods, and thought they ought to sacrifice to the majesty of divers deities; but the king, offering both vows and peace-offerings to Utgarda-Loki, obtained that fair season of weather for which he prayed.

Coming home, and feeling that he had passed through all these seas and toils, he thought it was time for his spirit, wearied with calamities, to withdraw from his labours. So he took a queen from Sweden, and exchanged his old pursuits for meditative leisure. His life was prolonged in the utmost peace and quietness; but when he had almost come to the end of his days, certain men persuaded him by likely arguments that souls were immortal; so that he was constantly turning over in his mind the questions, to what abode he was to fare when the breath left his limbs, or what reward was earned by zealous adoration of the gods.

While he was thus inclined, certain men who wished ill to Thorkill came and told Gorm that it was needful to consult the gods, and that assurance about so great a matter must be sought of the oracles of heaven, since it was too deep for human wit and hard for mortals to discover.

Therefore, they said, Utgarda-Loki must be appeased, and no man would accomplish this more fitly than Thorkill. Others, again, laid information against him as guilty of treachery and an enemy of the king's life. Thorkill, seeing himself doomed to extreme peril, demanded that his accusers should share his journey. Then they who had aspersed an innocent man saw that the peril they had designed against the life of another had recoiled upon themselves, and tried to take back their plan. But vainly did they pester the ears of the king; he forced them to sail under the command of Thorkill, and even upbraided them with cowardice. Thus, when a mischief is designed against another, it is commonly sure to strike home to its author. And when these men saw that they were constrained, and could not possibly avoid the peril, they covered their ship with ox-hides, and filled it with abundant store of provision.

In this ship they sailed away, and came to a sunless land, which knew not the stars, was void of daylight, and seemed to overshadow them with eternal night. Long they sailed under this strange sky; at last their timber fell short, and they lacked fuel; and, having no place to boil their meat in, they staved off their hunger with raw viands. But most of those who ate contracted extreme disease, being glutted with undigested food. For the unusual diet first made a faintness steal gradually upon their stomachs; then the infection spread further, and the malady reached the vital parts. Thus there was danger in either extreme, which made it hurtful not to eat, and perilous to indulge; for it was found both unsafe to feed and bad for them to abstain. Then, when they were beginning to be in utter despair, a gleam of unexpected help relieved them, even as the string breaks most easily when it is stretched tightest. For suddenly the weary men saw the twinkle of a fire at no great distance, and conceived a hope of prolonging their lives. Thorkill thought this fire a heaven-sent relief, and resolved to go and take some of it.

To be surer of getting back to his friends, Thorkill fastened a jewel upon the mast-head, to mark it by the gleam. When he got to the shore, his eyes fell on a cavern in a close defile, to which a narrow way led. Telling his companions to await him outside, he went in, and saw two men, swart and very huge, with horny noses, feeding their fire with any chance-given fuel. Moreover, the entrance was hideous, the door-posts were decayed, the walls grimy with mould, the roof filthy, and the floor swarming with snakes; all of which disgusted the eye as much as the mind. Then one of the giants greeted him, and said that he had begun a most difficult venture in his burning desire to visit a strange god, and his attempt to explore with curious search an untrodden region beyond the world. Yet he promised to tell Thorkill the paths of the journey he proposed to make, if he would deliver three true judgments in the form of as many sayings. Then said Thorkill: "In good truth, I do not remember ever to have seen a household with more uncomely noses; nor have I ever come to a spot where I had less mind to live." Also he said: "That, I think, is my best foot which can get out of this foremost."

The giant was pleased with the shrewdness of Thorkill, and praised his sayings, telling him that he must first travel to a grassless land which was veiled in deep darkness; but he must first voyage for four days, rowing incessantly, before he could reach his goal. There he could visit Utgarda-Loki, who had chosen hideous and grisly caves for his filthy dwelling. Thorkill was much aghast at being bidden to go on a voyage so long and hazardous; but his doubtful hopes prevailed over his present fears, and he asked for some live fuel. Then said the giant: "If thou needest fire, thou must deliver three more judgments in like sayings." Then said Thorkill: "Good counsel is to be obeyed, though a mean fellow gave it." Likewise: "I have gone so far in rashness, that if I can get back I shall owe my safety to none but my own legs." And again: "Were I free to retreat this moment, I would take good care never to come back."

Thereupon Thorkill took the fire along to his companions; and finding a kindly wind, landed on the fourth day at the appointed harbour. With his crew he entered a land where an aspect of unbroken night checked the vicissitude of light and darkness. He could hardly see before him, but beheld a rock of enormous size. Wishing to explore it, he told his companions, who were standing posted at the door, to strike a fire from flints as a timely safeguard against demons, and kindle it in the entrance. Then he made others bear a light before him, and stooped his body through the narrow jaws of the cavern, where he beheld a number of iron seats among a swarm of gliding serpents. Next there met his eye a sluggish mass of water gently flowing over a sandy bottom. He crossed this, and approached a cavern which sloped somewhat more steeply. Again, after this, a foul and gloomy room was disclosed to the visitors, wherein they saw Utgarda-Loki, laden hand and foot with enormous chains. Each of his reeking hairs was as large and stiff as a spear of cornel. Thorkill (his companions lending a hand), in order that his deeds might gain more credit, plucked one of these from the chin of Utgarda-Loki, who suffered it. Straightway such a noisome smell reached the bystanders, that they could not breathe without stopping their noses with their mantles. They could scarcely make their way out, and were bespattered by the snakes which darted at them on every side.

Only five of Thorkill's company embarked with their captain: the poison killed the rest. The demons hung furiously over them, and cast their poisonous slaver from every side upon the men below them. But the sailors sheltered themselves with their hides, and cast back the venom that fell upon them. One man by chance at this point wished to peep out; the poison touched his head, which was taken off his neck as if it had been severed with a sword. Another put his eyes out of their shelter, and when he brought them back under it they were blinded. Another thrust forth his hand while unfolding his covering, and, when he withdrew his arm, it was withered by the virulence of the same slaver. They besought their deities to be kinder to them; vainly, until Thorkill prayed to the god of the universe, and poured forth unto him libations as well as prayers; and thus, presently finding the sky even as before and the elements clear, he made a fair voyage.

And now they seemed to behold another world, and the way towards the life of man. At last Thorkill landed in Germany, which had then been admitted to Christianity; and among its people he began to learn how to worship God. His band of men were almost destroyed, because of the dreadful air they had breathed, and he returned to his country accompanied by two men only, who had escaped the worst. But the corrupt matter which smeared his face so disguised his person and original features that not even his friends knew him. But when he wiped off the filth, he made himself recognizable by those who saw him, and inspired the king with the greatest eagerness to hear about his quest. But the detraction of his rivals was not yet silenced; and some pretended that the king would die suddenly if he learnt Thorkill's tidings. The king was the more disposed to credit this saying, because he was already credulous by reason of a dream which falsely prophesied the same thing. Men were therefore hired by the king's command to slay Thorkill in the night. But somehow he got wind of it, left his bed unknown to all, and put a heavy log in his place. By this he baffled the treacherous device of the king, for the hirelings smote only the stock.

On the morrow Thorkill went up to the king as he sat at meat, and said: "I forgive thy cruelty and pardon thy error, in that thou hast decreed punishment, and not thanks, to him who brings good tidings of his errand. For thy sake I have devoted my life to all these afflictions, and battered it in all these perils; I hoped that thou wouldst requite my services with much gratitude; and behold! I have found thee, and thee alone, punish my valour sharpliest. But I forbear all vengeance, and am satisfied with the shame within thy heart—if, after all, any shame visits the thankless—as expiation for this wrongdoing towards me. I have a right to surmise that thou art worse than all demons in fury, and all beasts in cruelty, if, after escaping the snares of all these monsters, I have failed to be safe from thine."

The king desired to learn everything from Thorkill's own lips; and, thinking it hard to escape destiny, bade him relate what had happened in due order. He listened eagerly to his recital of everything, till at last, when his own god was named, he could not endure him to be unfavourably judged. For he could not bear to hear Utgarda-Loki reproached with filthiness, and so resented his shameful misfortunes, that his very life could not brook such words, and he yielded it up in the midst of Thorkill's narrative. Thus, whilst he was so zealous in the worship of a false god, he came to find where the true prison of sorrows really was. Moreover, the reek of the hair, which Thorkill plucked from the locks of the giant to testify to the greatness of his own deeds, was exhaled upon the bystanders, so that many perished of it.

After the death of Gorm, GOTRIK his son came to the throne. He was notable not only for prowess but for generosity, and none can say whether his courage or his compassion was the greater. He so chastened his harshness with mercy, that he seemed to counterweigh the one with the other. At this time Gaut, the King of Norway, was visited by Ber (Biorn?) and Ref, men of Thule. Gaut treated Ref with attention

311

and friendship, and presented him with a heavy bracelet.

One of the courtiers, when he saw this, praised the greatness of the gift over-zealously, and declared that no one was equal to King Gaut in kindliness. But Ref, though he owed thanks for the benefit, could not approve the inflated words of this extravagant praiser, and said that Gotrik was more generous than Gaut. Wishing to crush the empty boast of the flatterer, he chose rather to bear witness to the generosity of the absent than tickle with lies the vanity of his benefactor who was present. For another thing, he thought it somewhat more desirable to be charged with ingratitude than to support with his assent such idle and boastful praise, and also to move the king by the solemn truth than to beguile him with lying flatteries. But Ulf persisted not only in stubbornly repeating his praises of the king, but in bringing them to the proof; and proposed their gainsayer a wager.

With his consent Ref went to Denmark, and found Gotrik seated in state, and dealing out the pay to his soldiers. When the king asked him who he was, he said that his name was "Fox-cub" The answer filled some with mirth and some with marvel, and Gotrik said, "Yea, and it is fitting that a fox should catch his prey in his mouth." And thereupon he drew a bracelet from his arm, called the man to him, and put it between his lips. Straightway Ref put it upon his arm, which he displayed to them all adorned with gold, but the other arm he kept hidden as lacking ornament; for which shrewdness he received a gift equal to the first from that hand of matchless generosity. At this he was overjoyed, not so much because the reward was great, as because he had won his contention. And when the king learnt from him about the wager he had laid, he rejoiced that he had been lavish to him more by accident than of set purpose, and declared that he got more pleasure from the giving than the receiver from the gift. So Ref returned to Norway and slew his opponent, who refused to pay the wager. Then he took the daughter of Gaut captive, and brought her to Gotrik for his own.

Gotrik, who is also called Godefride, carried his arms against foreigners, and increased his strength and glory by his successful generalship. Among his memorable deeds were the terms of tribute he imposed upon the Saxons; namely, that whenever a change of kings occurred among the Danes, their princes should devote a hundred snow-white horses to the new king on his accession. But if the Saxons should receive a new chief upon a change in the succession, this chief was likewise to pay the aforesaid tribute obediently, and bow at the outset of his power to the sovereign majesty of Denmark; thereby acknowledging the supremacy of our nation, and solemnly confessing his own subjection. Nor was it enough for Gotrik to subjugate Germany:

312

he appointed Ref on a mission to try the strength of Sweden. The Swedes feared to slay him with open violence, but ventured to act like bandits, and killed him, as he slept, with the blow of a stone. For, hanging a millstone above him, they cut its fastenings, and let it drop upon his neck as he lay beneath. To expiate this crime it was decreed that each of the ringleaders should pay twelve golden talents, while each of the common people should pay Gotrik one ounce. Men called this "the Fox-cub's tribute". (Refsgild).

Meanwhile it befell that Karl, King of the Franks, crushed Germany in war, and forced it not only to embrace the worship of Christianity, but also to obey his authority. When Gotrik heard of this, he attacked the nations bordering on the Elbe, and attempted to regain under his sway as of old the realm of Saxony, which eagerly accepted the yoke of Karl, and preferred the Roman to the Danish arms. Karl had at this time withdrawn his victorious camp beyond the Rhine, and therefore forbore to engage the stranger enemy, being prevented by the intervening river. But when he was intending to cross once more to subdue the power of Gotrik, he was summoned by Leo the Pope of the Romans to defend the city.

Obeying this command, Karl intrusted his son Pepin with the conduct of the war against Gotrik; so that while he himself was working against a distant foe, Pepin might manage the conflict he had undertaken with his neighbour. For Karl was distracted by two anxieties, and had to furnish sufficient out of a scanty band to meet both of them. Meanwhile Gotrik won a glorious victory over the Saxons. Then gathering new strength, and mustering a larger body of forces, he resolved to avenge the wrong he had suffered in losing his sovereignty, not only upon the Saxons, but upon the whole people of Germany. He began by subduing Friesland with his fleet.

This province lies very low, and whenever the fury of the ocean bursts the dykes that bar its waves, it is wont to receive the whole mass of the deluge over its open plains. On this country Gotrik imposed a kind of tribute, which was not so much harsh as strange. I will briefly relate its terms and the manner of it. First, a building was arranged, two hundred and forty feet in length, and divided into twelve spaces; each of these stretching over an interval of twenty feet, and thus making together, when the whole room was exhausted, the aforesaid total. Now at the upper end of this building sat the king's treasurer, and in a line with him at its further end was displayed a round shield. When the Frisians came to pay tribute, they used to cast their coins one by one into the hollow of this shield; but only those coins which struck the ear of the distant toll-gatherer with a distinct clang were chosen by him, as he counted, to be reckoned among the royal tribute. The result was that the collector only reckoned that money towards the treasury of which his distant ear caught the sound as it fell. But that of which the sound was duller, and which fell out of his earshot, was received indeed into the treasury, but did not count as any increase to the sum paid. Now many coins that were cast in struck with no audible loudness whatever on the collector's ear, so that men who came to pay their appointed toll sometimes squandered much of their money in useless tribute. Karl is said to have freed them afterwards from the burden of this tax. After Gotrik had crossed Friesland, and Karl had now come back from Rome, Gotrik determined to swoop down upon the further districts of Germany, but was treacherously attacked by one of his own servants, and perished at home by the sword of a traitor. When Karl heard this, he leapt up overjoyed, declaring that nothing more delightful had ever fallen to his lot than this happy chance.

ENDNOTES:

(1) Furthest Thule—The names of Icelanders have thus crept into the account of a battle fought before the discovery of Iceland.

The Battle of Bravalla

BOOK NINE

After Gotrik's death reigned his son OLAF; who, desirous to avenge his father, did not hesitate to involve his country in civil wars, putting patriotism after private inclination. When he perished, his body was put in a barrow, famous for the name of Olaf, which was built up close by Leire.

He was succeeded by HEMMING, of whom I have found no deed worthy of record, save that he made a sworn peace with Kaiser Ludwig; and yet, perhaps, envious antiquity hides many notable deeds of his time, albeit they were then famous.

After these men there came to the throne, backed by the Skanians and Zealanders, SIWARD, surnamed RING. He was the son, born long ago, of the chief of Norway who bore the same name, by Gotrik's daughter. Now Ring, cousin of Siward, and also a grandson of Gotrik, was master of Jutland. Thus the power of the single kingdom was divided; and, as though its two parts were contemptible for their smallness, foreigners began not only to despise but to attack it. These Siward assailed with greater hatred than he did his rival for the throne; and, preferring wars abroad to wars at home, he stubbornly defended his country against dangers for five years; for he chose to put up with a trouble at home that he might the more easily cure one which came from abroad. Wherefore Ring (desiring his) command, seized the opportunity, tried to transfer the whole sovereignty to himself, and did not hesitate to injure in his own land the man who was watching over it without; for he attacked the provinces in the possession of Siward, which was an ungrateful requital for the defence of their common country. Therefore, some of the Zealanders who were more zealous for Siward, in order to show him firmer loyalty in his absence, proclaimed his son Ragnar as king, when he was scarcely dragged out of his cradle. Not but what they knew he was too young to govern; yet they hoped that such a gage would serve to rouse their sluggish allies against Ring. But, when Ring heard that Siward had meantime returned from his expedition, he attacked the Zealanders with a large force, and proclaimed that they should perish by the sword if they did not surrender; but the Zealanders, who were bidden to choose between shame and peril, were so few that they distrusted their strength, and requested a truce to consider the matter. It was granted; but, since it did not seem open to them to seek the favour of Siward, nor honourable to embrace that of Ring, they wavered long in perplexity between fear and shame. In this plight even the old were at a loss for counsel; but Ragnar, who chanced to be present at the assembly, said: "The short bow shoots its shaft suddenly. Though it may seem the hardihood of a boy that I venture to forestall

316

the speech of the elders, yet I pray you to pardon my errors, and be indulgent to my unripe words. Yet the counsellor of wisdom is not to be spurned, though he seem contemptible; for the teaching of profitable things should be drunk in with an open mind. Now it is shameful that we should be branded as deserters and runaways, but it is just as foolhardy to venture above our strength; and thus there is proved to be equal blame either way. We must, then, pretend to go over to the enemy, but, when a chance comes in our way, we must desert him betimes. It will thus be better to forestall the wrath of our foe by reigned obedience than, by refusing it, to give him a weapon wherewith to attack us yet more harshly; for if we decline the sway of the stronger, are we not simply turning his arms against our own throat? Intricate devices are often the best nurse of craft. You need cunning to trap a fox." By this sound counsel he dispelled the wavering of his countrymen, and strengthened the camp of the enemy to its own hurt.

The assembly, marvelling at the eloquence as much as at the wit of one so young, gladly embraced a proposal of such genius, which they thought excellent beyond his years. Nor were the old men ashamed to obey the bidding of a boy when they lacked counsel themselves; for, though it came from one of tender years, it was full, notwithstanding, of weighty and sound instruction. But they feared to expose their adviser to immediate peril, and sent him over to Norway to be brought up. Soon afterwards, Siward joined battle with Ring and attacked him. He slew Ring, but himself received an incurable wound, of which he died a few days afterwards.

He was succeeded on the throne by RAGNAR. At this time Fro (Frey?), the King of Sweden, after slaying Siward, the King of the Norwegians, put the wives of Siward's kinsfolk in bonds in a brothel, and delivered them to public outrage. When Ragnar heard of this, he went to Norway to avenge his grandfather. As he came, many of the matrons, who had either suffered insult to their persons or feared imminent peril to their chastity, hastened eagerly to his camp in male attire, declaring that they would prefer death to outrage. Nor did Ragnar, who was to punish this reproach upon the women, scorn to use against the author of the infamy the help of those whose shame he had come to avenge. Among them was Ladgerda, a skilled amazon, who, though a maiden, had the courage of a man, and fought in front among the bravest with her hair loose over her shoulders. All-marvelled at her matchless deeds, for her locks flying down her back betrayed that she was a woman.

Ragnar, when he had justly cut down the murderer of his grandfather, asked many questions of his fellow soldiers concerning the maiden whom he had seen so forward in the fray, and declared that he had gained the victory by the might of one woman. Learning that she was of noble birth among the barbarians, he steadfastly wooed her by means of messengers. She spurned his mission in her heart, but feigned compliance. Giving false answers, she made her panting wooer confident that he would gain his desires; but ordered that a bear and a dog should be set at the porch of her dwelling, thinking to guard her own room against all the ardour of a lover by means of the beasts that blocked the way. Ragnar, comforted by the good news, embarked, crossed the sea, and, telling his men to stop in Gaulardale, as the valley is called, went to the dwelling of the maiden alone. Here the beasts met him, and he thrust one through with a spear, and caught the other by the throat, wrung its neck, and choked it. Thus he had the maiden as the prize of the peril he had overcome. By this marriage he had two daughters, whose names have not come down to us, and a son Fridleif. Then he lived three years at peace.

The Jutlanders, a presumptuous race, thinking that because of his recent marriage he would never return, took the Skanians into alliance, and tried to attack the Zealanders, who preserved the most zealous and affectionate loyalty towards Ragnar. He, when he heard of it, equipped thirty ships, and, the winds favouring his voyage, crushed the Skanians, who ventured to fight, near the stead of Whiteby, and when the winter was over he fought successfully with the Jutlanders who dwelt near the Liim-fjord in that region. A third and a fourth time he conquered the Skanians and the Hallanders triumphantly.

Afterwards, changing his love, and desiring Thora, the daughter of the King Herodd, to wife, Ragnar divorced himself from Ladgerda; for he thought ill of her trustworthiness, remembering that she had long ago set the most savage beasts to destroy him. Meantime Herodd, the King of the Swedes, happening to go and hunt in the woods, brought home some snakes, found by his escort, for his daughter to rear. She speedily obeyed the instructions of her father, and endured to rear a race of adders with her maiden hands. Moreover, she took care that they should daily have a whole ox-carcase to gorge upon, not knowing that she was privately feeding and keeping up a public nuisance. The vipers grew up, and scorched the country-side with their pestilential breath. Whereupon the king, repenting of his sluggishness, proclaimed that whosoever removed the pest should have his daughter.

Many warriors were thereto attracted by courage as much as by desire; but all idly and perilously wasted their pains. Ragnar, learning from men who travelled to and fro how the matter stood, asked his nurse for a woolen mantle, and for some thigh-pieces that were very hairy, with which he could repel the snake-bites. He thought that he ought to use a

318

dress stuffed with hair to protect himself, and also took one that was not unwieldy, that he might move nimbly. And when he had landed in Sweden, he deliberately plunged his body in water, while there was a frost falling, and, wetting his dress, to make it the less penetrable, he let the cold freeze it. Thus attired, he took leave of his companions, exhorted them to remain loyal to Fridleif, and went on to the palace alone. When he saw it, he tied his sword to his side, and lashed a spear to his right hand with a thong. As he went on, an enormous snake glided up and met him. Another, equally huge, crawled up, following in the trail of the first. They strove now to buffet the young man with the coils of their tails, and now to spit and belch their venom stubbornly upon him. Meantime the courtiers, betaking themselves to safer hiding, watched the struggle from afar like affrighted little girls. The king was stricken with equal fear, and fled, with a few followers, to a narrow shelter. But Ragnar, trusting in the hardness of his frozen dress, foiled the poisonous assaults not only with his arms, but with his attire, and, singlehanded, in unweariable combat, stood up against the two gaping creatures, who stubbornly poured forth their venom upon him. For their teeth he repelled with his shield, their poison with his dress. At last he cast his spear, and drove it against the bodies of the brutes, who were attacking him hard. He pierced both their hearts, and his battle ended in victory.

After Ragnar had thus triumphed the king scanned his dress closely, and saw that he was rough and hairy; but, above all, he laughed at the shaggy lower portion of his garb, and chiefly the uncouth aspect of his breeches; so that he gave him in jest the nickname of Lodbrog. Also he invited him to feast with his friends, to refresh him after his labours. Ragnar said that he would first go back to the witnesses whom he had left behind. He set out and brought them back, splendidly attired for the coming feast. At last, when the banquet was over, he received the prize that was appointed for the victory. By her he begot two nobly-gifted sons, Radbard and Dunwat. These also had brothers—Siward, Biorn, Agnar, and Iwar.

Meanwhile, the Jutes and Skanians were kindled with an unquenchable fire of sedition; they disallowed the title of Ragnar, and gave a certain Harald the sovereign power. Ragnar sent envoys to Norway, and besought friendly assistance against these men; and Ladgerda, whose early love still flowed deep and steadfast, hastily sailed off with her husband and her son. She brought herself to offer a hundred and twenty ships to the man who had once put her away. And he, thinking himself destitute of all resources, took to borrowing help from folk of every age, crowded the strong and the feeble all together, and was not ashamed to insert some old men and boys among the wedges of the strong. So he first tried to crush the power of the Skanians in the field which in Latin is called Laneus (Woolly); here he had a hard fight with the rebels. Here, too, Iwar, who was in his seventh year, fought splendidly, and showed the strength of a man in the body of a boy. But Siward, while attacking the enemy face to face, fell forward upon the ground wounded. When his men saw this, it made them look round most anxiously for means of flight; and this brought low not only Siward, but almost the whole army on the side of Ragnar. But Ragnar by his manly deeds and exhortations comforted their amazed and sunken spirits, and, just when they were ready to be conquered, spurred them on to try and conquer.

Ladgerda, who had a matchless spirit though a delicate frame, covered by her splendid bravery the inclination of the soldiers to waver. For she made a sally about, and flew round to the rear of the enemy, taking them unawares, and thus turned the panic of her friends into the camp of the enemy. At last the lines of HARALD became slack, and HARALD himself was routed with a great slaughter of his men. LADGERDA, when she had gone home after the battle, murdered her husband.... in the night with a spear-head, which she had hid in her gown. Then she usurped the whole of his name and sovereignty; for this most presumptuous dame thought it pleasanter to rule without her husband than to share the throne with him.

Meantime, Siward was taken to a town in the neighbourhood, and gave himself to be tended by the doctors, who were reduced to the depths of despair. But while the huge wound baffled all the remedies they applied, a certain man of amazing size was seen to approach the litter of the sick man, and promised that Siward should straightway rejoice and be whole, if he would consecrate unto him the souls of all whom he should overcome in battle. Nor did he conceal his name, but said that he was called Rostar. Now Siward, when he saw that a great benefit could be got at the cost of a little promise, eagerly acceded to this request. Then the old man suddenly, by the help of his hand, touched and banished the livid spot, and suddenly scarred the wound over. At last he poured dust on his eyes and departed. Spots suddenly arose, and the dust, to the amaze of the beholders, seemed to become wonderfully like little snakes.

I should think that he who did this miracle wished to declare, by the manifest token of his eyes, that the young man was to be cruel in future, in order that the more visible part of his body might not lack some omen of his life that was to follow. When the old woman, who had the care of his draughts, saw him showing in his face signs of little snakes; she was seized with an extraordinary horror of the young man, and suddenly fell and swooned away. Hence it happened that Siward got the widespread name of Snake-Eye.

Meantime Thora, the bride of Ragnar, perished of a violent malady, which caused infinite trouble and distress to the husband, who dearly loved his wife. This distress, he thought, would be best dispelled by business, and he resolved to find solace in exercise and qualify his grief by toil. To banish his affliction and gain some comfort, he bent his thoughts to warfare, and decreed that every father of a family should devote to his service whichever of his children he thought most contemptible, or any slave of his who was lazy at his work or of doubtful fidelity. And albeit that this decree seemed little fitted for his purpose, he showed that the feeblest of the Danish race were better than the strongest men of other nations; and it did the young men great good, each of those chosen being eager to wipe off the reproach of indolence. Also he enacted that every piece of litigation should be referred to the judgment of twelve chosen elders, all ordinary methods of action being removed, the accuser being forbidden to charge, and the accused to defend. This law removed all chance of incurring litigation lightly. Thinking that there was thus sufficient provision made against false accusations by unscrupulous men, he lifted up his arms against Britain, and attacked and slew in battle its king, Hame, the father of Ella, who was a most noble youth. Then he killed the earls of Scotland and of Pictland, and of the isles that they call the Southern or Meridional (Sudreyar), and made his sons Siward and Radbard masters of the provinces, which were now without governors. He also deprived Norway of its chief by force, and commanded it to obey Fridleif, whom he also set over the Orkneys, from which he took their own earl.

Meantime, some of the Danes who were most stubborn in their hatred against Ragnar were obstinately bent on rebellion. They rallied to the side of Harald, once an exile, and tried to raise the fallen fortunes of the tyrant. By this hardihood they raised up against the king the most virulent blasts of civil war, and entangled him in domestic perils when he was free from foreign troubles. Ragnar, setting out to check them with a fleet of the Danes who lived in the isles, crushed the army of the rebels, drove Harald, the leader of the conquered army, a fugitive to Germany, and forced him to resign unbashfully an honour which he had gained without scruple. Nor was he content simply to kill his prisoners: he preferred to torture them to death, so that those who could not be induced to forsake their disloyalty might not be so much as suffered to give up the ghost save under the most grievous punishment. Moreover, the estates of those who had deserted with Harald he distributed among those who were serving as his soldiers, thinking that the fathers would be worse punished by seeing the honour of their inheritance made over to the children whom they had rejected, while those whom they had loved better lost their patrimony. But even this did not sate his vengeance, and he further determined to attack Saxony, thinking it the refuge of his foes and the retreat of Harald. So, begging his sons to help him, he came on Karl, who happened then to be tarrying on those borders of his empire. Intercepting his sentries, he eluded the watch that was posted on guard. But while he thought that all the rest would therefore be easy and more open to his attacks, suddenly a woman who was a soothsayer, a kind of divine oracle or interpreter of the will of heaven, warned the king with a saving prophecy, and by her fortunate presage forestalled the mischief that impended, saying that the fleet of Siward had moored at the mouth of the river Seine. The emperor, heeding the warning, and understanding that the enemy was at hand, managed to engage with and stop the barbarians, who were thus pointed out to him. A battle was fought with Ragnar; but Karl did not succeed as happily in the field as he had got warning of the danger. And so that tireless conqueror of almost all Europe, who in his calm and complete career of victory had travelled over so great a portion of the world, now beheld his army, which had vanquished all these states and nations, turning its face from the field, and shattered by a handful from a single province.

Ragnar, after loading the Saxons with tribute, had sure tidings from Sweden of the death of Herodd, and also heard that his own sons, owing to the slander of Sorle, the king chosen in his stead, had been robbed of their inheritance. He besought the aid of the brothers Biorn, Fridleif, and Ragbard (for Ragnald, Hwitserk, and Erik, his sons by Swanloga, had not yet reached the age of bearing arms), and went to Sweden. Sorle met him with his army, and offered him the choice between a public conflict and a duel; and when Ragnar chose personal combat, he sent against him Starkad, a champion of approved daring, with his band of seven sons, to challenge and fight with him. Ragnar took his three sons to share the battle with him, engaged in the sight of both armies, and came out of the combat triumphant.

Biorn, having inflicted great slaughter on the foe without hurt to himself, gained from the strength of his sides, which were like iron, a perpetual name (Ironsides). This victory emboldened Ragnar to hope that he could overcome any peril, and he attacked and slew Sorle with the entire forces he was leading. He presented Biorn with the lordship of Sweden for his conspicuous bravery and service. Then for a little interval he rested from wars, and chanced to fall deeply in love with a certain woman. In order to find some means of approaching and winning her the more readily, he courted her father (Esbern) by showing him the most obliging and attentive kindness. He often invited him to banquets, and received him with lavish courtesy. When he came, he paid him the respect of rising, and when he sat, he honoured him with a set next to himself. He also often comforted him with gifts, and at times with the most kindly speech. The man saw that no merits of his own could be the cause of all this distinction, and casting over the matter every way in his mind, he perceived that the generosity of his monarch was caused by his love for his daughter, and that he coloured this lustful purpose with the name of kindness. But, that he might balk the cleverness of the lover, however well calculated, he had the girl watched all the more carefully that he saw her beset by secret aims and obstinate methods. But Ragnar, who was comforted by the surest tidings of her consent, went to the farmhouse in which she was kept, and fancying that love must find out a way, repaired alone to a certain peasant in a neighbouring lodging. In the morning he exchanged dress with the women, and went in female attire, and stood by his mistress as she was unwinding wool. Cunningly, to avoid betrayal, he set his hands to the work of a maiden, though they were little skilled in the art. In the night he embraced the maiden and gained his desire. When her time drew near, and the girl growing big, betrayed her outraged chastity, the father, not knowing to whom his daughter had given herself to be defiled, persisted in asking the girl herself who was the unknown seducer. She steadfastly affirmed that she had had no one to share her bed except her handmaid, and he made the affair over to the king to search into. He would not allow an innocent servant to be branded with an extraordinary charge, and was not ashamed to prove another's innocence by avowing his own guilt. By this generosity he partially removed the woman's reproach, and prevented an absurd report from being sown in the ears of the wicked. Also he added, that the son to be born of her was of his own line, and that he wished him to be named Ubbe. When this son had grown up somewhat, his wit, despite his tender years, equalled the discernment of manhood. For he took to loving his mother, since she had had converse with a noble bed, but cast off all respect for his father, because he had stooped to a union too lowly.

After this Ragnar prepared an expedition against the Hellespontines, and summoned an assembly of the Danes, promising that he would give the people most wholesome laws. He had enacted before that each father of a household should offer for service that one among his sons whom he esteemed least; but now he enacted that each should arm the son who was stoutest of hand or of most approved loyalty. Thereon, taking all the sons he had by Thora, in addition to Ubbe, he attacked, crushed in sundry campaigns, and subdued the Hellespont with its king Dia. At last he involved the same king in disaster after disaster, and slew him. Dia's sons, Dia and Daxo, who had before married the daughters of the Russian king, begged forces from their father-in-law, and rushed with most ardent courage to the work of avenging their father. But Ragnar, when he saw their boundless army, distrusted his own forces; and he put brazen horses on wheels that could be drawn easily, took them round on carriages that would turn, and ordered that they should be driven with the utmost force against the thickest ranks of the enemy. This device served so well to break the line of the foe, that the Danes' hope of conquest seemed to lie more in the engine than in the soldiers: for its insupportable weight overwhelmed whatever it struck. Thus one of the leaders was killed, while one made off in flight, and the whole army of the area of the Hellespont retreated. The Scythians, also, who were closely related by blood to Daxo on the mother's side, are said to have been crushed in the same disaster. Their province was made over to Hwitserk, and the king of the Russians, trusting little in his own strength, hastened to fly out of the reach of the terrible arms of Ragnar.

Now Ragnar had spent almost five years in sea-roving, and had quickly compelled all other nations to submit; but he found the Perms in open defiance of his sovereignty. He had just conquered them, but their loyalty was weak. When they heard that he had come they cast spells upon the sky, stirred up the clouds, and drove them into most furious storms. This for some time prevented the Danes from voyaging, and caused their supply of food to fail. Then, again, the storm suddenly abated, and now they were scorched by the most fervent and burning heat; nor was this plague any easier to bear than the great and violent cold had been. Thus the mischievous excess in both directions affected their bodies alternately, and injured them by an immoderate increase first of cold and then of heat. Moreover, dysentery killed most of them. So the mass of the Danes, being pent in by the dangerous state of the weather, perished of the bodily plague that arose on every side. And when Ragnar saw that he was hindered, not so much by a natural as by a factitious tempest, he held on his voyage as best he could, and got to the country of the Kurlanders and Sembs, who paid zealous honour to his might and majesty, as if he were the most revered of conquerors. This service enraged the king all the more against the arrogance of the men of Permland, and he attempted to avenge his slighted dignity by a sudden attack. Their king, whose name is not known, was struck with panic at such a sudden invasion of the enemy, and at the same time had no heart to join battle with them; and fled to Matul, the prince of Finmark. He, trusting in the great skill of his archers, harassed with impunity the army of Ragnar, which was wintering in Permland. For the Finns, who are wont to glide on slippery timbers (snowskates), scud along at whatever pace they will, and are considered to be able to approach or depart very quickly; for as soon as they have damaged the enemy they fly away as speedily as they approach, nor is the retreat they make quicker than their charge. Thus their vehicles and their bodies are so nimble that they acquire the utmost expertness both in advance and flight.

Ragnar was filled with amazement at the poorness of his fortunes when he saw that he, who had conquered Rome at its pinnacle of power, was dragged by an unarmed and uncouth race into the utmost peril. He, therefore, who had signally crushed the most glorious flower of the Roman soldiery, and the forces of a most great and serene captain, now yielded to a base mob with the poorest and slenderest equipment; and he whose lustre in war the might of the strongest race on earth had failed to tarnish, was now too weak to withstand the tiny band of a miserable tribe. Hence, with that force which had helped him bravely to defeat the most famous pomp in all the world and the weightiest weapon of military power, and to subdue in the field all that thunderous foot, horse, and encampment; with this he had now, stealthily and like a thief, to endure the attacks of a wretched and obscure populace; nor must he blush to stain by a treachery in the night that noble glory of his which had been won in the light of day, for he took to a secret ambuscade instead of open bravery. This affair was as profitable in its issue as it was unhandsome in the doing.

Ragnar was equally as well pleased at the flight of the Finns as he had been at that of Karl, and owned that he had found more strength in that defenceless people than in the best equipped soldiery; for he found the heaviest weapons of the Romans easier to bear than the light darts of this ragged tribe. Here, after killing the king of the Perms and routing the king of the Finns, Ragnar set an eternal memorial of his victory on the rocks, which bore the characters of his deeds on their face, and looked down upon them.

Meanwhile Ubbe was led by his grandfather, Esbern, to conceive an unholy desire for the throne; and, casting away all thought of the reverence due to his father, he claimed the emblem of royalty for his own head.

When Ragnar heard of his arrogance from Kelther and Thorkill, the earls of Sweden, he made a hasty voyage towards Gothland. Esbern, finding that these men were attached with a singular loyalty to the side of Ragnar, tried to bribe them to desert the king. But they did not swerve from their purpose, and replied that their will depended on that of Biorn, declaring that not a single Swede would dare to do what went against his pleasure. Esbern speedily made an attempt on Biorn himself, addressing him most courteously through his envoys. Biorn said that he would never lean more to treachery than to good faith, and judged that it would be a most abominable thing to prefer the favour of an infamous brother to the love of a most righteous father. The envoys themselves he punished with hanging, because they counselled him to so grievous a crime. The Swedes, moreover, slew the rest of the train of the envoys in the same way, as a punishment for their mischievous advice. So Esbern, thinking that his secret and stealthy manoeuvres did not succeed fast enough, mustered his forces openly, and went publicly forth to war. But Iwar, the governor of Jutland, seeing no righteousness on either side of the impious conflict, avoided all unholy war by voluntary exile.

Ragnar attacked and slew Esbern in the bay that is called in Latin Viridis; he cut off the dead man's head and bade it be set upon the ship's prow, a dreadful sight for the seditious. But Ubbe took to flight, and again attacked his father, having revived the war in Zealand. Ubbe's ranks broke, and he was assailed single-handed from all sides; but he felled so many of the enemy's line that he was surrounded with a pile of the corpses of the foe as with a strong bulwark, and easily checked his assailants from approaching. At last he was overwhelmed by the thickening masses of the enemy, captured, and taken off to be laden with public fetters. By immense violence he disentangled his chains and cut them away. But when he tried to sunder and rend the bonds that were (then) put upon him, he could not in any wise escape his bars. But when Iwar heard that the rising in his country had been quelled by the punishment of the rebel, he went to Denmark. Ragnar received him with the greatest honour, because, while the unnatural war had raged its fiercest, he had behaved with the most entire filial respect.

Meanwhile Daxo long and vainly tried to overcome Hwitserk, who ruled over Sweden; but at last he enrapped him under pretence of making a peace, and attacked him. Hwitserk received him hospitably, but Daxo had prepared an army with weapons, who were to feign to be trading, ride into the city in carriages, and break with a night-attack into the house of their host. Hwitserk smote this band of robbers with such a slaughter that he was surrounded with a heap of his enemies' bodies, and could only be taken by letting down ladders from above. Twelve of his companions, who were captured at the same time by the enemy, were given leave to go back to their country; but they gave up their lives for their king, and chose to share the dangers of another rather than be quit of their own.

Daxo, moved with compassion at the beauty of Hwitserk, had not the heart to pluck the budding blossom of that noble nature, and offered him not only his life, but his daughter in marriage, with a dowry of half

326

his kingdom; choosing rather to spare his comeliness than to punish his bravery. But the other, in the greatness of his soul, valued as nothing the life which he was given on sufferance, and spurned his safety as though it were some trivial benefit. Of his own will he embraced the sentence of doom, saying, that Ragnar would exact a milder vengeance for his son if he found that he had made his own choice in selecting the manner of his death. The enemy wondered at his rashness, and promised that he should die by the manner of death which he should choose for this punishment. This leave the young man accepted as a great kindness, and begged that he might be bound and burned with his friends. Daxo speedily complied with his prayers that craved for death, and by way of kindness granted him the end that he had chosen. When Ragnar heard of this, he began to grieve stubbornly even unto death, and not only put on the garb of mourning, but, in the exceeding sorrow of his soul, took to his bed and showed his grief by groaning. But his wife, who had more than a man's courage, chid his weakness, and put heart into him with her manful admonitions. Drawing his mind off from his woe, she bade him be zealous in the pursuit of war; declaring that it was better for so brave a father to avenge the bloodstained ashes of his son with weapons than with tears. She also told him not to whimper like a woman, and get as much disgrace by his tears as he had once earned glory by his valour. Upon these words Ragnar began to fear lest he should destroy his ancient name for courage by his womanish sorrow; so, shaking off his melancholy garb and putting away his signs of mourning, he revived his sleeping valour with hopes of speedy vengeance. Thus do the weak sometimes nerve the spirits of the strong. So he put his kingdom in charge of Iwar, and embraced with a father's love Ubbe, who was now restored to his ancient favour. Then he transported his fleet over to Russia, took Daxo, bound him in chains, and sent him away to be kept in Utgard. (1)

Ragnar showed on this occasion the most merciful moderation towards the slayer of his dearest son, since he sufficiently satisfied the vengeance which he desired, by the exile of the culprit rather than his death. This compassion shamed the Russians out of any further rage against such a king, who could not be driven even by the most grievous wrongs to inflict death upon his prisoners. Ragnar soon took Daxo back into favour, and restored him to his country, upon his promising that he would every year pay him his tribute barefoot, like a suppliant, with twelve elders, also unshod. For he thought it better to punish a prisoner and a suppliant gently, than to draw the axe of bloodshed; better to punish that proud neck with constant slavery than to sever it once and for all. Then he went on and appointed his son Erik, surnamed Wind-hat, over Sweden. Here, while Fridleif and Siward were serving under him, he found that the Norwegians and the Scots had wrongfully conferred the title of king on two other men. So he first overthrew the usurper to the power of Norway, and let Biorn have the country for his own benefit.

Then he summoned Biorn and Erik, ravaged the Orkneys, landed at last on the territory of the Scots, and in a three-days' battle wearied out their king Murial, and slew him. But Ragnar's sons, Dunwat and Radbard, after fighting nobly, were slain by the enemy. So that the victory their father won was stained with their blood. He returned to Denmark, and found that his wife Swanloga had in the meantime died of disease. Straightway he sought medicine for his grief in loneliness, and patiently confined the grief of his sick soul within the walls of his house. But this bitter sorrow was driven out of him by the sudden arrival of Iwar, who had been expelled from the kingdom. For the Gauls had made him fly, and had wrongfully bestowed royal power on a certain Ella, the son of Hame. Ragnar took Iwar to guide him, since he was acquainted with the country, gave orders for a fleet, and approached the harbour called York. Here he disembarked his forces, and after a battle which lasted three days, he made Ella, who had trusted in the valour of the Gauls, desirous to fly. The affair cost much blood to the English and very little to the Danes. Here Ragnar completed a year of conquest, and then, summoning his sons to help him, he went to Ireland, slew its king Melbrik, besieged Dublin, which was filled with wealth of the barbarians, attacked it, and received its surrender. There he lay in camp for a year; and then, sailing through the midland sea, he made his way to the Hellespont. He won signal victories as he crossed all the intervening countries, and no ill-fortune anywhere checked his steady and prosperous advance.

Harald, meanwhile, with the adherence of certain Danes who were cold-hearted servants in the army of Ragnar, disturbed his country with renewed sedition, and came forward claiming the title of king. He was met by the arms of Ragnar returning from the Hellespont; but being unsuccessful, and seeing that his resources of defence at home were exhausted, he went to ask help of Ludwig, who was then stationed at Mainz. But Ludwig, filled with the greatest zeal for promoting his religion, imposed a condition on the Barbarian, promising him help if he would agree to follow the worship of Christ. For he said there could be no agreement of hearts between those who embraced discordant creeds. Anyone, therefore, who asked for help, must first have a fellowship in religion. No men could be partners in great works who were separated by a different form of worship. This decision procured not only salvation for Ludwig's guest, but the praise of piety for Ludwig himself, who, as soon as Harald had gone to the holy font, accordingly strengthened him with Saxon auxiliaries. Trusting in these, Harald built a temple in the land of Sleswik with much care and cost, to be hallowed to God. Thus he borrowed a pattern of the most holy way from the worship of Rome. He unhallowed, pulled down the shrines that had been profaned by the error of misbelievers, outlawed the sacrificers, abolished the (heathen) priesthood, and was the first to introduce the religion of Christianity to his uncouth country. Rejecting the worship of demons, he was zealous for that of God. Lastly, he observed with the most scrupulous care whatever concerned the protection of religion. But he began with more piety than success. For Ragnar came up, outraged the holy rites he had brought in, outlawed the true faith, restored the false one to its old position, and bestowed on the ceremonies the same honour as before. As for Harald, he deserted and cast in his lot with sacrilege. For though he was a notable ensample by his introduction of religion, yet he was the first who was seen to neglect it, and this illustrious promoter of holiness proved a most infamous forsaker of the same.

Meanwhile, Ella betook himself to the Irish, and put to the sword or punished all those who were closely and loyally attached to Ragnar. Then Ragnar attacked him with his fleet, but, by the just visitation of the Omnipotent, was openly punished for disparaging religion. For when he had been taken and cast into prison, his guilty limbs were given to serpents to devour, and adders found ghastly substance in the fibres of his entrails. His liver was eaten away, and a snake, like a deadly executioner, beset his very heart. Then in a courageous voice he recounted all his deeds in order, and at the end of his recital added the following sentence: "If the porkers knew the punishment of the boar-pig, surely they would break into the sty and hasten to loose him from his affliction." At this saying, Ella conjectured that some of his sons were yet alive, and bade that the executioners should stop and the vipers be removed. The servants ran up to accomplish his bidding; but Ragnar was dead, and forestalled the order of the king. Surely we must say that this man had a double lot for his share? By one, he had a fleet unscathed, an empire well-inclined, and immense power as a rover; while the other inflicted on him the ruin of his fame, the slaughter of his soldiers, and a most bitter end. The executioner beheld him beset with poisonous beasts, and asps gorging on that heart which he had borne steadfast in the face of every peril. Thus a most glorious conqueror declined to the piteous lot of a prisoner; a lesson that no man should put too much trust in fortune.

Iwar heard of this disaster as he happened to be looking on at the games. Nevertheless, he kept an unmoved countenance, and in nowise broke down. Not only did he dissemble his grief and conceal the news of his father's death, but he did not even allow a clamour to arise, and

329

forbade the panic-stricken people to leave the scene of the sports. Thus, loth to interrupt the spectacle by the ceasing of the games, he neither clouded his countenance nor turned his eyes from public merriment to dwell upon his private sorrow; for he would not fall suddenly into the deepest melancholy from the height of festal joy, or seem to behave more like an afflicted son than a blithe captain.

But when Siward heard the same tidings, he loved his father more than he cared for his own pain, and in his distraction plunged deeply into his foot the spear he chanced to be holding, dead to all bodily troubles in his stony sadness. For he wished to hurt some part of his body severely, that he might the more patiently bear the wound in his soul. By this act he showed at once his bravery and his grief, and bore his lot like a son who was more afflicted and steadfast. But Biorn received the tidings of his father's death while he was playing at dice, and squeezed so violently the piece that he was grasping that he wrung the blood from his fingers and shed it on the table; whereon he said that assuredly the cast of fate was more fickle than that of the very die which he was throwing. When Ella heard this, he judged that his father's death had been borne with the toughest and most stubborn spirit by that son of the three who had paid no filial respect to his decease; and therefore he dreaded the bravery of Iwar most.

Iwar went towards England, and when he saw that his fleet was not strong enough to join battle with the enemy, he chose to be cunning rather than bold, and tried a shrewd trick on Ella, begging as a pledge of peace between them a strip of land as great as he could cover with a horse's hide. He gained his request, for the king supposed that it would cost little, and thought himself happy that so strong a foe begged for a little boon instead of a great one; supposing that a tiny skin would cover but a very little land. But Iwar cut the hide out and lengthened it into very slender thongs, thus enclosing a piece of ground large enough to build a city on. Then Ella came to repent of his lavishness, and tardily set to reckoning the size of the hide, measuring the little skin more narrowly now that it was cut up than when it was whole. For that which he had thought would encompass a little strip of ground, he saw lying wide over a great estate. Iwar brought into the city, when he founded it, supplies that would serve amply for a siege, wishing the defences to be as good against scarcity as against an enemy.

Meantime, Siward and Biorn came up with a fleet of 400 ships, and with open challenge declared war against the king. This they did at the appointed time; and when they had captured him, they ordered the figure of an eagle to be cut in his back, rejoicing to crush their most ruthless foe by marking him with the cruellest of birds. Not satisfied with imprinting a wound on him, they salted the mangled flesh. Thus Ella was done to death, and Biorn and Siward went back to their own kingdoms.

Iwar governed England for two years. Meanwhile the Danes were stubborn in revolt, and made war, and delivered the sovereignty publicly to a certain SIWARD and to ERIK, both of the royal line. The sons of Ragnar, together with a fleet of 1,700 ships, attacked them at Sleswik, and destroyed them in a conflict which lasted six months. Barrows remain to tell the tale. The sound on which the war was conducted has gained equal glory by the death of Siward. And now the royal stock was almost extinguished, saving only the sons of Ragnar. Then, when Biorn and Erik had gone home, Iwar and Siward settled in Denmark, that they might curb the rebels with a stronger rein, setting Agnar to govern England. Agnar was stung because the English rejected him, and, with the help of Siward, chose, rather than foster the insolence of the province that despised him, to dispeople it and leave its fields, which were matted in decay, with none to till them. He covered the richest land of the island with the most hideous desolation, thinking it better to be lord of a wilderness than of a headstrong country. After this he wished to avenge Erik, who had been slain in Sweden by the malice of a certain Osten. But while he was narrowly bent on avenging another, he squandered his own blood on the foe; and while he was eagerly trying to punish the slaughter of his brother, sacrificed his own life to brotherly love.

Thus SIWARD, by the sovereign vote of the whole Danish assembly, received the empire of his father. But after the defeats he had inflicted everywhere he was satisfied with the honour he received at home, and liked better to be famous with the gown than with the sword. He ceased to be a man of camps, and changed from the fiercest of despots into the most punctual guardian of peace. He found as much honour in ease and leisure as he had used to think lay in many victories. Fortune so favoured his change of pursuits, that no foe ever attacked him, nor he any foe. He died, and ERIK, who was a very young child, inherited his nature, rather than his realm or his tranquillity. For Erik, the brother of Harald, despising his exceedingly tender years, invaded the country with rebels, and seized the crown; nor was he ashamed to assail the lawful infant sovereign, and to assume an unrightful power. In thus bringing himself to despoil a feeble child of the kingdom he showed himself the more unworthy of it. Thus he stripped the other of his throne, but himself of all his virtues, and cast all manliness out of his heart, when he made war upon a cradle: for where covetousness and ambition flamed, love of kindred could find no place. But this brutality was requited by the wrath of a divine vengeance. For the war between

331

this man and Gudorm, the son of Harald, ended suddenly with such slaughter that they were both slain, with numberless others; and the royal stock of the Danes, now worn out by the most terrible massacres, was reduced to the only son of the above Siward.

This man (Erik) won the fortune of a throne by losing his kindred; it was luckier for him to have his relations dead than alive. He forsook the example of all the rest, and hastened to tread in the steps of his grandfather; for he suddenly came out as a most zealous practitioner of roving. And would that he had not shown himself rashly to inherit the spirit of Ragnar, by his abolition of Christian worship! For he continually tortured all the most religious men, or stripped them of their property and banished them. But it were idle for me to blame the man's beginnings when I am to praise his end. For that life is more laudable of which the foul beginning is checked by a glorious close, than that which begins commendably but declines into faults and infamies. For Erik, upon the healthy admonitions of Ansgarius, laid aside the errors of his impious heart, and atoned for whatsoever he had done amiss in the insolence thereof; showing himself as strong in the observance of religion as he had been in slighting it. Thus he not only took a draught of more wholesome teaching with obedient mind, but wiped off early stains by his purity at the end. He had a son KANUTE by the daughter of Gudorm, who was also the granddaughter of Harald; and him he left to survive his death.

While this child remained in infancy a guardian was required for the pupil and for the realm. But inasmuch it seemed to most people either invidious or difficult to give the aid that this office needed, it was resolved that a man should be chosen by lot. For the wisest of the Danes, fearing much to make a choice by their own will in so lofty a matter, allowed more voice to external chance than to their own opinions, and entrusted the issue of the selection rather to luck than to sound counsel. The issue was that a certain Enni-gnup (Steep-brow), a man of the highest and most entire virtue, was forced to put his shoulder to this heavy burden; and when he entered on the administration which chalice had decreed, he oversaw, not only the early rearing of the king, but the affairs of the whole people. For which reason some who are little versed in our history give this man a central place in its annals. But when Kanute had passed through the period of boyhood, and had in time grown to be a man, he left those who had done him the service of bringing him up, and turned from an almost hopeless youth to the practice of unhoped-for virtue; being deplorable for this reason only, that he passed from life to death without the tokens of the Christian faith.

But soon the sovereignty passed to his son FRODE. This man's fortune, increased by arms and warfare, rose to such a height of prosperity that he brought back to the ancient yoke the provinces which had once revolted from the Danes, and bound them in their old obedience. He also came forward to be baptised with holy water in England, which had for some while past been versed in Christianity. But he desired that his personal salvation should overflow and become general, and begged that Denmark should be instructed in divinity by Agapete, who was then Pope of Rome. But he was cut off before his prayers attained this wish. His death befell before the arrival of the messengers from Rome: and indeed his intention was better than his fortune, and he won as great a reward in heaven for his intended piety as others are vouchsafed for their achievement.

His son GORM, who had the surname of "The Englishman," because he was born in England, gained the sovereignty in the island on his father's death; but his fortune, though it came soon, did not last long. He left England for Denmark to put it in order; but a long misfortune was the fruit of this short absence. For the English, who thought that their whole chance of freedom lay in his being away, planned an open revolt from the Danes, and in hot haste took heart to rebel. But the greater the hatred and contempt of England, the greater the loyal attachment of Denmark to the king. Thus while he stretched out his two hands to both provinces in his desire for sway, he gained one, but lost the lordship of the other irretrievably; for he never made any bold effort to regain it. So hard is it to keep a hold on very large empires.

After this man his son HARALD came to be king of Denmark; he is half-forgotten by posterity, and lacks all record for famous deeds, because he rather preserved than extended the possessions of the realm.

After this the throne was obtained by GORM, a man whose soul was ever hostile to religion, and who tried to efface all regard for Christ's worshippers, as though they were the most abominable of men. All those who shared this rule of life he harassed with divers kinds of injuries and incessantly pursued with whatever slanders he could. Also, in order to restore the old worship to the shrines, he razed to its lowest foundations, as though it were some unholy abode of impiety, a temple which religious men had founded in a stead in Sleswik; and those whom he did not visit with tortures he punished by the demolition of the holy chapel. Though this man was thought notable for his stature, his mind did not answer to his body; for he kept himself so well sated with power that he rejoiced more in saving than increasing his dignity, and thought it better to guard his own than to attack what belonged to others: caring more to look to what he had than to swell his havings.

This man was counselled by the elders to celebrate the rites of marriage, and he wooed Thyra, the daughter of Ethelred, the king of the English, for his wife. She surpassed other women in seriousness and shrewdness, and laid the condition on her suitor that she would not marry him till she had received Denmark as a dowry. This compact was made between them, and she was betrothed to Gorm. But on the first night that she went up on to the marriage-bed, she prayed her husband most earnestly that she should be allowed to go for three days free from intercourse with man. For she resolved to have no pleasure of love till she had learned by some omen in a vision that her marriage would be fruitful. Thus, under pretence of self-control, she deferred her experience of marriage, and veiled under a show of modesty her wish to learn about her issue. She put off lustful intercourse, inquiring, under the feint of chastity, into the fortune she would have in continuing her line. Some conjecture that she refused the pleasures of the nuptial couch in order to win her mate over to Christianity by her abstinence. But the youth, though he was most ardently bent on her love, yet chose to regard the continence of another more than his own desires, and thought it nobler to control the impulses of the night than to rebuff the prayers of his weeping mistress; for he thought that her beseechings, really coming from calculation, had to do with modesty. Thus it befell that he who should have done a husband's part made himself the guardian of her chastity so that the reproach of an infamous mind should not be his at the very beginning of his marriage; as though he had yielded more to the might of passion than to his own self-respect. Moreover that he might not seem to forestall by his lustful embraces the love which the maiden would not grant, he not only forbore to let their sides that were next one another touch, but even severed them by his drawn sword, and turned the bed into a divided shelter for his bride and himself. But he soon tasted in the joyous form of a dream the pleasure which he postponed from free loving kindness. For, when his spirit was steeped in slumber, he thought that two birds glided down from the privy parts of his wife, one larger than the other; that they poised their bodies aloft and soared swiftly to heaven, and, when a little time had elapsed, came back and sat on either of his hands. A second, and again a third time, when they had been refreshed by a short rest, they ventured forth to the air with outspread wings. At last the lesser of them came back without his fellow, and with wings smeared with blood. He was amazed with this imagination, and, being in a deep sleep, uttered a cry to betoken his astonishment, filling the whole house with an uproarious shout. When his servants questioned him, he related his vision; and Thyra, thinking that she would be blest with offspring, forbore her purpose to put off her marriage, eagerly relaxing the chastity for which she had so hotly prayed. Exchanging celibacy for love, she granted her husband full joy of herself, requiting his virtuous self-restraint with the fulness of permitted intercourse, and telling him that she would not have married him at all, had she not inferred from these images in the dream which he had related, the certainty of her being fruitful.

By a device as cunning as it was strange, Thyra's pretended modesty passed into an acknowledgment of her future offspring. Nor did fate disappoint her hopes. Soon she was the fortunate mother of Kanute and Harald. When these princes had attained man's estate, they put forth a fleet and quelled the reckless insolence of the Sclavs. Neither did they leave England free from an attack of the same kind. Ethelred was delighted with their spirit, and rejoiced at the violence his nephews offered him; accepting an abominable wrong as though it were the richest of benefits. For he saw far more merit in their bravery than in piety. Thus he thought it nobler to be attacked by foes than courted by cowards, and felt that he saw in their valiant promise a sample of their future manhood.

For he could not doubt that they would some day attack foreign realms, since they so boldly claimed those of their mother. He so much preferred their wrongdoing to their service, that he passed over his daughter, and bequeathed England in his will to these two, not scrupling to set the name of grandfather before that of father. Nor was he unwise; for he knew that it beseemed men to enjoy the sovereignty rather than women, and considered that he ought to separate the lot of his unwarlike daughter from that of her valiant sons. Hence Thyra saw her sons inheriting the goods of her father, not grudging to be disinherited herself. For she thought that the preference above herself was honourable to her, rather than insulting.

Kanute and Harald enriched themselves with great gains from sea-roving, and most confidently aspired to lay hands on Ireland. Dublin, which was considered the capital of the country, was beseiged. Its king went into a wood adjoining the city with a few very skilled archers, and with treacherous art surrounded Kanute (who was present with a great throng of soldiers witnessing the show of the games by night), and aimed a deadly arrow at him from afar. It struck the body of the king in front, and pierced him with a mortal wound. But Kanute feared that the enemy would greet his peril with an outburst of delight. He therefore wished his disaster to be kept dark; and summoning voice with his last breath, he ordered the games to be gone through without disturbance. By this device he made the Danes masters of Ireland ere he made his own death known to the Irish.

Who would not bewail the end of such a man, whose self-mastery

335

served to give the victory to his soldiers, by reason of the wisdom that outlasted his life? For the safety of the Danes was most seriously endangered, and was nearly involved in the most deadly peril; yet because they obeyed the dying orders of their general they presently triumphed over those they feared.

Germ had now reached the extremity of his days, having been blind for many years, and had prolonged his old age to the utmost bounds of the human lot, being more anxious for the life and prosperity of his sons than for the few days he had to breathe. But so great was his love for his elder son that he swore that he would slay with his own hand whosoever first brought him news of his death. As it chanced, Thyra heard sure tidings that this son had perished. But when no man durst openly hint this to Germ, she fell back on her cunning to defend her, and revealed by her deeds the mischance which she durst not speak plainly out. For she took the royal robes off her husband and dressed him in filthy garments, bringing him other signs of grief also, to explain the cause of her mourning; for the ancients were wont to use such things in the performance of obsequies, bearing witness by their garb to the bitterness of their sorrow. Then said Germ: "Dost thou declare to me the death of Kanute?" (2) And Thyra said: "That is proclaimed by thy presage, not by mine." By this answer she made out her lord a dead man and herself a widow, and had to lament her husband as soon as her son. Thus, while she announced the fate of her son to her husband, she united them in death, and followed the obsequies of both with equal mourning; shedding the tears of a wife upon the one and of a mother upon the other; though at that moment she ought to have been cheered with comfort rather than crushed with disasters.

ENDNOTES:

(1) Utgard. Saxo, rationalising as usual, turns the mythical home of the giants into some terrestrial place in his vaguely-defined Eastern Europe.

(2) Kanute. Here the vernacular is far finer. The old king notices "Denmark is drooping, dead must my son be!", puts on the signs of mourning, and dies.